Enterprise Modeling and Computing with UML

Peter Rittgen
University College of Borås, Sweden

T0325219

IDEA GROUP PUBLISHING

Hershey • London • Melbourne • Singapore

Acquisition Editor:	Michelle Potter
Senior Managing Editor:	Jennifer Neidig
Managing Editor:	Sara Reed
Development Editor:	Kristin Roth
Copy Editor:	Angela Thor
Typesetter:	Marko Primorac
Cover Design:	Lisa Tosheff
Printed at:	Integrated Book Technology

Published in the United States of America by
Idea Group Publishing (an imprint of Idea Group Inc.)
701 E. Chocolate Avenue
Hershey PA 17033
Tel: 717-533-8845
Fax: 717-533-8661
E-mail: cust@idea-group.com
Web site: http://www.idea-group.com

and in the United Kingdom by
Idea Group Publishing (an imprint of Idea Group Inc.)
3 Henrietta Street
Covent Garden
London WC2E 8LU
Tel: 44 20 7240 0856
Fax: 44 20 7379 3313
Web site: http://www.eurospan.co.uk

Library of Congress Cataloging-in-Publication Data

Enterprise modeling and computing with UML / Peter Rittgen, editor.
       p. cm.
   Summary: "This book bridges two fields that, although closely related, are often studied in isolation: enterprise modeling and information systems modeling. The principal idea is to use a standard language for modeling information systems, UML, as a catalyst and investigate its potential for modeling enterprises"--Provided by publisher.
   ISBN 1-59904-174-X (hardcover) -- ISBN 1-59904-175-8 (softcover) -- ISBN 1-59904-176-6 (ebook)
   1. Application software--Development. 2. UML (Computer science) 3. Business enterprises--Data processing.
I. Rittgen, Peter, 1964-
   QA76.76.A65E58 2006
   005.3--dc22
                                    2006019122

British Cataloguing in Publication Data
A Cataloguing in Publication record for this book is available from the British Library.

All work contributed to this book is new, previously-unpublished material. The views expressed in this book are those of the authors, but not necessarily of the publisher.

Enterprise Modeling and Computing with UML

Table of Contents

Section I: UML Extensions for Enterprise Modeling

Section II: UML as Meta-Language for Enterprise Modeling

Section V: Quality and Consistency in Enterprise Modeling

Foreword

This book is important: I will tell you why. I will also say a few words about me so that you get an idea of this person advising you on how to spend your time. Finally, I will outline my wishes about the direction I would like the future research on enterprise modeling to take.

In general terms, this book is focused on tools for the management and change of enterprises. The basis for this is the systems approach: viewing the enterprise itself as the main enterprise system, with the information system as a subsystem. The general idea is that we have to be able to grasp both the enterprise system and the information system in a thorough and comprehensive way to be able to manage change. If we do not know anything about the "enterprise boat," it sure is risky to try and steer it. This book outlines some individual tools and methods on how to get optimum ideas about the "enterprise boat" with all its information systems. To be able to grasp both the enterprise system and the information system, we have to apply modeling languages. These modeling languages are used to produce models of the modeled systems. These models, in turn, can be employed as tools both for integration, that is, making it easier to merge different parts of systems together, and for comprehension, making it easier to gather relevant aspects of the modeled systems.

This is of major importance simply because if we cannot coordinate the different parts of the enterprise boat, it will be almost impossible to steer it. More seriously, if we do not have a good comprehensive view of the boat, we do not know what it is exactly that we are steering. And moreover, we do not know how to steer and how to improve the steering information systems.

Today many enterprises are more or less blind, and they survive more by pure luck than by using rational thinking and tools. More than that, communication between the people building and maintaining information systems and the people building and maintaining the enterprise is often poor. New tools and a new way of thinking are needed. This is why this book is so important.

Then, who am I that you should trust such bold statements? First, from a more theoretical point of view, you might know that I have been a coworker with C. West Churchman who, for many people, is the main designer of the systems approach to enterprise management. When he was invited as the keynote speaker of a major conference, he wrote to me and asked if I could go there in his place, since as he said "You can say this as well as I can do." So I have taken that as proof that I am a systems thinker. From a practitioner's point of view, I have been working with big companies, banks, and cities in Europe for the last 15 years. I have been very much involved in the new type of IT applications where customers and other stakeholders are directly involved in what we nowadays call communities and e-power infrastructure.

Against this background, I can see a desperate need to develop better languages able to overcome the barriers between the more technically oriented IT system builders and the more economically oriented enterprise management builders. The book accepts this challenge and presents state-of-the-art ideas and solutions.

What I foresee as becoming increasingly important in the future is the modeling of customer requirements and their integration into the language. Successful companies of today are well into the thinking that their customers are coproducers of value that becomes manifest in services and products.

What I also observe is that the general direction of the work presented in this book goes towards trying to develop and design a more common modeling language that can be used by more people more easily. In my opinion, this aspect is of growing importance. Maybe someone will oppose, putting forward the argument that it is important to have many languages because they all contribute by emphasizing a special view of reality, and only in their entirety can they provided a comprehensive picture. According to the systems approach developed by Churchman and others (Ackoff, 1981; Checkland, 1988; Churchman, 1968; Mitroff & Mason, 1981), this is not enough. Every view also relates to possible actions and solutions, and these are of different values for different stakeholders. In order to act or steer the enterprise boat, someone will have to select or codesign (Albinsson & Forsgren, 2005; Forsgren, 1991) the acting model and the modeling language behind, though. Without this creative and ethical step, the enterprise will be hard to steer, as this book shows. Following this line of thinking, we have to try to codesign better modeling languages, always keeping in mind that acting models have to be challenged. For that reason, we also have to design better arenas for the codesign of new acting models.

This book can be regarded as such an arena, and the aim is to codesign better acting-modeling languages. The reflective reader will ask how we can judge whether one modeling language is better than another. A crucial question, indeed, and I look forward to more discussions about that.

Olov Forsgren
Sjuhärad Swedbank Distinguished Professor
University College of Borås, Sweden

REFERENCES

Ackoff, R. L. (1981). *Creating the corporate future*. New York: Wiley.

Albinsson L. & Forsgren, O. (2005). Codesign metaphors and scenarios — two elements in a design language for codesign. In *Proceedings of the 10th International Conference on the Language Action Perspective*, Kiruna, Sweden (pp. 131-1380).

Checkland, P. B. (1988). Soft systems methodology: An overview. *Journal of Applied Systems Analysis, 15*, 27-30.

Churchman, C. W. (1968). *The systems approach*. New York: Dell Publishing.

Forsgren, O. (1991) Coconstructive computer applications: Core ideas and some complementary strategies in the development of a humanistic computer science. In M. Bazewicz (Ed.), *Information systems architecture and technologies — ISAT'91* (pp. 45-53). Politechnika Wroclawska, Wroclaw.

Mitroff, I. I., & Mason, R. O. (1981). *Creating a dialectical social science*. Dordrecht, The Netherlands: Reidel.

Preface

Although enterprise modeling as a discipline is relatively young, enterprises have been using models to describe their business for quite some time. A business plan, for example, can be seen as a first-draft model of a business yet to be founded. And already at this early stage, we need something tangible to go upon: Potential investors and banks want to know about the chances and the risks of this new endeavor. Government agencies require some information in this model for deciding on approval. Likewise, business associates and top-level managers are interested in such a model. During a company's life, many more models come into play, very often in the context of planning situations: Production plans, marketing plans, project plans, personnel schedules, organizational charts, and so on. Enterprise modeling adds to those only two new aspects: comprehensiveness and integration. Comprehensiveness means that the set of all enterprise models covers the whole enterprise, that is, allows us to see the business from all relevant perspectives. Integration forces us to make sure that the models form a network of tightly coupled units that support each other. For example, if two models represent different views on an enterprise but overlap partially, that is, they contain descriptions of the same part of reality, then the overlapping parts should be consistent with each other, that is, the two descriptions must coincide.

Achieving comprehensiveness and integration in modeling is an ambitious task, and for many companies enterprise modeling is therefore rather a vision than reality. But the development towards that vision is driven by real forces. These forces have their origin in a changing economic environment that requires companies to respond at such a pace that change has become a constant process rather than an occasional endeavor. Among these changes is the increasing complexity of products and services that leads to value networks that mirror this complexity. Increased product complexity is in turn the result of any of the following factors (or a combination thereof):

- Technological advancement
- Additional product features
- New combinations of services
- Additional product-related services
- New or improved services
- Aggregated products

In other words, in order to provide an "attractive" package of complementing products and services to the market, enterprises often have to join forces because they cannot manage the inherent complexity of that task themselves. They do so by forming value networks, that is, by collaborating closely in a way that goes beyond the traditional value chain. These networks are relatively instable. They are formed, restructured, and abandoned to adapt to the changing needs of the market. For each organization in such a network, this has, naturally, a substantial impact on almost all aspects of their business. Changing supplier relations affect procurement processes; changing customer relations affect sales and marketing. In the same way, changing characteristics of products and services affect production and service provision.

Managing organizational changes of that magnitude requires a new form of knowledge. This knowledge is organized in a discipline called enterprise engineering (Davenport & Short, 1990; Fox, Gruninger, & Zhan, 1994; Gustas & Gustiene, 2004; Jochem, 2002). It provides the methods and tools to align the business processes with the strategic goals of the organization and the requirements posed by network partners. Like in other engineering disciplines, blueprints of the system to be engineered are at the heart of enterprise engineering. These blueprints, called models, are a prerequisite of any engineering activity such as the design of a new organization or the redesign of an existing one. They are provided by a discipline called enterprise modeling (Barrios & Nurcan, 2004; Fox, 1994; Fox, Barbuceanu, & Gruninger, 1996; Fox, Barbuceanu, Gruninger, & Lin, 1998; Fox & Gruninger, 1998; Gruninger & Fox, 1996; Jureta & Faulkner, 2005; Liles & Presley, 1996; Shinkawa & Matsumoto, 2001). Enterprise modeling provides a number of potential benefits such as better understanding of the enterprise, support for information systems development, more flexibility in organizational design, and a solid foundation for reorganizing the business.

According to ATHENA (2004), enterprise modeling can be structured in three parts:

- Enterprise frameworks and architectures
- Enterprise modeling languages
- Other approaches by industrial initiatives, standardization bodies, and organizations working on enterprise modeling concepts

An enterprise framework is "a fundamental structure which allows defining the main sets of concepts to model and to build an enterprise" (ATHENA, 2004). Some frameworks are used for integrating enterprise modeling, others for integrating enterprise applications. Among the frameworks that address integrated enterprise modeling are

- The **Zachman** Framework (Sowa & Zachman, 1992; Zachman, 1987)
- The **GERAM** (generalised enterprise reference architecture and methodology) Framework (Bernus & Nemes, 1996)
- The **GRAI** (graphs with results and activities interrelated) Framework (Chen & Doumeingts, 1996; Doumeingts, Vallespir, & Chen, 1998)
- The **ARIS** (achitecture of integrated information systems) Framework (Scheer, 1999a, 1999b)
- The **CIMOSA** (computer integrated manufacturing open systems architecture) Framework (ESPRIT Consortium AMICE, 1993; Zelm, 1995)
- The **DoDAF** (Department of Defense architecture framework) Architecture Methodology (DoD, 2003a, 2003b)

- TOGAF (The Open Group architecture framework) Architecture Methodology (Open Group, 2005)
- AKM (active knowledge modeling) (Lillehagen & Krogstie, 2002)

Frameworks for enterprise application integration include ISO 15745 (ISO, 2003b) and MISSION (Popplewell, Harding, & Rabe, 2001). Enterprise modeling languages are languages that allow us to express knowledge about an enterprise in an explicit, semiformal way. It is done with the help of models that capture this knowledge in a diagrammatic and/or textual form. The knowledge concerns organization and operations of the enterprise, that is, processes, behavior, activities, information, objects, material flows, resources and organizational units, system infrastructure, and architecture. The models describe the enterprise from different points of view such as functional, process, data, and economic. Examples of enterprise modeling languages are:

- **IEM:** Integrated enterprise modelling (Mertins & Jochem, 1999; Spur, Mertins, & Jochem, 1996),
- **Metis ITM, BPM, and UML** (Lillehagen, Dehli, Fjeld, Krogstie, & Jørgensen, 2002)
- **PN:** Petri nets (Aalst, Desel, & Oberweis, 2000)
- **CIMOSA:** Computer integrated manufacturing open systems architecture (ESPRIT Consortium AMICE, 1993)
- **GRAI:** Graphs with results and activities interrelated (Chen & Doumeingts, 1996; Doumeingts et al., 1998)
- **IDEF:** Integrated DEFinition (Menzel & Mayer, 1998)
- **PSL:** Process specification language (ISO, 2003a)
- **XPDL:** XML process definition language (Shapiro, 2005)
- **UML-EDOC:** UML profile for enterprise distributed object computing specification (OMG, 2004a)
- **UML-EAI:** UML profile for enterprise application integration (OMG, 2004b)
- **ebXML:** Electronic business eXtensible markup language (http://www.ebxml.org)
- **PIF:** Process interchange format (Lee, Yost, & PIF Working Group, 1994)
- **UEML:** Unified enterprise modeling language (Vernadat, 2002)
- **BPDM:** Business process definition metamodel (OMG, 2004d)
- **BPMN:** Business process modeling notation (OMG, 2004c)

As enterprise modeling is of significant interest to many industries, they have formed their own consortia and initiatives to establish industry standards. Many of the conventional standardization bodies are also involved in that work. The following is a noncomprehensive list of relevant organizations:

- **BPMI:** Business Process Management Initiative (now part of OMG)
- **WfMC:** Workflow Management Coalition
- **OAG:** Open Applications Group
- **OASIS:** Organization for the Advancement of Structured Information Standards
- **UN/CEFACT:** United Nations Centre for Trade Facilitation and Electronic Business
- **RosettaNet** (http://www.rosettanet.org)
- **W3C:** World Wide Web Consortium
- **OMG:** Object Management Group

Standards that concern enterprise modeling include:

- **EN/ISO 19439:** Enterprise integration — Framework for enterprise modeling
- **EN/ISO 19400:** Enterprise integration — Constructs for enterprise modeling
- **CEN TS 14818:** Enterprise integration — Decisional reference model
- **ISO CD 18629:** Process specification language (PSL)
- **ISO 15704:** Requirements for enterprise architecture and methodologies
- **ISO 14258:** Concepts and rules for enterprise models
- **ISO/IEC 15414:** Open distributed processing — Reference model — Enterprise language

The large number of methods and languages listed in the previous paragraphs represent only a fraction of available enterprise modeling options. In the face of this overwhelming multitude, it is not surprising that some proponents suggest the use of a single, standardized modeling language such as the unified modeling language (UML). But the diversity of approaches to enterprise modeling is not so much a sign of the immaturity of the field as an expression of its extraordinary complexity. An enterprise can be viewed from many angles and at the same time, we can focus on different facets of the enterprise. Any combination of angles and facets will yield a different methodology, each of them equally justifiable. Nevertheless, we cannot afford to maintain an almost infinite repertoire of methodologies from which the enterprise engineer selects the most appropriate one for the task at hand. This would imply that different tasks within the same enterprise might be performed with different methodologies, so that the whole enterprise would have to be modeled again from scratch for each new task. In such a situation, it is more feasible to develop an extensible set of integrated language components for each modeling purpose. The UML can play an important integrative role in this context.

The common factor of all enterprise modeling approaches is that they view the enterprise as a system where the information system is a subsystem of that system. The information system is that part of the overall system of the enterprise that collects, stores, administrates, processes, and retrieves information required for operating the business. Both systems are so tightly coupled that none of them can be seriously studied in isolation. This means that a modeling language for information systems must take into account enterprise modeling issues. And by the same argument, enterprise modeling cannot neglect the information system. As mentioned before, one of the major reasons for modeling an enterprise is precisely that the models can support us in developing or improving the information system.

While enterprise modeling is characterized by a multitude of approaches, information systems modeling is largely dominated by only one language: UML. This, and the fact that enterprise modeling and information systems modeling are so closely related, leads many to believe that the UML should also play a major role in enterprise modeling. The purpose of this book is to investigate this issue. To do so, we have divided the book into sections that deal with different approaches to it:

- Section I: UML Extensions for Enterprise Modeling
- Section II: UML as Meta-Language for Enterprise Modeling
- Section III: Enterprise Modeling Frontends for UML
- Section IV: Applying UML in Enterprise Modeling
- Section V: Quality and Consistency in Enterprise Modeling

The chapters in the first section start from the assumption that the UML itself can be used to model the whole enterprise when we extend the language in a suitable way. Specifically for this purpose, the UML provides a number of extension mechanisms such as stereotypes and profiles. There are three chapters in that section. Lars Bækgaard's chapter, "Extending UML to Support Business Activity Modeling," extends UML's activity diagrams by an important concept for business process modeling, that is, events. The second chapter, "Modeling and Specification of Collaborative Business Processes with an MDA Approach and a UML Profile," is written by Pablo David Villarreal, Enrique Salomone, and Omar Chiotti. It proposes a UML profile that can be used to model collaborative processes. The third and final chapter of this section investigates the user requirements notation (URN): "Enterprise Modeling with the Joint Use of User Requirements Notation and UML" by Anna Medve. The URN is a UML extension that supports requirements analysis.

The second section subsumes approaches that employ the UML as a metalanguage, which is, as a language for defining other, more specific languages for enterprise modeling. The first chapter in Section II, "Enterprise Architecture Modeling with the Unified Modeling Language" by Pedro Sousa, Artur Caetano, André Vasconcelos, Carla Pereira, and José Tribolet, specifies a language to describe the architecture of an enterprise based on the UML. Stefan Dietze does the same to arrive at a language for modeling software development processes. The title of his chapter is "Adaption of the UML to Formalized Software Development Process Assessment and Modeling: Dedicated Metamodel and Case Study." The final chapter in this second section, "Enterprise Modeling with ODP and UML," is written by the team of Sandy Tyndale-Biscoe, Antonio Vallecillo, and Bryan Wood. They make use of UML as a metalanguage for expressing enterprise viewpoint specifications of the reference model of open distributed processing (RM-ODP).

The third section, "Enterprise Modeling Frontends for UML" represents a fundamentally different approach. The two chapters in this section deny that the UML, as such, is sufficient for enterprise modeling, even if we allow for certain extensions and alterations. They claim that we need completely different types of languages because of differences in the natures of enterprises and information systems, respectively. The enterprise modeling language in this scenario functions as a kind of front-end for the system design in UML. A suitable procedure has to be established that helps with "translating" enterprise models into information system models. The first chapter in this section, "A Language-Action Approach to the Design of UML Models" by Peter Rittgen, describes such a (semiformal) procedure for a particular enterprise modeling language, dynamic essential modeling of organization (DEMO). The second chapter studies the differences between enterprises and information systems that we have mentioned, by comparing the characteristics of the metamodels of business action theory and the UML. The authors identify the conceptual deficiencies of the UML with respect to enterprise modeling, and thereby support the necessity of a separate enterprise modeling language. The title of the chapter is "Using UML Notation for Modeling Business Interaction," and it is written by Sandra Haraldson, Mikael Lind, and Jan Olausson.

The fourth section, "Applying UML in Enterprise Modeling," subsumes papers that apply the UML as it is in an enterprise modeling context. The first chapter of this section, "Using UML for Reference Modeling" by Peter Fettke, Peter Loos, and Jörg Zwicker investigates the suitability of the UML for reference modeling. Reference modeling implies the (re)use of existing (standard) models with the aim of improving the quality of new models and reducing the costs of developing them. The second chapter, "Modeling the Resource Perspective of Business Processes by UML Activity Diagram and Object Petri Net" by

Kamyar Sarshar and Peter Loos, employs activity diagrams to model the resources of a business processes and compares them to object petri nets.

The fifth and final section addresses issues of "Quality and Consistency in Enterprise Modeling" with UML. Herman Balsters opens this section with a chapter on "Merging and Outsourcing Information Systems with UML." This chapter suggests how models of businesses can be merged when the corresponding businesses have likewise been merged, or how the models can be split if a part of a business is to be outsourced to another business. This is achieved by so-called view transformations that are aimed at ensuring model consistency. András Pataricza, András Balogh, and Lázló Gönczy contribute the final chapter, "Verification and Validation of Nonfunctional Aspects in Enterprise Modeling." They take up the issue of model quality in general, and dependability in particular.

Together, the five sections and 12 chapters offer a fairly broad set of perspectives on the topic of enterprise modeling. The book is a joint effort of 27 scholars and practitioners from around the globe. We hope that our readers, whether they may be academics or practitioners, can benefit from this comprehensive view, and that the book provides them with helpful insights into the dynamic field of enterprise modeling. We firmly believe in the importance of enterprise modeling and engineering as major tools for creating and maintaining competitive advantage in today's and tomorrow's cutting-edge enterprises, in line with the "old" saying: If you can't model it, you can't manage it!

Peter Rittgen
Borås, Sweden
January, 2006

REFERENCES

Aalst, W. v. d., Desel, J., & Oberweis, A. (2000). *Business process management* (LNCS 1806). Berlin: Springer.

ATHENA. (2004). *First version of state of the art in enterprise modeling techniques and technologies to support enterprise interoperability* (EU IP Project No. 507849). Retrieved December 7, 2005, from http://www.athena-ip.org/

Barrios, J., & Nurcan, S. (2004, June 7-11). Model driven architectures for enterprise information systems. In A. Persson & J. Stirna (Eds.), *Advanced information systems engineering, Proceedings of the 16th International Conference, CAiSE 2004,* Riga, Latvia (pp. 3-19). Berlin: Springer.

Bernus, P., & Nemes, L. (1996). A framework to define a generic enterprise reference architecture and methodology. *Computer Integrated Manufacturing Systems, 9*(3), 179-191.

Chen, D., & Doumeingts, G. (1996). The GRAI-GIM reference model, architecture, and methodology. In P. Bernus et al. (Eds.), *Architectures for enterprise integration.* London: Chapman & Hall.

Davenport, T. H., & Short, J. E. (1990). The new industrial engineering: information technology and business process redesign. *Sloan Management Review 32*(5), 554-571.

DoD. (Ed.). (2003a). *DoD architecture framework* (Version 1.0). Volume I: Definitions and Guidelines. Washington, DC: Office of the DoD Chief Information Officer, Department of Defense.

DoD. (Ed.). (2003b). *DoD architecture framework* (Version 1.0). Volume II: Product Descriptions. Washington, DC: Office of the DoD Chief Information Officer, Department of Defense.

Doumeingts, G., Vallespir, B., & Chen, D. (1998). Decisional modelling using the GRAI grid. In P. Bernus, K. Mertins, & G. Schmidt (Eds.), *Handbook on architectures of information systems* (pp. 313-338). Berlin: Springer.

ESPRIT Consortium AMICE (Ed.). (1993). *CIMOSA: Open system architecture for CIM* (Research report ESPRIT, Project 688/5288) (Vol. 1, 2nd revised and extended edition). Berlin: Springer.

Fox, M. S. (1994). Issues in enterprise modelling. In S. Y. Nof (Ed.), *Information and collaboration models of integration* (pp. 219-234). The Netherlands: Kluwer Academic.

Fox, M. S., Barbuceanu, M., & Gruninger, M. (1996). An organisation ontology for enterprise modelling: Preliminary concepts for linking structure and behaviour. *Computers in Industry, 29*, 123-134.

Fox, M. S., Barbuceanu, M., Gruninger, M., & Lin, J. (1998). An organisation ontology for enterprise modeling. In M. Prietula, K. Carley, & L. Gasser (Eds.), *Simulating organizations: Computational models of institutions and groups* (pp. 131-152). Menlo Park, CA: AAAI/MIT Press.

Fox, M. S., & Gruninger, M. (1998). Enterprise modeling. *AI Magazine, 19*(3), 109-121.

Fox, M. S., Gruninger, M., & Zhan, Y. (1994). Enterprise engineering: An information systems perspective. In L. Burke & J. Jackman (Eds.), *3rd Industrial Engineering Research Conference Proceedings* (pp. 461-466). Norcross, GA: Institute of Industrial Engineers.

Gruninger, M., & Fox, M. S. (1996). The logic of enterprise modelling. In P. Bernus & L. Nemes (Eds.), *Modelling and methodologies for enterprise integration.* Cornwall: Chapman and Hall.

Gustas, R., & Gustiene, P. (2004). Towards the enterprise engineering approach for information system modelling across organisational and technical boundaries. In *Enterprise information systems V* (pp. 204-215). The Netherlands: Kluwer Academic Publisher.

ISO. (2003a). *ISO 18629-1 Industrial automation system and integration — Process specification language: Part 1: Overview and basic principles.* Geneva, Switzerland: International Organization for Standardization.

ISO. (2003b). *ISO 15745-1 Industrial automation systems and integration — Open systems application integration framework: Part 1: Generic reference description.* Geneva, Switzerland: International Organization for Standardization.

Jochem, R. (2002). Enterprise engineering: The basis for successful planning of e-business. In L. M. Camarinha-Matos (Ed.), *Collaborative business ecosystems and virtual enterprises* (pp. 19-26). Kluwer Academic Publishers.

Jureta, I., & Faulkner, S. (2005, October 24-28). An agent-oriented metamodel for enterprise modelling. In J. Akoka, S. W. Liddle, I. -Y. Song, M. Bertolotto, I. Comyn-Wattiau, S. Si-Said Cherfi, et al. (Eds.), *Perspectives in Conceptual Modeling, Proceedings of the ER 2005 Workshops AOIS, BP-UML, CoMoGIS, eCOMO, and QoIS*, Klagenfurt, Austria (pp. 151-161). Berlin: Springer.

Lee, J., Yost, G., & the PIF Working Group (1994, December 22). *The PIF process interchange format and framework* (Version 1.0). Retrieved from http://ccs.mit.edu/pif7.html

Liles, D. H., & Presley, A. R. (1996). Enterprise modeling within an enterprise engineering framework. In J. M. Charnes, D. J. Morrice, D. T. Brunner, & J. J. Swain (Eds.), *Proceedings of the 28th Winter Simulation Conference* (pp. 993-999). New York: ACM.

Lillehagen, F., Dehli, E., Fjeld, L., Krogstie, J., & Jørgensen, H. D. (2002). *Active knowledge models as a basis for an infrastructure for virtual enterprises.* Paper presented at the IFIP Conference on Infrastructures for Virtual Enterprises (PRO-VE), Sesimbra, Portugal.

Lillehagen, F., & Krogstie, J. (2002). Active knowledge models and enterprise knowledge management. In K. Kosanke, R. Jochem, J. G. Nell, & A. Ortiz Bas (Eds.), *Enterprise inter- and intra-organizational integration* (pp. 91-99). Dordrecht, The Netherlands: Kluwer Academic Publishers.

Menzel, C., & Mayer, R. J. (1998). The IDEF family of languages. In P. Bernus, K. Mertins, & G. Schmidt (Eds.), *Handbook on architectures of information systems* (pp. 209-242). Berlin: Springer.

Mertins, K., & Jochem, R. (1999). *Quality-oriented design of business processes.* Boston/ Dordrecht; London: Kluwer Academic Publishers.

OMG (Ed.). (2004a, February). *UML profile for enterprise distributed object computing specification.* Needham: OMG. Retrieved from http://www.uml.org

OMG (Ed.). (2004b, March). *UML profile and interchange models for enterprise application integration (EAI) specification.* Needham: OMG. Retrieved from http://www. uml.org

OMG (Ed.). (2004c, May). *Business process modeling notation (BPMN)* (Version 1.0). Needham: OMG. Retrieved from http://www.bpmn.org

OMG (Ed.). (2004d, August). *Business process definition metamodel* (Version 1.0.2). Needham: OMG. Retrieved from http://www.bpmn.org/Documents/BPDM%20Res ponse%20Revised%20Submission%2004-08-03.pdf

Open Group. (2005). *The Open Group architectural framework (TOGAF)* (Version 8). Retrieved from http://www.opengroup.org/togaf/

Popplewell, K., Harding, J. A., & Rabe M. (Eds.). (2001). *Deliverable D24: Final report from MISSION project* (ESPRIT Project No. 29 656). Retrieved from http://www. ims-mission.de/

Scheer, A.W. (1999a). *ARIS, business process framework* (3rd ed.) Berlin: Springer.

Scheer, A.W. (1999b). *ARIS, business process modelling* (3rd ed.). Berlin: Springer.

Shapiro, R. (2005). *Workflow process definition interface: XML process definition language.* (Document No. WfMC-TC-1025). Lighthouse Point, FL: Workflow Management Coalition. Retrieved December 12, 2005, from http://www.wfmc.org

Shinkawa, Y., & Matsumoto, M. J. (2001). Identifying the structure of business processes for comprehensive enterprise modeling. *IEICE Transactions on Information and Systems, 84D*(2), 239-248.

Sowa, J. F., & Zachman, J. A. (1992). Extending and formalizing the framework for information systems architecture. *IBM Systems Journal, 31*(3).

Spur, G., Mertins, K., & Jochem, R. (1996). *Integrated enterprise modelling.* Berlin: Beuth Verlag GmbH.

Vernadat, F. (2002). UEML: Towards a unified enterprise modelling language. *International Journal of Production Research, 40*(17), 4309-4321.

Zachman, J. A. (1987). A framework for information systems architecture. *IBM Systems Journal, 26*(3), 276-291.

Zelm, M. (Ed.). (1995). *CIMOSA: A primer on key concepts, purpose, and business value* (Technical Report). Stuttgart, Germany: CIMOSA Association.

Acknowledgments

The editors would like to acknowledge the help of all involved in the collation and review process of the book, without whose support the project could not have been completed. A further special note of thanks goes also to all the staff at Idea Group Inc., whose contributions throughout the whole process, from inception of the initial idea to final publication, have been invaluable. Deep appreciation and gratitude is due to University College of Borås for providing a unique research and teaching environment that stimulated and supported this year-long project.

Most of the authors of chapters included in this book also served as referees for articles written by other authors. Thanks go to all those who provided constructive and comprehensive reviews. However, some of the reviewers must be mentioned, as their reviews set the benchmark. Reviewers who provided the most comprehensive, critical, and constructive comments include Pablo David Villarreal of Universidad Tecnológica Nacional Santa Fe in Argentina; Ali H. Dogru of Middle East Technical University Ankara in Turkey; Artur Caetano of Technical University of Lisbon in Portugal; and Vince Kellen of DePaul University in Chicago.

Special thanks also go to the publishing team at Idea Group Inc. In particular to our development editor, Kristin Roth, who continuously prodded via e-mail for keeping the project on schedule, and to Mehdi Khosrow-Pour, senior academic editor, whose enthusiasm motivated me to initially accept his invitation for taking on this project.

Special thanks go to my colleagues at University College of Borås who gave me many new insights and provided inspiring thoughts while enduring my lack of understanding. And last but not least, I am grateful to my colleague, Mikael Lind, for his unfailing support and encouragement during the months it took to give birth to this book.

In closing, I wish to thank all of the authors for their insights and excellent contributions to this book. I also want to thank all of the people who assisted me in the reviewing process. Finally, I want to thank my partner for her love and support throughout this project.

Peter Rittgen, PhD
Borås, Sweden
June 2006

Section I

UML Extensions for Enterprise Modeling

Chapter I

Extending UML to Support Business Activity Modeling

Lars Bækgaard, Aalborg University, Denmark

ABSTRACT

This chapter presents an extension that makes UML better suited for business activity modeling. We extend UML's activity diagrams with events in order to make UML more oriented towards modeling of business concepts. The resulting event-activity diagrams have several modeling advantages. They can be used to model a business as a set of concurrent activities that are synchronized by means of shared events and shared objects. This means that business activities can be modeled in a way that resembles the distributed and concurrent activities of real-world business actors. By staying inside UML, we ensure that business analysts and software designers can use the same framework when they collaborate in a systems development project.

INTRODUCTION

Business activity modeling plays important roles in information systems development. In recent years, we have witnessed increased integration between human activity and activity performed by IT-systems. Internet-based businesses use IT-systems to maintain relations with customers, and to facilitate business transactions like ordering and payment. Hospitals use IT-systems to support medication, patient diaries, and patient administration. Educational institutions use IT-systems to support learning activities. In order to develop relevant IT-systems in such situations, it is necessary to obtain and express an understanding of the business activities (existing or new) within which the IT-systems are going to operate.

The integration of human activity and activity performed by IT-systems forces us to focus on business activities and the roles played by information and IT-systems herein. It is necessary to escape from the software-dominated perspective that characterizes many systems development methods (Jackson, 1983; Jacobson, Booch, & Rumbaugh, 1999; Mathiassen, Munk-Madsen, Nielsen, & Stage, 2000). The underlying assumption of such methods is that analysis and design of human work is outside the scope of systems development.

During the past 30 years, several attempts have been made to support business activity modeling (Avison & Wood-Harper, 1990; Goldkuhl, 1996; Lundeberg, Goldkuhl, & Nilsson, 1978; Nüttgens & Rump, 2002; Rittgen, 2003; White, 2004). Contextual design is a relatively new method for which success indicates that business activity modeling is being re-recognized as an essential systems development activity (Beyer & Holtzblatt, 1998).

UML is a collection of languages that primarily support object-oriented modeling of software systems in terms of flows, objects, and messages (Rumbaugh, Jacobson, & Booch, 1999). UML's strength is its support for object-oriented software development (Rittgen 2003). Parts of UML support some forms of business activity modeling, but the underlying perspective of such modeling is dominated by object-oriented software concepts rather than business-oriented concepts.

Before UML entered the scene, the world of systems development was dominated by structured methods like structured analysis (De Marco, 1978). These methods recommend that development activities are based on an analysis of current information activities, design of new information activities, and design of software that can perform selected information activities. Ironically, one of the arguments in favour of newer object-oriented methods is that the structured methods focus too much on business activity analysis (Mathiassen et al., 2000).

The purpose of this chapter is to improve UML's support for business activity modeling. We extend UML's activity diagrams with shared events. The resulting event-activity diagrams can be used to model relations between triggering events and triggered activity. They can be used to model relations between interrupting events and interrupted activity. They can be used to model business transactions like ordering and payment. Events can be used to synchronize two or more independent activities that are performed by independent actors. Previous versions of our modeling approach were discussed in Bækgaard (2001, 2004).

We begin by providing background information in terms of a discussion of activity systems and languages that support business activity modeling. Next, we present event-activity diagrams in order to extend UML with support for event modeling. We discuss our results and compare them to related work. Following that, we discuss possible future trends and conclude the chapter.

BACKGROUND

Our modeling approach is based on the assumptions that information systems are human activity systems that may or may not contain IT-systems, and that all information systems are contained in larger human activity systems that involve manipulation of physical things.

In this section, we present a view on business activities that can be used to evaluate modeling languages, and to inspire potential improvements of such languages. We discuss some of the most widely used languages as well as some of the newer languages that indicate the directions in which modeling languages evolve.

Business Activity

We view business systems, information systems, and IT-systems as activity systems in which actors perform activities. We use the terms activity, actor, thing, information, and event to characterize activity systems. The activity systems view makes it possible to talk about people-oriented and IT-oriented matters within a single linguistic framework.

We view a business system as an activity system in which actors manipulate things and information. Business activities include movement, manipulation, and consumption of things and information, and they include coordination activities that deal with requests for, agreements about, control of, and evaluation of work activities (Denning & Medina-Mora, 1995).

Our notion of an activity system is inspired by Checkland's notion of human activity systems. Checkland (1981) characterizes a human activity system in terms of the customers that benefit from a transformation that is caused by the actions of participating actors. A human activity system has one or more owners, and it operates within a specific environment. In order to support information systems analysis and modeling, we have added the categories IT-actors, information, events, and things. This is similar to Alter's (1999) notion of a work system that contains customers, products, business processes, participants, information, and technology.

We view an information system as an activity system in which actors use, interpret, manipulate, store, and exchange information. Many information systems operate in ways that are deeply integrated in material business activities. They are part of the business activity system rather than merely systems that support business activity.

Our notion of an information system is inspired by Buckingham, Hirschheim, Land, and Tully (1987), Alter (1999), and Goldkuhl and Ågerfalk (1998). Buckingham et al. describe an information system as a human activity system that may or may not involve computers. An information system assembles, stores, processes, and delivers information in a way that is accessible and useful for those that use the information. Alter views an information system as a work system that captures, moves, stores, retrieves, manipulates, and displays information. According to Goldkuhl and Ågerfalk, information systems consist of action potential, actions, and action memory. Information systems can support actions, they can perform actions, and they can remember past actions.

Checkland and Holwell (1998) characterize an information system as a system that delivers information in support of purposeful activity. Our notion of an information system is broader because it includes information activities that are integrated parts of the purposeful activity of actors. Unlike Checkland and Holwell, we do not view information systems as merely support systems.

Actors perform actions. They use, create, manipulate, and exchange things and information with or without the support of tools. We use the term actor as a reference to both persons and IT-systems. Even though there are many fundamental differences between people and IT-systems (Dreyfus & Dreyfus, 1986), it is useful to focus on an important similarity between people and IT-systems, namely their ability to perform actions.

An action is an atomic activity that is performed by an actor. An activity is a set of interrelated actions that constitutes a whole. An information activity is an activity that captures, stores, modifies, or presents information.

Events are significant occurrences without duration. Events have participants and properties. Shared events have more than one participant. When a book is borrowed in a library, the situation may be represented by an event that has a borrower and a book as participants. Occurrence dates and times are typical event properties. An event can be used to model a named time point in which actors, things, and information meet and interact. For example, an ordering event can be viewed as a time point where a customer and a product meet. Events have activity-like characteristics in the sense that something is changed when an event occurs. And events have information-like characteristics in the sense that they can be observed and described.

Flow

Flow-based modeling languages focus on the flow of activities, things, and information.

A data flow diagram defines a set of activities that manipulate and exchange information (De Marco, 1978). The activities interact in terms of information exchange, either directly or via information stores. Activities that manipulate and exchange physical things are not modeled. A data flow diagram can be divided into a set of related diagrams that interact in terms of information exchange. Data flow diagrams do not support event modeling. The development method SA uses data flow diagrams to model business activities that manipulate and exchange information (De Marco, 1978). SA uses data flow diagrams to model existing information activities and to define visions about new information activities. SA uses data flow diagrams to experiment with the content of information activities, and with the division of labour between persons and IT-systems.

The development method ISAC uses flow graphs that are similar to data flow diagrams, with the exception that they support modeling of the flow and manipulation of both information and things (Lundeberg et al., 1978). Goldkuhl (1996) uses action diagrams to model the flow of activities, things, and information.

An activity diagram defines a set of activities and their temporal dependencies (Rumbaugh et al., 1999). Sequencing of activities can be controlled by means of conditions. Two activity diagrams can synchronize their execution by sending and receiving signals. Activity diagrams can be subdivided into swim lanes. Each swim lane represents activities that are performed in a particular location, department, or by a specific actor.

Activity diagrams offer little more than data flow diagrams. And activity diagrams are not easily related to or translated into the more software-focused types of UML diagrams. The most serious disadvantage of activity diagrams is their lack of support for event modeling. The development method RUP uses activity diagrams to model business activities (Jacobson et al., 1999).

Objects

Object-based modeling languages focus on objects and exchange of messages between objects. An object is a unique unit that is composed of a set of state attributes and a set of methods that can be invoked by messages from other objects. The development method RUP uses class diagrams, state charts, and sequence diagrams to support object-oriented modeling of software (Jacobson et al., 1999).

A class diagram defines sets of associated objects. An object class defines a set of objects that has the same types of state attributes and methods. An association class defines a set of object pairs. Class diagrams can be used to model information structures and actor's action potential.

A state chart models a state-dependent object in terms of its ability to receive and send messages in terms of constraints on the sequencing of messages. For each state the object can respond to a given set of messages. All other messages will be rejected. As a response to an accepted message the object may send a message and/or change its state.

A sequence diagram models interaction between a set of objects in terms of messages that are passed among the objects.

Individual objects can be defined by class diagrams and state charts. Interaction between objects can be defined in terms of sequence diagrams. State charts define the internal flow of actions (messages) performed by an object. Sequence diagrams define the external flow of actions (messages) between objects.

Events

Event-based modeling languages focus on events and their roles in activities.

Yourdon (1989) introduced the notion of essential activities. The idea is that events in a system's environment trigger subsets of the system's activity. Each essential activity is triggered by events of a certain type. When such an event occurs the corresponding essential activity is executed. For example, a specific essential activity may represent the activity that is triggered when an order is received.

The notion of a use case is similar to the notion of an essential activity. A use case represents a coherent unit of functional behaviour that is offered by a system to one or more actors (Jakobson et al., 1989). It defines the behaviour of the system and its interaction with the involved actors. The behaviour is triggered by an action performed by one of the actors. RUP uses use cases to define functional requirements and to define the scope of a software system.

The behaviour of an essential activity or a use case can be defined by languages like activity, diagrams, state charts, sequence diagrams, and activity diagrams. Consequently, essential activities and use cases represent a simple extension of these languages by adding triggering events.

Event-driven process chains (EPC) are activity models in which the basic building blocks are events and activities (Nüttgens & Rump, 2002). Events can be used to control the flow of subactivities.

BPD-diagrams (business process diagrams) extend activity diagrams with events (Rittgen, 2003). BPD is inspired by EPC, and it uses events to control the flow of activities.

Business process modeling notation (BPMN) supports business activity modeling in terms of events and activities (White, 2004). Events can be used to control the flow of subactivities. Interaction between independent activities can be modeled in terms of information exchange.

Languages like EPC, BPD, and BPMN support modeling of events and their roles in business activities. However, they share a serious weakness. Neither of these languages supports rich modeling of interacting activities. We will discuss this in more detail at the end of the following section.

EVENT-ACTIVITY DIAGRAMS

In this section, we extend UML activity diagrams with shared events and asynchronous object sharing. The resulting event-activity diagrams contain a notation for events that may be shared by two or more activities. An event-activity diagram models a set of activities and the flow of things and information between the activities.

Real-world activities are composed of interacting, concurrent activities that synchronize from time to time. For example, the activities of customers and sales persons must synchronize when a customer buys an item. At other times, the activities of customers and sales persons are mutually independent.

We use events with participants to control synchronization between concurrent activities.

We have based our modeling approach on activity diagrams because they are part of UML and contain languages that support modeling of software. By staying inside UML, we ensure that business analysts and software designers can use the same framework when they collaborate in a systems development project.

Event Signatures

Events are significant occurrences without duration. Events have participants and properties. For example, ordering events may have participants like customers and products, and they may have properties like quantities and ordering dates.

We use expressions of the form "Name [ParticipantTypes] (PropertyTypes)" to define event signatures. An event signature defines a type of conforming event. The element "ParticipantTypes" defines the types of participants that can participate in events of the defined type. The element "PropertyTypes" defines the types of properties of events of the defined type.

An event expression conforms to a signature expression if it has the same name as the signature, and if its participants and properties conform to the participant and property types of the signature. For example, the event expression Borrow [$Borrower_1$, $BookCopy_4$] (September 29, 2001) conforms to the signature expression Borrow [Borrower, BookCopy] (Date).

Triggering and Interrupting Events

We symbolize an event by a circle (or oval) that contains parts of an event signature. As a minimum, the name of the event type must be present. If participant types and/or event properties are included, they define bindings of the actual participants and properties of executed events.

Figure 1. Generic event-activity diagram

An event-activity diagram defines an activity type and it is composed of triggering events, interrupting events, and an activity (Figure 1). The activity is initiated when a triggering event occurs. The activity runs until it reaches an exit point or until an interrupting event occurs. One or more actors carry out the activity.

Participant Roles

Events may have multiple participants. Shared events define synchronization points for two or more activities. Event-activity diagrams can model passive event participation and two types of active event participation (Figure 2).

If the event name is preceded by a question mark, the containing activity is passive relative to the event. The containing activity waits for another activity to request the event. If the event name is preceded by an exclamation mark, the containing activity is active relative to the event and it requests the event to be executed immediately. Otherwise, the containing activity is active relative to the event, and it can request the event to be executed now or later.

Object Sharing

Event-activity diagrams support modeling of concurrent activities that can share and exchange objects in an asynchronous manner.

Figure 2. Event participation roles

Figure 3. Maintain Book Collection

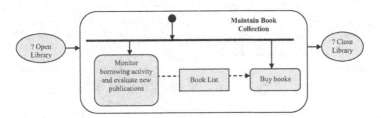

The diagram in Figure 3 models an activity that is concerned with maintenance of a book collection in a library. The activity Maintain Book Collection is triggered by the occurrence of an OpenLibrary event, and it is interrupted by the occurrence of a CloseLibrary event. The question marks mean that OpenLibrary and CloseLibrary must be requested by other activities. Two activities are carried out in parallel as indicated by the horizontal bar. They interact via the object Book List. The dotted arrow that connects the two activities represents the interaction. A dotted line does not represent transfer of control.

Triggered Events

Event-activity diagrams can be used to define rules for event triggering. The event-activity diagram in Figure 4 defines a book monitor in a library.

A Book Monitor instance is created each time a Borrow event occurs in order to ensure that unreturned books are recalled after 30 days, and that the borrower must pay a fine if the book is not returned after another 5 days. After 30 days, a Recall event is requested. After another 5 days, a Fine event is requested and the activity terminates. A Book Monitor is terminated if an interrupting Return event occurs. If such a Return event occurs within 30 days no Recall event is requested. If an interrupting Return event occurs within 35 days no Fine event is requested. Recall and Fine events are requested immediately. Therefore, a Recall event is requested after exactly 30 days, and a Fine event is requested after exactly 35 days.

The Borrower instance that participates in Recall, Fine, and Return events must be identical to the Borrower instance that participates in the triggering Borrow event. The BookCopy instance that participates in Recall and Return events must be identical to the BoookCopy instance that participates in the triggering Borrow event. This is indicated by

Figure 4. Book Monitor

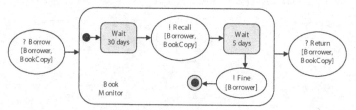

Figure 5. Book Monitor instance

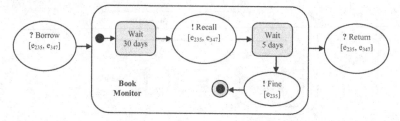

Figure 6. Borrower

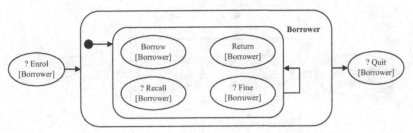

the explicit parameter names. Borrow and Return events are requested by Borrower activities (Figure 6).

Activity Instances

An event-activity diagram defines an activity type that can have multiple, concurrent instances. An instance of an activity type is generated by the occurrence of an event that conforms to a triggering event type.

Figure 5 contains an instance of the event-activity diagram Book Monitor (Figure 4). The participating Borrower is e_{235} and the participating BookCopy is e_{347}. Many Book Monitor instances can be active at a given point in time. Each such instance monitors the returning of a specific book copy.

Independent Events

Some events (and activities) are mutually dependent in the sense that they occur in certain sequences. Other events are independent in the sense that they can occur in any sequence. The following example illustrates how event-activity diagrams can be used to model independent events.

The diagram in Figure 6 models life-cycles of borrowers in a library. A Borrower activity is triggered by the occurrence of an Enrol event, and it is interrupted by the occurrence of a Quit event. A Borrower activity is a sequence of Borrow, Return, Reserve, Recall, and Fine events. These events are independent. This can be seen from the fact that these four event types occur isolated inside an activity box. The Borrower activity chooses one of these events each time this box is activated. Enrol, Recall, Fine, and Quit must be requested by other activities (indicated by the question marks).

Synchronization

Events with multiple participants represent time points where multiple activities must be synchronized. The event-activity diagram Book Monitor in Figure 4 contains several events that have a Borrower instance as participant. Book Monitor instances and Borrower instances must synchronize when Borrow, Recall, Fine, and Return events occur.

The diagram in Figure 7 models life cycles of book copies in a library. A book copy is a physical copy of a certain book title. A BookCopy activity is triggered by the occurrence of a RegisterCopy event, and it is interrupted by the occurrence of a DropCopy event. A

Figure 7. BookCopy

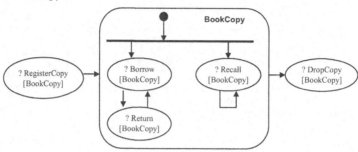

BookCopy activity is composed of two parallel activities. One of these activities is composed of an alternating sequence of Borrow and Return events. The other activity is composed of a sequence of Recall events. All events must be requested by other activities.

The event-activity diagrams in Figure 6 and Figure 7 are synchronized via the shared events Borrow, Return, and Recall. For example, when a Borrower instance requests a Borrow event, the event is executed if and only if the corresponding BookCopy instance is ready to participate.

Discussion

Event-activity diagrams are based on events with participants. This perspective on events is different from the event perspective used by EPC (Nüttgens & Rump, 2002), BPD (Rittgen, 2003), and BPMN (White, 2004). These languages do not consider the participants of events. Event-activity diagrams use events with participants to synchronize two or more concurrent activities. The subdivision of activities into concurrent, interacting activities that is facilitated by this mechanism makes it possible to define activities in a distributed manner that resembles the distribution of activity among actors in a business.

EPC, BPD, and BPMN view events as named points in time that can be used to control the flow of subactivities. Event-activity diagrams can use events in the same manner. Furthermore, event-activity diagrams can use the signatures of triggering events to instantiate multiple instances of a specific activity type.

Activity diagrams can communicate in terms of signals (Rumbaugh et al., 999). This mechanism can be used to synchronize two or more activity diagrams, but it is a very cumbersome method in comparison to the event participant synchronization used in event-activity diagrams. Activity diagrams support modeling of activities that exchange objects when control is transferred from one activity to another. Event-activity diagrams support modeling of asynchronous sharing of objects that is not coupled to transference of control. BPMN supports asynchronous exchange of objects in a similar manner.

FUTURE TRENDS

Early modeling languages, like data flow diagrams, supported activity modeling in terms of activities that manipulate and exchange information. Later, the object-oriented perspective almost completely replaced data flow diagramming and the structured methods. Recently, flow-based languages have gained renewed interest.

The most significant difference between data flow diagrams and more recent languages like EPC, BPD, and BPMN is the fact that the latter are based on events. Ironically, Yourdon (1989) extended data flow diagrams with triggering events and the notion of essential activities a few years before structured analysis was replaced by object-oriented methods.

Business events are important in many ways. They represent business transactions. They initiate and terminate workflow activities. They define time points where important information is registered and stored in databases. The notion of shared events and the corresponding modeling constructs of event-activity diagrams can be used to support analysis of business events. And they can be used to support design of new business activities—new ways of doing business.

We believe that the current interest in events and event modeling will continue, and that new language constructs based on events will appear in the near future. It is likely that the use of events in such languages will make the transition from business activity analysis to object-oriented software design smoother. The reason is that events indicate potential points in time where there may be interaction between human actors and IT-systems. And events are conceptually closer to object-oriented concepts, like messages, than general activities are.

Also, we believe that the notion of events will play an increasingly important role in business analysis and IT-systems. In these years, we witness an increasing integration of human activity and activity performed by IT-systems. Events are the atoms of business activities and they can be used to define business activity rules, and they represents the points in time in which relevant business information can be recorded.

CONCLUSION

We have discussed and analyzed UML's current support for business activity modeling. UML support relevant activity modeling in many ways. However, UML was initially created to support object-oriented software modeling. Consequently, its support for business activity modeling is somewhat inferior.

We have extended UML's activity diagrams with shared events and asynchronous sharing of objects. The resulting event-activity diagrams can be used to define business activities that include business transactions. It is possible to define entity life cycles in a way that resembles entity modeling in JSD (Jackson, 1983). It is possible to define triggering events that resemble the notion of essential events. And it is possible to use events to synchronize multiple, concurrent activities.

Event-activity diagrams can be used to support important modeling activities like analysis of business events, determination of borders between people and IT-systems, determination of the future activities of actors, determination of the degree of autonomy of IT-actors, and identification of use cases.

REFERENCES

Alter, S. (1999, March). A general, yet useful theory of information systems. *Communications of the Association for Information Systems, 1*(13).

Avison, D. E., & Wood-Harper, A. T. (1990). *Multiview*. Oxford, UK: Blackwell Scientific Publications.

Bækgaard, L. (2001). Event modeling. In M. Rossi & K. Siau (Eds.), *Information modeling in the new millennium*. Hershey, PA: Idea Group Publishing.

Bækgaard, L. (2004). Event-based activity modeling. In *Proceedings of the ALOIS'04 — Action in Language, Organisation and Information Systems*. Linköping, Sweden.

Beyer, H., & Holtzblatt, K. (1998). *Contextual design. Designing customer-centered systems*. San Fransisco: Morgan Kaufmann Publishers.

Buckingham, R. A., Hirschheim, R. A., Land, F. F., & Tully, C. J. (Eds.). (1987). *Information systems education: Recommendations and implementation*. Cambridge: Cambridge University Press.

Checkland, P. (1981). *Systems thinking, systems practice*. West Sussex, UK: Wiley.

Checkland, P., & Holwell, S. (1998). *Information, systems, and information systems*. West Sussex, UK: Wiley.

De Marco, T. (1978). *Structured analysis and system specification*. New York: Yourdon.

Denning, P. J., & Medina-Mora, R. (1995, May-June). Completing the loops. *Interfaces, 25*(3), 42-57.

Dreyfus, P. J., & Dreyfus, S. E. (1986). *Mind over machine*. New York: The Free Press.

Goldkuhl, G. (1996). Generic business frameworks and action modeling. *First International Workshop on Communication Modeling*, Tilburg, The Netherlands.

Goldkuhl, G. & Ågerfalk, P. J. (1998). Action within information systems: Outline of a requirements engineering method. In *Proceedings of the 4th International Workshop on Requirements Engineering: Foundation for Software Quality (REFSQ'98)*, Pisa, Italy.

Jackson, M. (1983). *System development*. Hertfordshire, UK: Prentice Hall International.

Jacobson, I., Booch, G., & Rumbaugh, J. (1999). *The unified software development process*. Reading, MA: Addison-Wesley.

Lundeberg, M., Goldkuhl, G., & Nilsson, A. (1978). *Systemeering* (in Swedish). Lund, Sweden: Studentlitteratur.

Mathiassen, L., Munk-Madsen, A., Nielsen, P. A., & Stage, J. (2000). *Object-oriented analysis & design*. Aalborg, Denmark: Marko Publishing House.

Nüttgens, M., & Rump, F. J. (2002). Geschäftsprozessmanagement mit Ereignisgesteuerten Prozessketten. *EPK2002*, Trier, Germany, November 21-22, 2002.

Rittgen, P. (2003). Business processes in UML. In L. Favre (Ed.), *UML and the unified process*. Hershey, PA: Idea Group Publishing.

Rumbaugh, J., Jacobson, I., & Booch, G. (1999). *The Unified Modeling Language reference manual*. Reading, MA: Addison-Wesley.

White, S. A. (2004). *Introduction to BPMN*. Retrieved August 5, 2005, from http://www.bpmn.org

Yourdon, E. (1989). *Modern structured analysis*. Upper Saddle River, NJ: Prentice-Hall.

Chapter II

Modeling and Specification of Collaborative Business Processes with an MDA Approach and a UML Profile

Pablo David Villarreal, CDIDI - Universidad Tecnológica Nacional, Argentina

Enrique Salomone, INGAR-CONICET, Argentina

Omar Chiotti, Universidad Tecnologica Nacional & INGAR-CONICET, Argentina

ABSTRACT

This chapter describes the application of MDA (model driven architecture) and UML for the modeling and specification of collaborative business processes, with the purpose of enabling enterprises to establish business-to-business collaborations. The proposed MDA approach provides the components and techniques required for the development of collaborative processes from their conceptual modeling to the specifications of these processes and the partners' interfaces in a B2B standard. As part of this MDA approach, a UML profile is provided that extends the semantics of UML2 to support the analysis and design of collaborative processes. This UML profile is based on the use of interaction protocols to model collaborative processes. The application of this UML profile in a case study is presented. Also, an overview is provided about the automatic generation of B2B specifications from conceptual models of collaborative processes. In particular, the generation of B2B specifications based on ebXML is described.

INTRODUCTION

To compete in the current global markets, enterprises are focusing on setting up business-to-business (B2B) collaborative relationships with their partners in order to improve their performance, as well as the global performance of the supply chain (Liu & Kumar, 2003). A B2B collaboration implies the integration of enterprises in two levels: a business level and a technological level. In order to accomplish inter-enterprise integration at both levels, one of the main challenges is the modeling and specification of *collaborative business processes*. Through these processes, enterprises undertake to jointly carry out decisions to achieve common goals, coordinate their actions, and exchange information.

On the one hand, the definition of interenterprise integration at business level requires the conceptual modeling of collaborative processes. Business engineers and system designers have to rely on a language that allows them to model these processes without considering the technology used to implement them. Moreover, such modeling language has to support the particular requirements of the B2B collaborations: enterprise autonomy, decentralization, global view of the collaboration, peer-to-peer interactions, and the use of suitable abstractions to model communicative actions and negotiations among partners.

On the other hand, collaborative process models defined at business level have to be translated into specifications of collaborative processes and systems' interfaces based on a B2B standard so that partners can execute these processes. Currently, however, the development of collaborative processes, from the conceptual modeling up to the specifications in a B2B standard, is costly, time consuming, and complex. In addition, collaborative process models must be consistent with the specifications generated at the technological level. Hence, an approach is required to allow business engineers to focus on the business level, and automatically generate the technological solutions required to carry out a B2B collaboration from the conceptual models of collaborative processes, in order to maintain the consistency between both levels.

The objective of this chapter is to show how the MDA (model driven architecture) initiative (OMG, 2003) can be applied to the development of collaborative processes in order to address the aforementioned issues. Through an MDA approach, collaborative process models play an important role. Hence, business engineers can focus mainly on the design of collaborative process models to define partners' business integration and the behavior of the B2B collaborations. Then, they can transform these models to automatically generate the XML code of the specifications of the collaborative processes and the partners' interfaces in a B2B standard. In this way, an MDA approach intends to reduce the inherent complexity and costs which partners have to incur during the development of collaborative processes and B2B systems, and to ensure that a business solution is consistent with their respective technological solutions.

In addition, this chapter describes how to extend the semantics of UML2 for supporting the conceptual modeling of collaborative processes. A UML profile for collaborative processes is presented that has the aim of supporting the particular requirements of B2B collaborations. These requirements are met through the use of interaction protocols to model collaborative processes. Interactions protocols are based on speech act theory (Searle, 1975) and hence, by means of this UML profile, business engineers can define, in a richer way, communicative actions and negotiations between partners in collaborative processes.

This chapter is organized in the following way. The first section introduces the main concepts of B2B collaborations, then it describes the requirements for both the conceptual modeling of collaborative processes and the automatic generation of B2B specifications, and finally it discusses limitations of current proposals. The second section describes the MDA approach for the development of collaborative processes. The third section describes the UML Profile for Collaborative Business Processes Based on Interaction Protocols (UP-ColBPIP). The fourth section provides an overview of the automatic generation of the specifications of collaborative processes and partners' interfaces from UP-ColBPIP models. In particular, the transformation of UP-ColBPIP models into ebXML specifications is described. Finally, the fifth section outlines future trends, and the last section presents conclusions.

BACKGROUND

A B2B collaboration implies integration of enterprises at two levels: a business level and a technological level. The *business level* refers to the problem domain, that is, business engineers' view of the B2B collaboration. At this level, integration is addressed through the application of a collaborative business model. Examples of these models for the supply chain management are vendor managed inventory (VMI) (CompTIA EIDX, 2004); collaborative forecasting, planning and replenishment (CPFR) (VICS, 2002); and the Partner-to-Partner Collaborative Model (Villarreal, Caliusco, Zucchini, Arredondo, Zanel, Galli, & Chiotti, 2003a). A collaborative model defines the generic rules and parameters to be considered in inter-enterprise collaboration. However, the concrete behavior of the collaboration is formalized in *collaborative business processes* that define the roles performed by partners and how they coordinate their actions and exchange information. Therefore at this level, enterprises have to focus mainly on the definition of these processes, according to the features of the collaborative model agreed by enterprises.

An important requirement at business level is the definition of collaborative processes without considering the technology used to implement them. This is due to the fact that the people involved at this level are not acquainted with or are not interested in dealing with the technical details of the implementation. Furthermore, the modeling of these processes should not be driven by a specific technology (Baghdadi, 2004). The technology should be decided later.

The *technological level* refers to the solution domain, that is, system architects and developers' view on the solution. At this level, integration is addressed through the implementation of a B2B information system. This type of system is composed of autonomous, heterogeneous, and distributed components that are deployed by each enterprise to jointly execute collaborative processes with other partners. Interoperability between these components is a key issue. It can be achieved by using a B2B standard that provides the languages to specify the so-called B2B protocols (Bernauer, Kappel, & Kramler, 2003; Bussler, 2001). Two important interoperability aspects are supported by these protocols: the specification of the collaborative processes and the specification of partners' interfaces that compose the B2B information system, both based on executable languages.

In this way, technology-independent collaborative processes should be modeled at business level, and then specified at the technological level through B2B protocols. Both definitions must have a mutual correspondence in order to make sure that the technological solution is consistent and supports the collaborative processes agreed by the partners. In addition, for the purpose of taking advantage of new market opportunities, enterprises need to reduce cost, time, and complexity in the generation of technological solutions. To address such issues, several authors (Baghdadi, 2004; Bernauer et al., 2003) have recognized the convenience of providing approaches for the design of collaborative processes, regardless of the idiosyncrasies of particular B2B standards; and the automatic generation of B2B specifications based on a B2B standard from those processes.

To achieve the above requirements, model-driven development (MDD) has been identified as an appropriate software development philosophy to be exploited in a method for the development of collaborative processes (Villarreal, Salomone, & Chiotti, 2005). Two premises of MDD are (Selic, 2003) models play an important role, since they are the main development products instead of the programs; the code has to be generated in an automatic way from these models. Therefore, by applying an MDD approach, business engineers and system developers can build and transform collaborative process models in order to generate the XML code of the B2B specifications.

In addition, the OMG's MDA initiative (OMG, 2003) proposes a conceptual framework, along with a set of standards to build model-driven development methods. A key MDA standard is UML. The use of standards provides a significant importance because it allows communication of the best design practices, enables and encourages reuse, facilitates interoperability among complementary tools, and encourages specialization (Selic, 2003).

One principle of MDA is that the development of information systems can be organized around a set of models by imposing a series of transformations between models, organized into an architectural framework of layers and transformations. The components of MDA are platform independent models (PIMs), platform specific models (PSMs), transformations from PIMs into PSMs, and transformations from PSMs into source code (Figure 1). A platform makes reference to the technology that supports the system being built. In this way, the development process consists of: defining the PIMs; selecting the platform and executing the transformations that generate PSMs; and finally, generating the code from the selected PSM.

In order to define an MDA approach for the development of collaborative processes, two main tasks have to be supported :

- Conceptual modeling of collaborative processes to support the analysis and design of these processes without considering the technological issues.
- Automatic generation of B2B specifications from models of collaborative processes.

The requirements to support the above tasks are now discussed and analyzed.

Requirements for the Conceptual Modeling of Collaborative Processes

The traditional approach to model business processes has been the use of workflow modeling languages. However, as it has been previously discussed in several works (Bussler,

Figure 1. Development process based on MDA

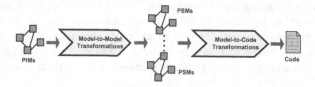

2001; Chen & Hsu, 2001), the use of workflows to manage collaborative processes is not appropriate. This is due to the particular characteristics of the B2B collaborations that impose several requirements (Villarreal, Salomone, & Chiotti, 2003b). Therefore, to support such requirements in the conceptual modeling of collaborative business processes, a suitable modeling language is required.

A first requirement is to represent the global view of the interactions between the partners. Public behavior and responsibilities of each partner, in terms of sending and receiving messages, should be explicitly defined in a collaborative process model.

Second, in B2B collaborations, enterprises behave as autonomous entities that collaborate while they hide their internal activities and decisions. This autonomy should be preserved in collaborative process models; that is, internal activities each partner performs for processing the received information or producing the information to be sent should not be defined.

Third, the decentralized management of collaborative processes can be achieved through peer-to-peer (P2P) interactions between the partners (Chen & Hsu, 2001), where each of them manages the role it performs in a B2B collaboration. Therefore, P2P interactions should be also expressed in a collaborative process model. This is correlated with the global-view requirement since this view allows describing P2P interactions.

Fourth, in the supply chain management through B2B collaborations, enterprises carry out joint decision making in order to agree on common demand forecasts, production plans, order plans, and so forth. Therefore, a modeling language for collaborative processes should provide appropriate primitives that enable representing complex negotiations in these processes.

Fifth, as it is discussed later, the definition of B2B interactions in collaborative processes cannot be restricted to the mere information exchange. It is also necessary to support communicative actions and the creation of commitments in the interactions between the parties.

Finally, there are different perspectives that a business process model has to support: functional (actions or activities), behavioral (control flow), informational (exchanged documents), operational (applications), and organizational (roles) (Jablosnky & Bussler, 1996). Although most of them are appropriate in collaborative process models, the operational perspective should not be defined by them, because the knowledge of the private applications that a partner uses to support collaborative processes reduces the enterprise autonomy.

Requirements for the Automatic Generation of B2B Specifications

As it was described previously, collaborative processes are implemented through B2B protocols that contain the specifications of these processes, and the corresponding partners' interfaces. Currently, there are two main technologies proposed for the specification of B2B protocols (Bernauer et al., 2003): standards based on Web services composition, such as BPEL (Business Process Execution Language) (BEA, IBM, Microsoft, SAP, & Siebel, 2003) and Web Services Choreography Description Language (WS-CDL) (W3C, 2004); and standards based on business transactions, such as ebXML (electronic business XML) (OASIS, 1999) and RosettaNet (1999).

On the one hand, standards based on business transactions and standards based on Web services composition are not compatible, and thus enterprises have to decide which ones to use. Furthermore, B2B standards are in constant evolution: new ones are proximate to appear, and there are different versions of them. As a consequence, the automatic generation of B2B specifications requires a particular transformation procedure for each standard and version.

On the other hand, an enterprise should be able to collaborate with several partners using different B2B standards (Medjahed, Benatallah, Bouguettaya, Ngu, & Ahmed, 2003). Moreover, a partner may require implementing the same collaborative processes with several partners using different B2B standards. This requirement can be solved reusing technology-independent collaborative process models to generate technological solutions in different standards.

Limitation of the Current Proposals

Several works have been proposed to support the modeling and specification of business processes in B2B settings. Some of them are MDD approaches, proposed to generate technological solutions based on Web services composition (Baïna, Benatallah, Cassati, & Toumani, 2004; Koehler, Hauser, Kapoor, Wu, & Kumaran, 2003). They focus on the modeling and automatic code generation of business or conversation protocols based on BPEL. This type of protocol refers to the message exchange between a composite Web service and a client of the Web service, without defining the internal business logic of the service. A conversation protocol defines the order in which a partner sends messages to and receives messages from its partners. Therefore, they focus on the modeling and specification of the behavior of collaborative processes, but from the point of view of only one partner. As a result, these approaches do not fulfill the requirement of representing the global view of the interactions between the partners. Also, they only consider as implementation technology the use of a Web services composition standard.

Gardner (2003) proposes an MDD approach, and provides a UML profile for modeling of business processes based on BPEL. Therefore, in this approach the definition of technology-independent process models is not supported, and it is also focused on a specific standard. In addition, BPEL only supports collaborative processes defined as conversation protocols.

Hofreiter and Huemer (2004a) propose the generation of ebXML BPSS (business process specification schema) (UN/CEFACT & OASIS, 2003) specifications from conceptual models of collaborative processes. The modeling language used to support the analysis and design of collaborative processes is that provided by UN/CEFACT modeling methodology (UMM). Such language was defined as a UML profile. Although UMM claims independence of the technology, the main conceptual elements are those used in BPSS, because the BPSS metamodel is a subset of the UMM metamodel. Hence, although the transformation of UMM into BPSS is simple and almost direct, this language influences the adoption of one standard. Moreover, UMM encourages defining collaborative processes in a hierarchical way, first defining business collaborations and then defining business transactions. This hierarchical approach does not enable representing the interactions and partners' responsibilities within a collaborative process in a high abstraction level. They are defined within business transactions, but not in the business collaboration realizing the collaborative process.

In addition, the interaction patterns proposed by UMM to define business transactions do not support complex negotiations. As an example, the *commercial (offer-acceptation)* pattern describes a negotiation with an offer that can be only accepted or rejected. However, in complex negotiations, there may exist different options and counterproposals. In this way, the different stages of a negotiation into a business collaboration cannot be identified without additional effort. This effort results in a higher complexity to model negotiations in collaborative processes.

Hofreiter and Huemer (2004b) also propose the transformation of collaborative processes defined with UMM into BPEL specifications. However, this approach does not consider the application of an MDD or MDA approach to support the development of collaborative processes.

Table 1 synthesizes the strengths and limitations of these approaches. In brief, although the benefits of MDA for the domain of collaborative processes and B2B specifications are clear, currently, it has not been completely exploited in this domain. First, there is a lack of technology-independent modeling languages that support the identified requirements for the conceptual modeling of collaborative processes: in particular, the requirements of global view of the interactions, support for negotiations, and support for the definition of communicative aspects. Second, some of the described approaches are not based on a conceptual

Table 1. Strengths and limitations of the current approaches

Current approaches	Strengths	Limitations
MDD approach for Web services composition Baïna et al., 2004)	• A MDD approach to generate technological solutions based on Web services composition • Processes are modeled by using extended state machines	• No support to model the global view of interactions • Focus only on a web services composition standard • Use of MDA and UML is not considered • No support for negotiations and communicative actions
MDD approach for Web services composition (Koehler et al., 2003)	• A MDD approach to generate technological solutions based on Web services composition • Explicit separation of the business view and the technological view • Use of UML Activity Diagrams to model processes	• MDA is not considered • No support to model the global view of the collaborative processes • Focus only on a web services composition standard • No support for negotiations and communicative actions.
UML Profile for BPEL (Gardner, 2003)	• Use of MDA and a UML Profile (it essentially uses activity diagrams to model BPEL processes)	• No support to model the global view of interactions • A technology-independent UML Profile is not considered • No support for negotiations and communicative actions.

Table 1. continued

| UMM (Hofreiter and Huemer , 2004a),Hofreiter and Huemer , 2004b) | • Provide a UML Profile to model business collaborations
• Support the global view of the interactions
• Support to define commitments in the interactions between the partners | • Focus mainly one bXML.
• Hierarchical definition of the collaborative processes do not highlight the interactions and the partners' responsibilities in a high abstraction level
• Stages of a negotiation into a business collaboration cannot be identified without to exploit the business transactions
• MDA is not considered
• No support to model transformations. |

framework such as MDA and therefore, neither the use of standards such as UML nor the use of model transformation mechanisms to generate code is considered. Finally, most of the above approaches consider only one type of implementation technology, such as the use of Web services composition standards.

An MDA Approach for Collaborative Business Processes

In order to exploit the benefits of the model-driven development for the collaborative process domain, an MDA approach, which aims at enterprises at the different stages of the development of collaborative processes, is proposed.

In MDA, the concept of system does not only refer to the software, but can also refer to an enterprise, a set of enterprises, parts of different systems, and so forth. In the MDA approach proposed in this chapter, the system to be built includes the specifications of the collaborative processes, and the partners' interfaces of the B2B information system, both based on a B2B standard.

In addition, MDA provides the guidelines and the general components that a model-driven development method has to contain, but it does not provide the concrete techniques to be used in each domain. Although UML can be considered as a generic standard modeling language that can also be used to model organizational aspects, it is important to use languages and techniques that are more suitable and closer to the application domain.

Therefore, with the purpose of providing an MDA approach for collaborative processes, the components to be taken into account, along with the languages and techniques proposed to build these components, are described (Figure 2):

- **Collaborative business process models based on UP-ColBPIP:** These are the technology-independent collaborative process models and, hence, the main development products. For the building of these models, the *UML Profile for Collaborative Business Processes Based on Interaction Protocols (UP-ColBPIP)* is proposed, which is described later.
- **The collaborative business process models based on a B2B standard:** These are the collaborative process models specific to the technology. This MDA approach

Figure 2. MDA approach for collaborative processes

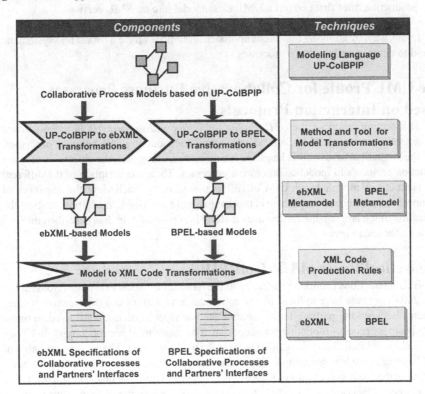

focuses on the generation of two types of technological solutions that can be derived from UP-ColBPIP models: solutions based on the ebXML standard; or solutions based on Web services composition standards, such as BPEL and WS-CDL. For building these models, it is necessary to define their corresponding metamodels. They can be derived from the XML schemas provided by the languages of the B2B standards. In this way, the metamodel of a B2B standard language corresponds to its XML schema, and the models correspond to the XML documents that contain the B2B specifications. Although the XML documents may be generated directly from the UP-ColBPIP models, this intermediate representation allows a more modular and maintainable process transformation and it is in line with the principles of MDA.

- **Transformations of UP-ColBPIP models into models based on a B2B standard:** These transformations allow the generation of technology-dependent process models from UP-ColBPIP models. To support the definition and automatic execution of the transformations, a method and a tool for model transformations is required.
- **B2B specifications:** The final output of the transformations is one or more XML documents that contain the process and the partners' interfaces specifications based on a B2B standard. The transformation of technology-dependent models into the cor-

responding specifications is almost direct. This transformation is supported by XML production rules that convert a UML class model into an XML version.

In this way, by applying this MDA approach, enterprises have a robust and systematic method to develop collaborative processes.

The UML Profile for Collaborative Business Processes Based on Interaction Protocols

This section describes the *UML Profile for Collaborative Business Processes Based on Interaction Protocols (UP-ColBPIP)* proposed for modeling collaborative processes. First, the theoretical bases of this language are discussed, along with the objectives of using interaction protocols to model collaborative processes. Then, a description of the different views that can be modeled with UP-ColBPIP is provided. For each view, the semantics of the conceptual elements incorporated in this language are described. In addition, to show the application of the language, a complete case study is presented, which is described through examples for each view.

Theoretical Bases of UP-ColBPIP

B2B interactions cannot be restricted to the mere information exchange (Goldkuhl & Lind, 2004), but they have to focus on the communicative actions and the creation of commitments between the parties. These communicative aspects are not considered in many of the business process modeling languages such as those used for modeling workflows (GoldKuhl and Lind, 2004; Weigand, Heuvel, & Dignum, 1998). The theoretical bases of these languages are less sound and rigid because they have to rely on the intuitive understanding of their axiomatic notions, such as the concept of activity or task (Dietz, 2002). The consequence of this is the ambiguity in the definition of the activities, because two business engineers can have different interpretations of the same model.

The communicative aspects of B2B interactions can be captured by applying the principles of the language/action perspective (LAP) theory (GoldKuhl & Lind, 2004). The main premise of LAP is that communication is a type of action that creates commitments between the parties. LAP emphasizes what the parties do, how the language is used to create a common understanding, and how the activities are coordinated through the language. Its theoretical foundations are built on speech acts theory (Searle, 1975). A speech act is the speaker's expression of a propositional attitude (utterance) toward some proposition. In other words, a speech act represents the intention of the speaker with respect to some propositional content. An argument of the speech act theory is that different intentions (request, propose, accept, and so on) can be applied to the same content. For example *request (order)* and *propose(order)* have the same propositional content, but clearly express different intentions from the speaker.

Through the use of speech acts, the language is used to create a common understanding between the parties because the semantics of speech acts are known and understood by parties. This is important in B2B collaborations in which partners collaborate to establish commitments and achieve common goals. If such understanding cannot be established, it will be very difficult to achieve the collaboration.

There are several approaches based on LAP for modeling business processes: action workflow (Medina-Mora, Winograd, Flores, & Flores, 1992), DEMO (Dietz, 1999) and layer patterns approaches (Lind & Goldkuhl, 2001; Weigand et al., 1998). These approaches emphasize the use of communication patterns that group a set of interactions based on speech acts. The patterns are generic and predefined. Business processes are defined through the composition of these patterns. Moreover, in some approaches, a pattern represents a specific concept, that is, a business transaction (Dietz, 1999; Lind & Goldkuhl, 2001).

In this way, with these approaches, business engineers have to focus on the modeling of processes using concepts such as generic patterns or business transactions, instead of focusing on the most appropriate speech acts to describe the interactions. Although the speech act is the atomic concept, it is not the main concept used to model processes. Therefore, the use of speech acts to define processes is left in a second place. This leads to a loss of descriptive power in business process models viewed as communicative processes. Furthermore, predefined communication patterns are less flexible for the design; there are situations that cannot be contemplated by these patterns. This has been identified as one of the main weaknesses of these approaches (GoldKuhl & Lind, 2004).

These difficulties can be overcome if speech acts are considered not only as the atomic concept, but also as the main concept used to describe interactions between the parties at a high level. Thus, business engineers may focus on the interactions and the creation of commitments between the parties using speech acts as the first-class construction blocks of the processes.

To fulfill this requirement, the UML profile proposed in this chapter incorporates the concept of *interaction protocol* to represent the behavior of collaborative processes. Interaction protocols are based on the application of speech acts, and have been used in the area of multiagent systems for representing interactions between software agents (Bauer, Müller, & Odel, 2001). Since the properties of software agents (such as autonomy, heterogeneity, decentralization, social interactions) are also desirable for enterprises involved in B2B collaborations, the use of interaction protocols to define B2B interactions arises as a very promising approach to be explored (Villarreal et al., 2003b; Villarreal, Salomone, & Chiotti, 2003c).

In the context of B2B collaborations, an interaction protocol describes a high-level communication pattern through an admissible sequence of business messages between enterprises playing different roles (Villarreal et al., 2003b). A business message is an interaction between two parts that is based on a speech act to represent the intention associated to a business document that a partner is communicating to another partner.

The main objective of modeling collaborative processes through interaction protocols is to fulfill the identified requirements for the conceptual modeling of these processes.

- **Enterprise autonomy:** In contrast to activity-oriented process models, interaction protocols focus on the message exchange between enterprises. Activities each partner performs for processing the information to be received or producing the information to be sent are not defined in the interaction protocols. They are kept hidden to the remaining partners.
- **Global view of the interactions, decentralization, and peer-to-peer interactions:** Through the modeling of interaction protocols, the focus is on the representation of the global view of the interactions between the partners. The message choreography describes peer-to-peer interactions and partners' responsibilities in the roles they play. It also shows the decentralized feature of the interactions.

- **Support for negotiations:** Through the use of business messages based on speech acts, interaction protocols also provide an intentional perspective to process models. Decisions and commitments made by the partners can be known from the speech acts. This enables the definition of complex negotiations in collaborative processes.
- **Support for modeling the communicative aspects of B2B collaborations:** The communicative aspects of B2B collaborations can be represented by modeling interaction protocols because they are based on the use of speech acts. In addition, messages based on speech acts are used at a high level, and are the first-class construction blocks. In this way, business engineers have to focus on the semantics of each message selecting the most appropriate speech act.

Description of the Modeling Language UP-ColBPIP

The modeling language UP-ColBPIP has been defined as a UML profile that extends the semantics of UML2 to model collaborative processes. A UML profile is defined using the extension mechanisms provided by UML: stereotypes, tagged values, and constraints. *Stereotypes* define new conceptual elements as extensions of UML metaclasses. *Tagged values* define attributes of the stereotypes. *Constraints* may be defined on the stereotypes or the UML metaclasses to restrict the way in which the original concepts of UML or the stereotypes can be used. One of the purposes behind UP-ColBPIP is to provide the best possible correspondence with UML, so that its graphical notation is intuitive for a business process designer who has worked with UML. Therefore, the semantics of the conceptual elements (stereotypes) of UP-ColBPIP is similar, or there is a correspondence with the semantics of the extended UML2 elements. Appendix A contains a summary of the UP-ColBPIP stereotypes and the UML metaclasses they extend. They can be used to implement this UML profile in any UML case tool that supports it.

UP-ColBPIP encourages a top-down approach to model collaborative processes because it supports the modeling of four views: *B2B collaboration view, collaborative processes view, interaction protocols view* and *business interfaces view*. Each view is a refinement of the previous one.

Following, the conceptual elements of UP-ColBPIP that support the modeling of the above views are described. Furthermore, the application of UP-ColBPIP is illustrated through a case study of a B2B collaboration between two manufacturer enterprises. The purpose of this B2B collaboration is that partners carry out a collaborative replenishment based on a vendor-managed inventory (VMI) collaborative model. In this model, the supplier determines when to ship materials and how much to ship for replenishing the customer's inventory. Calculation of the replenishment may be based on a forecast, or only on consumption data. Particularly, the B2B collaboration is defined according to the forecast-based VMI model proposed by EIDX (EIDX, 2004), a consortium of enterprises of the electronics industry.

Defining the B2B Collaboration View

This view captures the participants and their communication relationships in order to provide an overview of the B2B collaboration. To support this view, UP-ColBPIP extends the semantics of the UML collaborations. Therefore, a *B2B collaboration* is defined in a UML composite structure diagram and is represented by the stereotype <<B2B Collaboration>>. A B2B collaboration represents a set of cooperating *trading partners* performing a specific *role*. Communication between the partners is represented by a *B2B relationship* that

Figure 3. A composite structure diagram describing a B2B collaboration

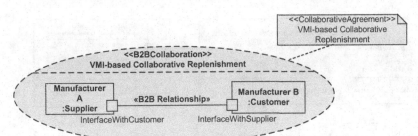

is represented by a connector with the stereotype <<B2B Relationship>>. Trading partners own *public business interfaces* (*ports* in UML) that allow them to engage in a B2B relationship to interact with another partner and fulfill a specific role. Furthermore, the name of the *collaborative agreement* is associated to the B2B collaboration.

As an example, Figure 3 shows the B2B collaboration of the collaborative replenishment based on a VMI model of the case study. This B2B collaboration indicates *Manufacturer B* performs the role *Customer,* and *Manufacturer A* performs the role *Supplier*. *Manufacturer A* contains the public business interface *InterfaceWithCustomer,* and *Manufacturer B* contains the public business interface *InterfaceWithSupplier*. Partners communicate through these interfaces. The name of the collaborative agreement is associated to the B2B collaboration.

Furthermore, the B2B collaboration view describes the parameters of the *collaborative agreement* and the hierarchy of common *business goals* that partners have agreed. To represent it, UP-ColBPIP extends the semantics of the UML classes and objects. A *collaborative agreement* defines the parameters (attributes) that govern the B2B collaboration, which are defined in a class with the stereotype <<Collaborative Agreement>>. The collaborative agreement has also an associated hierarchy of common *business goals* that indicates the requirements to be fulfilled in the B2B collaboration. A business goal represents a common objective to be achieved by the partners. Through the definition of common business goals, partners can later evaluate the collaboration performance.

Business goals are defined based on the goal patterns proposed in Eriksson and Penker (2000) to model organizational goals. A business goal can have several subgoals, and there can be one root business goal. Subgoals have to be fulfilled for the achievement of their upper goal. The name of a goal should be defined in terms of a desire state about some information shared by partners, or in terms of optimization such as improve sales, reduce inventory, and so forth. Two types of predefined business goals are included in the profile: *quantitative goal* and *qualitative goal*. Quantitative goals are defined on the basis of performance measurements (such as key performance indicators) about some information shared by the partners. This type of goal is described by a current value (if known), a target value, the measurement unit being used, the computation method (metric), and the update frequency of the defined metric. Qualitative goals are informally described, and they rely on human judgment rather than a specific value. Business goals are defined in a class diagram as instances of the *QuantitativeGoal* or the *QuanlitativeGoal* classes that are stereotyped <<Business Goal>>. Goals and their subgoals are associated by the use of dependency relationships.

Figure 4. Class diagram describing the collaborative agreement and the business goals

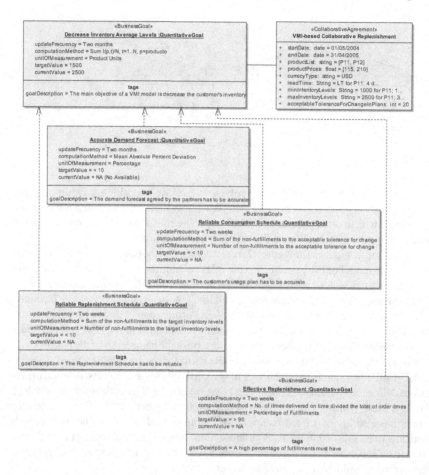

Figure 4 shows the class diagram with the collaborative agreement and the business goals that partners have agreed in relation to the above defined B2B collaboration. The collaborative agreement has several attributes. The first two attributes define the agreement period. The next three attributes refer to commercial aspects, such as the products to be considered in the collaboration, the price of products, and the money used for the commercial transactions. The other attributes define the parameters to be used for the inventory management.

The hierarchy of business goals indicates that the root goal defines the main purpose of a VMI model: *decrease inventory average levels*. To achieve this goal, four subgoals have to be fulfilled. All the goals have been defined as quantitative goals with their corresponding attributes. For example, the main goal indicates that the current inventory average level is "2,500 units," the target value to be achieved is "1,500 units," the measurement unit is "product units," the metric is "the sum of the inventory average values of each product," and the update frequency of the metric is "2 months."

Defining the Collaborative Business Processes View

This view is concerned with the identification of the collaborative processes that are required to achieve the business goals defined in the previous view. To support this view, UP-ColBPIP extends the semantics of the UML use cases. In UML, a use case is used to capture the system's requirements, that is, what a system is supposed to do. In UP-ColBPIP, a *collaborative process* is used to capture the actions that partners will perform and the business documents they will exchange as part of the B2B collaboration. In this way, a collaborative process is defined as an informal specification of a set of actions performed by trading partners to achieve a goal. In UML use cases diagrams, collaborative processes are defined using the use case notation with the stereotype <<collaborative business process>>.

Two or more roles performed by trading partners can be involved in a collaborative process. Roles and partners have to correspond to those defined in this view. They are represented with the notation of *actor* and are associated to the collaborative processes.

A business goal can be only achieved through the execution of collaborative processes. Hence, the dependency relationship stereotyped <<Achieves>> indicates the allocation of a business goal to a collaborative process. Through business goals, the performance of collaborative processes can be also evaluated later.

A collaborative process can be composed of *subprocesses* to indicate that a process contains the behavior provided by other processes. To represent it, the *include* relationship of UML is extended with the stereotyped <<subprocess>>. In addition, a collaborative process can be also composed of exception processes. An *exception process* is a specific type of collaborative process that is used to manage a predefined exception that can occur in a collaborative process. The exception process indicates how the collaborative process can be finished or corrected in case the exception occurs. The place where an exception can occur in a collaborative process is indicated through exception points defined within the process.

The stereotyped <<exception>> represents the relationship between an exception process and a collaborative process. This stereotype extends the semantics of the *extend* relationship of UML. The place where the exception can occur in the behavior of a collaborative process and the condition to be evaluated for enacting the exception process is indicated with a comment associated to the relationship exception.

A collaborative process has several attributes that can be defined with expressions in natural language or in OCL (object constraint language). The *startEvent* attribute defines the events that trigger the process. The *preCondition* attribute defines the condition that has to be satisfied before the execution of the process. This condition can be defined according to the state (ready, executing, or finished) of an instance of another process, or the state of a business document. The *postCondition* attribute defines the condition that has to be satisfied after the execution of the process.

Finally, this view also contains the *business documents*, that is, the information to be exchanged by the partners in the collaborative processes. Because business documents can be exchanged in different processes, they are defined in an independent way. UP-ColBPIP does not support the modeling of the business documents structure, but it just makes reference to them. Business documents and their types are defined in class diagrams, and are stereotyped <<BusinessDocument>> and <<BusinessDocumentType>> respectively. Syntaxes and semantics of the business documents are out of the scope of UP-ColBPIP. Semantics should be defined with specific modeling languages, such as proposed in Caliusco, Maidana, Galli, & Chiotti (2004). Syntax is already provided by the content B2B standard to be used.

Figure 5. Use case diagram describing the collaborative processes

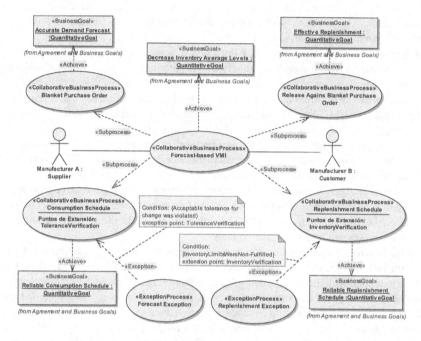

The business documents to be exchanged in a collaborative process are defined as attributes of the process, where the document type corresponds to one of those provided by the B2B standard to be used. The class notation of use cases (with an ellipse in the upper-right corner) can be used to visualize the attributes of the collaborative processes in a class diagram.

As an example, Figure 5 shows the collaborative processes required by the VMI-based collaborative replenishment of the case study. For each business goal defined, a collaborative process has been defined. The *forecast-based VMI* collaborative process is the main process and hence, it has allocated the main goal. According to the hierarchy of business goal, the following collaborative processes have been defined: *blanket purchase* order, *consumption schedule, release against blanket purchase order* and *replenishment schedule* processes. They are the subprocess of the *forecast-based VMI* process. Each collaborative process has an associated business goal to fulfill.

Furthermore, two exception processes have been defined. In the *consumption schedule* collaborative process, its *SupplierVerification* exception point indicates that an exception can occur when the supplier verifies the customer's consumption plan. If this exception occurs, it is managed by the *ForecastException* process, as the *exception* relationship indicates. The comment on this relationship describes the condition to be satisfied for executing this exception process, and also makes reference to the exception point on which the condition is verified. In a similar way, another exception process is associated to the *ReplenishmentSchedule* process.

Figure 6. Class diagram describing the attributes of the collaborative processes

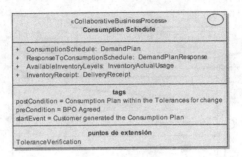

Figure 6 shows the attributes of the collaborative process *consumption schedule*. The attribute *startEvent* indicates this process is initiated when the client generates a consumption schedule. The *precondition* indicates that before the execution of this process, the *blanket purchase order (BPO)* business document must be agreed. The *postCondition* indicates this process has to finish with a consumption schedule that fulfills the change tolerances defined in the agreement. Finally, two business documents will be exchanged in this process: the consumption schedule to be sent by the customer, and the schedule response to be sent by the supplier.

Defining the Interaction Protocols View

This view focuses on the definition of the formal behavior of the collaborative processes that are realized through interaction protocols. UP-ColBPIP extends the semantics of the UML interactions to support the modeling of interaction protocols. Therefore, interaction protocols can be visualized in UML2 interaction diagrams: sequence diagram, communication diagram, interaction overview diagram and timing diagram. The former is the best known, and provides a more expressive concrete syntax for interaction protocols. The sequence diagrams describing interaction protocols are stereotyped <<protocol>>.

The behavior semantics of an interaction protocol, that is, the choreography of messages, is defined by the ordered sequence of the following elements: business messages, control flow segments, interaction paths, protocol references, and terminations.

Following, the main conceptual elements used to define interaction protocols are described. Figure 7 shows the notations for the elements of an interaction protocol through a typical protocol that can be used when a partner asks another one to carry out some action or produce some information for the former. In this example, a partner playing the role of supplier is requesting a demand forecast to another partner playing the role of customer.

Trading Partner and Role

The trading partners participating in an interaction protocol and the role they fulfill are represented in *lifelines* (see notation in Figure 7).

Figure 7. Notations for the elements of the interaction protocols

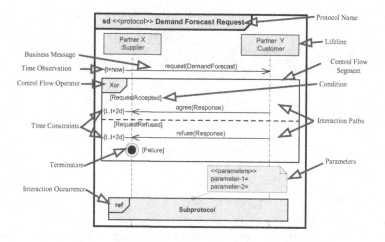

Business Message, Speech Acts and Business Documents

A business message defines an interaction or communication between two roles: a sender and a receiver. A business message contains a speech act and a business document (see notation in Figure 7). The semantics of a business message is defined by its associated speech act. A business message expresses the sender has done an action that generates the communication of a speech act representing the sender's intention with respect to the exchanged business document. Also, the message indicates the sender's expectation, and the receptor then acts according to the semantics of the speech act.

As an example (Figure 7), in the message "request(DemandForecast)," the speech act "request" indicates the supplier's intention of requesting a demand forecast from the customer. It also implies the customer cannot respond with any speech act but a suitable speech act, such as agree, or refuse, indicating the reasons of the acceptance or refusal in its associated business document. Hence, the speech act to use for describing a business message depends on its semantics. To define messages of the protocols, we have used the speech acts provided by FIPA ACL library. The semantics of these speech acts can be found in FIPA (2002).

A business message also represents a one-way asynchronous communication. This feature is essential in B2B interactions because the sender's internal control must not be subordinated to the receptor's response. A business message is managed by the receptor just as a signal that has to be interpreted to activate the internal behaviors of the receptor. In addition, a business message may require the sending of acknowledgments by the receiver toward the sender. A *receipt acknowledgement* indicates that the receptor has to send an acknowledgment if the message has been received. A *read acknowledgement* indicates the receptor has to send an acknowledgment if the message has been validated and understood.

To represent business messages, the semantics of the messages used in the UML interactions is extended. In UML, the *signature* of a *message* can refer to a signal or an operation. However, in our modeling domain, trading partners cannot invoke private behaviors of other trading partners, but they can only manage asynchronous reception signals used to internally activate their behaviors. Therefore, the *signature* of a *BusinessMessage* must only refer to a *signal*, and not to an *operation*. In addition, since the signature of a business message refers to the associated speech act, the stereotype *SpeechAct* extends the semantics of the UML signals.

The acknowledgments of a business message can be added as its tagged values. If these attributes are true, the acknowledgments have to be done.

Finally, a business message can have a condition to indicate when the message can be sent. The condition on a message is indicated before its signature with the following syntaxes: "[<condition expression>]:". Furthermore, a business message may be sent several times. In this case, the acknowledgments must be returned each time the message is sent. The repetition of a message is indicated before its condition or signature. The symbol "*" indicates the message can be sent while the condition is satisfied. Or else, the repetition of a message can be indicated with a natural number.

Control Flow Segment

It is used to represent complex message sequences in the choreography of an interaction protocol. It contains a control flow operator and one or more interaction paths. An interaction path (interaction operand in UML) can contain any element of a protocol: messages, terminations, interaction occurrences, and nested control flow segments. The stereotype *control flow segment* extends the semantics of the *combined fragment* of UML interactions in order to provide well-known control flow operators for defining collaborative processes. It is represented as a box with a rounded rectangle in the upper-left corner that contains a *control flow operator*. The interaction paths are divided by a dashed horizontal line (see notation in Figure 7).

The semantics of a control flow segment depends on the control flow operator being used. The operators provided by UP-ColBPIP are Xor, Or, And, If, Loop, Transaction, Exception, Stop, and Cancel. The *And* operator represents the execution of parallel (concurrent) interaction paths in any order. The execution of the messages of the different paths can be interleaved, but the message sequence in each path must be fulfilled. The *Xor* operator represents that in a set of alternative paths, only one can be executed in case its condition is evaluated to true. The *Or* operator represents two or more paths that can be executed, and at least one of them must be executed. Also, all paths can be executed in case its condition is evaluated to true. The *If* operator represents a path that is executed when its condition is true, or nothing is executed. This can also have an *else* path that is executed when the condition of the first path is false. The *Loop* operator represents a path that can be executed while its condition is satisfied. Two types of *Loop* segments can be defined: a loop "For" with the condition "(1,n)," where the segment path must be executed at least once; and a loop "While" with the condition "(0,n)," where the path can be executed zero or *n* times. The *Transaction* operator represents that the messages and paths of the segment have to be done atomically, and the messages cannot be interleaved with messages of other paths. If a failure occurs in this type of segment, the messages executed and the assumed commitments are discharged. The *Exception* operator represents the path to be followed as a consequence of an exception (defined in the condition of the path) that can occur in the specific point of the protocol where the segment is defined. The *Stop* operator is similar to the *Exception*, but is used to require the abrupt termination of the protocol. The *Cancel* operator represents the paths to be followed to manage an exception. Unlike *Stop* and *Exception* operators, the exception to be managed can occur in any point of the interaction protocol. Hence, a segment with this operator has to be defined at the end of the protocol. This type of segment can be used to define the paths to be followed in case of time exceptions, acknowledgment exceptions, and so forth.

Conditions and Time Constraints

Conditions represent logical expressions that constrain the execution of a message or a path into a control flow segment. They can be defined in natural language or using OCL expressions. Time constraints are used to define deadlines on messages or protocols. A time constraint can be defined using relative or absolute dates. It defines a duration representing the deadline for the execution of a message or protocol. Conditions and time constraints are already provided by UML (see Figure 7 for the notations of these elements).

Interaction Occurrence

This UML element is used to represent that another interaction protocol is being invoked, which is referred to as the nested or subprotocol. Its notation is a rectangle with a pentagon with the keyword *ref* (see notation in Figure 7). When the roles of a protocol and its nested protocol are different, the correspondence between the roles has to be defined as parameters associated to the interaction occurrence.

Terminations

Terminations represent the end of a protocol (see notation in Figure 7). Two termination types can be defined: *success* and *failure*. The former implies the protocol has ended in a successful way. A failure indicates the protocol has not ended as it was expected. This only indicates the protocol did not follow the expected business logic. The semantics of the element *stop* of UML is extended to represent *success* and *failure* terminations.

Protocol Template

It represents a reusable pattern of interaction used to define interaction protocols. It has the same features of an interaction protocol. The difference lies in the fact that a protocol template is not a directly usable protocol, but a parameterized protocol. A sequence diagram with the stereotype <<template>> defines a protocol template. To create a protocol based on a template, each protocol parameter is assigned a value. The parameters are the roles and messages' business documents defined in the protocol template. These parameters are not bounded with any business documents and roles defined in the B2B collaboration. Parameters have to be bound to the specific business documents and roles of a B2B collaboration when a protocol is defined. Instantiations of parameters are indicated with a comment stereotyped <<parameters>> linked to the sequence diagram.

Examples of Interactions Protocols Defined for the Case Study

Following, some of the interaction protocols, which realize the collaborative processes of the case study defined in the collaborative processes view, are described.

Figure 8 shows the sequence diagram corresponding to the protocol *Blanket Purchase Order*. This represents a negotiation process between a *customer* and a *supplier* for agree-

Figure 8. Sequence diagram of the protocol blanket purchase order

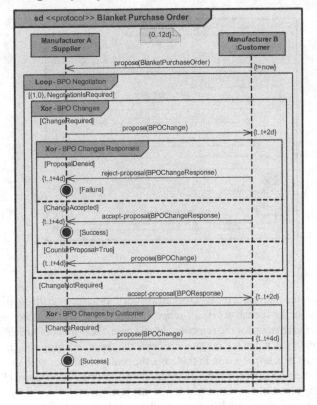

ing on a *Blanket Purchase Order (BPO)*, that is, an order forecast for the agreement period against which multiple short-term releases will be generated to satisfy the customer's requirements. The BPO business document contains total quantity, conditions, and pricing terms on items.

The protocol starts with the *customer*, who based on the results of its internal process of materials requirements planning, sends a business message proposing a BPO, as it is indicated by the speech act *propose* and the business document *BPO* associated to the first message. Then, several negotiation cycles can occur. This is represented by the segment *BPO Negotiation*, which is executed at least once and while the condition *NegotiationIsRequired* is true, that is, while the partners are still interested in following the negotiation. In this loop, the *supplier* internally evaluates the *BPO,* and one of two paths can occur. This is specified by the control flow segment *BPOChanges* with the *Xor* operator.

If changes to the *BPO* are required by the supplier, the first path is executed. The supplier proposes changes to the *BPO* making a counterproposal (message *propose(BPOChanges)*). Then, the customer evaluates the proposed changes, and it can respond in three different ways as it is indicated by the segment *BPOChangeResponses*. One alternative is when the

Figure 9. Sequence diagram of the protocol consumption schedule

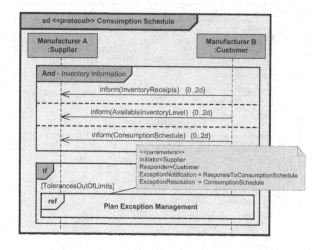

customer rejects the changes to the BPO because it does not agree with the *supplier's* proposal. The message with the speech act *reject-proposal* indicates it. Its associated business document contains the reasons for the rejection. In this case, the protocol finishes with a failure. Another alternative is when the *customer* accepts the *supplier's* proposal, as it is indicated by the speech act *accept-proposal*. In this case, the protocol finishes with success. The third alternative is when the *customer* makes a counterproposal (message *propose(BPOChange)*). In this case, the protocol continues with a new negotiation cycle.

Within the segment *BPOChanges,* if the *supplier* does not require changes, the second path (segment *BPOChanges*) is executed. The *supplier* responds with an *accept-proposal* that represents its acceptance to the BPO proposed by the *customer*. In addition, if the *customer* wants to initiate changes (segment *BPO Changes By Customer*), it makes a counterproposal sending the *propose(BPOChanget)* message. In this case, the protocol continues with a new negotiation cycle, according with the loop segment. Else, the protocol finishes with success.

In this protocol, several cycles of negotiation can occur. However, the duration constraint {0..12d} on the protocol determines that it cannot be executed for more than 12 days. In addition, deadlines are defined on the messages of this protocol through time constraints.

Figure 9 shows the sequence diagram of the protocol *Consumption Schedule*. The objective of this protocol is to make customer notifies to the supplier of some information (segment *Inventory Information*) that will be used by the latter to calculate and do the replenishment. The messages are based on the speech act *inform,* so that the supplier comes to know about the inventory information and the consumption schedule calculated by the customer.

Then, based on the acceptable tolerances for the consumption plan defined in the agreement, if the supplier detects exceptions on the consumption plan, the *Plan Exception Management* protocol is invoked. It realizes the exception process *Forecast Exception* defined in the analysis stage. In order to realize this protocol, and because it was defined as a protocol

Figure 10. Sequence diagram of the protocol plan exception management

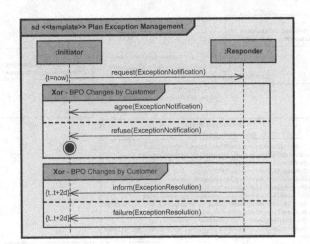

template, the corresponding values are assigned to the required parameters, as it is indicated in the comment associated to the interaction occurrence referencing to this protocol.

Figure 10 shows the protocol template *Plan Exception Management*, which can be reused to define different protocols that manage exceptions in any type of plan or schedule. This protocol starts with the initiator requesting a change on some information to resolve an exception. Then, the responder sends an *agree* message that represents the commitment of the responder to resolve the exception in the future; or the responder refuses the requested changes and the protocol finishes. Once the responder made the changes and resolved the exceptions, it informs the initiator of the results.

Defining the Business Interfaces View

This view offers a static view of the collaboration through the business interfaces of the roles performed by the partners. The business interfaces contain the required business services to support the exchange of messages in the interaction protocols defined in this view.

A *business interface* extends the semantics of the UML *interfaces* to declare the public responsibilities and obligations of a role to interact with another one. A role can have a set of *provided* and *required interfaces* that have to be contained in one of its *public business interfaces*. A provided interface gives a view of the messages that a role expects to receive, according to the protocols in which it interacts with another role. A required interface gives a view of the business messages that a role can send to another role.

A business interface is composed of *business services* that manage the asynchronous reception of the business messages. Therefore, business services extend the semantics of the UML receptions. The name of a business service corresponds to the speech act of the message to receive, and it also contains as a parameter the business document transported by the message.

Figure 11. Class diagram describing the business interfaces view

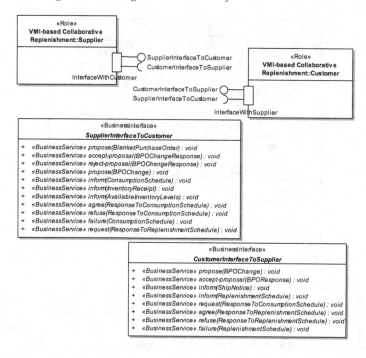

The provided and required business interfaces of the roles are derived from the protocols in which they are involved. The business services are derived from the business messages of these protocols. The notation of the business interfaces and business services is that used in UML for interfaces and operations. Also, the notation of the provided and required business interfaces is that used in UML for the provided and required interfaces of a port.

Figure 11 shows the class diagram describing the business interfaces of the roles *customer* and *supplier*. As an example, the business interface *SupplierInterfaceToCustomer* indicates the business services provided by the supplier to interact with the customer in the protocols defined in this view. It is the provided interface of the supplier and the required interface of the customer. The business services of this interface were defined from the business messages that the supplier can receive in the above protocols.

Generation of Technological Solutions from UP-ColBPIP Models

This section describes how UP-ColBPIP models can be used to generate technological solutions that enable the execution of these processes. Not all concepts used in UP-ColBPIP will have a correspondence with concepts used in the technological level. The main views of a UP-ColBPIP model to be considered to generate B2B specifications are the interaction protocols and business interfaces views. Specifications of the processes can be derived from the former, and specifications of the interfaces required by the partners can be derived from the latter.

In particular, the main mappings to generate specifications in the ebXML standard from UP-ColBPIP models are described. Then, an overview of the implementation of the transformations is provided.

Generating ebXML Specifications from UP-ColBPIP Models

The ebXML standard consists of a set of languages for enabling B2B interactions through the exchange of XML-based messages. Two languages are relevant for generating B2B specifications in the proposed MDA approach: Business Process Specification Schema (BPSS) (UN/CEFACT and OASIS, 1999), and collaboration-protocol profile and agreement (CPPA) (OASIS, 2002). BPSS is used to specify collaborative processes, and CPPA is used to specify the partners' interfaces.

BPSS uses the concept of binary collaboration to represent a collaborative process. A binary collaboration consists of two roles that interact through business transactions by exchanging business documents. It defines a choreography in terms of business states, which can be business activities or control flow elements as fork, join, decision, transition, start, success, and failure. A business activity can be either a collaboration activity or a business transaction activity. The former represents the execution of a binary collaboration within another binary collaboration. The latter represents the execution of a business transaction, which consists of a requesting activity and the responding activity executing one or two business document flows. It may also support one or more business signals.

Table 2 presents the main mappings of UP-ColBPIP elements into BPSS elements. Some aspects of these mappings are now described in order to provide a better understanding of this transformation.

Table 2. Mapping of UP-ColBPIP elements to BPSS elements

UP-ColBPIP Elements	BPSS Elements
B2B Collaboration	Process Specification
Business Document	Business Document
Interaction Protocol	Binary Collaboration
Partner Role	Role
Fragments	Business States
Business Message	Business Transaction Activity
Speech Act	Business Transaction
Interaction Ocurrence	Collaboration Activity
Success	Success
Failure	Failure
Control Flow Segment	Binary Collaboration

An interaction protocol realizing a collaborative process having two roles is transformed into a binary collaboration. Fragments of interaction protocols are mapped into business states of the generated binary collaboration. In particular, a business message is transformed into a business transaction activity. The *fromRole* and the *toRole* attributes of a business transaction activity are derived from the roles involved in the message. A business transaction activity only represents the order of the business message into the choreography. Interaction between the roles is defined by the business transaction associated to the business transaction activity that realizes the message. Therefore, for representing business messages based on speech acts, business transactions are derived from the speech acts and defined only with the requesting activity that indicates the speech act. The responding activity is not generated. This represents the asynchronous feature of the business messages. The requesting activity is defined with a document envelope referencing the business document to be sent, according to the business document associated to the business message. In addition, if the business message has a time constraint, the *timeToPerform* attribute is generated in the business transaction activity.

To transform the interaction protocol's choreography of business messages into a binary collaboration's choreography of business states, control flow segments (CFSs) are transformed into subbinary collaborations. In the binary collaboration realizing the interaction protocol, a collaboration activity is added with a reference to the new binary collaboration created from the CFS. The reasons for this decision are BPSS does not support complex control flows, such as loops; operators of CFSs have not a direct counterpart in BPSS; CFSs can contain sub-CFSs, hence, their mapping into binary collaborations reduces the complexity in the binary collaboration realizing the interaction protocol.

The mapping of a CFS into a binary collaboration is performed according to the operator contained in the CFS. Table 3 summarizes this mapping. As an example, a CFS with an XOR operator is mapped to a binary collaboration having a fork state with an "XOR" value in its

Table 3. Mapping of a control flow segment into a binary collaboration

ControlFlow segment	Binary Collaboration with the following business states		
operator	Fork.type	Join.waitForAll	Decision
Xor	XOR	False	--
Or	OR	False	--
And	OR	True	--
If	--	--	Defined after a start states
Loop (0,n)	--	--	Defined after a start states
Loop (1,n)	--	--	Defined before the completion states
Transaction	A binary collaboration is generated without these states		
Stop	Idem to above. A failure state is included in the BC realizing the IP		
Exception	A binary collaboration is generated without these states		
Cancel	Cannot be mapped in a direct way into a BC		

attribute *type,* and a join state with the attribute *waitForAll* settled in false. A CFS with a *Loop* operator is mapped to a binary collaboration having a decision as the first business state if it is a "Loop (0,n)," or else the decision state is defined before the completion states.

More details about the generation of BPSS specifications and an example for that can be found in (Villarreal et al., 2005).

With respect to CPPA, it supports the specification of the interface of a partner in a Collaboration Protocol Profile (CPP). A CPP specifies the way a partner will interact with another one performing the binary collaborations defined in a BPSS specification. The main elements to be derived are the *CollaborationRole* that specifies the BPSS file and the role a partner plays; the *ServiceBinding* that specifies the incoming (element *CanReceive*) and outgoing (element *CanSend*) messages of the role according to the requesting and responding activities of business transactions; and the business signals of a business transaction. *CanReceive* and *CanSend* elements are derived from the provided and required interfaces of the role that a partner performs in the source UP-ColBPIP model. The remaining elements of a CPP specification cannot be generated from UP-ColBPIP because they correspond to the technical details, such as the transport protocol to be used.

Implementation of Transformations

The transformation of UP-ColBPIP models into ebXML specifications was implemented using a model transformation tool prototype proposed in Villarreal (2005). This tool enables the definition of model transformations for generating specifications based on different B2B standards from UP-ColBPIP models. Briefly, this tool implements a model transformation language that supports the declarative definition of transformation rules and their composition in rule modules that consist of a hierarchy of rules. For each mapping between elements of the source and target languages, a transformation rule is defined. Transformation rules consist of input and output patterns defined according to the metamodels of the source language and the target language. These patterns are specified in an imperative way using Java code. With this tool, a model transformation to translate UP-ColBPIP models into ebXML specifications has been defined, according to the mappings described in the previous section.

Then, this model transformation can be executed for generating the XML code of the B2B specifications. In this case, the tool uses a transformation engine that takes as an input a UP-ColBPIP model in an XMI format and generates ebXML (BPSS and CPPA) models. Then, it generates the XML documents (corresponding to the ebXML specifications) from the ebXML models through the production rules of XML code incorporated within the tool. In order to manipulate UP-ColBPIP models and import them in an XML format, the tool uses the APIs of the implementation of the UML2 metamodel based on the eclipse modeling framework (EMF) (Eclipse, 2004). Also, for manipulating ebXML models, EMF was also used to generate the API that allows the manipulation of these models.

Future Trends

The benefits of using an MDA approach and a UML profile can be enhanced if they are not only considered to generate technological solutions, but they are also used to verify models. Verification of models means using a tool and formal techniques to analyze the models for the presence of desirable properties and the absence of undesirable ones (Selic, 2003). In the context of B2B collaborations, the verification of collaborative processes is very important to assure the right behavior of the inter-enterprise collaboration. Therefore, the verification of functional requirements of these processes, such as the absence of "dead-looks" and "livelocks," should be done.

Currently, there are proposals for the verification of process' specifications based on a specific standard, such as BPEL (Ferrara, 2004). This implies that the verification is done after the technological solution is generated. However, since an MDA approach encourages the use of models as the main development products, the verification of collaborative processes should be done at the earlier stages of the development, when business engineers make the most important decisions. To support it, it is necessary to verify technology-independent process models, such as those based on UP-ColBPIP. Therefore, future work consists of the formalization of UP-ColBPIP models of collaborative processes and the transformation of these models into formal models, in order to enhance the proposed MDA approach.

On the other hand, Web services are having more and more interest in supporting the execution of collaborative processes. In addition, currently, vendor support is stronger for Web services than ebXML. Therefore, specifications based on Web services composition standards, such as BPEL and WS-CDL, should be also generated from conceptual models of collaborative processes based on UP-ColBPIP. The most important aspect to consider is that some languages, such as BPEL, support the definition of collaborative processes using abstract conversation protocols. This means the choreography is defined considering the view of only one role. Hence, from UP-ColBPIP models, the abstract conversation protocol required by each partner has to be generated. This is possible because interaction protocols show the global view as well as the view of each role.

To generate collaborative process specifications that focus on the global view, the use of the new standard WS-CDL is more appropriate because it supports this requirement. In the same way, it has been demonstrated that ebXML specifications and BPEL specifications can be generated from UP-ColBPIP models (Villarreal, 2005). Our ongoing work is about the generation of WS-CDL specifications from these models.

CONCLUSION

This chapter has described the application of MDA and UML for the domain of collaborative business processes. An MDA approach and a UML profile have been proposed in order to support the modeling of collaborative processes and the automatic generation of technological solutions (B2B specifications) based on B2B standards.

The components and techniques required by the MDA approach for collaborative processes have been described. The main benefits of this MDA approach are

- Increase of the abstraction level in the design of B2B collaborations, because the main development products are the technology-independent collaborative process models. This means business engineers and system designers can design collaborative process models by using the proposed UML profile in order to define the business aspects of the B2B collaboration (e.g., responsibilities and common business goals of the partners, communicative aspects of the interactions), instead of dealing with technical details. In this way, this MDA approach encourages partners to focus mainly on the business aspects, and provides the guidelines and techniques required for deciding and generating technological solutions.

- Reduction of development time and costs, because technological solutions (B2B specifications) are automatically generated from the conceptual models of collaborative processes defined at business level. This automatic generation of the B2B specifications is enabled by applying the model transformations corresponding to the B2B standard to be used.
- The generated technological solutions are consistent with the processes defined at business level. This allows partners to be sure that the generated B2B specifications really support the collaborative processes and eventually, the business goals agreed by the partners at business level. This consistency between the business solutions and the technological solutions is achieved by applying transformations to the collaborative process models for generating their corresponding B2B specifications.
- Independence of the collaborative process models from the B2B standards, which increases the reuse of these models. A collaborative process defined with the UML profile proposed is independent of the B2B standards. To generate the B2B specifications with different B2B standards, it is necessary to define a particular transformation for each case. The MDA approach enables a partner to use a same collaborative process model in several B2B collaborations with different partners, and for each B2B collaboration to generate the process and interfaces' specifications in a different B2B standard.

In order to exploit these benefits, an important requirement is the use of a suitable modeling language. The proposed UML profile is a solution towards that direction. UP-ColBPIP provides the appropriate conceptual elements for modeling technology-independent collaborative processes. It supports the definition of different views of the B2B collaboration and collaborative processes. In this way, UP-ColBPIP encourages a top-down process design from the definition of the business goals to be fulfilled in the B2B collaboration, and the identification of the collaborative processes for achieving those goals, up to the modeling of the interaction protocols that realize these processes and the definition of the partners' business interfaces.

The main theoretical base of UP-ColBPIP is the use of the interaction protocol concept to model the behavior of the collaborative processes, along with the application of the speech act theory. On the one hand, the main purpose of using interaction protocols is to fulfill the identified requirements for the conceptual modeling of collaborative processes. On the other hand, UP-ColBPIP can be considered as a communication-oriented process modeling language. Through the modeling of interaction protocols, business engineers can focus not only on information exchange, but also on the communicative aspects of collaborative processes, allowing for a better understanding of B2B collaborations. Business messages based on speech acts allow representing the intentions of partners when they exchange information in collaborative processes. By means of speech acts, parties can create, modify, cancel, or fulfill commitments. In addition, the use of speech acts simplifies the design of collaborative processes. Designers can use intuitive concepts closer to the natural language and social interactions between human beings. However, for a common understanding of collaborative processes, the semantics of the speech acts must be known and understood in the same way by all the parties. Therefore, the use of a library of well-defined speech acts is important. In this chapter, the FIPA ACL library has been used. However, other standard or proprietary libraries may be used.

Through the use of this UML profile based on UML2, business engineers can apply well-known notations for modeling collaborative processes. Moreover, the use of this UML profile allows extending the semantics of UML for the domain of collaborative processes, providing a more suitable vocabulary for this domain than the original UML; and reusing the existing UML case tools to model collaborative processes.

Finally, this chapter has provided an overview of the aspects required for the automatic generation of technological solutions. Particularly, the mappings of UP-ColBPIP elements into the ebXML standard elements have been described. The main ebXML elements can be derived from UP-ColBPIP models. This indicates that UP-ColBPIP do not only provide the conceptual elements required to model collaborative processes in a high-abstraction level, but also to derive executable specifications based on a B2B standard. In addition, although in this chapter we focused on ebXML solutions according to the components and techniques defined in the MDA approach, from UP-ColBPIP models it is also possible to generate solutions based on Web services composition standards such as BPEL or WS-CDL.

REFERENCES

Baghdadi, Y. (2004). ABBA: An architecture for deploying business-to-business electronic commerce applications. *Electronic Commerce Research and Applications, 3,* 190-212.

Baïna, K, Benatallah, B., Cassati, F., & Toumani, F. (2004). Model-driven Web service development. In A. Persson & J. Stirna (Ed.), *CAiSE'04, LNCS* (Vol. 3084, pp. 290-306).

Bauer, B., Müller, J. P., & Odel, J. (2001). Agent UML: A formalism for specifying multiagent software systems. *Int. Journal of Software Engineering and Knowledge Engineering, 11(3),* 1-24.

BEA, IBM, Microsoft, SAP, & Siebel (2003). *Business process execution language for Web services (BPEL).* Retrieved June 1, 2003, from: http://www-106.ibm.com/developerworks/library/ws-bpel/

Bernauer, M., Kappel, G., & Kramler, G. (2003). Comparing WSDL-based and ebXML-based approaches for B2B protocol specification. In *Proceedings of Int. Conference on Service-Oriented Computing 2003, LNCS, Vol. 2910* (pp. 225-240).

Bussler, C. (2001). The role of B2B engines in B2B integration architectures. *ACM SIGMOD Record, Special Issue on Data Management Issues in E-Commerce, 31(1).*

Caliusco, M. L., Maidana, C., Galli, M. R., & Chiotti, O. (2004). Contextual ontology definition metamodel. In *Proceedings of the IV Iberoamerican Conference on Software Engineering and Knowledge Engineering* (pp. 261-275).

Chen, Q., & Hsu, M. (2001) Interenterprise collaborative business process management. In *Proceedings of the 17th International Conference on Data Engineering (ICDE).*

CompTIA Electronics Industry Data Exchange (EIDX). (2004). *Replenishment scenario 4 - forecast-based supplier-managed inventory (SMI), V. 1.0.* Retrieved May 2004, from http://www.comptia.org/sections/eidx/business_process/replenishment/replmodl4.asp

Dietz, J. L. (1999). Understanding and modelling business processes with DEMO. In *Proceedings of Conceptual Modeling - ER '99, LNCS* (Vol. 1728, pp. 188-202).

Dietz, J. L. G. (2002). The atoms, molecules, and matter of the organizations. In *Proceedings of the 7th International Workshop on the Language Action Perspective on Communication Modeling (LAP 2002).*

Eclipse. (2004). *Eclipse modeling framework*. Retrieved August 2004, from http://www. eclipse.org/emf/

Eriksson, H., & Penker, M. (2000) *Business modeling with UML: Business patterns at work*. New York: John Wiley & Sons.

Ferrara, A. (2004). Web services: A process algebra approach. In *The Proceedings of the 2nd International Conference on Service Oriented Computing (ICSOC 2004)*. ACM.

FIPA (Foundation for Intelligent Physical Agents). (2002). *FIPA Communicative Act Library Specification*. Retrieved September 2003, from http://www.fipa.org/specs/ fipa00037/.

Gardner, T. (2003). UML modelling of automated business processes with a mapping to BPEL4WS. In *First European Workshop on Object Orientation and Web Services (EOOWS)*.

Goldkuhl, G., & Lind, M. (2004). Developing e-Iiteractions — A framework for business capabilities and exchanges. In *Proceedings of the 12th European Conference on Information Systems (ECIS-2004)*.

Hofreiter, B., & Huemer, C. (2004a). ebXML business processes — Defined both in UMM and BPSS. In *Proceedings of the 1st GI-Workshop XML Interchange Formats for Business Process Management* (pp. 81-102).

Hofreiter, B., & Huemer, C. (2004b). Transforming UMM business collaboration models to BPEL. In *International Workshop on Modeling InterOrganizational Systems (MIOS)*.

Jablonski, S., & Bussler, C. (1996). *Workflow management: Modeling concepts, architecture and implementation*. London: International Thompson Computer Press.

Koehler, J., Hauser, R., Kapoor, S., Wu, F., & Kumaran, S. (2003). A model-driven transformation method. In *Seventh International Enterprise Distributed Object Computing (EDOC 2003)*.

Lind, M., & Goldkuhl, G. (2001). Generic layered patterns for business modelling. In *Proceedings of the Sixth International Workshop on the Language-Action Perspective on Communication Modelling (LAP 2001)* (pp. 21-22).

Liu, E., & Kumar, A. (2003). Leveraging information sharing to increase supply chain configurability. In *Proceedings of The Twenty-Fourth International Conference on Information Systems*.

Medina-Mora, R., Winograd, T., Flores, R., & Flores, F. (1992) The action workflow approach to workflow management technology. In *Proceedings of the 4th Conference on Computer Supported Cooperative Work*.

Medjahed, B., Benatallah, B., Bouguettaya, A., Ngu, A. H. H., & Ahmed, K.E. (2003). Business-to-business interactions: Issues and enabling technologies. *The VLDB Journal, 12(1)*, 2041-2046.

OASIS (1999). *Electronic business using eXchange markup language (ebXML)*. Retrieved 2001, from http://www.ebxml.org

OASIS ebXML CPP/A Technical Committee (1999). *Collaboration-protocol profile and agreement specification, Versión 2.0*. Retrieved from http://www.ebxml.org/specs/

Object Management Group. (2003). *Model-driven architecture (MDA) guide, Versión 1.0.1*. Retrieved May 20, 2004, from http://www.omg.org/mda

RosettaNet Consortium. (1999) *RossetaNet*. Retrieved May 2001, from http://www.rosettanet.org/RosettaNet/Rooms/DisplayPages/LayoutInitial

Searle, J. R. (1975). A taxonomy of illocutionary acts. In K. Gunderson (Eds.), *Language, mind and knowledge*. Minneapolis, MA: University of Minnesota.

Selic, B. (2003). The pragmatics of model-driven development. *IEEE Software, 20(5)*,19-25.

UN/CEFACT, & OASIS (2003). *ebXML business specification schema, Version 1.10*. Retrieved March 2004, from http://www.untmg.org/downloads/General/approved/

Villarreal, P. (2005). *Modeling and specification of collaborative business processes*. PhD Thesis. Santa Fe, Argentina: CERIDE.

Villarreal, P., Caliusco, M., Zucchini, D., Arredondo, F., Zanel, C., Galli, M. R., & Chiotti, O. (2003a). Integrated production planning and control in a collaborative partner-to-partner relationship. In S. Sharma & J. Gupta (Eds.), *Managing e-business in the 21st century* (pp. 91-110). Victoria, Australia: Heidelberg Press.

Villarreal, P., Salomone, E., & Chiotti, O. (2003b). Managing public business processes in B2B relationships using B2B interaction protocols. *XXIX Conferencia Latinoamérica de Informática (CLEI 2003)*.

Villarreal, P., Salomone, E., & Chiotti, O. (2003c). B2B relationships: Defining public business processes using interaction protocols. *Journal of the Chilean Society of Computer Science, Special Issue on the Best Papers of the JCC 2003, 4(1)*. Retrieved November 2003, from http://www.dcc.uchile.cl/~mmarin/revista-sccc/sccc-web/volumen4-1.html

Villarreal, P., Salomone, E, & Chiotti, O. (2005). Applying model-driven development to collaborative business processes. In *Proceedings Iberoamerican Workshop on Requirement Engineering and Sowftare Environments (IDEAS'05)*.

Voluntary Interindustry Commerce Standard (VICS). (2002). *Collaborative planning, forecasting, and replenishment - Voluntary guidelines, V 2.0*. Retrieved May 2004, from http://www.vics.org/committees/cpfr/voluntary_v2/

Weigand, H., Heuvel, W., & Dignum, F. (1998) Modelling electronic commerce transactions - A layered approach. In *Proceedings of the Third International Workshop on the Language Action Perspective (LAP'98)*.

World Wide Web Consortium (W3C). (2004). *Web services choreography description language Version 1.0*. Retrieved May 2005, from http://www.w3.org/TR/2004/WD-ws-cdl-10-20041217/

APPENDIX A

Summary of the UP-ColBPIP Stereotypes and the UML Metaclass they Extend

UP-ColBPIP stereotype	UML metaclass	Parent
B2BCollaboration	Collaborations::Collaboration	
TradingPartner	StructuredClasses::Class	
PartnerRole	StructuredClasses::Class InternalStructures::Property UseCases::Actor	
B2BRelationship	InternalStructures::Connector	
PublicBusinessInterface	Ports::Port	
CollaborativeAgreement	Kernel::Comment; Kernel::Class	
BusinessGoal	Class	
CollaborativeBusiness Process	UseCases::UseCase	
ExceptionProcess		CollaborativeBusiness Process
Subprocess	UseCases::Include	
Exception	UseCases::Extend	
ExceptionPoint	UseCases::ExtensionPoint	
Achieves	Dependencies::Dependency	
InteractionProtocol	BasicInteractions::Interaction	
ProtocolTemplate		InteractionProtocol
BusinessMessage	BasicInteractions::Message	
ControlFlowSegment	Fragments::CombinedFragment	
ControlFlowOperators	Kernel::Enumeration	
SpeechAct	Communication::Signal	
BusinessDocument	Kernel::Class	
Failure	Stop	
Success	Stop	
ProtocolParameters	Kernel::Comment	
BusinessInterface	Interfaces::Interface	
BusinessService	Communications::Reception	

Chapter III

Enterprise Modeling with the Joint Use of User Requirements Notation and UML

Anna Medve, Pannon University, Hungary

ABSTRACT

This chapter introduces the user requirements notation (URN) standardized formal methods and its joint use with unified modeling language (UML) in enterprise modeling. It argues that the joint use of URN and UML can enhance enterprise models and coevolve with enterprise engineering processes. URN combines goals and scenarios to help reasoning and to capture user requirements prior to detailed design. Furthermore, URN can be integrated partially or entirely into an existing business process modeling approach without replacing current ways of creating and analyzing models in order to be useful. Modeled in the UML, a URN model may be incorporated into the rest of a system's UML design documentation, seamlessly linking the documentation for the requirements elicitation part of a project to the whole, and to be fully integrated with the rest of the design documentation for a software system.

BACKGROUND

Enterprise roles must aid in the design of information technology (IT) infrastructure and its interfaces between software systems that adapt enterprise organizational structure to maintain a consistent overview of all processes (ATHENA, 2004). Enterprise roles are involved in modeling processes via their facility to help designers to link the modeling, optimization, and execution of business processes with their physical configurations, IT, and software systems. In order to have a common language that is understandable by all participants, the modeling language should be a common language between the stakeholders and the system designers.

Two aspects important in object orientation in modeling practices must be highlighted: The first aspect is that the object management group (OMG) defines object management as software development that models the real-world through representation of "objects." These objects are the encapsulation of the attributes, relationships, and methods of software-identifiable program components. Object management results in faster application development, easier maintenance, enormous scalability, and reusable software (OMG, 2003).

The second aspect is that open distributed processing –reference model (ODP-RM) is a standard elaborated by the joint working group ISO/IEC/ITU. ODP supports the modeling of distributed processing entities using UML metamodel. The term "object" in ODP means "a model of entity." An entity is any concrete or abstract thing of interest. An object

Figure 1. UCMs as a missing piece of the UML puzzle (Amyot,He, He, & Cho, 1999)

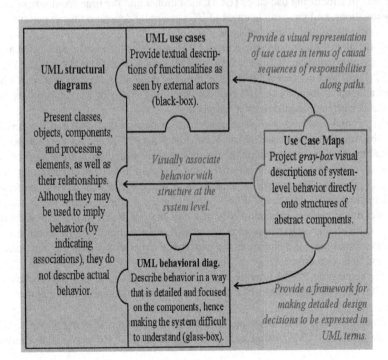

is characterized by its behavior and, dually, by its state. Depending on the viewpoint, the emphasis may be placed on behavior or on state. When the emphasis is placed on behavior, an object is informally said to perform functions and offer services (ITU-T, 2151, 2003).

The enterprise modeling viewpoints identify roles, processes, policies, and their relationships among enterprise objects (Fox & Gruninger, 1998). While OMG object term helps to make a conceptual basis for model-based enterprise engineering, ODP, like object term, helps to make enterprise specifications that support the specification users at the application and software level. Both object viewpoints can be transformed from URN specification. URN has notations to make statements about domain elements and abstractions of software objects also.

Weiss and Amyot (2005) demonstrate how the URN can be used to model business processes. Through an illustrative example, they present that URN posed suitable and useful features for modeling and analyzing business processes, and that it satisfies the goals of a BPM (business process management) language.

UCM AND UML

In August 2003, OMG adopted the revised de facto standard (UML 2.0) (OMG, 2003). In the superstructure, that is the part of the language visible by the modeler, some well-known and established formal methods features like message sequence charts (MSC) (ITU-T-Z.120,1999), specification and description language (SDL) (ITU-T-Z.100,1999), real-time object-oriented modeling (ROOM) (Selic, 2004), and others are introduced.

The way of structuring use cases (UCs), the number and the time requirement of the necessary iterations, and the completeness of UCs generally depend on the experience and routine of workgroups and system analysts.

Amyot et al. (1999) presents the current UML pieces of the puzzle, and UCM as the missing piece-an adaptation of Buhr's view of UML and UCM (Buhr, 1998) (see Figure 1). The UCM notations contain features for expressing dynamic situations that span whole systems in a compact form by several rational "grey-box" steps of traceable progression from use cases with visible information designed.

The rigorous UCM scenario-based approach for designing distributed systems has introduced by Amyot and discussed in Amyot and Eberlein (2003b) and Amyot (2004a). The advantage of this method is to separate the functions to the underlying structures; provide a visual representation of use cases in terms of causes, responsibilities, and effects along paths; and also part provide a framework for making detailed design decisions to be expressed with more appropriate UML views. When this structure is modified or refined, UCMs require simpler modifications consisting only of a new binding between the responsibilities and the components. In comparison with them, UML interaction diagrams would need to be rebuilt as soon as there is a change in the underlying structure because the functions are tightly bound to the structure.

At the same time, UCM provides a bird's-eye view of activities from behavioral diagrams allocated to organizations of components and objects in structural diagrams (see Figure 15).

This enables architectural reasoning throughout the evolution of a system design. Architectural viewpoints of UCM's features are offered in Buhr (1998) to learn and to exercise.

THE USER REQUIREMENTS NOTATION (URN) STANDARD

The URN standard (ITU-T-Z.150, 2003) is defined to provide facilities to express the relationship between business objectives and goals, and system requirements, expressed as scenarios and global constraints over the system and its development, deployment, maintenance, evolution, and operational processes. The URN elaborated by the International Telecommunication Union (ITU-T) is the first standardization effort of a formally defined notation used for capturing and analyzing user requirements. URN focuses on user requirement desired goals or functions that users or other stakeholders expect the system to achieve.

URN capabilities allow to

1. Support different views according to the needs of the enterprise stakeholders.
2. Derive specifications from one model without additional transformation.
3. support new ways of thinking, and provide concepts to handle role changes of enterprise objects.
4. Provide logical and structural connectors to integrate business technology supporting interoperability with existing applications.
5. Solve the problem of building new applications by coupling existing ones.
6. Provide abstract components and constructs to support all traditional objectives from information systems for enterprise modeling and understanding as a sociotechnical system.

Figure 2. Basic elements of a UCM path

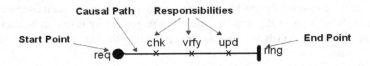

Figure 3. UCM stub plug-in notations

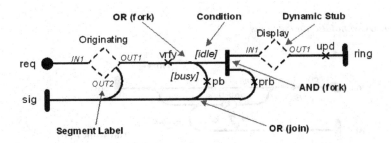

URN combines two complementary notations: the *goal-oriented requirement language (GRL)* for goal-modeling techniques built in the well-established nonfunctional requirement (URN-NFR) by a graphical notation that allows reasoning about (*nonfunctional*) requirements and *use case maps (UCMs)* for scenarios modeling functional requirement (URN-FR) by a graphical *scenario notation* for describing causal relationships between responsibilities superimposed on organisational structure of abstract components (Amyot, 2003a, 2004; Buhr, 1998).

Business objectives and product quality attributes are modelled using the URN-NFR. An integrated view of behavior and structure is modelled using the URN-FR. The URN is applicable within standards bodies, industry, and commercial organizations.

USE CASE MAPS (UCM) NOTATIONS

The language used for the URN-FR is the use case map (UCM) notation (ITU-T – Z.152, 2003).

UCM specifications employ scenario paths to illustrate causal relationships among responsibilities. A system specification is essentially a set of path specifications. The constraints on presenting a path specification to a human viewer dictate that a large system specification is composed of a set of root maps. Each root map contains one or more path specifications.

Elements of the path notation (see Figures 2, 3, & 4) allow the specification of the handling of a class of events in one path specification.

Basic elements of UCMs are start points, responsibilities, end points, and components. *Start points* are filled circles representing preconditions or triggering causes. *End points* are bars representing postconditions or resulting effects. *Responsibilities* are crosses representing actions, tasks, or functions to be performed. *Components* are boxes representing entities or objects composing the system. Use case *paths* are wiggle lines that connect start points, responsibilities, and end points. In case that a responsibility is said to be bound to a component, the component is responsible for performing the action, task, or function represented by the responsibility.

A lengthy path specification can be fitted into a root map by moving segments of it to child maps, using the stub plug-in mechanism (see Figure 3). Conditions can be attached to alternative paths and plug-ins. The plug-in maps are submaps that describe locally how a feature modifies the basic behavior.

Figure 4. UCM notational elements

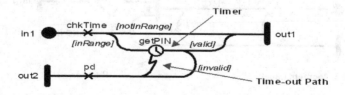

The diamond symbol indicates a stub notion. The stub on the parent map represents the plug-in on the child map. Multiple levels of stubs and plug-ins can be used, structuring and integrating scenarios in various ways, for example sequentially, as alternatives with OR-forks/joins, or concurrently with AND-forks/joins. Integration may involve *static stubs* that contain only one submap, or *dynamic stubs* that may contain multiple submaps whose selection can be determined at run-time according to a *selection policy*.

Other notational elements include numerous control elements OR-join, OR-fork, AND-join, AND-fork, timer, abort, failure point, and shared responsibilities.

A detailed introduction to and examples of these concepts can be found in Buhr (1998) and ITU (2003).

- **Scenario interactions:** Shown by multiple paths through the same component, and by one path triggering and another disabling. The UCM notation combines behavioral scenarios with structures of abstract components.
- **Components:** Represent, at the requirements level, abstract entities corresponding to actors, processes, objects, containers, agents, and so forth
- **Responsibilities:** Processing tasks, for example procedures, functions, and actions. Preconditions and postconditions can be associated with a responsibility.

UCM notations are very useful in stage 1 descriptions of service functionalities. In stage 1, requirements usually suffer from heavy instabilities, whereas scenarios and potential component topologies (structures of functional and network entities) are volatile. UCMs fit well in approaches that intend to bridge the gap between requirements and an abstract system design (stage 2), where a tentative distribution of system behaviors over a structure is being

Figure 5. UCMNav framework

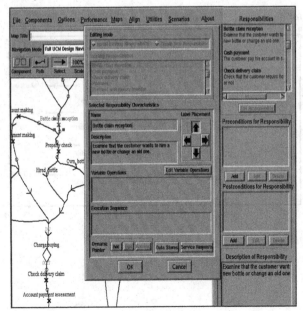

introduced. Thus, they represent useful and powerful tools for the support of the thinking process and the evaluation of functional alternatives. Further details can be found in Amyot (2004a), Buhr (1995, 1998) and Virtual Library at Use Case Maps Group (2005).

UCM support is provided by the UCM navigator tool (UCMNav). It is a free graphical environment, (see Figure 5) developed at Carleton University, Canada, for editing, exploring, and analyzing UCMs. This tool is available at http://www.UseCaseMaps.org/tools/ucmnav/ (UCMNav, 2005). The current version requires an X Window server, the XForms libraries, and a UNIX variant (Solaris, Linux, and Windows/Cygwin are supported).

Another tool, jUCMNav, is available at http://jucmnav.softwareengineering ca/twiki/ bin/view/ProjetSEG/WebHome/, an Eclipse-based graphical editor for use case maps that breaks dependencies on XForms and X Window servers.

GOAL-ORIENTED REQUIREMENT LANGUAGE (GRL)

The language used for the URN-NFR is the *goal-oriented requirement language (GRL)* notation (ITU-T-Z.151, 2003) (ITU-T-Z.153, 2003). GRL is a graphical notation that allows reasoning about (*nonfunctional*) requirements. GRL is concerned with *intentional* elements, actors, and their relationships.

GRL offers a graphical means of describing and structuring various concerns. Softgoals, which represent *goals* that are somewhat fuzzy in nature and can never be entirely satisfied, capture high–level objectives. Softgoals can be connected to each other using qualitative *contribution links* (see Figure 6 and 7). Contribution links represent various degrees of impact, including positive and sufficient, positive but insufficient, unknown positive, and

Figure 6. GRL notations

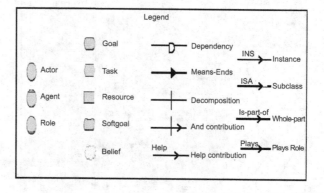

Figure 7. Correlation relationship

Figure 8. Contribution relationship

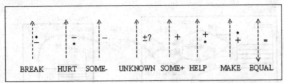

their corresponding contributions on the negative side (see Figure 8). Softgoals can be decomposed and refined until they reach the point where they become quantifiable goals or potential operational solutions. *Tasks* are used to operationalize softgoals.

GRL visualizes static relations existing between the various goals, their interactions, and accompanying rationales.

Figure 11 presents the problem of determining a contribution link and evaluation of a candidate combination of solutions. The propagation in a GRL model is usually bottom-up, and no cycles are caused by contributions links.

The OME framework available at OME (2004) is a GRL support provided by the organization modeling environment (OME) developed at Carleton University, Canada.

SOLUTIONS AND RECOMMENDATIONS
Requirements Engineering and URN Relationship

When used at an early stage in the development process, namely in the user requirements elicitation and specification, URN results in a more precise specification of user requirements. Stakeholder involvement in the elicitation process and tool-based support of conversations between stakeholders and developers are essential for obtaining a good requirements definition (Laamswerde & Willemet, 1998; Whittle & Krüger, 2005). URN specification facilitates detection and avoidance of undesirable interactions between features, and has a significant multiplier effect on the potential reduction in costs of understanding, analysis, and testing (Amyot, 1999; ITU, 2003).

Figure 9. Static context view of an intelligent cardiac telemonitoring system

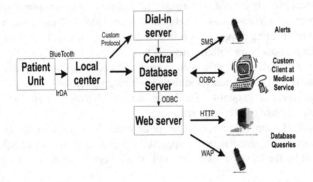

Figure 10. Dynamical context view of telemonitoring system by UCM model

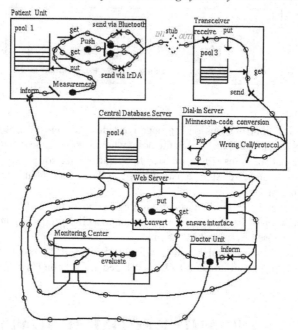

We explain readability of UCMs and GRL models of user requirements by intelligent cardiologic telemonitoring system (Medve, 2005b). The patient will receive 24-hour real-time ECG monitoring in their home during which sensors on the body will supply high-quality medical data. Sensors can be developed for several health parameters, respiratory rate, ECG (1-, 3-, and 12-leads), pulse, temperature, blood saturation, and blood pressure (surveillance, constant screening, and dependence on technology.). Doctors are provided with the information and the tools needed to optimize the number of therapy adjustments and patients' education that are the key points to achieve a positive impact in the patient's control (see Figure 9). Data from these sensors are sent to the patient's local computer through wireless communication, and the computer will analyze and store the data. Intelligent software may trigger medical supervision, treatment, or care by establishing two-way communication over the Internet with remote" arrive-on-call" treatment/care providers. This is a quite advanced system of medical monitoring at home, as it is based on an automatic (i.e., computer triggered) wireless alarm connection with the nearest hospital.

Figure 10 shows a UCM scenario with events paths for intelligent cardiologic telemonitoring system (ICTS) components and their main responsibilities.

It improves and documents quality of collaboration between medical staff and computer scientists during the capture of user requirements.

The technological support is meaningful in the cardiologic monitoring system. The harmony of the knowledge base has been supported by the requirement engineering. It is illustrated very well by the work of Sik-Lányi and co-workers. They developed two multi-

Figure 11. GRL specification of system mobility requirements

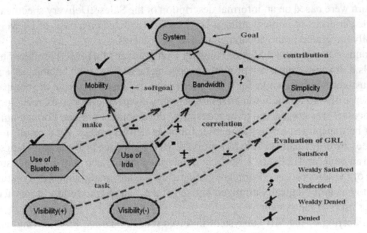

media rehabilitation programs for stroke patients, and some educational software for visually impaired users (Sik-Lányi, 2005a,b,c).

After making clear the misinformation, there may be some little mistakes. In their concrete example for stroke patients, there were some errors. They would never have caught these little errors earlier during the developing phase of the software. These mistakes came up only during the testing phase with the patients. The other problem was during the tests they realized that the experience of using computers plays an important role, so they needed to give the patients time to practise. One could have prevented these mistakes if the developer and the user could have harmonised the user's needs.

Figure 11 shows a GRL evaluation of a candidate combination of solutions of system mobility.

The combined view of behavior and structure offers an opportunity to consider alternative architectural solutions for the desired behavior specified by reusable scenario specifications, refining in collaboration with medical staff.

In the case of a new system based on COTS components, or in the case of extension of an existing system, both specifications involve the use of existing subsystem components. If, however, there is no URN-FR model of the existing system, the developers must first construct one. Where the scenario requires a responsibility that is not implemented by one of the COTS components, as it can be seen in the case study, the requirements engineer draws the causality flow outside the components and places the notation for the responsibility there.

A CASE STUDY

This case study is concerned with the development of a portion of the UCM model, and transformed in UML model elements.

Through an example, we first give an overview of a case study on sales and delivery and the corresponding UCM model that was constructed for supply and distribution of industrial cases. The case study is based on technical reports by Molnár (2005) and Menyhárt (2005), which, in turn were based on an informal description of the Sales&Delivery specifications, and on the experiences of implementing a UML model (realized on a basis of UCM model that was fully integrated in the documentation of the system).

The industrial unit named Messer Hungary Dunaföldvár MbH (MH) produces butane gas and sells it. It's most important profile is supplying tanks filled with butane gas, and exchanging customers' empty tanks for filled ones (tanks can be rented from the company).

In the case of MH, for the automatization of premises-specific processes, reengineering of sales processes was considered to be a desirable development project. For example, the amounts to be transported may change after filling in delivery notes. As a result, interim delivery notes are only finalized after transportation has been done by the acknowledgement of modified amounts and delivery. Lists of both interim and finalized delivery notes support controlling of the sales process. For raising efficiency, the information recorded on the two lists needs to be chronologically arranged in one list that can help to follow stores actually available for users of the system.

Reengineering of the MH subsystem involves redocumenting, reorganizing, and restructuring the subsystem, including reengineering all data.

This reengineering creates new subsystem documentation and makes it easier to understand. The strategy of user interface design modified this way will be user interface distribution, in order to take advantage of the local processing capacity available on desktop PCs. Therefore, there is no need to change the system itself, and only writing screen management middleware and user interface software for the client computer is required. User interface services (presentation, interaction control, and validation) are implemented in the client desktops, where the data are processed, while application services remain in the server system. The user interfaces services are implemented with character-based forms interfaces; calls are made to functions in the client operating system to implement the user interface.

In the case of ordering, a product goes along the logistics chain via integrated processes. The sales department accounts for the sale of the manufactured goods, customer service, and the ongoing provision of stores. By means of a document chain, a Sales&Delivery workflow is established that starts with the first contact with the customer, and it lasts until invoicing of the shipped goods, and passing of the data to Accounting. All phases and options appear on sales documents, enabling all the sales activities to be processed, the elements of the logistics chain to be identified, and real times recorded. Sales and marketing activities can be planned and controlled on the basis of these data.

Customers can purchase the goods in person or, if transportation is required, they can place the order by phone or fax. The remainder of the clientele is a group of warehouses. Normally, a factory unit only supplies warehouses in its vicinity, but it may supply others as well. Depending on the available stock, the goods required by warehouses are transported according to a preliminary order. Goods are transported daily by lorries, and empty cylinders are taken back by return. A delivery note is written and attached to each and every order.

The notes are not validated immediately because so-called "interim delivery notes" are supplied, and it is these notes from which the final ones are recorded by the system. For example, the amounts to be transported may change after the completion of the delivery note. As a result, the interim delivery note is finalized after transportation has been carried out by including acknowledgment of the modified amounts and transport. A list of the interim delivery notes and another list of the finalized delivery notes support controlling of the sales process.

The information in the two lists, as mentioned before, needs to be recorded chronologically into one list that can help to clarify what is actually available for the users of the system. Otherwise, the interim delivery notes may reduce actual stock, and the final stock will appear in the system, but it will not appear in any sort of summary. The solution to the problem involves giving intermediate information to the finance and sales departments for decisions to be made on stock management.

Proposed problem solution: reengineering sales and distribution services, modeling with UCM and UML. Requirements: elicitation and specification with UCMs can, with ease, be explained to, and used by different stakeholders and end-users who have been involved in the process.

UCMs can provide an overview of organizations, with the help of which stakeholders can recognize their own role, their work context, and the interrelations between several activities. Shared features are needed to identify various users and their requirements (both technical and organisational) in each node during cooperation.

Requirements Specification of Sales and Distribution Services with UCM

Based on the reports on informal requirements of sales and distribution services acquired during interviews with the employees, we can obtain a UCM of the context view of the sales subsystem, as shown in Figure 12 and Figure 13, the final sales subsystem.

UCM capabilities enable early reasoning about the choice of substructures for implementing the specifications on the basis of this UCM model. The structural and organizational concepts of the *sales and delivery* domain will match the causal relationship concepts of UCM.

Figure 12. The main processes in the root-UCM

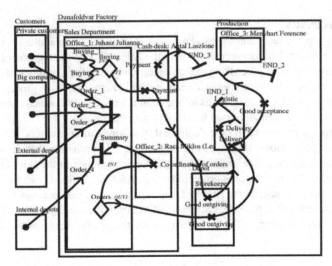

Figure 13. Root map of the sales and delivery UCM

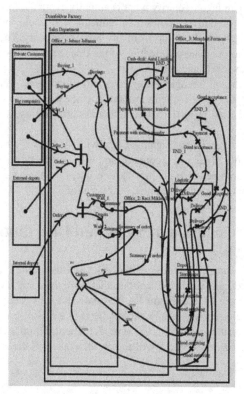

Basic Processes

As a first step, we represent the two basic processes in UCM. In addition to the UCM diagrams, we also get full documentation with the help of UCM-descriptions explaining the main processes, that is, purchasing and ordering. Only the rough outlines of these processes are represented: the newly revealed requirement elicitation of the processes can be visualized on the same UCM diagram as information is gathered until we can consider it as accomplished and all information is at hand for reengineering.

In the process of purchasing we distinguish two kinds of consumers, that is, small consumers and corporations. Both types of consumers can purchase either directly or by ordering the products by phone or fax. Customer service belongs to the sales department and within that, to the staff member arranging the transaction (Office 1), whose job is taking orders and serving customers. The next step is payment, which belongs to the job of the cashier. After payment, the goods are brought out from the store, and then logistics is responsible for their delivery. The customer receives the goods (Receive) and this is the end (END_1) of the process.

As regards ordering, the orders that have been received during the day are cross-checked at the end of each day. The orders are sorted, with the contribution of the manager (Office 2Coordination of orders). After this, the goods are transported to the customers, who pay (cash_desk payment by cash, end_2 payment by money transfer) the bill upon delivery, with the exception of the company's own depository, because transport to the depot is considered as in-firm materials handling.

Production, as its name suggests, deals with producing the goods. Production is always controlled according to the orders received. At the same time, it is in continuous contact with the stores (stock registry) and with sales (stock control). All production processes are dealt with by production staff (Office 3).

Figure 12 represents the main components of the system as the actual places of these activities (sales, production, Offices 1 to 3, depot, logistics, etc.), while the paths represent the revealed main processes. On the left side, the depositories and the customers can be seen, who may either purchase or order goods. The steps of purchasing and ordering processes are given in submaps.

Analysis of Processes

When analyzing the main components of the processes, we seek answers to the following questions: who is interacting with whom, and when is a certain job dealt with at a given location? The steps of the processes are represented in the submaps.

Figure 14. UCMNav description of responsibilities in the root-UCM

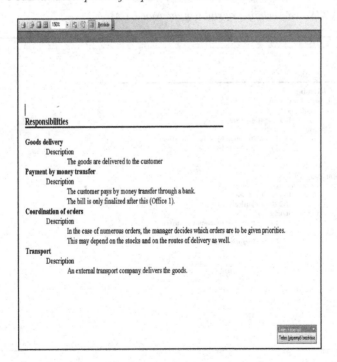

The UCM-descriptions of the processes (in the form of textual documentation) explain the details. A major advantage of this is that, together with requirement elicitation, certain constraints and attributes can be fixed; rendered to the components and the responsibilities of the system.

UCMNav tools contain features for documenting the informal requirements relating to the responsibilities, components, and stubs of submaps plug-ins, as shown in Figures 14 and 15.

Components and responsibilities that conform to the domain of business processes can easily be identified and specified in sub-UCM diagrams, then integrated in a global UCM that covers all cases.

In the process of directly purchase the BUYING in OFFICE_1, we can see, at Figure 16, who we distinguish as old and new consumers in the steps of payment and the CHARGE BUYING submap process.

In Figure 13, we can see the bird's-eye view of a root-UCM model that is improved with submaps connector stubs for integration of BUYING and ORDERING subsystems, and alternative paths discovered by way of iterations.

The ORDERS sub-UCM contains guarded alternative paths, with input and output conditions documented in stub descriptions, as shown in Figures 14 and 15, for example, path (*customers, payments by cash,*) and (*customers, payment by money transfer*) when the guarded condition is related on payments mode.

The UCM model can be used either manually or automatically by various methods, depending on the tools used and the model goals. We have used a UCM model to construct

Figure 15. UCMNav description of stubs in the root-UCM

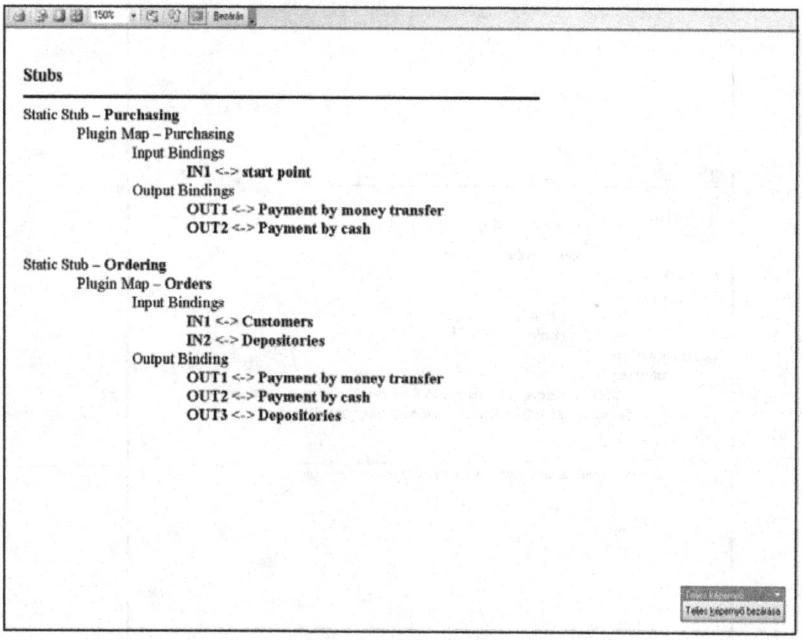

```
Stubs
─────────────────────────────────────────────────

Static Stub – Purchasing
        Plugin Map – Purchasing
                Input Bindings
                        IN1 <-> start point
                Output Bindings
                        OUT1 <-> Payment by money transfer
                        OUT2 <-> Payment by cash

Static Stub – Ordering
        Plugin Map – Orders
                Input Bindings
                        IN1 <-> Customers
                        IN2 <-> Depositories
                Output Binding
                        OUT1 <-> Payment by money transfer
                        OUT2 <-> Payment by cash
                        OUT3 <-> Depositories
```

interaction diagrams modeling interobject relationships. Use case diagrams and sequence diagrams can be constructed step by step along UCM paths. To realize use cases and sequence diagrams with UML, we applied manual translation.

Externally visible actions of a component have input and output statements that can be used by the external behavior of an arbitrary component, and can be described by sub-UCM diagrams that communicate with the rest of the system and the environment. We can use this to advantage in separating the functions of the underlying structure. When this structure is refined, UCM diagrams require simple modifications consisting only of a new binding between the responsibilities and the components.

In contrast, UML interaction diagrams would need to be rebuilt as soon as there is a change in the underlying structure, because the functions are tightly bound to the structure, and need several iterations and rebuilding of diagrams. UCM capabilities allow early reason-

Figure 16. BUYING submap

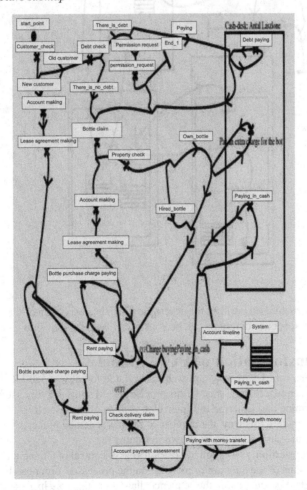

Figure 17. ORDERS submap

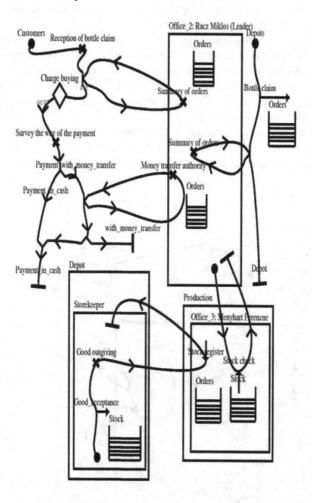

ing to choose substructures to perform the description. On the basis of this UCM model, use case diagrams and sequence diagrams can be constructed step by step along a path.

Manual Transformation of UCM Model

First, we use a root UCM in which stubs are related to convert sub-UCM diagrams into use cases and sequences diagrams. In this process, UCM stubs are very useful, because they help to determine and describe the interrelationships of the use cases "include" and "extend" relationships. In this way, the number of iterations can be reduced.

A part of the use cases diagram is shown in Figure 18.

During the preparation, as we realize a certain kind of control of the sequence diagram, possible imperfections of the diagram or mistakes in the processes' order can be identified. This is very important because using the sequence diagram in this way increases the chance

Figure 18. Part of use cases diagram constructed from UCM path

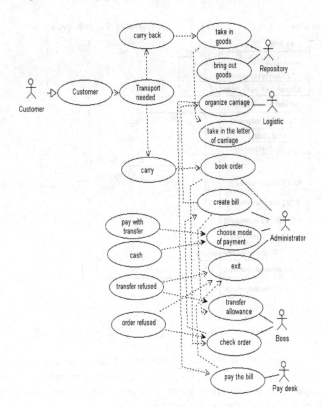

of continuing without a mistake. With this early discovery of mistakes, only the reconstruction of the diagram is needed, leading to a significant time saving.

The collaboration diagrams express the structural position of the objects participating in the given activity, but here a particular marking is needed to describe the temporal order of the messages. The preparation of the collaboration diagram is made possible most simply by using the sequence diagram and the UCM scenario.

Second, we realized class diagrams to components after modeling SDs. The necessary requirements documentation, containing UCM scenarios, UML sequence diagrams, and UML collaboration diagrams can specify the requirements extension.

UCM startpoints and endpoints are converted to messages; components to instances, responsibilities to actions; guarding conditions to conditions; timestamps to timers.

A basis of this UCM can be constructed UCDs and SDs step by step in a way of paths. These SDs show a flattened view of the scenarios, and the hierarchical structure of UCMs with stubs and plug-ins disappears.

We used UCMs to construct manually the UML activity diagrams from the Amyot method described in Amyot (1999), where the elements of state machine are diagrams mes-

Figure 19. Part of sequence diagram constructed from UCM path

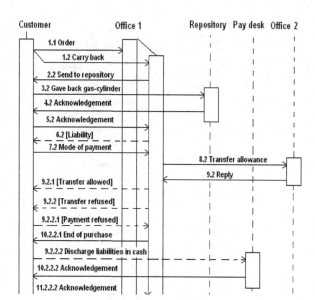

sages and process names generated from UCM path, responsibilities actions and states, and conditions as states. In this way, to verify the completeness of the model, there is no need to analyze SDs to obtain their overlapped parts: SDs serve only as intermediate steps that help to abstract from UCMs and follow the test events.

Modelled in the UML, a UCM model may be incorporated into the rest of a system's UML design documentation, seamlessly linking the documentation for the requirements elicitation part of a project to the whole, and can be fully integrated with the rest of the design documentation for a software system.

The Modeling Process Using Tools and Model Transformation

- UCM-based model engineering process can use tools such as the UCM navigator (UCMNav) to create, maintain, and transform UCM models. Scenario is a good basis for reuse of requirements model for validation by deriving test goals, and is more realistic (Amyot, 2004b).
- Tools for GRL and UCM (OME, 2004; UCMExporter, 2004; UCMNav, 2005) are available for free. UCMExporter is a recent tool that takes the resulting XML scenarios as input and converts them to MSCs (message sequence charts–able to specify sequence diagrams for use cases scenarios) or to UML 1.5 sequence diagrams (in XMI format). OME is a tool for GRL specifications, capable of exporting models into XML format (for integration with UCM, UML)

- UCMNav - UCM scenarios and UCMNav scenario specification converted to XML.
- UCMExporter supports the conversion of XML to message sequence charts (MSC) - able to specify sequence diagrams for use cases scenarios).

FUTURE TRENDS

UCM and GRL method have previously been used in the design of telecommunication infrastructures to provide views of multiagent systems and complex network systems. Our research focused on using the URN notations both for health systems engineering (Medve, 2005a-b) and reengineering of legacy systems (Menyhárt, 2005; Molnár, 2005).

As suggested and demonstrated in Amyot and Weiss (2005), URN can be integrated partially or entirely into an existing business process modeling approach, without replacing current ways of creating and analyzing models in order to be useful.

We are planning for future research mapping UCM2UML steps for modeling the reengineering situations of COTS systems.

URN can provide an overview of organizations where stakeholders can recognize their own role, their work context, and interrelationships between activities and goals. It also contributes to better communication in, collaboration with, and participation by other stakeholder groups.

ACKNOWLEDGMENTS

The author is grateful to Prof. György Kozmann for her inspiring research work and for her comments in stimulating discussions. Ferenc Menyhárt and Tamás Molnár (students) and Miklós Rácz Sales and Delivery Department chief at Messer Hungary Dunaföldvár MbH (MH), collaborated in UCM model constructions in industrial case study.

REFERENCES

Amyot, D. (2003a). *Introduction to the user requirements notation: Learning by example.* Retrieved September 2, 2003, from http://www.usecasemaps.org/pub/comnet03.pdf

Amyot, D., Echihabi, A., & He, X. (2004b). UCM exporters: Supporting scenario transformation from use case maps. In *NOTERE '04*. Retrieved September 30, 2005, from http://www.site.uottowa.ua/n/damyot/pub/NOTERE04.pdf

Amyot, D., & Eberlein, A. (2003b). An evaluation of scenario notations and construction approaches for telecommunication systems development. *Telecommunication Systems Journal, 24*(1), 61-94.

Amyot, D., He, X., He, Y., & Cho, D.Y. (1999). *Generating scenarios from use case map specifications.* Retrieved January 10, 2002, from http://www.usecasemaps.org/pub/UCM_UML99.pdf

Amyot, D., Patriu, D. B., & Woodside, M. (2004A). Scenario-based performance engineering with UCMnav. In *Proceedings of the 11th SDL Forum (SDL '03)* (LNCS 27081, pp. 18-35).

Amyot, D., Weiss, M., & Logrippo, L. (2004b). *UCM-based generation of test goals* (Report ISSRE04:WITUL) Retrieved November 2004, from http://www.sdl-forum.org

ATHENA. (2004). *D.A1.1.1First version of state of the art in enterprise modeling techniques and technologies to support enterprise interoperability on.* Retrieved October 3, 2004, from http://www.athena-ip.org/index.php?option=content?task=view&id=2 5&Itemid=60#A1

Buhr, R. J. A (1995). *Use case maps for object-oriented systems.* Retrieved September 25, 2003, from http://www.usecasemaps.org/pub/UCM_book95.pdf

Buhr, R. J. A. (1998). Use case maps as architectural entities for complex systems. *IEEE Transactions on Software Engineering, 24*(12), 1131-1155.

Fox, M. S., & Gruninger, M. (1998). Enterprise modeling. *AI Magazine 19*(3), 109-121.

ITU-T - International Telecommunications Union. (1999). *Recommendation Z.100, Specification and description language (SDL); Recommendation Z.120, Message sequences charts (MSC),* Geneva, Switzerland. Retrieved September 30, 2003, from http://www.itu.int/ITU-T/publications/index.html

ITU-T – International Telecommunications Union. (2003). *Draft recommendation Z.153 (02/03) URN: Methodological approach. Geneva, Switzerland; Draft recommendation Z.151 (02/03) GRL: Goal-oriented requirement language; Recommendation Z.150 (02/03) URN: User requirements notations — Language requirements and framework; Draft recommendation Z.152 (02/03) UCM: Use case map notation.* Geneva, Switzerland. Retrieved September 30, 2003, at http://www.itu.int/ITU-T/publications/index.html

Lamsweerde, A. V., & Willemet, L. (1998). Inferring declarative requirements specifications from operational scenarios. *IEEE Transactions on Software Engineering. Special Issue on Scenario Management, 24*(12), 1089-1114.

Medve, A. (2005a). Standardized formal languages for reliable model engineering. In *International Scientific Conference, MicroCAD2005* (pp. 315-321), Miskolc, Hungary.

Medve, A., Szakolczay, K., & Kozmann, G. (2005b). IT models for e-health application processes. In M. Duplaga & K. Zielinski (Eds.), *Overcoming the barriers to e_health growth in enlarged Europe* (pp. 9-23). Kraków: Health and Management Press.

Menyhárt, F. (2005). *Termékgyártó vállalat értékesítési folyamatának újratervezése és SAP illesztése.* MSc Thesis (in Hungarian: Reengineering of supply and delivery process and SAP integration), University of Veszprém, Faculty of Information Technology, Veszprém, Hungary.

Molnár, T. (2005). *Követelményelemzés- és specifikálás egy termékgyártó vállalat értékesítési folyamatának újratervezéséhez.* MSc thesis (in Hungarian: Requirements engineering for reengineering of supply and delivery process and SAP integration), University of Veszprém, Faculty of Information Technology, Veszprém, Hungary.

ODP-RM. (2005). *Open distributed processing — Reference model — Enterprise language* (ITU-T 10 Recommendation X.911 (05/05)). Retrieved June 10, 2005, form http://www.itu.int/rec/recommendation.asp?type=folders&lang=e&parent=T-REC-X.911

OME. (2004). Retrieved March 2004, from http://www.cs.toronto.edu/km/OME/; http://usecasemaps.org/TOOLS

OMG. (2003). *Unified modeling language: Superstructure, Version 2.0* (OMG Final Adopted Specification ptc/03-08-02). Retrieved January 10, 2003, from http://www.omg.org

Regev, G. (2001). *Goal-driven requirements engineering overview.* Retrieved September 25, 2003, from http://lamswww.elpf.ch/Reference/Goal

Selic, B. V. (2004). On the semantic foundations of standard UML 2.0. In *SFM-RT 2004* (LNCS 3185, pp. 181-199).

Sik-Lanyi, C., Bacsa, E., Matrai, R., Kosztyán, Z., & Pataky, I. (2005a). The design question of development of multimedia educational software for aphasia patients. In K. Miesenberger, et al. (Eds.), *Computers helping people with special needs* (LNCS 3118, pp. 6-13). Heidelburg, Germany: Springer Press.

Sik-Lanyi, C., Martai, R., Molnar, G., & Lanyi, Z. (2005c). User Interface design for visually impaired children. *E&I Elektrotechnik und Informationstechnik, 122*(12), 488-494.

Sik-Lanyi, C., Szabo, J., Pall, A., & Pataky, I. (2005b) Computer-controlled cognitive diagnostics and rehabilitation method for stroke patients. *ERCIM News, 61*, 53-54.

Telelogic, A. B.(2005). *Tau G2 Reference MSC2SDL Synthesizer Tutorial, Version G2 2.4.* Retrieved September 2, 2005, from http://www.telelogic.com

UCMExporter. (2004). *UCM user group UCMExporter.* Retrieved September 25, 2003, from http http://ucmexporter.sourceforge.netUCMNav. (2005). *UCM user group, UCMNav 2.* Retrieved September 2, 2003, from http://usecasemaps.org/tools/ucmnav/index.html

Virtual Library at Use Case Maps Group. (2005). Retrieved September 2, 2003, fromhttp://www.usecasemaps.org/Virtual Library/

Weiss, M.,& Amyot, D. (2005). Business process modeling with URN. *International Journal of E-Business Research, 1*(3), 63-90.

Whittle, J., & Krüger, I. (2005). *A methodology for scenario-based requirements capture.* Retrieved January 10, 2005, from http://www.cse.ucsd.edu/~ikrueger/publications/WhittleKrueger_SCESM04_final.pdf

Section II

UML as Meta-Language for Enterprise Modeling

Chapter IV

Enterprise Architecture Modeling with the Unified Modeling Language

Pedro Sousa, Technical University of Lisbon, Portugal

Artur Caetano, Technical University of Lisbon, Portugal

André Vasconcelos, Technical University of Lisbon, Portugal

Carla Pereira, Link Consulting, S.A., Portugal

José Tribolet, Technical University of Lisbon, Portugal

ABSTRACT

Organizations make extensive use of information systems to support planning, decision making, controlling, and to leverage competitive advantage. Organizations are also complex entities that integrate contrasting concepts such as strategy, people, processes, technology, and information. These concepts must be aligned towards the same purpose to ensure that the organization is able to evolve while maximizing the usage of its resources. However, misalignment issues often occur despite large investments in management, organizational, and technological infrastructures. Misalignment also hinders change since it makes it difficult to understand the organization and seamlessly communicate its concepts. This chapter describes the key concepts for modeling an organization's enterprise architecture using the unified modeling language. Enterprise architecture consists of defining and understanding the different elements that shape the organization and how these elements are interrelated with the purpose of understanding and facilitating organizational evolution and change. To achieve this goal, the chapter proposes an enterprise architecture model that separates core organizational concerns as different architectural views, allowing both the modeler and the model user to focus in isolation on organizational, business, information, application and technological aspects.

INTRODUCTION

Organizations are complex entities that deal with contrasting concepts such as people, value chains, business processes and information systems, and technology. Representing the knowledge about an organization proves to be a challenging task since it requires multiple concepts to be represented in a coherent and integrated way, and not as a set of unrelated and independent elements. Failing to deliver such an integrated representation contributes to the materialization of heterogeneous and misaligned views on the organization that would hinder the detection of problems and improvements, as well the ability to assess the overall organization.

For an organization to change it must be self-aware, meaning the knowledge on the organizational concepts is comprehensively shared and understood. This allows minimizing the mismatch between the organization's actual state of affairs and the state as perceived by the different stakeholders. This gap will hold back the definition and implementation of the changes that are required for an organization to evolve. In addition, with the ubiquitous proliferation of information systems and technology, the above-mentioned problems are accentuated as the pressure to change grows and the systems facilitate information sharing and process automation, regardless of its quality and how processes are actually aligned with the organization goals. Indeed, despite the investments made on the research and development of systems and technology, most organizations still do not have adequate tools or methodologies that enable the management and coordination of these systems in such a way as to support planning, changing, decision making, controlling and, especially, as a means to use these systems to explicitly leverage competitive advantage.

Identifying the architecture of the enterprise should therefore be considered as a fundamental step for any organization that renders important to be ready to act rather than react, and to be able to understand whether its elements are aligned. The enterprise architecture results from the continuous process of representing and keeping aligned the elements that are required for managing the organization. In this paper, the term architecture stands for the fundamental arrangement of the components within any kind of sociotechnical system, as well as their relationships to each other and the environment, and the design rules for developing and structuring the system (IEEE, 2000). The components are depicted in the form of a model, while reducing insignificant and redundant aspects. The design rules, on the other hand, stipulate the development and structuring of the model that specifies the types of components, the types of relationships and consistency conditions for the use of components, and their relationships.

Therefore, and set in the context of an organization, the definition of the enterprise architecture strategically aims at:

- Modeling the role of information systems and technology in the enterprise in order to control its life cycle.
- Assessing the alignment between enterprise-wide concepts so that suitable corrective actions can be defined.
- Aligning information systems with business processes and information, thus establishing a reference for efficient resource management.
- Planning sustainable changes.
- Providing the means to generate enterprise knowledge to assist management decisions in an agile and competitive environment.

Target Audience

Since an enterprise architecture allows perspectives with different levels of detail to be created, the concepts addressed in this paper are suitable to a wide target audience, including managers, modelers and architects, and software designers and developers. Managers can make use of the enterprise architecture to understand how the multiple aspects of the organization are interconnected, namely, how strategy is realized in business processes, and how processes depend on and are supported by the organizational service infrastructure. Modelers and architects use the architecture as the organizational lingua franca to represent and communicate strategy, business processes, information, and systems, and to assess and evaluate the alignment between them. Finally, system and software designers exploit the architecture as a means to identify business-driven service requirements, and to explore opportunities for service reuse.

Scope and Contributions

An organization is a complex man-made system that comprises a formal group of people that share one or more goals (Scott, 1997). A system is a collection of interrelated elements within a unified whole. The system concept is often used to describe a set of entities that interact, and for which a model can often be constructed. There exist multiple ways to describe complex systems, including system dynamics (Forrester, 1961) and systems thinking (Senge, 1990). System thinking makes use of techniques to study systems in a holistic way rather than in reductionist terms. It aims to gain insights into the whole by understanding the interactions and processes between the elements that comprise the whole system. Systems thinking can help avoid the silo effect, where a lack of organizational communication can cause a change in one area of a system to adversely affect another area of the system.

The first step into defining an enterprise architecture model is establishing the properties that the model stands for, and the architectural perspectives or views that must exist so that these properties can be successfully architected. It is a requirement that the enterprise concepts and models should be simple enough so that they may be used as a communication, analysis, and discussion tool. The enterprise models need to be defined with simple common sense rules, but also be sound and coherent. This means the models must provide a high-level view that abstracts technical details and interconnections, while keeping a complex structure traceable and coherent.

An architecture must be designed bearing in mind its expected usage. It is about specifying how the things on the enterprise should operate and interact, having a means specified. It should allow, on the one hand, describing organizations, business processes, business information, and systems and, on the other, assessing the alignment between these concepts. This is accomplished by defining the semantics of a set of modeling concepts and a set of five traceable architectural views to represent and relate these concepts in the context of enterprise architecture. These artifacts will be expressed using the unified modeling language (OMG, 2004), confining and extending its generic modeling mechanisms using the standard profiling mechanisms to adapt it to the enterprise-modeling domain.

The five architectural views on the enterprise focus individually on organizational, business, information, applications, and technological concerns. The organizational view focuses on the things that are defined independently of the business and are shared by the whole enterprise, from the management's standpoint. This view addresses concepts related with the enterprise vision and strategic goals. The business view deals with the issues related to a specific business, including specifying the value chain and its business processes, and other concepts related to the operational behavior of the business. The information view concerns the management of the enterprise information that is required to support all strategic and operational processes and decisions. The application view focuses on the specification of a technological independent architecture of services that are put in place to support the business. Finally, the technological view concerns the specification and description of the information, computational, and other technology that is required to support the organization.

The key contribution of this chapter is expressing the components and semantics of an architectural model for process-oriented organizations using five views that separately address different concerns related to the organization, business, information, application, and technology. These aspects are then coherently integrated in the enterprise architecture model that aims at fulfilling the goals previously discussed. The proposed framework relies on a metamodel that defines the fundamental concepts and their relationships. It also makes use of the object-oriented paradigm, exploiting mechanisms such as specialization and aggregation, with the goal of maximizing reusability and facilitating the discussion and communication of the models, thus promoting understandability. The representation of the models relies on the syntax and semantics of the unified modeling language 2.0. In brief, the proposed framework will address the following questions:

- How to model business activities and business processes?
- How to model the resources consumed, modified, and produced that result from executing an activity?
- How to model business services, that is, the operations an activity requires to be executed?
- How to model system services, that is, the services provided by systems supporting business services?
- How to model the architecture of the business support systems?
- How to express the alignment between business processes, business activities, business information, and support systems?
- How to express the alignment between the requirements of an activity and the services provided by business support systems?

However, we will not address a method to evaluate an enterprise architecture or model. Also out of scope is a detailed representation of the organization's strategy as well as the alignment between the organization strategy, strategic and operational goals, and indicators and business processes.

Chapter Structure

This chapter is structured as follows: the next section reviews the concept of enterprise architecture and the significant work in this area. Next, the "enterprise architecture views" section presents the five components of the proposed enterprise architecture model. These architectural components detail the organizational, business, information, application, and technological aspects of the organization. The fundamental modeling concepts used in the enterprise architecture model and the corresponding UML representation are then described in the "enterprise architecture model" section. This section also synthesizes the overall model, describing its structural and dynamic aspects. "Assessing the alignment" provides a set of rules to analyze and assess the alignment between the architecture elements and views. Finally, the last section provides the chapter concluding remarks.

ENTERPRISE ARCHITECTURE

Enterprise architecture is a concept that has been around for almost 20 years. In the meantime, areas such as business process management (Burlton, 2001; Smith & Fingar, 2003), business process redesign and reengineering (Davenport & Short, 1990; Malhotra, 1998; Stoddard & Jarvenpaa, 1995) and total quality management (Juran & Godfrey, 1999; Senge, 1990), just to name a few, shed light on the relationship between process-oriented management and business process support through information technology. However, most approaches that stemmed from these fundamental studies do not provide holistic models on the enterprise's components as put forward by orthodox enterprise architecture. This holistic vision is shared by many references on enterprise architecture found in mainstream literature:

- Enterprise architecture consists of defining and understanding the different elements that make up the enterprise, and how those elements are interrelated (Open Group, 2003).
- Enterprise architecture is the holistic expression of an organization's key business, information, application, and technology strategies and their impact on business functions and processes. The approach looks at business processes, the structure of the organization, and what type of technology is used to conduct these business processes (Meta Group, 2005).
- Enterprise architecture is a relatively simple and straightforward model, framework, or template that can be used by everyone within your enterprise to assess how things are going, to facilitate their work, and to design new projects (Egan, 1988).
- Enterprise architecture is the set of representations required to describe a system or enterprise regarding its construction, maintenance, and evolution (Zachman, 1987).
- Enterprise architecture is a strategic information asset base that defines the business mission, the information necessary to perform the mission, the technologies necessary to perform the mission, and the transitional processes for implementing new technologies in response to the changing mission needs (FEAPMO, 2003).
- Enterprise architecture is a complete expression of the enterprise; a master plan that "acts as a collaboration force" between aspects of business planning such as goals, visions, strategies, and governance principles; aspects of business operations such as business terms, organization structures, processes, and data; aspects of automation such

as information systems and databases; and the enabling technological infrastructure of the business such as computers, operating systems, and networks (Schekkerman, 2004).

The preceding definitions share a common concern: enterprise architecture is about the structure of the things of relevance in the enterprise, their components, and how these components fit and work together to fulfill a specific purpose. In the remainder of this section, we will review a set of significant approaches to enterprise architecture.

The ANSA project (ANSA, 1989; Herbert, 1994) focused on developing a basic understanding of distributed architectures. ANSA recommends a set of components, rules, recipes, and guidelines to help designers make design decisions. This project was most likely the first to propose specific projections that were claimed to provide complete coverage of information processing systems. The projections on enterprise, information, computation, engineering, and technology views were later taken up in the open distributed processing standards, such as CORBA. This concept enables separating the multiple concerns of a complex system in such a way that they can be individually addressed and later composed in a global representation of the system. Thus, the concept of enterprise projection shares a common goal with other approaches to enterprise architecture, such as Zachman's framework, and the one proposed in this chapter. One of the first standards to embrace enterprise projections was ISO's RM-ODP. The reference model for open distributed processing (Farooqi, Loggripo, & Loggripo, 1995; ISO, 1995; Schurmann, 1995) aimed at integrating a wide range of distributed systems standards, and maintaining consistency across such systems. To do so, RM-ODP includes descriptive as well as prescriptive elements. The descriptive elements provide a common vocabulary, while the five prescriptive elements, known as viewpoints, constrain what can be built as required by a system. Specifically, it defines the enterprise viewpoint for system boundaries, policies, and purpose; the information viewpoint to represent distributed information; the computational viewpoint for decomposition of the system into distributable units; the engineering viewpoint for description of components needed and, finally, the technology viewpoint for describing the implementation details of components.

The Zachman framework for enterprise architecture (O'Rourke, Fishman, & Selkow, 2003; Sowa & Zachman, 1992; Zachman, 1987) is amongst the recognized works on enterprise architecture from both modeling and management perspectives. It provides a view of the subjects and models needed for developing and documenting a complete enterprise architecture, and is described in a matrix that provides, on the vertical axis, multiple perspectives of the overall architecture and on the horizontal axis, a classification of the various artifacts of the architecture. The framework is structured around the perspectives related to the user roles involved in planning, designing, building, and maintaining enterprise information systems. These perspectives are:

- **Scope (planner's perspective).** Concerns the strategic aspects of the organization, the context of its environment, and scope.
- **Enterprise model (owner's perspective).** Concerns the business perspective of the organization, how it delivers value, and how it will be used.
- **System model (designer's perspective).** Concerns the systems of the organization, ensuring they fulfill the owner's expectations.

- **Technology model (builder's perspective).** Concerns the technology used to support the systems and the business in the organization.
- **Detailed representations (subcontractor's perspective).** Concerns the builder's specifications of the system components to be subcontracted internally or to third parties.

The six columns focus on separating different domain concerns:

- **Data (what).** Concerns the definition and understanding of the organization's information.
- **Function (how).** Describes the process of translating the mission of the organization into the business, and into successively more detailed definitions of its operations.
- **Network (where).** Concerns the geographical distribution of the organization's activities and artifacts, and how they relate with each perspective of the organization.
- **People (who).** Describes who is related with each artifact of the organization, namely business processes, information, and IT. At higher-level cells, the "who" refers to organizational units, whereas in lower cells it refers to roles and system users.
- **Time (when).** Describes how each artifact of the organization is organized in time.
- **Motivation (why).** Describes the translation of goals in each row into actions and objectives in lower rows.

The Zachman framework contains suggested specification documents for each cell of the matrix (Zachman, 1987). For example, it suggests using ER technique for modeling the data description in the owner's view business model, or using functional flow diagrams for modeling the owner's view process description. However, it does not define a metamodel to integrate the information within each cell, nor does it describe how to trace such information (Frankel, Harmon, & Mukerji, 2003). Nevertheless, the framework is independent of specific methodologies. In addition, there are no specific techniques described to create the suggested specification documents in each cell of the framework.

Cap Gemini Ernst & Young has developed an approach to the analysis and development of enterprise and project-level architectures known as the integrated architecture framework (Goedvolk, Bruin, & Rijsenbrij, 1999). It can be considered a design tool, aiming at the development of mutually aligned business and IT systems through a unified architecture. IAF breaks down the overall problem into a number of areas covering people and processes, information and knowledge, information systems, and technology infrastructure. There are two special areas addressing the governance and security aspects across all the other areas. Analysis of each of these areas is structured into four levels: contextual, conceptual, logical, and physical, representing phases of the design process and not different levels of management attention. The contextual view justifies the organization and describes its contextual environment. It corresponds largely to Zachman's planner's perspective row. The conceptual view describes what the requirements are, and what the vision for the solution is. The logical view describes how these requirements and vision are met. Finally, the physical view describes the artifacts of the solution. These views are not related to Zachman's perspectives since in IAF, business, information, information systems, and technological infrastructure are the artifacts of the architecture whereas in Zachman, business, information systems, and technology are perspectives.

TOGAF, the open group architecture framework (Open Group, 2003), is an industry standard architecture framework used to develop enterprise architecture descriptions. It enables designing, evaluating, and building the architecture for an organization. The key to TOGAF is the architecture development method (ADM), an approach for developing enterprise architecture descriptions that meet the needs of the specific business. TOGAF mainly consists of three parts: the ADM, the enterprise continuum, and the resource base. None of the three parts delivers a metamodel to assure a consistent reuse of components during an iterative use of the procedure. The ADM is iterative, over the whole development process, between phases, and within phases (architecture development cycle). The cycle consists of eight phases: architecture vision, business architecture, information system architectures, technology architecture, opportunities and solutions, migration planning, implementation governance, and architecture change management. Each of these eight phases contains further detailed steps. The use of reference models (which are provided by the TOGAF enterprise continuum) and guidelines (which are provided by the TOGAF resource base) can be regarded as other important activities in the developing process. TOGAF uses a set of activities that build a detailed procedure model for developing enterprise architecture descriptions. Even though TOGAF ADM describes the different inputs and outputs for each phase of the architecture development cycle, there are no specification documents that describe the output, and no instructions that clearly describe in which phase of the development cycle that specification documents have to be generated. From that point of view, specification documents only exit in part within the TOGAF framework.

In the next sections, we propose an enterprise architecture model that naturally follows the approach and several goals of the work here described. However, it emphasizes the traceability, alignment, and assessment between enterprise components, facilitating their reuse and independent codevelopment. The enterprise architecture model, graphically expressed in the UML, relies on a metamodel to define its elements and corresponding relationships.

ENTERPRISE ARCHITECTURE VIEWS

We propose modeling the multidimensional aspects of the enterprise architecture and, based on that, defining and evaluating the alignment between business processes, business information, and the corresponding support systems and technology. The first step in this direc-

Figure 1. The five enterprise architecture components

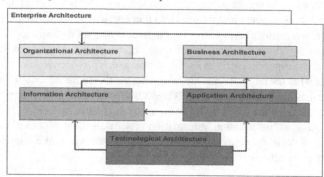

tion is identifying a minimal set of components able to represent the required organizational concepts, while ensuring that the alignment between these concepts can be assessed.

The enterprise architecture model comprises five architectural components: organizational architecture, business architecture, information architecture, application architecture, and technological architecture. Each of these subarchitectures is individually represented and organized as a UML package, as depicted in Figure 1. Each package owns its model elements, and its elements cannot be owned by more than one package. The relationships, depicted as dotted arrows, represent the dependencies of each package. The following subsections detail each of the architecture components.

Organizational Architecture

The organizational architecture deals with the aspects directly related with the organization that are not related with the specific business it conducts, nor with the mechanisms used to accomplish the creation of value. It therefore includes concepts such as the enterprise mission, vision and strategy, and the definition of organizational units.

The enterprise mission and vision state what the enterprise is and does, defining why the organization exists. The mission is a concise and internally focused statement of the reason for the organization's existence, defining the purpose toward which its activities are directed and the values that guide employee's activities. The mission also describes how the organization expects to compete and deliver value to customers. On its turn, the vision points out where the enterprise aims to be in the future through the enterprise strategy, defining the mid- to long-term goals of the organization. The vision statement should be market-oriented and made publicly available. It describes, often in visionary terms, how the organization wants to be perceived by the world (Kaplan & Norton, 2004).

The enterprise strategy states the key decisions and actions the enterprise is willing to do in order to accomplish its vision, and describes how it intends to create value for its shareholders, and customers. Strategy is about selecting the set of processes in which an organization will excel to create a sustainable difference in the marketplace.

The organizational architecture includes other concepts such as organizational policies, organizational units, as well as human resource issues like people roles, carrier, goals, and so on.

Business Architecture

The business architecture results from the implementation of business strategies and the definition of processes. The functional requirements of business process support systems, that is, the information systems that will operationally support the business, are derived from this architecture.

The core concept within the business architecture is the business process. A business process is a set of value-adding activities that operates over input entities producing output entities. The activities comprised in the process are coordinated, meaning they are either orchestrated by a central controlling entity or choreographed. The actual coordination mechanism is only relevant when detailing how the process is enacted. What distinguishes an arbitrary set of coordinated activities from a business process is the fact that the process must add value to some customer, whether internal or external to the organization. Thus, although an organization always comprises multiple sets of coordinated activities, each may or may not be classified as an actual business processes. Business processes are orthogonal to the organization's units. In fact, they frequently cross the boundaries of several units. Macroscopically, business processes are abstracted as value chains (Porter, 1985).

An activity describes the business roles required for its operation. These roles are played by the organization entities and usually include actor role, resource role, and observable state role. An activity requires one actor, or a combination or team of actors to be executed. The actor represents a person, a machine or device, or an information system. An actor provides the services required for fulfilling the business role required by the activity. A resource is used as input or output of an activity during its operation. A resource is usually created, used, transformed, or consumed during the operation of the activity. An observable state is a specific resource role that is used as a means to observe the status of an activity. An activity is performed during a specific period. As a precondition for its enactment, all of the business roles must be fulfilled by specific entities. These entities will be engaged in playing their roles for the duration of the activity. The activity postcondition is that all of the roles will have finished playing their part.

Information Architecture

The information architecture describes what the organization needs to know to run its processes and operations as described in the business architecture. It defines a view on the business information that is system and technology independent. It is an abstraction of the information requirements of the organization, and provides a high-level logical representation of all the key information elements that are used in the business, as well as the relationship between them (Gilchrist & Mahon, 2004; Inmon, 1999).

Business information is structured as a collection of informational entities. An entity can result from the composition or specialization of other entities in the object-oriented sense. Information entities are classes, meaning they can be typified. Entities describe most artifacts of the enterprise, namely those resources required by processes, including business, support, and management processes. As such, they have an identifier, defined from a business perspective, and a set of attributes. Attributes are related to the roles the entities play. Therefore, each role integrates its set of attributes into the entity. The overall set of attributes results from merging each individual set of attributes derived from each role the entity is able to play.

Application Architecture

The application architecture fulfills two major goals: supporting the business requirements and allowing efficient management of the organization's entities. To satisfy these goals, the application architecture should be derived top-down from the analysis of the business and information architectures.

The application architecture defines the applications needed for data management and business support, regardless of the actual software used to implement systems (DeBoever, 1997). It functionally defines what application services are required to ensure processes and entities are supported in acceptable time, format, and cost (Spewak & Hill, 1992). According to the International Enterprise Architecture Center (2005), it should describe the characteristics, styles, and interactions among multiple applications.

Thus, the application architecture defines the applications required to enable the business architecture. This includes identifying how the applications interact with each other, how they will interact with other business integration elements, and how the application and data will be distributed throughout the organization. It typically includes descriptions of automated services that support the business processes, and of the interaction and interdependencies between an organization's application systems, plans for developing new applications, and revision of old applications based on the enterprises objectives.

The architecture of a business process support system is described using a structure of information system block, or IS block for short, that depicts an information system or application building blocks. An IS block is then defined as an organized collection of services, mechanisms, and operations designed to handle organization information (Spewak & Hill, 1992). We extend this definition to allow an IS block to handle not only information, but also the coordination and other mechanisms required to support business process. Each block may state several attributes, such as availability, scalability (ability to scale up performance), and profile-based access (ability to identify who does what).

Technological Architecture

The technological architecture represents the technologies behind application implementation as well as the infrastructure and environment required for the deployment of the business process support systems.

The technological architecture addresses a large number of concepts since it must cope simultaneously with continuous technological evolutions and the need to provide different specialized technological perspectives, such as those centered on security and hardware. These concepts are abstracted as an information technology block. An IT block is the infrastructure, application platform, and technological or software component that realizes or implements a set of IS blocks. It encompasses three parts:

- **IT infrastructure block:** Represents the physical and infrastructural concepts existing in the information systems architecture: the computational nodes (e.g. servers, personal computers, or mobile devices), and the noncomputational nodes (e.g. printers, network components) that support application platforms.
- **IT platform block:** Describes the implementation of the services used in the IT application deployment, such as the operation system, the Web platform, and the EAI platform.
- **IT application block:** Is the technological implementation of an IS block. It classifies the type of implementation, such as presentation, logic, data, or coordination block, as well as the technological concepts used in the implementation, such as object or component-oriented architecture and types of modules. An IT application block makes use of services provided by the IT platform.

Two other concepts are also important in the description of the information system architecture:

- **Operation:** An abstract description of an action supported by a service (W3C, 2002). An operation is the finer-grain concept in the information technology architecture
- **Service:** The aggregation of a set of operations provided by an architectural block. It can be seen as a generalization of the concept of Web service notion (W3C, 2002). We consider three distinct types of service:
  - **Business service:** A set of operations provided by IS blocks supporting business processes.

- ◦ **IS service:** A set of operations provided by an IS block to other IS blocks. This is used to aggregate multiple IS blocks.
- ◦ **IT service:** A set of technological services provided by the specific application platforms.

ENTERPRISE ARCHITECTURE MODEL

The architectural views describe and relate the fundamental concepts that, as a whole, describe the enterprise architecture. Each is represented as a class within a specific package, as depicted in Figure 2. This section details the fundamental concepts and the relationships that are required to represent the enterprise architecture according to the five views that were defined earlier.

Fundamental Concepts

An organization can be modeled as a collection of business nouns that interact as described by a number of verbs. The nouns represent things within the organization that are of interest regarding the purpose of the model. The verbs stand for the enterprise activities that define how work is done and how value is added, thus describing its business processes and activities. Here we define the fundamental concept of entity and activity, and that of role.

Figure 2. The fundamental concepts within each of the five enterprise architecture views

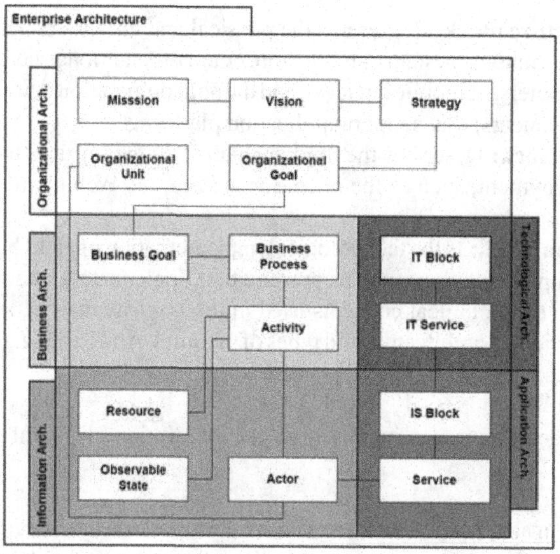

Figure 3. Relationships between activity, role and entity

These three concepts allow complex interactions of entities to be abstracted. The relationships between these three elements are depicted in Figure 3.

Entity

An organization is composed of entities. Entities are nouns that have a distinct, separate existence, though it need not be of material existence. There is also no presumption that an entity is animate. An animate entity is able to exhibit active behavior. In enterprise modeling, an entity can be a person, place, machine, concept, or event that has meaning in the context of the business, and about which some information may be stored because it is relevant for the purpose of the model.

Entities can be classified according to its attributes and methods. Entities may relate structurally to other entities, as in the case of an entity composed by other entities (e.g. an inventory is composed of products). An entity may also be specialized to restrict the features of a more general entity.

An entity is characterized by its attributes and methods. These features can be either intrinsic or extrinsic. Intrinsic features describe the entity in isolation, while extrinsic features arise from the relationships with other entities. For example, the entity Person has intrinsic features such as Age and Sex, and extrinsic features such as Job Position and Salary, which derive from a transitory relationship between the Person and the Organization. The state of the intrinsic features may change over time (e.g., Age), but always characterize the object. Extrinsic features only manifest themselves while a relationship is valid, and may become unsuitable when the relationship is no longer valid. For example, the Job Position or Salary properties are not appropriate to characterize an unemployed person. This means an entity's extrinsic features are directly constrained by the potential relationships it may have in a given context, such as its whole lifespan, a bounded business collaboration, or specific time interval.

When entities interact with other entities, they do so through roles. In this case, we say the entities are collaborating, and that each of the entities is playing a set of roles in the context of a specific business activity.

UML Representation

An entity is a UML Class. The features of this class represent the intrinsic attributes and methods of the entity. Intrinsic means that the features exist per se, regardless of its collaborations. An entity may relate to other entities via aggregation or generalization. An entity may only relate structurally to other entities. The collaboration or interaction between activities is mediated by roles.

Figure 4 shows a class diagram depicting three entity classes along with the corresponding attributes. In this example, the Inventory entity aggregates Products.

Figure 4. Entity class

Role

A role is the observable behavioral of an entity in the scope of a specific collaboration context. Hence, a role represents the external visible features of that entity when it collaborates with a set of other entities in the context of some activity. An entity relates to zero or more role classes through the stereotyped «play» relationship. Each role represents a subset of its external or extrinsic features in the context of a specific collaboration defined in a role model.

Roles aim at separating the different concerns that arise from the collaborations between the entities fulfilling an activity. A role may be bound to multiple entities via the «play» relationship. Binding a role to an entity means that a specific instance of that entity is able to express the behavior defined by the role. It also means that the attributes and method of the role will be part of the entity's feature set.

A role is also a type and may be classified according to its attributes and methods. Therefore, it can be generalized and aggregated as a regular class.

Roles are described in role models. A role model describes how roles are structured and how they collaborate in order to fulfill a task. The role model may also specify constraints.

UML Representation

Roles are described as UML classes. A role may be specialized to restrict its behavior and may be composed of other roles. A composed role is able to put into play the behavior of each of the roles it comprises. The structural relationships between roles are shown on class diagrams.

Roles relate to entities through the «play» classifier relationship stereotype. Actually, entity instances play role instances. Role models are packages that comprise a class diagram to describe the role structure and a UML dynamic diagram to describe its collaborations.

The class diagram depicts the roles and the role associations required to fulfill a task. It also describes any constraints or business rules that govern the role associations. Constraints can be expressed in OCL or in natural language, depending on the level of formality that is required.

Figure 5 shows the structural dependencies between two roles, Employee and Employer, both defined in the Works For role model. It also depicts the binding between two entities, Person and Organization, and the two roles Employee and Employer.

It is important to contrast the definition of the Person class in Figure 5 and Figure 4. Figure 4 depicts the attributes of the Person without making clear what attributes derive from what collaborations. This mixes its intrinsic attributes (age and sex) with the external

Figure 5. The Works For *role model showing the dependencies between two related roles (left) and binding roles to entities (right)*

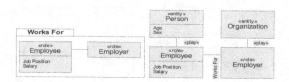

attributes that are only relevant when the person behaves as an employee (job position and salary). In opposition, the diagram in Figure 5 uses roles to separate the Person's external attributes from its intrinsic attributes. It can be observed that the job position and salary are extrinsic attributes and are dependent on the specific role Employee. Moreover, the role model makes clear that the Employee role relates with the Employer role, in the context of the Works For collaboration. Separating the intrinsic from extrinsic features allows for a more efficient informational architecture and application since entities may be designed so that they are independent of the specific activities that use them, not only improving the reusability of the entities, but also the ability to understand why a specific feature exists in a business entity.

Activity

An activity is an abstraction representing how a number of entities collaborate through roles in order to produce a specific outcome. Similar to an algorithm, an activity aims accomplishing some task that, given an initial state, will always end in finite time and in a recognizable end-state. An activity may also be functionally decomposed into a finite set of further activities, thus adding detail to the specification.

An activity specifies what entities are required to realize a task. As seen earlier, roles are used to separate the description of the actual entity features from the features required by the collaboration in context of the activity. In this way, activities and entities are described separately, and roles may be reused in different activities.

UML Representation

An activity is described by a number of role collaborations as shown earlier in the previous section. To improve readability and use a notation closer to that of BPMN (BPMI,

Figure 6. Role-typed entity association mediated by an activity classifier

Figure 7. Common generic roles played by entities in the course of an activity

Figure 8. Activity decomposition methodology according to observable states

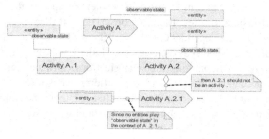

2004) and IDEF-0 (ICAM, 1981), we can alternatively represent an activity as in Figure 6, using UML's action or send signal action icons.

An activity often results from a number of interacting entities playing a set of roles specialized from four generic roles: resource, actor, observable state, and business goal (v. Figure 7). The resource role is played by the entities that are used as input to the activity operation. These resource entities are handled by a number of actors to generate another set of output resource entities. An entity plays an actor role whenever it is performing active behavior, that is, putting into action its skills or capabilities. Actors may be played by entities modeling people, mechanical devices, or information systems. During these operations, actors may or may not contribute to the achievement of business goals. These goals are themselves entities.

Finally, and from a methodological viewpoint, activities must relate to at least one entity playing the role of observable state. An observable state models a state of affairs that is of interest to a stakeholder in the context of the enterprise architecture. It can be seen as an indicator that results from performing the activity. If there is no observable state related to a collaboration, this means the collaboration should not be modeled as an activity. This criterion can be used as a stop condition when deciding whether to decompose an activity any further. If the decomposition results in at least one activity that produces no observable state, then the decomposition should either be deemed invalid, or else be rearranged so that every decomposed activity produces at least one observable state (Figure 8). It is noteworthy that the set of observable states depends on the purpose of the enterprise architecture. For instance, the set of observable states in an architecture that will be used to identify system requirements will probably be much more detailed than the set used to describe the core activities of an organization from a strategic perspective. Likewise, observable states are completely detached from how activities are coordinated. Until now, we have only discussed activities and activity decomposition at a structural level, and have not mentioned how to coordinate activities through the specification of activity flows or other mechanisms. This will be the subject of next section.

Business Processes and Activity Coordination

Coordination means integrating or linking together different parts of a system to accomplish a collective set of tasks. In the case of activity coordination, it means describing how activities are linked together so that they define a business process. Several definitions of business process can be found in the literature, such as:

- The set of internal activities performed to serve a customer. The purpose of each business process is to offer each customer the right product or service, with a high degree of performance measures against cost, longevity, service, and quality.
- A set of coherent activities that creates a result with some value for an internal or external customer; it is a meaningful whole of value-adding activities.
- The manner in which work is organized, coordinated, and focused to produce a valuable product or service (Laudon & Laudon, 2000).
- A collection of activities that takes one or more kinds of inputs and creates an output that is of value to the customer (Hammer & Champy, 2001).

A common factor in these definitions is that a business process is a coordinated set of activities that is able to add value to the customer, and to achieve business goals. This definition means that only the coordinated activities that fulfill these requirements can be classified as a business process. In this sense, classification of coordinated activities as a business process is an assessment that can be made *a posteriori*.

Figure 9. Activity diagram representing the "frying an omelet" process

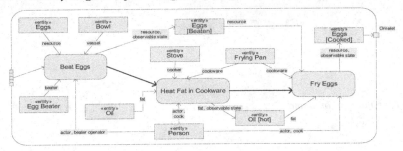

Figure 10. Role models depicting the relationships between the roles

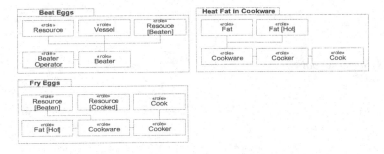

Coordination may mean either orchestration or choreography. Orchestration occurs when activities are coordinated by a centralized element that holds the coordination script. Choreography corresponds to autonomous coordination in the sense every activity decides its own actions according to a set of rules shared by every participant. While describing the business architecture, it is possible to describe the activity coordination in different ways, such as using explicit control or data flow between activities or using events or preconditions.

UML Representation

Coordination is represented using any of UML's dynamic diagrams. Figure 9 shows a UML activity diagram depicting a process by making explicit the control flow between the activities and the data flow between the data objects. The structural part of the role model is depicted in Figure 10. For instance, Beat Eggs is an activity where a Person acts as a Beater Operator while using a Beater and a Vessel to change the state of a Resource to beaten. The activity diagram shows the actual entities playing these roles while the role model describes the role relationships.

Figure 11. Organizational unit

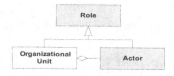

Figure 12. Chain of command

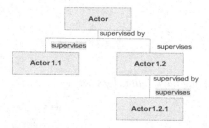

Figure 13. Business goal

Role Types

Business entities are able to play a number of different roles during its lifetime. The basic roles we require to describe the enterprise architecture as earlier described (see Figure 2) correspond to the business nouns considered in the organizational, business, information, application, and technological architecture views. This subsection describes each of these roles.

Organizational Unit

An organizational unit includes information about the organizational units that make up an organization, the human resources that belong to those organizational units, as well as the structure and relationships that connect them all together.

Another important concept is that of chain of command, which refers to an interconnected and unbroken set of reporting relationships extending from the top of the organization to the bottom. Each level in the structure from the bottom-up is accountable to a superior (Hampton, 1986). The chain of command is modeled relating actors with a «supervisor» and «supervised by» association.

Business Goal

A business goal represents a measurable state that the organization intends to achieve. Goals are achieved by the entities involved in performing activities.

Figure 14. Resource

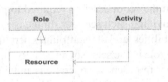

Figure 15. Observable state

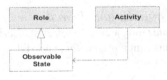

Figure 16. Actor

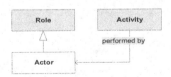

Resource

A resource is the role of an entity that models capacity to be used and produced by business processes. The capacity may be consumed, incorporated, monopolized, or accessed (Taylor, 1995).

Observable State

An observable state models a state of affairs that is of interest to a stakeholder in the context of the enterprise architecture. Observable states can guide the task of functional decomposing an activity as discussed earlier in section Activity.

Actor

An actor is an animate entity capable of exhibiting active behavior. Actors model people, computer systems, mechanical tools, or any other devices used to perform the operations required by an activity.

Since entities only collaborate through roles, classifying an entity as an actor depends on the roles the entity is able to play, that is, on the type of collaborations it participates in. This means that some entities may be potential actors, but in a specific organizational case, they are just inanimate entities. Moreover, the status of an actor is transient and context dependent, meaning that the same entity could be an actor in the context of a process and a resource in another. For example, in a social security benefits process, the entity that represents a pensioner, although modeling a person, would not be modeled as an actor since the roles this entity plays are not related to executing any activity. However, if the same person works for the social security and is involved in playing some operational roles in that same process, then he or she would be regarded as an actor in that context. This means that the criteria for deciding whether an entity is an actor are the roles it is able to play.

Actors are able to perform the set of services required to play a role. This means an actor is then responsible for providing such services. In the case of people, these services are correlated to the skills, capabilities, and other attributes pertaining to the person that are relevant to assign his or her to a role in the scope of an activity. In the case of computerized systems or machines, the services represent the operations and functions that these devices put into play during the role assignment. This topic will be further discussed in section under "Roles and Entities."

Mission, Vision, Strategy, Organizational Goal

The mission states the organization's purpose of existence. Having the mission as a motto, the vision is the way to transform it in something possible to achieve in a near future.

Figure 17. The strategy role model

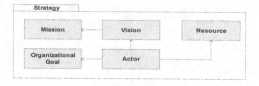

Figure 18. The strategy business process

Figure 19. Roles provided by entities and required by an activity

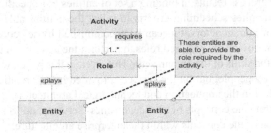

On its turn, strategy is a high-level business process that describes how to accomplish the vision. The goals that this strategic process achieves are called organizational goals. This is depicted in Figure 17.

As seen earlier in sections Activity and Business Processes and Activity Coordination, a business process is performed by actors who act upon resources, thus achieving goals. Figure 18 shows how these roles relate in the context of the strategy process. This process is a means of coordinating the enterprise. It explicitly defines who the actor responsible for conducting the strategic process is. This actor uses the vision and a set of resources to produce organizational goals.

Roles and Entities

The business architecture defines the business processes of the organization. To do so, it makes use of the repository of activities and entities specified in the organization's information architecture. Activities describe how the entities collaborate through roles in order to produce a specific outcome. This outcome results from actors performing operations or services over the other collaborating entities.

This means we can model this interaction as a marketplace where activities are the demand and actors (i.e., active entities able to express behavior) are the offer. The activity describes what roles are required for its operation. Entities are able to play these roles, thus providing the required service.

Figure 20. Services

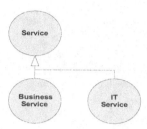

The scheduling process results in binding a set of entities to a specific instance of an activity. To do so, it applies scheduling criteria to select the entities able to perform the activity. In the case of human actors, this can be accomplished by selecting the available actors that are able to provide the required roles to perform the activity. In this case, a role must be translated to the skills of the human actor. However, in this paper, we will not focus on the task provided by people, but on the services provided by information systems and technology as described in the application and technological architectures.

We will next define the concepts of service, business service, and IS and IT block, to conclude the definition of the concepts within the enterprise architecture.

Business Services and IT Services

A service is an aggregation of a set of operations provided by an architectural block. The operations provided by a service are implemented in other architectural blocks, such as IS block and IT block. It is represented in UML as an interface element, restricting it to the interfaces provided by the IS block and the IT block.

A business service is a collection of operations provided by IS blocks that support business processes. This is the key concept in service-oriented architectures; the business service aggregates the set of operations used by business processes and, thus, provides the interface between business and information systems.

The IT service is an interface provided by an IT block to other IT blocks. This is the lower level concept of service that includes software services (implemented, for example in

Figure 21. Definition of IS and IT blocks (left) and example showing an IS block A providing a business service to a role and to another IS block B that is realized by an IT block (right)

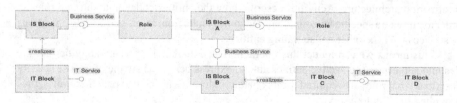

a Web service), the technological services provided by application platforms (e.g., operation system services, security services, data services, integration services), and the infrastructure services (e.g., the services provided by the network).

Application Block and IT Block

An application block or IS block denotes an application that aggregates an organized collection of mechanisms and operations that are able to manipulate organization data. It is represented as a UML component. An IS block provides business services to roles or to other IS Blocks.

The IT block represent the infrastructure, platform, technological, or software component that realizes an IS block. It is a UML class.

ASSESSING THE ALIGNMENT

This section outlines the rules to assess the alignment between the architecture views and its elements. Figure 22 shows the alignment dependencies between the architecture views. The next sections present a set of alignment rules between business and information architectures, business and application architectures, and information and application architectures. The final subsection summarizes the integrity rules that deal with the relationships between the architectural components.

Business and Information Architectures

Information and business architectures are aligned when business people have the information they need to run the business. This means accurate, on-time information, with the right level of detail. The impact of misalignments between these architectures is mostly the inability of getting the information relevant for the business. For instance, a manager asks for a report where sales figures need to be decomposed by service type. Assuming the report has either actual or foreseen business relevance, the ability to produce such a report is evidence of the alignment between information and business architectures. To produce the report, the organization must possess the adequate data and applications. Common rules to assess the alignment between the business and information architectures are:

Figure 22. Dependencies between the architecture views while assessing the alignment

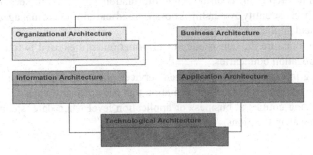

- Business activities create, update, or delete at least one information entity.
- The attributes of entities are read at least by one business activity.
- Entities must be classified and named only within the information architecture.
- Entities have an identifier that is clearly understood by business people.
- Entities must have a means of being communicated to the appropriate audience using enterprise-standard applications and tools.
- Entities must be owned by someone responsible for their coherency, accuracy, and relevance to the business.

Business and Application Architectures

The alignment between business and applications does not imply a flexible and agile IS architecture. A measure of flexibility and agility is the effort required to enable the information systems to provide services to the business. Misalignments often drive people to engage in other tasks than those required by the activities being performed. Common rules required to assess the alignment between the business and application architectures are:

- Business data is introduced only once.
- Business activities related to information processing should be automated as business services.
- Each business service must support at least one activity.
- There are no redundant business services. This means that if an application service is removed, at least one business activity would no longer be supported.
- Information required for critical processes should be supported by services with high availability.

Information and Application Architectures

Misalignments between information and application architectures increase the effort required to ensure applications have the right data for processing. This means that IT people focus on keeping information entity replicas coherent or in integration projects that serve no purpose other than ensuring the coherency between information replicas. In both cases, the extra effort is an evidence of misalignment between information and application architectures. There are other evidences of misalignment between information and application architectures, such as:

- The need to keep replicas of the same information entity, and to keep such replicas coherent because entity ownership is not specified and entities are managed by multiple independent application services.
- The need to assure the consistency of information entities used in transactions that cross application boundaries.
- Retrieving information from unrelated services and applications to produce a view on the organization's business information that has no clear owner.
- Transforming entities at business or application level when data is changed within technological applications.

Table 1. Integrity rules

Concept relationship		Integrity rule
OA::Mission	**OA::Vision**	Every organization should have a mission defined. For that mission, there should be a vision.
OA::Vision	**OA::Strategy**	The vision should be accomplished by one or more strategies. A strategy is only defined for a single vision.
	OA::Organizational goal	A vision should have one or more goals to achieve. A goal is only defined for one vision.
OA::Strategy	**OA::Organizational goal**	A strategy should contribute to one or more goals. A goal can be supported by one or more strategies.
OA::Organizational Goal	**BA::Business goal**	A goal can be decomposed in one or more business goals. A business goal is only related to one organizational goal.
BA::Business Goal	**BA::Business process**	A business process can have one or more business goals to achieve. A business goal can be supported by one or more business process.
IA::Activity	**OA::Strategy**	A business process can have one or more strategies to achieve. A strategy can be supported by one or more business process
	OA::Organizational unit	A business process can be associated to one or more organizational units. An organizational unit can handle one or more business process.
	IA::Resource	A business process can relate to multiple resources. A resource can be related to one or more business process.
	IA::Observable state	An activity must have at least one observable state associated to it, thus justifying its functional decomposition.
	IA::Actor	An activity must be owned and enacted by at least one actor. The actor is not necessarily the same.
	AA::Business service	An activity must be supported by at least one business service.
IA::Actor	**OA::Organizational unit**	An organizational unit comprises one or more actors. An actor reports only to a single organizational unit.
	AA::Business service	An automated actor must provide one or more business services.
AA:Business service	**AA::IS block**	A business service must be provided by at least one IS block.
TA::IT block	**TA::IT service**	An IT service must be provided by at least one IT block.
	AA::IS block	Each IS block must be implemented in at least one IT block.

To mitigate the above issues, the views of information and application architectures must be consistently updated. The fundamental rules required to assess the alignment between the information and application architectures are:

- An information entity is managed by a single application.
- The business services that update the same information entity must be supported by the same application.
- The business service that manages an information entity must provide the means to share and distribute it across the organization using agreed-on protocols and formats as defined by the business.
- Exporting and distributing information entities across organization applications should be made imposing the minimum dependencies between application as possible. The usage of a common data store is often preferable to point-to-point application integration. Applications managing a given information entity should export its contents to the data store when its contents have changed. Applications requiring an information entity should inquire the data store for up-to-date information.

Integrity Rules

The following table summarizes a set of integrity rules that apply between pairs of enterprise concepts. The list is far from being complete. The concept names are qualified and preceded by OA, BA, IA, AA, TA, standing for organizational, business, information, application and technological architecture, respectively. These integrity rules should be observed while creating and assessing the enterprise architecture model.

CONCLUSION

Enterprise architecture consists of defining and understanding the different elements that shape an organization, and how those elements are interrelated. In this chapter, we have proposed a set of concepts and their relationships to describe an organization with the purpose of understanding and facilitating its evolution. These concepts are part of an enterprise architecture that is decomposed in five architectural views, each focusing on separate concerns within the enterprise.

Enterprise architecture defines the concepts that allow an organization to be described at multiple levels of detail allowing multiple dimensions of analysis. In architecture and civil engineering, for instance, the concepts and computer-aided tools already exist, allowing the design and analysis of a structure from different perspectives, ranging from electrical wire details to its macrostructural properties, and continually assessing the coherence and alignment of such perspectives. Representing the enterprise architecture with the UML is a step towards achieving a similar goal. Such concepts can ultimately allow an organization to be assessed and controlled so that the alignment becomes the process of continuously guiding the enterprise resources to exploit opportunities and cope with environmental changes.

REFERENCES

ANSA. (1989). *The ANSA reference manual, release 01.00*. Cambridge: Architecture Projects Management Ltd.

BPMI. (2004). *BPMN 1.0*. Retrieved December, 15, 2005, from http://www.bpmn.org/Documents/BPMN V1-May 3 2004.pdf

Burlton, R. (2001). *Business process management: Profiting from process*. Indianapolis, IN: Sams Publishing.

Davenport, T., & Short, J. (1990). The new industrial engineering: Information technology and business process redesign. *Sloan Management Review, 31*(4), 11-27.

DeBoever, L. (1997). *Enterprise architecture boot camp & best practices: A workshop*. Salt Lake City, UT: Meta Group.

Egan, G. (Ed.). (1988). *Change-agent skills A: Assessing and designing excellence*. San Diego, CA: San Diego University Associates.

Farooqi, K., Loggripo, L. , & Loggripo, J. (1995). The ISO reference model for open distributed processing: An Introduction. *Computer Networks and ISDN Networks, 27*(8), 1215-1229.

FEAPMO. (2003). *Business reference model version 2.0*. Retrieved December, 15 2005, from http://www.cio.gov/documents/secure/BRM_v2_Comment_Response.pdf

Forrester, J. (Ed.). (1961). *Industrial dynamics*. Waltham, MA: Pegasus Communications.

Frankel, D., Harmon, P., & Mukerji, J. (August, 2003). The Zachman framework and the OMG's model driven architecture. *Business Process Trends*.

Gilchrist , A., & Mahon, B. (2003*). Information architecture: Designing information environments for purpose*. London: Facet Publishing.

Goedvolk, J., Bruin, H., & Rijsenbrij, D. (August, 1999). Integrated architectural design of business and information systems. In *Proceedings of the Second Nordic Workshop on Software Architecture (NOSA 1999)*, Sweden.

Hammer, M., & Champy, J. (Ed.) (2001). *Reengineering the corporation: A manifesto for business revolution*. London: Nicholas Brealey Publishing.

Hampton, D. (Ed.). (1986). *Management*. Singapore: McGraw-Hill.

Herbert, A. (1994). An overview of ANSA. *IEEE Network, 8*(1), 18-23.

ICAM. (1981). *Architecture part II-volume IV — Function modeling manual (IDEF0)*. Wright-Patterson Air Force Base, OH: Government Printing Office for Air Force Materials Laboratory.

IEEE. (2000). *IEEE recommended practice for architectural description of software-intensive systems*. IEEE Architecture Working Group, Std 1471-2000.

Inmon, W. (Ed.). (1999). *Data architecture — the information paradigm*. Wellesley, MA.: QED Technical Publishing Group.

International Enterprise Architecture Center. (2005). Retrieved December, 15 2005, from http://www.ieac.org/about/index.htm

ISO. (January, 1995). *ODP reference model: Descriptive model*. ITU-T/ISO/IEC Reccomendation X.902, International Standards Organization *10746-2*.

Juran, J. M., & Godfrey, A. B. (1999). Juran's quality handbook (5th ed.). New York: McGraw-Hill.

Kaplan, R., & Norton, D. (2004). *Strategy maps: Converting intangible assets into tangible outcomes*. Boston: Harvard Business School Press.

Labovitz , G., & Rosansky, V. (Ed.). (1997). *The power of alignment: How great companies stay centered and accomplish extraordinary things*. New York: John Wiley & Sons.

Laudon, K., & Laudon, J. (Ed.) (2000). *Management information systems.* NJ: Prentice Hall.

Luftman, J. (Ed.). (1996). *Competing in the Information Age: Strategic alignment in practice.* New York: Oxford University Press, Inc.

Malhotra, Y. (1998). Business process redesign: An overview. *IEEE Engineering Management Review, 26*(3), 27-32.

Meta Group (2005). Retrieved December, 15 2005, from http://www.metagroup.com/products/insights/eas_1_sc.htm

OMG. (2004). *Unified modeling language: Superstructure* (Version 2.0). Object Management Group. Retrieved December 15, 2005, from http://www.omg.org/cgi-bin/doc?ptc/2004-10-02

Open Group. (2003). *The Open Group architectural framework (TOGAF)* (Version 8.1). The Open Group.

O'Rourke, C., Fishman, N., & Selkow. W. (Ed.). (2003). *Enterprise architecture using the Zachman framework.* Boston: Course Technology, Inc.

Papp, R. (Ed.). (2001). *Strategic information technology: Opportunities for competitive advantage.* Hershey, PA: Idea Group Publishing.

Porter, M. (Ed.). (1985). *Competitive advantage.* New York: The Free Press.

Schekkerman, J. (Ed.). (2004). *How to survive in the jungle of enterprise architecture framework: Creating or choosing an enterprise architecture framework.* Victoria, Canada: Trafford Publishing.

Schurmann, G. (1995). The evolution from open systems interconnection (OSI) to open distributed processing (ODP). *Computer Standards and Interfaces, 17,* 107-113.

Scott, R. (1997). *Organizations: Rational, natural, and open systems.* NJ: Prentice Hall.

Senge, P. (Ed.). (1990). *The fifth discipline: The art & practice of the learning organization.* New York: Currency Doubleday.

Smith, H., & Fingar P. (2003). *Business process management: The third wave.* Tampa, FL: Meghan-Kiffer Press.

Sowa, J., & Zachman, J. (Eds.) (1992). Extending and formalizing the framework for information systems architecture. *IBM Systems Journal, 31,* 590-616.

Spewak, S., & Hill, S. (Eds.) (1992). *Enterprise architecture planning: Developing a blueprint for data, applications and technology.* New York: Wiley-QED Publication.

Stoddard, D., & Jarvenpaa, S. (1995). Business process redesign: Tactics for managing radical change. *Journal of Management Information Systems, 12*(1), 81-107.

Taylor, D. (Ed.). (1995). *Business engineering with object technology.* New York: John Wiley & Sons.

W3C. (2002). *Web services: World Wide Web Consortium.* Retrieved December, 15 2005, from http://www.w3.org/2002/ws/

Zachman, J. (1987). A framework for information systems architecture. *IBM Systems Journal, 26*(3), 276-292.

Chapter V

Adaption of the UML to Formalized Software Development Process Assessment and Modeling:
Dedicated Metamodel and Case Study

Stefan Dietze, Fraunhofer Institute for Software
and Systems Engineering ISST, Germany

ABSTRACT

This chapter introduces a conceptual metamodel that enables the assessment and semiformal modeling of business processes in the domain of software engineering based on the UML metamodel. In addition to the definition of an appropriate process modeling method, a basis for performing empirical case studies and structured process assessments is provided by defining and structuring the relevant process entities (artifacts, roles, tools) and process elements, and their interdependencies on the metamodel level. Above all, some example models are presented that were developed by applying the introduced metamodel during an initial case study. The described metamodel allows the opportunity to create detailed organizational UML-based models that describe the relevant roles, workflows, artifacts, as well as the used tools and their interdependencies. Thus, it can facilitate a founded assessment, evaluation, and reengineering of organizational software development processes.

INTRODUCTION

Enterprise and business process modeling are very important activities that provide the well-founded basis for further assessment, reengineering, and support of existing processes. Besides that, well-structured and comparable qualitative process descriptions, developed with formalized and standardized modeling methods, enable the benchmarking of different process models across organizational boundaries. Also, in the specific domain of formal software engineering, business process modeling is considered to be an important discipline that provides the well-founded basis for software requirements analysis and management (Kroll & Kruchten, 2003). Since the UML is the de facto modeling standard for software and system modeling, it would be desirable to adapt the elaborate UML specification for process and business modeling as well.

This chapter introduces a UML-based metamodel that enables the analysis and formalized description of organizational and business processes in the domain of software engineering, and also facilitates their reengineering. This provides the opportunity to create detailed organizational UML-based models that describe the relevant roles, workflows, produced artifacts, as well as the used tools and their interdependencies. Therefore, the metamodel represents an innovative extension of the UML, and is a contribution to the areas of enterprise and organizational modeling with the UML.

The metamodel was developed as part of a joint research project between the Fraunhofer ISST (Berlin) and Potsdam University, aimed at the identification, semiformal description, and adaptation of typical open source software development (OSSD) processes and organizational mechanisms (Dietze, 2004). During the project, it was used successfully to empirically analyze software development processes based on comparative case studies, and to develop a generalized model of OSSD in a formalized representation.

The following will provide an overview of the metamodel, which itself was specified by using class diagrams of the UML. The used and referenced modeling elements are completely based on the UML metamodel (Object Management Group, 2002).

The metamodel is divided into two central parts. The first part describes and structures the software development process on the metamodel level, and is explained in section three after an introduction to background and motivation. The second part defines UML-based viewpoints and model elements that enable the formalized description of the software development process. These are explained in section four. The fifth section of this chapter subsequently introduces a first application of the metamodel to real-life software development processes. The last section of this chapter gives a summarizing conclusion.

BACKGROUND

This section provides a brief overview of basic modeling concepts, issues, and needs in the area process modeling, as well as metamodeling concepts in the software engineering domain.

Figure 1. Typical modeling cycle

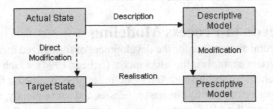

Modeling Cycle and Metamodeling

According to Ludewig (2002), models can be classified as descriptive or prescriptive models. A descriptive model is aimed at describing the actual state of a specific subject matter, whereas a prescriptive model is aimed at describing an intended state of a specific subject matter. Thus, a descriptive model can serve as a well-founded basis for modification into an improved prescriptive model. Figure 1 presents this typical model life cycle.

The main reason for process modeling, and modeling in general, is to provide abstract and understandable views of real-world aspects. Therefore, a model can be created on different levels of abstraction in order to gradually refine the model. The Table 1 describes the different abstraction levels based on the four-level metamodeling architecture of the UML (Object Management Group, 2002):

The four abstraction levels described in Table 1 define the terminology that is used in this chapter, and differ only slightly from the UML metamodel. The primary purpose of such a gradual, model-development architecture is to ensure that the produced models are formalized at every stage, as much as possible. This supports a high level of readability and sustainability.

The lowest level represents the instance of a model and is, therefore, the most specific of all levels. The model level that is one level higher defines the language to describe a model instance of a specific information domain. Furthermore, the metamodel level above defines the framework to specify a model, whereas a meta-metamodel represents the most abstract level and enables the definition of a metamodel. For example, the patch artifact represents

Table 1. Overview metamodeling architecture

Layer	Description	Example
meta-metamodel	The infrastructure for a metamodeling architecture. Defines the language for specifying metamodels.	Class, Attribute, Operation
metamodel	An instance of a meta-metamodel. Defines the language for specifying a model.	Role, Tool, Artifact
model	An instance of a metamodel. Defines a language to describe an information domain.	Developer, Bug Tracking System, Patch
instance	An instance of a model. Defines a specific information domain.	Developer A, Bugzilla, Patch #2386

an instantiation of an artifact, whereas a specific patch with a specific patch number (e. g. # 2386) represents an instantiation of the patch artifact.

Issues and Needs in Process Modeling

There exist several approaches for the development of formalized models of business processes. One important example is the ARIS model (Scheer, 1994), which describes a very complex and comprehensive architecture and modeling approach aimed at the development of exhaustive descriptions of existing business processes and consequently, their assessment and reengineering. Since the ARIS approach is not domain specific and originally was intended to enable the exhaustive modeling of business processes in many different domains, it is a very elaborate framework, and intricate to apply.

Especially in the domain of software engineering, the ARIS approach is not established very widely because the UML can be perceived as an informal standard for software modeling. As the UML metamodel (Object Management Group, 2002) provides an extensive set of modeling facilities, it is also used in many ways for the modeling of business processes. Since the original intension of the UML is to support the design and specification of software systems within model-based software development approaches, it is not very well suited to process modeling in general. The UML metamodel is a very complex specification that is time-consuming to comprehend and tedious to apply for process modeling. Furthermore, the UML specification describes several formal modeling approaches that are only necessary for software specification and not for process modeling, for example, component diagrams, sequence diagrams, and deployment diagrams. Moreover, it is important to notice that even though the UML metamodel provides a very useful and comprehensive set of modeling elements, it does not provide sufficient methodical information about how these should be deployed. Thus, the UML specification contains no information on the way a consistent and exhaustive design model could be created from scratch. Nevertheless, the UML describes a well-founded and widely established modeling approach that can build an appropriate basis for process modeling in general. To take these aspects into consideration, the adapted metamodel described in this chapter introduces an approach for process modeling in the domain of software engineering and the underlying metamodel that is based on the UML metamodel. The proposed metamodel therefore reduces the complexity of the UML by defining some specific viewpoints appropriate for process modeling. Furthermore, methodical aspects were incorporated in the metamodel by defining an abstract conceptual metamodel of software development, and assigning its process elements and entities to specific viewpoints and model elements of the modeling approach.

Metamodeling in the Software Engineering Domain

In order to develop well-structured descriptive models, it is necessary to utilize a metamodel that defines and structures the assessment process as well as the process modeling approach. In the domain of software engineering, some approaches already exist that follow similar purposes and describe aspects related to the metamodel in this chapter.

In this context, the traditional software development process metamodels aimed at assuring process and product quality such as the capability maturity model (CMM), the capability maturity model integrated (CMMI) or the SPICE (software process improvement and capability determination) have to be mentioned. SPICE (Software Quality Institute, 2005) as well as CMM (Raynus, 1998) are international standards for software process improvement. Both are primarily aimed at process assessment, enable the association of maturity levels to a software development process, and provide guidance in improving software development processes. These models also include an informal process categorization of software development processes on the metamodel level, but both SPICE and CMM do not provide a metamodel or modeling method that supports the formal description of the assessed processes.

Another very important approach to software development process metamodeling is the software process engineering metamodel (SPEM) (Object Management Group, 2003) that was released by the Object Management Group (OMG) in November 2002. The SPEM defines a UML-based metamodel for describing software development processes. Since SPEM is very complex and generic, it exhibits disadvantages in its usability in real-world software development process analysis. Furthermore, SPEM does not provide a categorization of software development process elements and entities similar to the categorization that is an integral part of the metamodel described in the following sections.

CONCEPTUAL SOFTWARE DEVELOPMENT PROCESS METAMODEL

This section describes the first part of the original metamodel introduced in this chapter. It describes the software development process on the metamodel level in order to enable a structured realization of software development process assessments and comparative case studies. The definition of a common metamodel for software process assessment and empirical case studies enables a well backed-up and structured process analysis, and ensures the comparability of different assessment results (Scacchi, 2001; Scacchi, 2002).

Figure 2. Process decomposition and process specialization

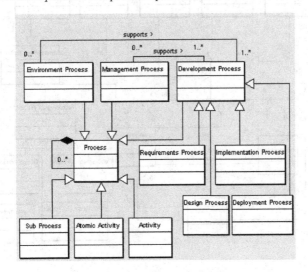

Process Decomposition

To enable a detailed analysis of all processes on different levels of abstraction, a process is perceived as a composition of subprocesses, activities, and atomic activities. In the complete metamodel specification (Dietze, 2004), each of these process elements was defined in detail to enable a precise demarcation between them. The decomposition of a process is displayed in the following figure:

Figure 2 represents the process decomposition as well as a process specialization based on Scacchi (2002). Specialized process categories are visualized as metaclasses that enable the categorization of a process as an environmental process, a management process, or as a development process. The development processes are the primary processes of every software development project, whereas the environmental and the management processes support these processes, and are aimed at process coordination and providing an appropriate environment for successful software development.

Metamodel of Entities

The metamodel of entities defines and categorizes all aspects that should be considered when analyzing individual software development processes. Figure 3 specifies the process entities and their dependencies that should be identified and analyzed during a detailed assessment.

Figure 3 displays the core aspects as metaclasses and some specialized classes that represent certain categories. Specialized metaclasses were defined at this level of abstraction in the process description to enable a structured analysis and categorization of the diverse aspects of software development processes. The central entities within this metamodel and software development processes, in general, are:

Figure 3. Overview metamodel of entities

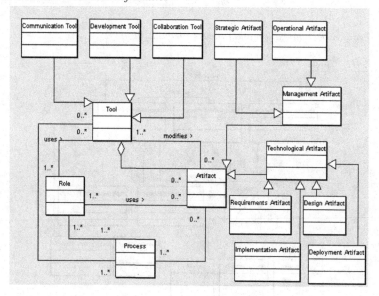

- Role
- Tool
- Artifact
- Process

According to Acuna and Ferré (2001), a role describes a set of responsibilities, rights, and skills required to perform a specific software process activity. Thus, a role can be represented by an individual person or a group of people.

In addition, an artifact represents an information object that can be created, modified, and used by a specific process (Kroll & Kruchten, 2003). In order to enable a further categorization of identified artifacts, several specialized artifact categories were defined. The primary artifacts within a software development process are the technological artifacts. These artifacts are produced within a software development project, and thus are the direct input and output objects of specific development activities. A further categorization was defined by associating artifacts to specific software engineering disciplines and creating appropriate subcategories: requirements artifact, design artifact, implementation artifact, test artifact. In contrast to technological artifacts, artifacts of the category management artifact are aimed at supporting the primary software development activities by enabling process planning, controlling, and managing the project and its progress. Regarding the scope and planning horizon of a specific management artifact, it can be characterized as strategic or operational.

In addition to these classifications, the entity tool refers to software tools that are involved in specific activities within a software developed project. Thus, a tool is aimed at using and modifying artifacts and is deployed by a specific role. According to Scacchi (2002), the software engineering support tools were divided into three specific categories regarding their intended primary purpose: collaboration tool (e.g., bug tracking system), communication tool (e.g., newsgroup), and development tool (e.g., editor or diff).

VIEWPOINTS AND MODEL ELEMENTS

The metamodel not only defines entities and processes that are necessary for consideration in the assessment of software development processes or business processes in general, but also describes an approach for documenting these analyzed aspects. Therefore, several UML-based viewpoints were defined that enable the exhaustive description of a software development process in all of its facets with formalized model elements. These viewpoints represent the framework for the process modeling approach and are introduced in this section.

Categorization of Viewpoints

The metamodel selects and adapts some viewpoints of the UML specification and defines some new ones in order to create an appropriate process modeling method based on the UML metamodel.

Each of the viewpoints is focused on a specific aspect of the software development process such as static relationships of entities, process structures, or workflow chronology. Every individual viewpoint is aimed at the representation of one or more specific entities and process elements, and specifies the necessary model elements to describe these aspects.

Figure 4. Viewpoints and their categorization

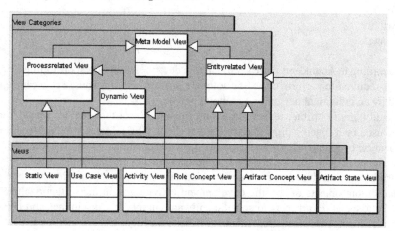

These viewpoints differentiate between process-related viewpoints and entity-related viewpoints. A process-related view is used to model a certain aspect of a specific process, subprocess, or activity, whereas an entity-related view should be used to model a certain aspect of a specific entity or a group of entities across several processes.

The process-related views include the static view, which adapts the static view of the UML metamodel and enables the description of relationships between certain process entities within a specific process. The use case view and the activity view extend this static view by considering the dynamic aspects of a process. The use case view is aimed at identifying and structuring the relevant processes and the involved roles, whereas the activity view is used to describe the necessary activities and their pre- and postconditions in detail.

The role concept view and the artifact concept view are entity-related views aimed at providing a general overview of the role and the artifact model of a software development project. The artifact state view is also an entity-related view, but enables the description of states of a specific artifact and their dependencies over the entire artifact life cycle.

Process-Related Viewpoints and Associated UML Diagram Types

Figure 5 presents the correlation of process-related viewpoints to certain diagram types of the UML metamodel (Object Management Group, 2002) and to specific process elements.

Whereas the process elements were presented at the lowest level in Figure 5, a package containing the process-related viewpoints is located there. Furthermore, the related diagram types of the UML specification are shown at the top of the figure. The figure illustrates that certain process elements could be presented by instantiating one or more views, but could also be part of another viewpoint. For example, a process could be described in a static and a use case view, but could also be part of another use case view as a specific use case. Consistently, a subprocess could also be part of a use case view as a specific use case and

Figure 5. Correlation between process-related viewpoints, UML diagram types, and process elements

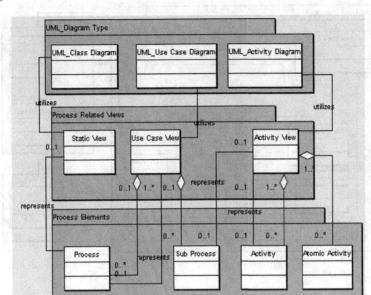

besides that, could be described in a specific activity view in order to specify the chronological sequence of activities. In addition, an activity itself can be presented in an activity view, which in turn can contain activities and atomic activities.

Example Viewpoint: Use Case View

For each individual viewpoint, a UML model type and appropriate model elements were selected from the UML metamodel. These should be used when creating models in this specific viewpoint to describe the entity from this perspective. The following figure shows exemplarily the use case view, in order to provide an example of a viewpoint metamodel.

Figure 6 shows the relationships between UML model elements, process elements, and process entities within this specific view. This metamodel serves as the foundation for developing a formalized, use case view of a specific process.

The use case view is dedicated to identifying and describing the key roles and processes, and also to enable the structuring of a process into subprocesses. Thus, several use case views are typically developed as part of an entire descriptive model. A use case diagram can contain several use cases, whereas each represents a specific subprocess or process according to this metamodel. Furthermore, a specific actor represents a responsible role or an involved role. In order to describe relationships between a role and a use case, or between several use cases, some appropriate model elements of the UML specification (Object Management Group, 2002) were selected. These relationships can be used to describe responsibilities

Figure 6. Metamodel of the use case view

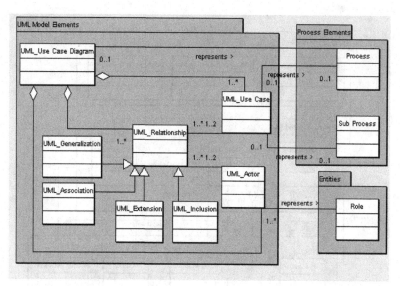

of specific roles or dependencies between several subprocesses. In order to illustrate the deployment of this view and furthermore, the entire metamodel, the next section will show some example models that were created based on this specification.

CASE STUDY

This section outlines the background and results of a comparative case study of open source software development processes where the described metamodel was deployed in order to analyze and describe a specific process model.

Application Context: Open Source Software Development

Open source software (OSS) has reached a remarkably high popularity in many different application domains throughout the last years. The success of famous OSS products, such as the Linux Kernel or the Apache HTTPD Web Server, has lead to the hypothesis that the underlying OSS development model, which obviously has the ability to produce successful software products, should be considered as a reliable and viable approach in the areas of software engineering (SE) and of cooperative work in general.

Despite the growing popularity of OSS, this new paradigm of software development has not yet been researched much, in contrast to proprietary SE processes. Therefore, these practices were analyzed in detail in order to determine whether the advantages of these methods can contribute to nonsoftware-related industries as well.

An appropriate explanation of the open source term is provided by the Open Source Initiative (OSI), which has developed the open source definition (OSD). This definition contains a set of criteria that have to be considered in the software license models used for OSS in accordance with the OSD (Open Source Initiative, 2002):

- Free distribution and redistribution
- Publicly available source code
- Possibility of source code modification and redistribution
- No discrimination of certain users/groups or employment domains

All license models that follow the criteria defined in the OSD can be considered to be compatible to the understanding of OSS as defined by the OSI. In addition, the OSI provides a list of all certified software licenses (Open Source Initiative, 2003). These characteristics have significantly determined the evolution of the entire OSS development model, and especially the requirements definition processes.

Although many existing OSS projects have successfully developed individual practices and specific processes, it is possible to define some common characteristics that can be identified in most OSS development projects (Cubranic, 2002; Fogel & Bar, 2002; Gacek, Lawrie, & Arief, 2002; Scacchi, 2001; Vixie, 1999).

- Collaborative development
- Globally distributed actors
- Voluntariness of participation
- High diversity of capabilities and qualifications of all actors
- Interaction exclusively through Web-based technologies
- Individual development activities executed in parallel
- Dynamic publication of new software releases
- No central management authority
- Truly independent, community-based peer review
- "Bug-driven" development

According to Raymond (2001), these characteristics lead to the metaphor of a "bazaar" that represents the characteristics of the OSS development practices in contrast to a "cathedral" representing the centralized and strictly controlled traditional software development.

The OSS development processes are often characterized as "bug-driven." This results from the typical practice of every software modification being based on a specific bug report or, more generally, on a change request that represents the central requirements artifact within the OSSD approach. This characteristic also clarifies the importance of the requirements definition processes within OSSD projects.

Research Approach

The metamodel was used as the formal foundation for a research project aimed at the identification and formalized specification of a descriptive process model for open source software development (OSSD) processes (Dietze, 2004, 2005). These activities were based on case studies that were performed by participating in several projects, analyzing the projects' information sources, and carrying out interviews and a literature review.

The following OSSD projects were empirically assessed:

- Apache HTTPD[1]
- Linux Kernel[2]
- Mozilla project[3].

The research was focused on the processes, roles, artifacts, and the deployed software infrastructure that is used to support the whole development approach, and especially requirements engineering practices. The identification and formal presentation of a descriptive process model enabled the further improvement of the identified processes and its software infrastructure, as well as providing the opportunity to consider the integration of these practices into traditional software development approaches.

The following sections contain some results of the case study, and should provide an idea of how instantiated models of the described metamodel can look and which aspects

Figure 7. Identified roles and responsibilities

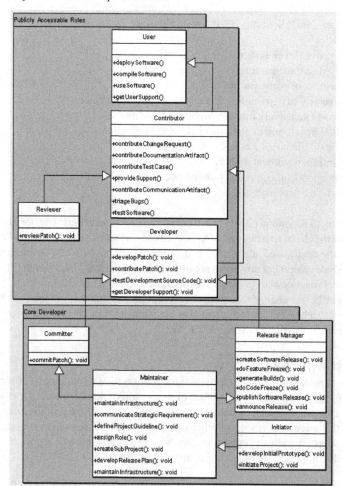

can be captured. This should present an idea about the applicability, potential, and open issues of the metamodel.

Results: Entity-Related Views

This section introduces the entity-related views of the metamodel that were created to provide information about a specific entity or a group of entities.

Figure 7 presents the key roles in OSSD as an instantiation of the role concept view of the metamodel. Figure 7 provides an overview of all the identified roles and their typical responsibilities, and is an example of an entity-related viewpoint in the metamodel. All collaborative development activities are performed by distributed actors who were aggregated to the following roles:

- User
- Contributor
- Developer
- Reviewer
- Committer

Figure 8. Artifact state view of a change request

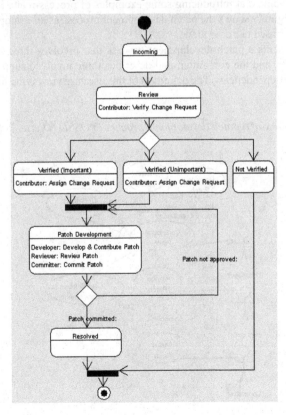

These roles are not usually defined explicitly, but describe a certain set of actors who fulfill a defined set of functions and tasks. A common set of characteristics can also be defined, for example, user privileges that all actors fulfilling a certain role are associated with. An actor is usually associated with more than one role. For example, the development of source code as a developer implies the use of the OSS as a passive user, and the submission of patches makes a developer also become a contributor.

Another important entity-related viewpoint in the metamodel is the artifact state view that enables the visualization of the life cycle of a specific artifact. Figure 8 is a state view that describes the typical life cycle of a change request that has to be perceived as an important artifact in OSSD.

The artifact state view captures typical states of an artifact and their dependencies. A change request, for example, is described with metadata through a bug or request tracking system (e.g., bugzilla), and its state is typically defined explicitly with a dedicated attribute (*state*). Every actor performing an activity that is related to a particular change request can make this information available to the whole community by setting the *Status* attribute of the change request to a certain value that describes what he is going to do. Thus, this life cycle provides a very important functionality for the documentation and coordination of subsequent processes.

Results: Process-Related Views

This section is aimed at introducing some examples of process-related views of the OSSD processes. Figure 9 shows the patch development process as an example process in the described UML-based use case view:

Figure 9 represents a patch development process that involves three roles: the developer, the reviewer, and the committer, and describes three involved subprocesses (use cases) and their interdependencies. The definition of this use case view is the first step in the

Figure 9. Use case view of a patch development process in OSSD (Dietze, 2004)

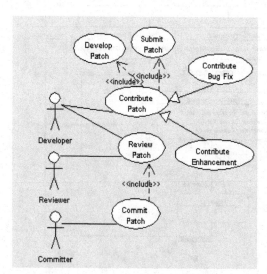

Figure 10. Activity view of a patch development process OSSD (Dietze, 2004)

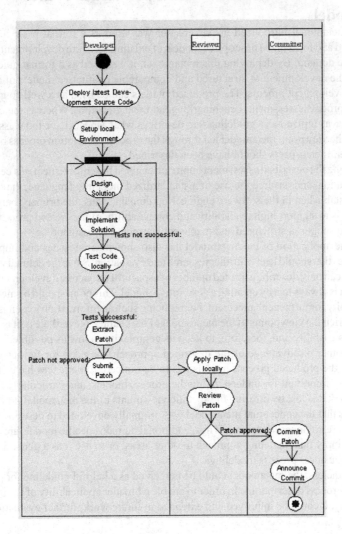

description of a specific process, and has to be enriched with more information by detailing each subprocess in more views, such as the activity or static view. Figure 10 describes this process in the activity view of the metamodel.

In this viewpoint, all activities are presented as action states of the UML metamodel, and the responsible role is visualized with swimlanes that assign the activities to a specific role.

The subprocess "Contribute patch" is performed by the role "Developer," and includes the subprocesses aimed at developing and submitting the patch. A group of reviewers is responsible for reviewing the patch. If the review was successful and the patch was approved, the committers commit the patch into the central source code repository.

Lessons Learned: Benefits and Open Issues of the Metamodel

The metamodel introduced in this chapter was used as a formal basis for creating standardized and formalized descriptive models of existing software development processes in a specific domain. By deploying this metamodel, it was used as a formal guideline that supported the development of structured and comparable qualitative models of a concrete software development process. The produced models can be used as a well-founded basis for further process assessment, benchmarking, and reengineering. Whereas the conceptual metamodel was utilized as a guideline that describes what aspects have to be assessed and described, the viewpoint metamodel led through the process description process by defining how the identified aspects should have been described.

Utilizing the described assessment approach enabled the enforcement of a certain level of formalization, and ensured the use of a standardized modeling language, the UML, that is widely established in the software engineering domain. Thus, the primary benefit of the metamodel is to support high readability and comparability of the created process descriptions, and to support a structured and manageable process assessment.

But the application of the metamodel has also shown some issues and improvement opportunities that should lead to further research and evaluation. Since the defined viewpoints and models can only describe a limited number of aspects of a concrete development process, information is always lost by creating a descriptive model. This point should be mentioned as an opportunity for further enhancement. For reducing such an information loss, it is probably useful to enrich the viewpoints of the metamodel of the chapter. Nevertheless, it is important to ensure its usability and, therefore, to keep its complexity as low as possible.

As another disadvantage of the described approach, the need for further verbal description of the produced process models has to be noticed. Experiences have shown this as being very important for understanding the process models, and particularly for adding information that is lost by creating the specific viewpoints of the metamodel. Furthermore, it is obvious that the conceptual metamodel was originally developed to describe processes in the software engineering domain. Thus, additional domain specific models are necessary in order to apply this modeling approach to other areas, or to use it as a general modeling method for business process modeling.

Nevertheless, the metamodel could be perceived as a helpful guideline for producing formalized process descriptions. In order to enable a broader applicability of the introduced methodology, it could be improved and extended in future work; further evaluation is necessary.

CONCLUSION

This chapter has shown a modeling method that enables semiformal modeling of business processes, and especially software development processes based on the UML metamodel, and that has been verified during comparative case studies of real-world software projects. Besides the definition of an appropriate process modeling method based on the UML metamodel, a well-founded basis for performing empirical case studies and structured process assessments was provided. This has been achieved by defining and structuring the relevant process entities (artifacts, roles, tools), process elements (subprocesses, activities), and their interdependencies on the metamodel level. Above all, some example models were shown that were developed in a research project by applying the presented metamodel for empirical software development process research.

As was demonstrated, this metamodel represents an innovative contribution to the area of enterprise and organizational modeling with the UML in the domain of software engineering, and could lead to further research on this topic. Although the metamodel was primarily dedicated to process modeling in this specific domain, it could be adapted to other fields of application in future work. In addition, it would be an important next step to implement the metamodel as a specific UML profile, and to develop an appropriate software support to facilitate the entire process modeling method. This could lead to widespread future use of the presented approach.

REFERENCES

Acuna, S., & Ferré, X. (2001). Software process modelling. In *Proceedings of the 1ª Jornadas Iberoamericanas de Ingeniería del Software e Ingeniería del Conocimiento*, Buenos Aires, Argentina. Retrieved June 23, 2002, from http://www.unse.edu.ar/congres/jornadas/silvac/documentos/congres1.pdf

Cubranic, D. (2002). *Open source software development*. Retrieved March 26, 2002, from http://sern.ucalgary.ca/~maurer/ICSE99WS/Submissions/Cubranic/Cubranic.html

Dietze, S. (2004). *Model und Optimierungsansatz für Open Source Softwareentwicklungsprozesse*. Doctoral dissertation, Institute of Computer Science, Potsdam University.

Dietze, S. (2005). Collaborative requirements definition processes in open source software development. In J. L. Maté & A. Silva (Eds.), *Requirements engineering for sociotechnical systems* (pp. 189-208). Hershey, PA: Information Science Publishing.

Fogel, K., & Bar, M. (2002). *Open Source-Projekte mit CVS*. MITP.

Gacek, C., Lawrie, T., & Arief, B. (2002). *The many meanings of open source*. Retrieved May 28, 2002, from http://citeseer.nj.nec.com/485228.html

Kroll, P., & Kruchten, P. (2003). *The rational unified process made easy*. Addison Wesley.

Ludewig, J. (2002, March 25-27). Modele im Software Engineering — eine Einführung und Kritik. In *Proceedings of the Modelierung 2002*, Germany (LNI P-12 of the Gesellschaft für Informatik).

Mockus, A., Fielding, R., & Herbsleb, J. (2000). A case study of open source software development: The Apache server. In *Proceedings of the 22nd International Conference on Software Engineering*. IEEE Computer Society.

Object Management Group. (2002). *Unified modeling language specification* (Version 1.4). Retrieved October 30, 2002, from http://www.omg.org/cgi-bin/doc?formal/01-09-67

Object Management Group. (2003). *Software process engineering metamodel specification* (Version 1.0). Retrieved October 07, 2003, from http://www.omg.org/cgi-bin/apps/doc?formal/02-11-14.pdf

Open Source Initiative. (2002). *Open source definition*. Retrieved December 12, 2003, from http://opensource.org/docs/definition.php

Open Source Initiative. (2003). *OSI certified software licenses*. Retrieved January 15, 2003, from http://opensource.org/licenses/index.php

Raymond, E. S. (2001). *The cathedral and the bazaar*. O'Reilly.

Raynus, J. (1998). *Software process improvement with CMM.* Artech House Computer Science Library, Artech House Publishers.

Reis, C. R., & Pontin de Mattos Fortes, R. (2002). *An overview of the software engineering process and tools in the Mozilla Project.* Retrieved May 17, 2002, from http://www.async.com.br/~kiko/papers/mozse.pdf

Scacchi, W. (2001). *Software development practices in open software development communities: A comparative case study.* Position Paper for the 1st Workshop on Open Source Software Engineering. May 15, 2001 as part of the 23rd International Conference on Software Engineering (ICSE 2001).

Scacchi, W. (2002). *Comparative case analysis for understanding software processes.* Retrieved March 26, 2002, http://www.usc.edu/dept/ATRIUM/Papers/New/CCA-Draft.html

Scheer, A. W. (1994). *Business process engineering* (2nd rev. ed.). Springer-Verlag Telos.

Software Quality Institute. (2005). *Software process improvement and capability determination (SPICE) project Web site.* Australia: Griffith University. Retrieved from http://www.sqi.gu.edu.au/spice/

Vixie, P. (1999). Software engineering. In C. Dibona, S. Ockman, & M. Stone (Eds.), *Open sources — voices from the open source revolution.* O'Reilly & Associates.

ENDNOTES

[1]   http://httpd.apache.org/
[2]   http://www.kernel.org
[3]   http://www.mozilla.org

Chapter VI

Enterprise Modeling with ODP and UML

Sandy Tyndale-Biscoe, Open-IT Limited, UK

Antonio Vallecillo, University of Málaga, Spain

Bryan Wood, Open-IT Limited, UK

ABSTRACT

RM-ODP is a standard defining a framework for the specification of large distributed systems that is based on solid foundations, and that defines five generic and complementary viewpoints for structuring the system specifications in order to deal with their inherent complexity. One of these viewpoints, the enterprise viewpoint, focuses on the purpose, scope, and policies for the system and its environment. This viewpoint is independent from any computational and platform-specific concerns, and provides a well-defined approach to enterprise modeling. However, the fact that RM-ODP does not define any notation for describing its viewpoint languages has traditionally hampered its wide adoption by many industrial sectors. On the other hand, UML is a widely accepted notation for system specification but lacks formal semantics, and has limited structuring mechanisms for dealing with large and complex system specifications. In this chapter, we describe how ODP and UML can be combined for enterprise modeling, showing how enterprise viewpoint specifications can be written in UML to obtain the major benefits of both approaches. The work described here is part of an ISO/IEC and ITU-T initiative to define the use of UML for ODP system specifications.

INTRODUCTION

One of the common ways of dealing with the inherent complexity of specifying distributed systems is by dividing the design activity into a number of areas of concern, each one dealing with a specific aspect of the system. Current software architectural practices define several distinct viewpoints of systems, as described in IEEE Std. 1471 (2000), in order to accomplish such decomposition of a specification. Examples include the "4+1" view model (Kruchten, 1995), the Zachman framework (Sowa & Zachman, 1992; Zachman, 1987), and the reference model of open distributed processing (RM-ODP) (ISO/IEC 10746-1, 1998).

In particular, we are interested in the RM-ODP. The RM-ODP defines a framework for system specification based on five generic and complementary viewpoints on the system and its environment: enterprise, information, computational, engineering, and technology. Specifications of a system from these viewpoints provide abstractions that allow stakeholders to observe a system from different suitable perspectives (Linington, 1995). The viewpoints have been chosen as a necessary and sufficient set to meet the needs of ODP standards and of system specification. A language is defined for each viewpoint comprising concepts, rules, and structures for the specification of a system from that viewpoint.

Within the set of ODP viewpoint specifications, the enterprise specification focuses on the purpose, scope, and policies for the system and its environment. Its objective is to describe the structure and operation of the enterprise of which the system is a part in order to define the enterprise requirements on the system, and the system behaviour to meet these requirements, abstracted from other system considerations such as particular details of its implementation or of the technology used. The enterprise language (ISO/IEC 15414, 2002) comprises concepts, rules, and structures for the specification of a system from the enterprise viewpoint. Thus, it allows the representation of enterprise issues and provides an excellent basis for establishing technology- and tool-independent communication mechanisms between enterprise and IT stakeholders.

However, the viewpoint languages are abstract, in the sense that they define what concepts should be supported, but not how they should be represented. Although an advantage in theory, this really hinders the development of commercial tools for writing and analysing ODP system specifications.

So far, most of the notations proposed for the different viewpoints are based on formal description techniques such as Z, LOTOS, or SDL. They allow precise specifications of systems, and even some tool support for analysing and formally reasoning about the specifications produced. The main drawback of these approaches is that the formality and intrinsic difficulty of most formal description techniques have hampered their acceptance and wide use in industrial environments, and have encouraged the quest for more user-friendly notations. In this respect, the general purpose modeling notation UML (unified modeling language) is clearly the most promising candidate.

The wide adoption of UML by industry, the number of available UML tools, and the increasing interest in model-driven development and, in particular, in the MDA® initiative, motivated ISO/IEC and ITU-T to launch a joint project in 2004 that aims to define an approach for using UML for representing ODP system specifications, This standard, hereinafter known as UML for ODP (ISO/IEC 19793, 2005), or just simply as ISO/IEC 19793, targets three major audiences: first, ODP modellers, who could use the UML notation for expressing their ODP specifications in a standard graphical way; second, UML modellers, who could use the RM-ODP concepts and mechanisms to structure their UML system specifications; finally, modeling tool suppliers, who could be able to develop UML-based tools capable of expressing RM-ODP viewpoint specifications.

This chapter discusses the approach taken in ISO/IEC 19793 for using UML for representing ODP enterprise specifications. In particular, the chapter shows how the use of UML for ODP enterprise modeling addresses the current limitations of UML for dealing with many business concepts and issues. Modeling such concepts and issues is increasingly important for any organization, but UML itself provides little or no direct support for doing this.

The structure of the chapter is as follows. The first section is a brief description of the ODP enterprise language. Then follows an introduction of the example that is used to illustrate the approach that provides some text-based fragments of the enterprise specification for that example system. The following section explains how the RM-ODP enterprise language concepts are mapped to UML 2.0 in the form of a profile, and illustrates the use of this profile by some examples. We then discuss the benefits of the approach and some issues that relate to its use. Finally, we relate our work to other similar proposals and offer a set of conclusions.

THE ODP ENTERPRISE LANGUAGE

Description of the Concepts

An enterprise specification of an ODP system is a description of that system, and of the environment in which it exists, that focuses on the scope and objective of the system and the policies that apply to it in the context of its environment. The scope of the system is the behaviour that can be assumed by the people and things that interact with it, and the specification explicitly includes those aspects of the environment that influence this behaviour; environmental constraints are captured as well as usage and management rules.

In an enterprise specification, *enterprise objects* model *entities*, where an entity is any concrete or abstract thing of interest in the universe of discourse (which is the system and relevant parts of its environment). An enterprise object is characterized by its *behaviour*, which is a collection of *actions* (*internal actions* and *interactions* with other *enterprise objects*) associated with the enterprise object, with a set of constraints on when they may occur.

The fundamental structuring concept of an enterprise specification is that of a *community*. A community is a configuration of enterprise objects that models a set of entities (e.g. human beings, information processing systems, resources of various kinds, and collections of these) that has been formed for a particular *objective*, and where the entities are subject to some implicit or explicit agreement governing their collective behaviour.

The behaviour of a community is a collective behaviour consisting of actions in which the enterprise objects of the community participate, together with a set of constraints on when these actions may occur. The assignment of actions to the enterprise objects is defined in terms of *roles*, where roles specify decomposition of the behaviour of the community into separate parts that can each be performed by an enterprise object in the community. Each action of the community is either part of a single role behaviour or is an interaction that is part of more than one role behaviour.

The actions identified by roles, and the ordering of those actions, can be represented in terms of *processes*, where a process is an abstraction of the community behaviour that includes only those actions that are related to achieving some particular subobjective of the community.

An enterprise specification can include *policies* that specify behaviour, or constraints on behaviour that can be changed during the lifetime of the ODP system, or that can be changed to tailor a single specification to apply to a range of different ODP systems.

An enterprise specification may also identify *parties* that model natural persons or any other entities considered to have some of the rights, powers, and duties of a natural person, actions that involve *accountability* of such parties, and delegation of authority for such actions.

The *scope* of the ODP system is its intended behaviour, expressed in terms of roles that it fulfils, processes involving those roles, policies, and their relationships.

In the universe of discourse, at some level of abstraction, a collection of entities may itself be viewed as an entity (e.g., a business is treated as a legal entity for some purposes) and be part of a collection of such entities. Where it is necessary to model this situation in an enterprise specification, the community that models such a collection of entities is also, at some level of abstraction, viewed as a composite (enterprise) object (a *community object*), and may be part of a community of enterprise objects, including other community objects.

Summary of Enterprise Language Concepts

Figures 1 to 4 provide a summary of the concepts that have been discussed and the relationships between them. It should be noted that these four diagrams do not represent individual metamodels, but are illustrations based on the integrated set of concepts that are defined in the enterprise language standard (ISO/IEC 15414, 2002), with our representations of the concepts presented there.

Figure 1. Enterprise concepts

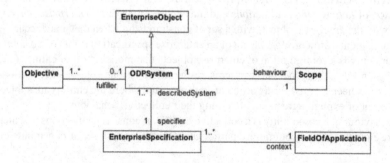

Figure 2. Community concepts

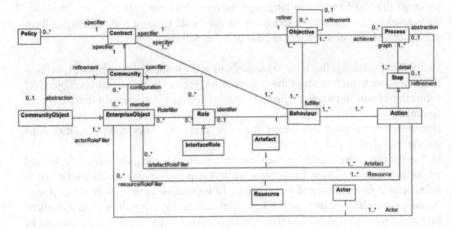

Figure 3. Policy concepts

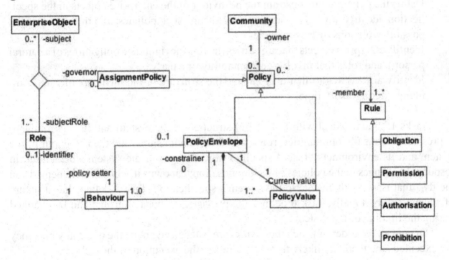

Figure 4. Accountability concepts

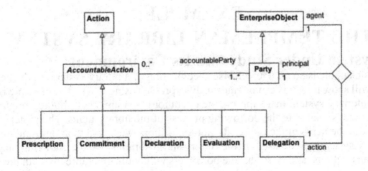

Producing an Enterprise Specification

Although the ODP enterprise language standard does not prescribe any particular method for developing an enterprise specification, practical experience has shown that there are a number of tasks involved that may be ordered as follows:

1.   Define the set of things that have to happen within the scope of the enterprise specification and relate them to a set of the communities, each with an appropriate objective; define the relationships among the communities and the behaviour required from each community.

2.   Define the roles in each community, the associated behaviours, and the relationships among the roles.

3.   Define the enterprise objects in each community and for each, the roles it fulfils and its participation in actions as an actor (it performs the action), as an artefact (it is referenced in the action), and as a resource (it is essential to the action in that it may become unavailable or used up). A key point here is that this will include identification of the roles played by the ODP system or systems, and these may be thought of as defining the "requirement" for the system.

4.   Define the policies that constrain the behaviour of the enterprise objects in the specification, identify any behaviour that may change such policies, and the effects of the possible violations of those policies.

5.   Identify enterprise objects that are parties (having the rights and obligations of a natural person), and roles that involve accountability of a party.

6.   Identify any behaviour that may change the structure or the members of each community during its lifetime.

Tasks 1, 2, and 3 deal with the (static) structure of the system and its environment, expressed in terms of communities, roles, and their relationships, and the behaviour of the system and its environment. Task 4 specifies how changes in the system's behaviour, in response to changes in the policies of the organisation that owns it, can be implemented "on the fly," that is, without change to the system's specification. Task 5 defines the structure of accountability. Finally, Task 6 defines the provision of behaviour that can be changed during the lifetime of the system.

Of course, the order in which these tasks are listed need not be the order in which they are executed, and there are likely to be iterations in the execution of the tasks.

EXAMPLE:
THE TEMPLEMAN LIBRARY SYSTEM
The System Under Study and Its Environment

This example is an ODP enterprise specification of a library system. In the next section, we will show how this can be rigorously expressed using UML. The example is about the computerized system that supports the operations of a university library, in particular those operations related to the borrowing process of the library items. The system should keep track of the items of the university library, its borrowers, and their outstanding loans. The library system will be used by the library staff (librarian and assistants) to help them record loans, returns, and so forth. The borrowers will not interact directly with the library system. Instead of a general and abstract library, this example is based on the regulations that rule the borrowing process defined at the Templeman Library at the University of Kent at Canterbury, a library that has been previously used by different authors for illustrating some of the ODP concepts.

In the following, the *library system* (or the *system*, for short) will refer to the computerized system that supports the library operations, while the *library* will refer to the business itself, that is, the environment of the *system*.

Rules for the System

The basic rules that govern the borrowing process of the library are as follows:

1. Borrowing rights are given to all academic staff, and to postgraduate and undergraduate students of the University.
2. Library books and periodicals can be borrowed.
3. The librarian may temporarily withhold the circulation of library items, or dispose of them when they are no longer appropriate for loan.
4. For requesting a loan, the borrower must hand the books or periodicals to a library assistant.
5. There are prescribed periods of loan and limits on the number of items allowed on loan to a borrower at any one time. These rules may vary from time to time, the librarian being responsible for setting the chosen policy. Typical limits are detailed below:
   - Undergraduates may borrow 8 books. They may not borrow periodicals. Books may be borrowed for 4 weeks.
   - Postgraduates may borrow 16 books or periodicals. Periodicals may be borrowed for 1 week. Books may be borrowed for 1 month.
   - Teaching staff may borrow 24 books or periodicals. Periodicals may be borrowed for 1 week. Books may be borrowed for up to 1 year.
6. Items borrowed must be returned by the due day and time that is specified when the item is borrowed.
7. Borrowers who fail to return an item when it is due will become liable to a charge at the rates prescribed until the book or periodical is returned to the library, and may have borrowing rights suspended.
8. Borrowers returning items must hand them in to an assistant at the main loan desk. Any charges due on overdue items must be paid at this time.
9. Failure to pay charges may result in suspension by the librarian of borrowing facilities.

These rules can be the starting point for the preparation of an ODP enterprise specification. However, it is important to note that the rules above leave many details of the system unspecified, such as when or how a borrower suspension is lifted by the librarian, or the precise information that needs to be kept in the system for each user and library item. The specification process followed here will help uncover such missing details progressively, so the appropriate stakeholders of the system can determine them by making the corresponding decisions.

Fragments of the Enterprise Specification in Plain English

Following the process outlined previously in the section titled Producing an enterprise specification, we first develop an outline of the things that have to happen, and the one or more communities that are needed to make them happen. In this simple example, the things that have to happen are that borrowers of various kinds borrow and return books and periodicals under the overall control of a librarian assisted by a library assistant, who is supported by the library system.

Thus, we can initially identify a community we call *Library* that has an objective that we can formally define as follows: **"To allow the use, by authorised borrowers, of the varying collection of Library items as fairly and efficiently as possible."**

Fulfilment of this objective is achieved by the following roles: *Librarian*; *Assistant*; *Borrower*; *Library System* (the names of model elements in the enterprise specification are in *bold italic* typeface.).

Membership of the community will vary over time as the roles fulfilled by enterprise objects change, where enterprise objects may be people such as Library staff or members of the university (undergraduates, postgraduate students, and teaching staff), as well as the hardware and software that make up the library system.

The behaviour identified by the roles is expressed as actions that are performed by enterprise objects as actors, and may or may not be about enterprise objects as artefacts. Actions may be structured in two ways: in the form of the interactions that must take place between each role, or in the form of processes. Which approach is used is a matter of choice and modeling purpose, and a model may contain both approaches.

For example, we can identify a set of interactions that take place between the roles *Borrower, Assistant,* and *Library System* when a book or periodical is borrowed from the library.

Similarly, we can detail the process that takes place when a book or periodical is borrowed in terms of a sequence of steps (a form of action) performed by some enterprise object, as an actor in a role such as *Borrower*, in which something happens, and during which information may flow about one or more enterprise objects that are involved in the action as artefacts.

For example, there is a process called *Borrow item* that is triggered by an actor in the role *Borrower* performing a step identified as *request loan* that concerns an enterprise object of type *Loan*. This step triggers the following step, performed by the enterprise object fulfilling the role *Assistant*, in which the details of the *Borrower* and the item that is the subject of the *Loan* are entered into the *Library System*. The enterprise object *Library System* (fulfilling the role *Library System*) performs the next step, which is to validate the *Loan* against the known details of the enterprise object fulfilling the role *Borrower*. And so the process continues until either the loan is approved or it is disallowed.

The details of this process may change depending on the *value* of *Lending limit policy*.

From the foregoing very prolix description of a small fragment of the enterprise specification for the library system, it can be seen why a visual notation such as UML is so urgently needed. The next section illustrates the approach to this that is adopted by the UML for ODP standard (ISO/IEC 19793, 2005).

EXPRESSION IN UML

A UML Profile

The use of UML for ODP system specification is not straightforward. For instance, the underlying object models that form the basis of UML and ODP do not match completely, for example, UML is class-based, whilst ODP is object-based, and the behavioural models are different. Let us try to explain these differences.

The UML object model imposes a mindset of using a single hierarchy of subclasses of isolated objects exchanging messages, and requires properties of collections of objects (both collective state and collective behaviour) to be expressed in terms of their refinement using attributes of individual objects. In contrast, a more general object model, such as the one followed by ODP, does not require invariants and operations to be owned by a single object: rather, it uses collective state for invariants, and collective behaviour for operation and interaction specifications (Johnson & Kilov, 1999). For example, an ODP action may be associated with more than one object and thus, is not necessarily a message; an ODP contract is defined as an agreement governing part of the collective behaviour of a set of objects; enabled behaviour is defined in ODP as behaviour characterizing a set of objects; and so on. Besides, ODP specifications are object-based, which means that instances (e.g., objects, actions, or roles) are first-class elements of the models, whilst classes and types are defined over such instances. (In ODP, a class is a collection of objects, and an object type is a predicate on objects.) However, UML is class-based, and therefore classes constitute the primary elements of the UML models, and objects are mere instances of these classes. (This difference can be expressed by saying that ODP is Aristotelian while UML is Platonic: this is a subtle difference, but implies a different attitude in the way ODP and UML specifications are formulated and developed.)

Another important problem comes from the fact that the semantics of UML are sometimes very loose (for example, with concepts such as aggregation or action). This may also be an impediment to achieving the precise specification and analysis of ODP systems and the development of tools. In our case, this issue can be mitigated by the use of a concrete subset of UML, whose semantics can be precisely defined by the ODP concepts they represent, as, for example, Haim Kilov (2002) and other authors successfully do in their approaches to business modeling. Furthermore, this method allows the definition of UML profiles for representing the ODP viewpoint languages that refine the semantics of the appropriate UML concepts to match the corresponding ODP concepts (this can be done if the original semantics of the UML concepts is respected, that is, not broken, by the profile extension). We have followed this approach in our work, selecting a set of UML concepts that can be used to represent the ODP enterprise viewpoint concepts, and defining a UML profile for them.

The new facilities in UML 2.0 for defining language extensions using profiles have been of great help, and have allowed us to represent many ODP enterprise concepts in a natural way. However, the task has not been easy, mainly because there is no clear way of representing some concepts (e.g., community) and because some other ODP concepts are difficult to express using UML (e.g., policy and accountability concepts).

Space does not permit a full description (or even listing) of the complex ways instances of the RM-ODP enterprise language concepts are expressed in UML that constitute the full UML Profile. We therefore restrict ourselves to describing how those concepts introduced in the example are expressed.

In this section, a distinction is made between normal English, RM-ODP concepts, and UML concepts: RM-ODP concepts are in *italics*; UML concepts are in sans-serif typeface.

Community and Objective

A *community* is expressed with a UML component stereotyped as «EV_Community» that is included in a package stereotyped as «EV_CommunityContract» that contains the specification of the *community*, that is, its *objective*, its *behaviour*, and any *enterprise objects* that are specific to the *community* concerned. Relationships between all these UML model elements may also be included in the package specifying the community. Moreover, the package may also contain some or all of the elements expressing the *enterprise objects* that fulfil its *roles*.

Any component expressing a *community* will have exactly one association, stereotyped as «EV_ObjectiveOf» to a class stereotyped as «EV_Objective», that expresses the *objective* of the *community*, and a set of realizations, each stereotyped as «EV_CommunityBehaviour», to the UML classifier model elements expressing its *roles* and the associated *behaviour* (*interactions, actions, steps,* and *processes*).

Enterprise Object

An *enterprise object* is expressed by a class stereotyped as «EV_EnterpriseObject». Where a specific individual entity is being referenced (e.g. the *ODP system*), the class concerned is a singleton. A class stereotyped as «EV_EnterpriseObject» may have associations (stereotyped as «EV_FulfilsRole») with one or more classes stereotyped as «EV_Role» in one or more *communities,* expressing the fact that the *enterprise object* fulfils (or may fulfil) these *roles*.

Community Object

A *community object* is an *enterprise object* that is refined in the model as a *community*. It is expressed by a class stereotyped as «EV_CommunityObject», with a dependency, stereotyped as «EV_RefinesAsCommunity» to the *community* that refines it.

Behaviour

Behaviour can be expressed in the form of interactions between *roles* or, alternatively and dually, in the form of *processes* performed by a set of *roles*. The two approaches provide alternative views of the same *behaviour*, the choice of which approach to use, or whether, indeed, to use both, depends on the modeling purpose and the target audience. Interaction modeling is more precise, but is intellectually more demanding. Process modeling may be more intuitive to some subject matter experts.

Behaviour as Interactions between Roles

Where the *behaviour* is expressed in terms of *interactions* between *roles* in a *community*, a *role* is expressed by a class stereotyped as «EV_Role», in the name space of the package, stereotyped as «EV_CommunityContract», that specifies the *community* in which the *role* exists. The *behaviour* identified by the *role* is expressed by the following combination of UML model elements:

- One or more classes, each having one or more associations with the class stereotyped as «EV_Role» mapping to the role being specified. Each of these classes is stereotyped as «EV_Interaction». These associations are stereotyped as «EV_InteractionInitiator» or «EV_InteractionResponder» depending upon the part played by the corresponding role in the interaction.
- Each class stereotyped as «EV_Interaction» will also, in general, have associations (also stereotyped as shown) with other classes that are stereotyped as «EV_Role» where there is an interaction between the enterprise objects fulfilling these roles.
- An *interaction* may be defined as a composition of *interactions*. When it is not defined as a composition, it has an association with a signal stereotyped as «EV_Artefact» mapping to an *artefact role* that also has an association with an «EV_EnterpriseObject» class, identifying the information that is exchanged in the *interaction*.
- A StateMachine for which the context is the «EV_Role» that defines the constraints on the receiving and sending of information by an *enterprise object* fulfilling the *role* and any associated internal *actions* of the *enterprise object*. This StateMachine shows the sending and receiving of the signals, each stereotyped as «EV_Artefact», associated with the *interactions* of the *role,* and thus shows the logical ordering of these *interactions,* and may define the *internal actions* of the *role* in terms of the behaviours associated with the states.

Behaviour as Processes and Steps

Where the *behaviour* is modelled in terms of *processes* of a *community*, a *process* is expressed by an activity stereotyped as «EV_Process» in the name space of the package stereotyped as «EV_CommunityContract» that specifies the *community* that uses this *process* to achieve its *objective*. In this activity:

- the steps of the process are expressed by actions, stereotyped as «EV_Step»;
- the enterprise objects fulfilling roles that perform the steps (as actors) are expressed by ActivityPartitions stereotyped as «EV_Role»;
- the enterprise objects that are referenced in the steps (as artefacts) are expressed by ObjectNodes, stereotyped as «EV_Artefact».

If there is a corresponding interaction model, the ActivityStates in a partition expressing a *role* must correspond to the *internal actions* identified in (the states of) the StateMachines for the class expressing the same *role* in the interaction model.

Actor (with Respect to an Action)

The concept *actor* is a relationship between an *enterprise object* and an *action*. There is no single UML model element that expresses an instance of the RM-ODP enterprise language concept, *actor. Actors* in a model may be identified from either or both of:

- An examination of the interaction model where the existence of actors will be indicated by the associations, stereotyped as «EV_FulfilsRole», between the classes stereotyped as «EV_Role» and «EV_EnterpriseObject», respectively, taken in combination with the StateMachine that expresses the behaviour of the relevant role.

- In an examination of the process model, the presence of an «EV_Step» in an «EV_Role» ActiviyPartition indicates that the enterprise object fulfilling the role is an *actor* for the *step* concerned.

Artefact (with Respect to an Action)

The concept *artefact* is also a relationship between an *enterprise object* and an *action*. In an *interaction* model, an *artefact* referenced in an *action* is expressed by a signal, stereotyped as «EV_Artefact», that has two associations: one association, stereotyped as «EV_ArtefactRole», will be with the «EV_EnterpriseObject» class that expresses the enterprise object that is an *artefact* with respect to the *action*; the other association, stereotyped as «EV_ArtefactReference», will be with the «EV_Interaction» class that expresses the *interaction* for which the *enterprise object* is an *artefact*.

If there is a *process* model, it is possible to express each instance of the RM-ODP enterprise language concept, *artefact,* with a single UML model element, namely an ObjectNode stereotyped as «EV_Artefact».

Expressing the Templeman Library Example in UML

In the figures that follow, to improve the clarity of the diagrams, icons have been used to represent certain UML stereotypes. These are summarised in Figure 5.

Figure 5. Icons

Concept	Stereotype Name	Icon
Community	«EV_Community»	
Objective	«EV_Objective»	
Enterprise Object	«EV_EnterpriseObject»	
Community Object	«EV_CommunityObject»	
ODP System	«EV_ODPSystem»	
Role	«EV_Role»	
Interaction	«EV_Interaction»	
Process	«EV_Process»	
Step	«EV_Step»	
Artefact	«EV_Artefact»	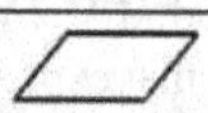

Model Structure

Figure 6 shows the overall structure of the UML model that expresses the enterprise specification. It shows the specification contained in a package, stereotyped as «Enterprise_Spec», that includes the **Library** at two levels of abstraction: at the higher level as a class stereotyped as «EV_CommunityObject», and at a lower level as a component stereotyped as «EV_Community» contained in a package, stereotyped as «EV_CommunityContract», that contains the details. The representation at two levels allows for modeling high-level interactions between the library and other enterprise objects, not members of its community (e.g., the **Academic Community** within the University).

The Library Community Package

Figure 7 shows the packaging of the detail of the **Library** community, where its objective, the processes, interactions and roles that support it, its locally owned enterprise objects, and its policies are detailed.

Figure 6. Top level structure of the enterprise specification in UML

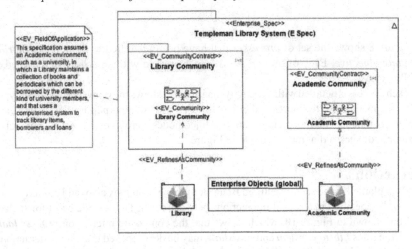

Figure 7. UML specification of the library community

Figure 8. Library processes

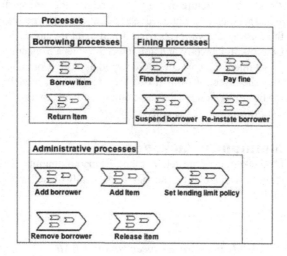

Figure 8 shows the set of *processes* that have been identified to support the ***Library community objective***. Each of these *processes* is expressed with an activity stereotyped as «EV_Process».

Each process is detailed with an activity diagram that shows the *steps* (Actions stereotyped as «EV_Step», the *roles* that perform them (ActivityPartitions stereotyped as «EV_Role»), and the *artefacts* that are referenced in the *steps* (Objectnodes stereotyped as «EV_Artefact»). An example of such a diagram is shown in Figure 9.

Interactions

As explained in the section entitled **Behaviour,** behaviour may also (and possibly more precisely) be specified in terms of interactions between roles. The starting point for such an exercise is shown in Figure 10, which shows that the composite interaction *process loan*, between the roles *Library system* and *Assistant*, may be decomposed into three interactions: *Request, Authorize,* and *Disqualify*, each of which is concerned with artefacts representing usages of the enterprise object (type) *Loan*.

Figure 10 also shows an aspect of the RM-ODP enterprise language that is extremely useful. This concerns policy modeling. The class, stereotyped as «EV_PolicyEnvelope» named *Lending limit policy*, is shown as having an «EV_AffectedBehaviour» dependency from the interaction *Process loan*, which shows that the specification of this interaction is governed by the value of this policy.

Roles and Enterprise Objects

Figure 11 shows the assignment rules of enterprise objects to roles. Note, this diagram is probably in error as it implies that just about anyone can be a librarian, whereas it is very likely that some qualifications would be necessary, which implies the existence of an enter-

Figure 9. Detail of the Borrow Item process

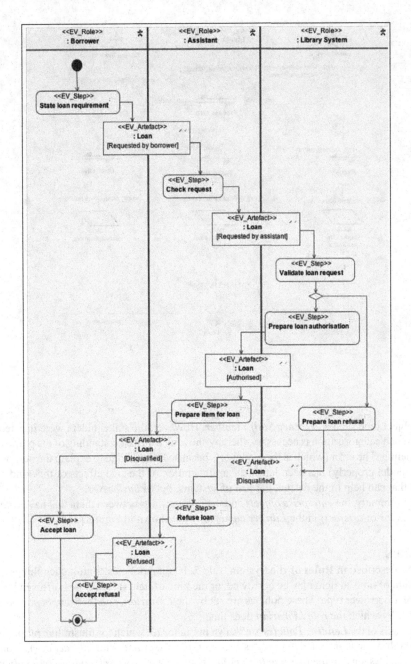

Figure 10. Process loan composite interaction

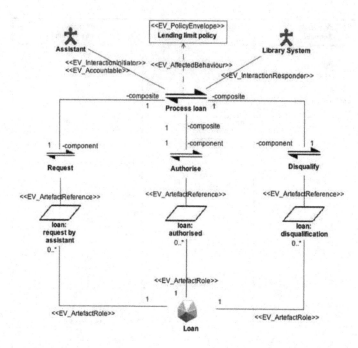

prise object type such as ***Library Staff member***. However, the stakeholders were insistent that no such categorisation is necessary, thereby showing a misunderstanding of the purpose of modeling. The error (which is the modeller's because he has failed to explain the purpose of the model properly) has been left in as an illustration of the side effects of this kind of model that can help in the design, not just of systems, but of *businesses*.

In summary, the *enterprise objects* and the relationships between them that have *roles* (either *actor* or *artefact*) in the ***Library*** community are shown in Figure 12.

Policies

As described in **Rules of the System**, rule 5, lending policies control such things as the length of time an item may be borrowed, or the kind of item that may be borrowed by a particular borrower type. These policies are set by the ***Librarian***, and there are *behaviours* specified by which the *role* **Librarian** does this.

Details of the ***Lending Policies*** are shown in Figure 13, which for illustrative purposes offers both behavioural modeling styles (i.e. with *processes* and with *interactions*). From this, it can be seen that the ***Lending limit policy*** is set by a *process* ***Set lending limit policy***, and impacts on the *role* ***Library System***, when taking part in the *process* ***Borrow Item***, or the *interaction* of the same name.

Figure 11. Role assignment rules

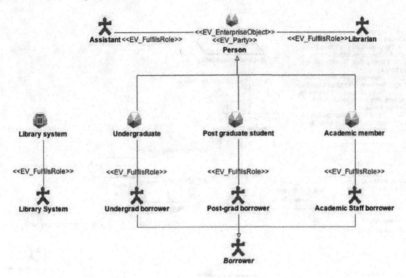

Figure 12. Enterprise objects

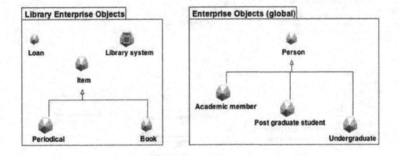

Similarly the ***Loan Duration policy*** is set by the *interaction **Set loan duration policy*** (located in the ***Administrative Interactions*** package), and impacts on the *role **Library System*** when taking part in the *process **Fine Borrower***, or the *interaction* of the same name.

Benefits and Issues

A fundamental benefit of the approach to enterprise modeling that has been outlined in this chapter is that, within its scope, it is an approach that combines the precision and rigour of the RM-ODP with the presentational benefits of UML. In effect, the enterprise language profile defined in UML for ODP (ISO/IEC 19793, 2005) defines a "domain specific language" that addresses the operational structure and behaviour of an enterprise.

Of equal importance, however, is the fact that the approach has evolved as part of a rigorous, structured, viewpoint-based approach to system specification as a whole, in which the enterprise language described here is one of a family of languages, each of which comprises

Figure 13. Lending policies

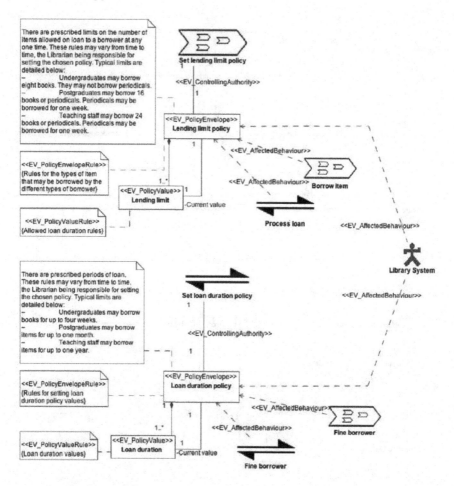

concepts, rules, and structures for the specification of an ODP system from one of a set of viewpoints that, together, cover all aspects of a system specification. All of these viewpoint languages are defined on the basis of a common set of concepts that are needed to perform the modeling of ODP systems and to provide the principles of conformance to ODP systems, so that the model of a system from one viewpoint can be related in a straightforward way to a model from another viewpoint.

Thus, the set of viewpoint specifications provides the basis for tracing the requirements on the system, specified by enterprise specification, to the details of the system implementation specified in the other viewpoint specifications; bridging the gap from business need to system operation. Furthermore, when allied with the definition of UML profiles for the information, computational, engineering, and technology viewpoints in UML for ODP (ISO/IEC 19793, 2005), the enterprise modeling approach described here can form part of a model-driven approach to system development that exploits the evolution of tools supporting model-driven development.

Nevertheless, there are a number of potential issues that need to be investigated arising from the use of an object-based approach for enterprise modeling.

The focus of the enterprise specification is on the specification of what the system is expected to do in the context of the enterprise: consequently, the focus of the enterprise language is on the operational structure and behaviour of the enterprise, and an object-based approach works well for this. Can such an approach be extended to cover other aspects of the enterprise, or be made compatible with other approaches that address these other aspects? Of equal importance, is the approach understandable and usable by business stakeholders, or can it be made understandable and usable by them? The enterprise specification is of no value if it does not represent the views of the business stakeholders but instead, only the views on the business of the system developers. On the other hand, it is of limited value if it is in a form that does not constitute a coherent and rigorous part of the overall system specification. Finally, can the approach take account of the insights of "soft" systems analysis (Checkland, 1981), and take account of differing views on the objectives and operation of the enterprise?

While investigation is, clearly, necessary, there seems to be no a priori reason why the issues of addressing other aspects of the enterprise and ensuring usability for business stakeholders cannot be dealt with satisfactorily, especially taking into account current developments in modeling technology in the context of MDA®. Thus, a key aspect of the MDA® programme is the provision of transformations between models in different modeling languages, where those languages are defined in terms of MOF-compatible metamodels (the MOF (Meta Object Facility) is specified in ISO/IEC 19502, 2005; OMG, 2005). Such transformations would allow enterprise models in different languages and addressing different issues to be formally related, and allow views of an ODP enterprise model to be presented in an appropriate form for business stakeholders.

Taking into account "soft" systems analysis, on the other hand, seems more likely to affect the process for developing the enterprise specification, rather than the form of the specification itself. The process must ensure that the differing views of the enterprise are all clearly articulated and reconciled where necessary, and then accommodated in the final specification.

Thus, it is our view that enterprise modeling using the ODP enterprise language can be successfully integrated with approaches that are, possibly, more suited to other aspects of the enterprise. Confirmation (or otherwise) of this view must come through feedback from the different companies and organizations that are starting to use ODP for their IT system specifications, since these are the ones who can really judge the practicality of the approach.

Related Work

Most of the initial proposals for modeling the ODP enterprise language were largely based on formal notations, such as Object-Z or Maude (see, e.g., the works by Durán & Vallecillo, 2003 or by Steen & Derrick, 2000). Formal notations provide precise and unambiguous system specifications and, more importantly, they also allow the rigorous analysis of the systems, with tools for quick-prototyping, model checking, or theorem proving. However, formal specifications are difficult to read and understand by most business people, who demand simpler and more user-friendly notations for handling business systems require-ments and specifications, and by system analysts and developers, who are increasingly using UML-based modeling tools.

A second group of works explored the use of UML for enterprise modeling. An in-teresting proposal is that of Chris Marshall (2000), who describes in his book many of the concepts involved in enterprise modeling, and provides some guidelines for representing them using plain UML. One of the limitations of this approach is that it is not connected or integrated to any development methodology, which may hinder its wide adoption.

A very good recent book about business modeling is that by Haim Kilov (2002). This provides a detailed and precise walk-through of the main modeling concepts and techniques involved in enterprise modeling, and reviews the factors that impact business models, sys-tems, and specifications. As a graphical notation, he shows how the key modeling concepts can be represented in a small subset of UML, whose semantics can be precisely defined. On top of this, business patterns and reuse techniques are also introduced, to benefit from gained experiences. However, the book remains at a descriptive level, without proposing any specific notation or methodology for developing comprehensive enterprise specifications.

Sheer (2000) describes in detail in his book how ARIS methods can model and real-ize business processes by means of UML, and can be used in concrete scenarios, including knowledge management, implementation of workflow systems, and standard solutions (e.g., SAP). However, the approach described is limited to the process aspect of an enterprise specification.

Other authors have studied the feasibility of using UML 1.4 to represent specific ODP enterprise concepts, such as accountability or policies. Examples include the works by Lin-ington (1999), Aagedal and Milosevic (1999), Blanc, Gervais, and Le Delliou (1999) and Kent (2001). Some of these represent the basics from which UML for ODP (ISO/IEC 19793) has evolved. A further source of inspiration is OMG's UML profile for EDOC (enterprise distributed object computing), which also allows enterprise modeling with UML. In particular, EDOC's enterprise collaboration architecture (ECA) specification (OMG, 2004) provides a whole set of models and mechanisms very well suited for enterprise modeling.

However, all these proposals share some common problems that are mainly due to the lack of expressiveness of UML 1.4 for representing business concepts. The size of this semantic gap has resulted in either too simplistic solutions (those that tried to cover only those issues that could be naturally expressed with UML 1.4), or too complex (those that tried to be complete and semantically sound, and therefore had to stretch UML 1.4 too much in order to cover all enterprise modeling concepts). The UML profile for EDOC is an ex-ample of the second group and, as a result, its final size and complexity represent, from our point of view, an important limitation for its wide acceptance by the software engineering community. With the advent of UML 2.0 the situation has changed, since not only are its semantics more precisely defined, but it also incorporates a whole new set of concepts more apt for modeling the structure and behaviour of distributed systems. Our work exploits the new features of UML 2.0 to represent, in a more natural way, the key enterprise concepts.

Finally, the model driven architecture® (MDA®, 2001) is the approach defined by OMG to achieve model driven development based on OMG standards. MDA® specifies three viewpoints on a system, and three corresponding models: computation independent model (CIM), platform independent model (PIM), and platform specific model (PSM). The CIM focuses on the requirements for the system, without showing details of its structure; a CIM is sometimes called a domain model. The PIM and PSM focus on the system functionality: the

PIM abstracts from the details necessary for a particular platform, while the PSM combines the functionality specified by the PIM, with an additional focus on the detail of the use of a specific supporting platform. Although the exact role of the CIM has not yet been precisely defined by OMG, it seems to be intended to capture similar information about the system to that provided by the ODP enterprise specification, and thus a CIM may be provided by an enterprise specification, together with relevant parts of an information specification.

CONCLUSION

In this chapter, we have briefly described an approach for enterprise modeling using the ODP enterprise language and UML. In particular, we have presented a UML profile that can be used for expressing the ODP enterprise specification of a system as an integral part of an ODP system specification. This can bring along the important benefits of enabling business need to be clearly related to system implementation, and exploiting the emerging tools that support model-driven development.

REFERENCES

Aagedal, J., & Milosevic, Z. (1999). ODP enterprise language: UML perspective. In *Proc. of the 3rd International Enterprise Distributed Object Computing Conference (EDOC '99)*, (pp. 60-71). Los Alamitos, CA: IEEE Computer Society Press.

Blanc, X., Gervais, M. P., & Le Delliou, R. (1999). Using the UML language to express the ODP enterprise concepts. In *Proc. of the 3rd International Enterprise Distributed Object Computing Conference (EDOC '99)* (pp. 50-59). Los Alamitos, CA: IEEE Computer Society Press.

Checkland, P. (1981). *Systems thinking, systems practice*. Chichester, UK: John Wiley & Sons.

Durán, F., & Vallecillo, A. (2003). Formalizing ODP enterprise specifications in Maude. *Computer Standards & Interfaces, 25*(2), 83-102.

IEEE Std 1471. (2000). *IEEE recommended practice for architectural description of software-intensive systems*.

ISO/IEC 10746-1. (1998). *Information technology — Open distributed processing — Reference model: Overview*. ITU-T Rec. X.901 (1998) | ISO/IEC 10746-1:1998. Geneva, Switzerland.

ISO/IEC 10746-2. (1995). *Information technology — Open distributed processing — Reference model: Foundations*. ITU-T Rec. X.902 (1995) | ISO/IEC 10746-2:1995. Geneva, Switzerland.

ISO/IEC 10746-3. (1995). *Information technology — Open distributed processing — Reference model: Architecture*. ITU-T Rec. X.903 (1995) | ISO/IEC 10746-3:1995. Geneva, Switzerland.

ISO/IEC 10746-4. (1997). *Information technology — Open distributed processing — Reference model: Architectural semantics*. ITU-T Rec. X.904 (1997) | ISO/IEC 10746-4:1997. Geneva, Switzerland.

ISO/IEC 15414. (2002). *Information technology — Open distributed processing — Reference model — Enterprise language*. ITU-T Rec. X.911 (2002) | ISO/IEC 15414:2002. Geneva, Switzerland.

ISO/IEC 19502. (2005). *Metaobject facility (MOF) Specification* (Version 1.4). Geneva, Switzerland.

ISO/IEC 19793. (2005). *Information technology — Open distributed processing – Reference model — Use of UML for ODP system specifications.* ITU-T Rec. X.906 | ISO/IEC 19793. 2nd Committee Draft. Bari, Italy.

Johnson, D. R., & Kilov, H. (1999). An approach to a Z toolkit for the reference model of open distributed processing. *Computer Standards & Interfaces, 21*(5), 393-402.

Kent, S. (2001). The unified modelling language. In *Formal methods for distributed processing: A survey of object-oriented approaches* (pp. 126-152). Cambridge: Cambridge University Press.

Kilov, H. (2002). *Business models: A guide for business and IT.* Upper Saddle River, NJ: Prentice Hall.

Kruchten, P. (1995). Architectural blueprints — The 4+1 view model of software architecture. *IEEE Software, 12*(6), 42-50.

Linington, P. (1995). RM-ODP: The architecture. In K. Milosevic & L. Armstrong (Eds.), *Open distributed processing II* (pp. 15-33). Paris: Chapman & Hall.

Linington, P. (1999). Options for expressing ODP enterprise communities and their policies by using UML. In *Proceedings of the 3rd International Enterprise Distributed Object Computing Conference (EDOC'99)* (pp. 72-82). Los Alamitos, CA: IEEE Computer Society Press.

Marshall, C. (2000). *Enterprise modelling with UML: Designing successful software through business analysis.* Reading, MA: Addison-Wesley.

OMG. (2004). *Enterprise collaboration architecture (ECA) specification* (Version 1.0). OMG document formal/04-02-01.

OMG. (2005). *Metaobject facility (MOF) specification* (Version 1.4). OMG document pas/05-05-01.

Scheer, A. (2000). *Aris-business process modeling* (3rd ed.). New York: Springer-Verlag.

Sowa, J. F., & Zachman, J. A. (1992). Extending and formalising the framework for information systems architecture. *IBM Systems Journal, 31*(3). IBM Publication G321-5488.

Steen, M., & Derrick, J. (2000). ODP enterprise viewpoint specification. *Computer Standards & Interfaces, 22*(3), 165-189.

Zachman, J. A. (1987). A framework for information systems architecture. *IBM Systems Journal, 26*(3). IBM Publication G321-5298.

Section III

Enterprise Modeling Frontends for UML

Chapter VII

A Language-Action Approach to the Design of UML Models

Peter Rittgen, University College of Borås, Sweden

ABSTRACT

The language-action perspective provides a communicative view on the organization. In it, an organization is characterized as a system of interacting agents. This view is helpful in understanding how the organization works, and it can also contribute to the design of information systems in support of it. This design is often done in UML, a language that views an information system as a system of message-passing objects. We suggest an approach to support this design by mapping action models onto UML models.

INTRODUCTION

In a reengineering project, it is not uncommon to encounter a situation where none of the available modeling methods can complete the whole task. We met such a situation in an interorganizational project where we used one such approach, the language-action perspective, to analyze the business process. This approach was useful for understanding the business situation, eliciting problems, and proposing the design of an improved organization. But some of the problems consisted of poor or missing information system support, and we considered that UML would be more useful for finding solutions to them. That left us with the task of "implementing" our organizational designs, which we developed in DEMO, in a new language, UML, a task that was by no means straightforward owing to the fact that both languages represent different views on a system (the following paragraphs elaborate this point). As a consequence, we developed a language-mapping framework to support this task. In the remaining sections, we introduce the languages involved, develop the mapping procedure, and relate empirical findings regarding this approach.

In his paper "Representation and Communication," Johannesson (1995, p. 291) writes: "There are several different views of the functional role of information systems. Two of the most important ones are the model view and the communicative action view. According to the model view, the primary purpose of an information system is to provide a model of a universe of discourse (UoD), thereby enabling people to obtain information about reality by studying the model. In this respect, an information system works as a passive repository of data that reflects the structure and behaviour of the UoD. In contrast, the communicative action view states that the major role of an information system is to support communication within an organisation by structuring and coordinating the actions performed by the organisation's agents. The system is seen as a medium through which people can perform social actions, such as stating facts, making promises, and giving orders."

He reconciles both views by suggesting a language that is similar to the data-flow diagrams of the model view, but which is founded on the speech acts of the communicative action view. The choice of terminology for the two views is unfortunate, though. On the one hand, proponents of the action view also employ models to picture the system in question (typically an organization). On the other hand, languages that provide a model view often define a concept of action. But the two views are based on ontological foundations that are so fundamentally different that the two concepts of "action" have little in common. The following paragraphs explore this issue.

In the action view, a system consists of a number of agents (people or organizational units) who interact with each other by communicating. The basic unit of communication is a speech act (Austin, 1962; Searle, 1969). An action pair is the smallest sequence of actions that has an effect in the social world (e.g. establishing a commitment). It consists of two speech acts: an utterance and the response (e.g. a request and the promise). On the third level, the workflow loop (or action workflow, Medina-Mora, Winograd, Flores, & Flores, 1992) describes a communicative pattern consisting of two consecutive transactions that aim at reaching an agreement about (1) the execution of an action, and (2) the result of that execution. The left side of Figure 1 shows three examples of workflow loops. Higher

Figure 1. Action view and reaction view

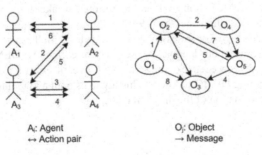

A_i: Agent
↔ Action pair

O_j: Object
→ Message

levels can be defined, such as contract and scenario, but the first three are sufficient for the purpose of this chapter.

In the model view, object orientation prevails today in most areas of software engineering. It has largely replaced the functional paradigm that characterized early approaches to software engineering (and is still used in certain areas such as databases). In object orientation, a system is seen as a collection of objects exchanging messages. Each object encapsulates data and functionality (or structure and behaviour, or attributes and operations). An object is, in principle, a passive (or reactive) unit that only acts if it receives a message. It will then carry out the appropriate operation, which might involve sending messages to other objects. Finally, it will deliver the result as a reply to the original message, but "communication" is essentially one-way (see Figure 1, right).

The major conceptual differences between the views are:

1.   The action view describes social systems that consist of human beings that can both act of their own accord and react to stimuli from the environment, whereas an object can only react. We will therefore call the model view "reaction view."

2.   By performing speech acts, agents create obligations for themselves or others. Having a conscience, they are fully aware of the consequences of entering into a commitment, and also of not fulfilling an obligation. An object is not equipped with a conscience, so it cannot commit itself. If an object behaves in the "desired" way, this is due to a preprogrammed automatism, and not the result of an individual decision based on free will. An object cannot be responsible for its "actions."

3.   Communicating is not just exchanging messages. We communicate to achieve a certain purpose for which we need the help of others. An object sends a message because its code prescribes this behaviour, and the message is received, processed, and "answered" for precisely the same reason. An object has no intentions.

In short, it can be said that the difference between agents and objects is the same as that between human beings and machines. In the light of these fundamental discrepancies, it seems doubtful whether a reconciliation of action view and reaction view can be successful. But both views play an important role in the development of information systems as sociotechnical systems, so we cannot drop either of them. It would be equally inadequate to describe a social system in terms of mindless objects as it would be to describe a technical artefact, such as software, in terms of responsible and conscious agents. But a mere coexistence of both views is not enough because the social and technical aspects of an information system are so tightly interwoven that we cannot neatly separate them into weakly connected areas of concern, each dominated by its respective view. So we have to think of ways to "mediate" between both views. Mediation is, in our definition, a weaker form of integration than reconciliation, as defined in Johannesson (1995).

The approach we suggest operates on the language level. In the next section, we argue for this decision and present our languages of choice for each view: DEMO and UML respectively. Assuming the precedence of the action view over the reaction view, we introduce a framework for mapping DEMO to UML. This involves both a mapping of the language concepts, and a transformation of the diagram types.

LANGUAGES FOR ACTION VIEW AND REACTION VIEW

Our approach to mediating between action view and reaction view proceeds at the language level. On the one hand, this gives us a richer understanding of each view by examining the details of the concepts of a language representing this view. In addition, it also offers the chance to provide more comprehensive and constructive support for mediation. But on the other hand, each language will also introduce additional features that are not a necessary prerequisite of the respective view. The results of such an approach should therefore be considered with care because they might not generalize to all languages of the action and reaction views. In particular, the selected languages might not even be "typical" representatives of their respective views.

Regarding the reaction view, the task of finding an appropriate language is not difficult. The software engineering community has subjected itself to a rigorous standardization process that resulted in the unified modeling language (UML). It follows the object-oriented paradigm, and is widely used in the design of information systems. Adhering to the reaction view, its focus is more on the technical part of the information systems than on the organizational (i.e. social) part, but the proponents of UML claim that it can also be used for the latter. As evidence for this standpoint, they mention use cases and business processes. For the former, UML provides a specific language construct: use case diagrams. The latter were originally supposed to be represented as activity diagrams (with swimlanes), but a language extension called enterprise collaboration architecture (ECA) (OMG, 2004) now takes care of business processes. Nevertheless, UML does not offer an action view because the concept of an actor is weakly integrated and restricted to the role of a user of the information system. This point is argued more thoroughly in the subsection "concept mapping."

The situation regarding the action view (or language-action perspective) is much more complex. The approaches assuming this view cover a wide range of epistemological orientations coming from disciplines as diverse as social sciences, political science, law, linguistics, cognitive science, organizational theory, artificial intelligence, and computer science. They have in common that they are based on speech-act theory (Austin, 1962; Habermas, 1984; Searle, 1969). Examples of such approaches are conversation-for-action (Winograd & Flores, 1986), DiaLaw (Lodder & Herczog, 1995), multiagent systems (Dignum & Weigand, 1995; Hulstijn, Dignum, & Dastani, 2004), dynamic essential modelling of organizations (DEMO) (Dietz, 1999; Dietz & Habing, 2004; Liu, Sun, Barjis, & Dietz, 2003), action workflow (Denning & Medina-Mora, 1995; Kethers & Schoop, 2000; Medina-Mora et al., 1992;), action-based modeling (Lehtinen & Lyytinen, 1986), business action theory and SIMM (Goldkuhl, 1996; Goldkuhl & Lind, 2004; Goldkuhl & Röstlinger, 1993), and discourse structures (Johannesson, 1995). As we aim at finding a language that is suitable for being mapped to UML, we would like it to exhibit certain external similarities with UML: on the syntactic level it should provide a diagram-like notation, and on the semantic level it should possess an appropriate degree of formality. We found that DEMO fulfils these criteria best. The following subsections give short introductions to both languages.

Dynamic Essential Modeling of Organization

In the action view, the structure of an organization is understood as a network of commitments. As these commitments are the result of communication, it follows that a model of

Figure 2. Architecture of DEMO (simplified)

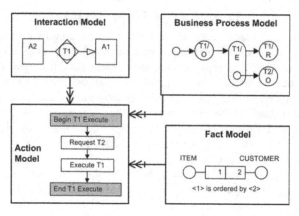

the organization is essentially a model based on purposeful, communicative acts. In DEMO, all acts that serve the same purpose are collected in a *transaction* in which two roles are engaged: the *initiator* and the *executor*. The definition of a transaction in DEMO is broader than that given in the introduction. It comes closer to that of a workflow loop, but it also includes a noncommunicative action, namely the agreed action that the executor performs in the object world. Hence, each transaction is assumed to follow a certain pattern that is divided into three sequential phases and three layers. The phases are *order* (O), *execute* (E), and *result* (R). The layers are success, discussion, and discourse. On the success layer, the phases are structured as follows. In the order phase, the contract is negotiated. This involves, typically, a *request* being made by the initiator and a *promise* by the executor to carry out the request. In the next phase, the contract is executed, which involves factual changes in the object world (as opposed to the intersubject world of communication). Finally, in the result phase, the executor *states* that the agreed result has been achieved, and the initiator *accepts* this *fact*. If anything goes wrong on the success layer, the participants can decide to move to the discussion or discourse layer. For details on these layers see Reijswoud (1996).

Figure 2 gives an overview of the architecture of DEMO. The interaction model shows actors and their relations to transactions, but abstracts from time. The business process model, on the other hand, abstracts from the actors, but refines the transactional logic in two ways: it breaks each transaction into its phases, and specifies how they are ordered causally and conditionally. This allows us to determine the order of the communicative acts in time. The fact model describes all information that is created or used by an organization. A fact is the result of a successful transaction, and implies that the proposition of the request has become true. The interstriction model (not shown in Figure 2) is similar to the interaction model, but in addition to the communication that is part of the transactions, it also exhibits informative communication. All models are linked to the action model, which gives a detailed account of activities carried out within a transaction phase (which can also involve links to other transactions).

Figure 3 gives examples of an interaction model and a business process model. They are taken from Reijswoud and Dietz (1999), and show a part of the business process of an organization called SGC, a nonprofit organization that mediates consumer complaints in The Netherlands.

Figure 3. Examples of an interaction model and a business process model

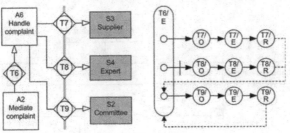

The transactions of the example are as follows:

- T6: Handling_complaint
- T7: Defending_complaint
- T8: Giving_advice
- T9: Passing_judgement

The actor A2, who is responsible for mediating the claim, requests that actor A6 handles the complaint. Both A2 and A6 are internal actors (represented by white boxes). The latter will give the supplier a chance to defend the complaint, ask an expert to give advice, and request that the committee passes a judgement. S2 – S4 are external actors, as the grey boxes show. A simple line connects the initiator with the transaction, an arrow points from it to the executor. The grey line represents the system boundary. Observe that Figure 3 shows only a fragment of the model.

The right side of Figure 3 contains a part of the business process model. It shows details of the execution phase of transaction 6: Handling_complaint. This phase is called T6/E. From inside it, the transactions T7, T8, and T9 are started. This is represented by arrows from the initiation points (small, white circles) to the order phases of the respective transactions. Solid arrows indicate a causal relation, dashed ones a conditional relation. The inside of a phase is viewed as a concurrent region, so all three triggered transactions could start at the same time if it were not for the dashed lines. An arrow that is crossed by a line represents an optional relation. In short, the supplier is asked to defend the complaint in any case, and the expert is possibly consulted. After T7 (and possibly T8) have been completed, the committee is asked to pass judgement. Only when T9/R has been finished can we also terminate T6/E. Observe that this is due to the dashed arrow between them. As a rule, the initiation points inside a phase trigger transactions in an asynchronous manner without waiting for their completion.

The Unified Modeling Language

The specification of the unified modeling language (OMG, 2003) is divided into two parts: semantics and notation. The first part introduces the concepts of UML with the help of metamodels and natural language. It is organized in packages (which are themselves a concept of UML). See Figure 4 for an overview of the relevant packages.

All concepts for structural models are defined in the foundation. They comprise static aspects of a system such as classes, interfaces, and attributes. Based on the foundation, the

Figure 4. Architecture of UML (simplified)

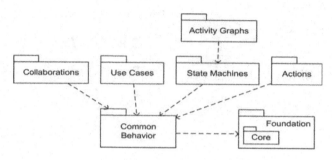

elements of the behavioral (dynamic) models are specified, which consist of common behavior (such as signals, procedures, instances, etc.) and diagram-specific behavior (one package for each, see Figure 4). Their purpose is defined in OMG (2003, p. 2-92 f.) as: "The Collaborations package specifies a behavioral context for using model elements to accomplish a particular task. The Use Case package specifies behavior using actors and use cases. The State Machines package defines behavior using finite-state transition systems. The activity graphs package defines a special case of a state machine that is used to model processes. The Actions package defines behavior using a detailed model of computation."

The notation part of the language specification introduces a number of diagrams that define how the elements of the semantics packages can be represented graphically. For the purpose of this chapter, the relevant diagrams (and the primary packages they refer to) are collaboration diagram (collaborations), statechart diagram (state machines), activity diagram (activity graphs), and class diagram (foundation). For a detailed description of these diagrams, refer to OMG (2003).

A LANGUAGE-MAPPING FRAMEWORK FOR DEMO AND UML

A General Framework for Mapping Languages

The Object Management Group (OMG) has suggested an architecture for language integration that is called model driven architecture (MDA) (Miller & Mukerji, 2003). In it, a system is specified from three different viewpoints: computation independent, platform independent, and platform specific. Although the scope of MDA is much broader, a typical assumption is that all models (views) can be constructed with the help of only one language, and UML is the preferred candidate for that role. But Evans, Maskeri, Sammut, and Willans (2003) argue that "a truly flexible model-driven development process should not dictate the language that practitioners should use to construct models, even an extensible one. Instead they should be free to use whichever language is appropriate for their particular domain and application, particularly as many languages cannot be shoe-horned into the UML family." We follow this argument and suggest extending the model mapping of MDA (Caplat & Sourrouille, 2003) to "language mapping."

Figure 5. A framework for language mapping

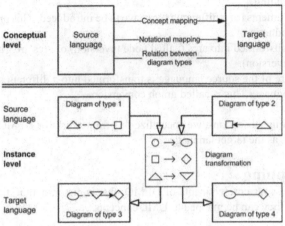

A general framework for mapping a modeling language to another one is shown in Figure 5. We distinguish between the conceptual level and the instance level. On the conceptual level, we first perform concept mapping. This step involves finding for each concept of the source language a matching one in the target language. A successful match implies that a significant part of the semantics of the source concept can also be expressed by the target concept. Note that concept mapping, as defined here, does not relate to the one known from (empirical) social research. For example, the DEMO concept of an action maps to the UML concept of an action state. The latter is something that is performed while the system is in a certain state. As this is very general, it encompasses the meaning of action in DEMO for which the same holds, but in addition to that, an action is restricted to being either an objective action in the object world, or a communicative action in the intersubject world (see subsection "concept mapping" for more details). Note that such a mapping is not always possible because the target language might not have a related concept at all, or the "common denominator" between both concepts is not a significant part of the semantics of the source concept (i.e., the two concepts have very little in common). This implies that language mapping cannot be done for any combination of languages, at least not in the way described here. Moreover, we cannot expect that we always succeed in establishing a one-to-one correspondence between concepts. Sometimes several source concepts jointly map to one target concept, or one source concept maps to a conjunction of target concepts.

The second step consists of a notational mapping. We assume that each concept is associated with a notational element in the respective language, so with concept mapping being done, this step is straightforward. The third and last step is about establishing a relation between the diagram types of both languages. This step provides rules for carrying out the actual diagram transformation on the instance level. In the example of Figure 5, this step is trivial: it involves only a (slight) change in the notation and a rearrangement of the six basic concepts (three node types and three relation types: solid arc, dashed arc, and arrow) into different diagrams. But for realistic modeling languages, the mapping rules can be much more complex. Typical types of transformations include:

- One element has to be mapped to a number of elements (e.g., a subgraph). This process is called unfolding.
- Additional elements (of a different type) have to be introduced. This process is called element introduction.
- Nodes are transformed into arcs (called node inversion) or arcs are transformed into nodes (arc inversion).
- A substructure of the source language is transformed into a different substructure of the target language. This is called graph conversion.

In the following subsections, we specialize this framework for DEMO as the source language and UML as the target language.

Concept Mapping

Let us look at four core concepts of DEMO, that is, actor, action, transaction, and category, and how they can be mapped to UML concepts.

Actor → Actor/Object

The concept of an actor in DEMO is mapped both to that of an actor and to that of an object in UML. An actor (in DEMO) is a role that a subject (human being) plays. An actor (in UML) "defines a coherent set of roles that users of an entity can play when interacting with the entity. An actor may be considered to play a separate role with regard to each use case with which it communicates" (OMG, 2003, p. 2-131). In UML, an actor can play many roles, in DEMO it can play only one role (i.e., the actor is the role). But in UML, actors can only interact with the information system. In DEMO, they interact with each other. As use cases (or a similar notion) are not defined in DEMO, the mapping actor → actor is valid, but not helpful. But if we also introduce a mapping actor → object, we can at least interpret (or view) the actor as a (re)acting object. This means that we will lose the mind of the actor, but we can still express a significant part of the semantics of an actor; the structure and behaviour of the actor are retained in the object.

Action → Action State

The concept of an action in DEMO is mapped to that of an action state in UML. In DEMO, actions are divided into communicative actions and objective actions. Communicative actions take place in the intersubject world and consist of speech acts. Material actions are performed in the object world and can be material or immaterial. Communicative actions can lead to changes in the social (intersubject) world (i.e., creating obligations), objective actions can lead to changes in the object world (i.e., the creation of facts). An action state refers to a state (of the system). Upon entering the state, the (entry) action is triggered. Upon completion of the action, the state is left. As the latter definition does not restrict the type of action, it also encompasses the action concept of the former. In DEMO, a state transition is the effect of an action that is compatible with UML's concept of a state where the completion of an action causes the system to leave its current state and thereby make a transition to the consecutive state

Transaction → State

The concept of a transaction in DEMO is mapped to that of a state in UML. A (business) transaction is a pattern that consists of the conversation for an (objective) action, the execution of that action, and the conversation for the result (of that action). This concept has no direct counterpart in UML. Instead, it has to map to a sequence of messages that represent the speech acts. Technically, this is done by unfolding on the instance level (i.e., transformation interaction model → collaboration diagram). On the conceptual level, we can only map a transaction to a state of UML. When the system enters this state, the transaction is initiated. When the transaction is finished, the system leaves the state.

Category → Class

The concept of a category in DEMO is mapped to that of a class in UML. A category is a primal class (derived classes are used to define roles in DEMO). Each object is an instance of exactly one category, but can also be an instance of many arbitrarily derived classes. In UML "a class is a description of a set of objects that share the same attributes, operations, methods, relationships, and semantics" (OMG, 2003, pp. 2-26). A category (as a primal class) is a class in the sense of this definition. Categories can have n-ary relations that correspond to association classes in UML. Categories and their relations are used to represent facts about the intersubject world and the object world.

Diagram Transformation

Figure 6 shows the overall framework for the language mapping. The DEMO diagrams are represented by rounded boxes, the UML diagrams by rectangular boxes. The mapping of concepts is visualized by single-headed arrows, the transformation of diagrams by double-headed arrows. Each diagram conversion involves a transformation of the notation, but will also require some more sophisticated transformation process (e.g., transaction unfolding). Concurrency explication and class association are graph conversions, Signal and infolink introduction are element introductions, and transaction unfolding is an unfolding in the sense of the general integration framework.

The interaction model introduces systems, actors, and transactions that all become classes in UML. But the transactions (the most important concept of DEMO) also form states in the statechart diagram. The business process model refines transactions into phases that in turn become substates of the respective transaction state in the statechart diagram. The basic elements of the fact model are the categories. They correspond to classes in UML. The interstriction model introduces fact and communication banks to store records of facts and communication. They also correspond to classes in UML. The action model introduces wait states that map to signal receipts in activity diagrams.

The interaction model is transformed into the collaboration diagram. Apart from a notational conversion, this requires an unfolding of the transactions, a concept that has no immediate dynamic counterpart in UML. Each transaction is split into its communicative acts, which then are represented by messages in UML. An example of that is given in the next section.

The business process model is transformed into the statechart diagram. Again, this involves a change in notation, but also an explication of the inherent concurrent behavior of a phase. A phase can have many concurrent initiation points, but each state has only one initial (sub)state. Dividing the state into concurrent regions is not feasible due to the asyn-

Figure 6. Framework for integrating DEMO and UML

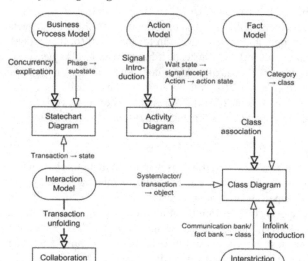

chronous nature of the threads triggered by the initiation points. Hence, the initial state is forked into as many threads as there are initiation points that have no arrows pointing at them (plus one that leads to the final state if no arrow points to the phase). An arrow pointing at a phase maps to one pointing at the corresponding final state. If more than one arrow points at a phase or initiation point, the respective arrows in the statechart diagram are joined by a synchronization bar. Optional relationships map to guarded transitions. An example for such a transformation is given in the next section.

The action model is transformed into the activity diagram. Apart from the usual notational conversion, this means that a signal receipt has to be introduced into the activity diagram for each wait state that is found in the action model. Likewise, a signal sending is introduced after the actitivity that corresponds to the action that is waited for.

The fact model is transformed into the class diagram. This involves that each fact (which is an *n*-ary relations between categories) is mapped to an association class that has associations to each of the classes corresponding to the categories. That process is called class association.

The interstriction model introduces further associations into the class diagram, one for each informational link between an actor and a transaction, fact bank, or communication bank. We call that process infolink introduction.

Examples of Diagram Transformation

Due to the limited space, we give examples for the first two transformations only. Figure 7 shows the collaboration diagram (upper half) for the interaction model of Figure 3 (left), and also the statechart diagram (lower half) for the business process model of Figure 3 (right). Each system or actor of the interaction model becomes an object (instance) in the collaboration diagram. A transaction is represented by a (communication) link that bears the name of the transaction (i.e., its purpose). This link is bidirectional (i.e., it does not have an arrowhead that restricts the navigability) because a transaction involves communication in both directions, from initiator to executor and back. This link can now be used to exchange the messages that correspond to the communicative acts in DEMO. Each executor has also a link to itself, which means that the execution phase is self-induced. A request and an accept message are introduced along the link with arrows that point from the initiator to the executor. They represent the first and the last communicative acts of a transaction, respectively. In the same way, a promise and a state message are attached to the link. They are passed from the executor to the initiator, and from the second and penultimate speech acts, respectively. Observe that a collaboration diagram does not require us to specify the order of messages, but we could do so with the help of sequence numbers in front of the message names.

The lower half of Figure 7 shows the statechart diagram that corresponds to the excerpt from the business process model of Figure 3. The execution phase of T6 becomes a state (which itself is a substate of the transaction state T6). Within T6/E, the initial state is forked into two concurrent threads to trigger transactions T7: Defending_complaint, and T8: Giving_advice. While T7 is triggered in any case, the transition to T8 is guarded by [c], which means that the expert is asked to give advice under a condition that has not yet been specified; the business process model only indicates that T8 is optional, not under which circumstances it is carried out. On completion of T7 (and possibly T8), T9: Passing_judgement is carried out. After that, we enter the terminal state of T6/E, which concludes the execution phase of T6.

Figure 7. Collaboration diagram and statechart diagram

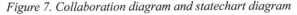

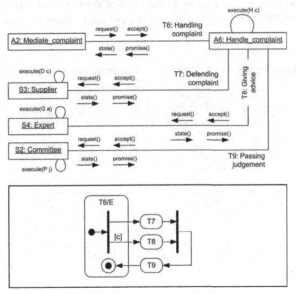

EMPIRICAL STUDIES
An Interorganizational Case Study

The ideas in this chapter were inspired by a project we carried out in spring 2004 together with two companies: a logistics provider and a large retail chain. The objective was to model the complex interorganizational business process as a basis for its reorganization. We found that the language-action perspective was successful in that scenario. One of the reasons for this is certainly the highly interactive nature of the process we studied, where communication is vital and frequent. But LAP also facilitated understanding among people who not only came from different organizations, but also worked in different domains: purchase, marketing, inbound and outbound logistics and so forth. It made a complex process more transparent to all participants (each of whom provided only a small puzzle piece to the overall picture), and it allowed them to discuss, in a constructive way, possible options for reorganization. As a result, two major areas for improvement were identified: a tighter integration between the different information systems of both companies, and a greater accuracy in the forecasts concerning incoming and outgoing commodity flows.

The framework that we have presented helped us in developing an approach to solve the first problem. The study proceeded in three steps. In the first step, we analyzed from a language-action perspective those parts of the two businesses that require cooperation. As a result, we created detailed models of information flows and information dependencies, problem graphs, and goal graphs, together with a comprehensive, textual description of the businesses and their problems in relation to their cooperation. Figure 8 shows a part of the data flows for receiving goods.

Both companies operate their own warehouse management system. The physical warehouse at the logistics provider is managed with DISA. During the night, a file detailing the goods received during the day is sent to the retail chain to update the "virtual" warehouse that is managed with SAP. This "double bookkeeping" often leads to inconsistencies between the two databases, for example, if a file is not received in order.

In the second step, we decided to address one of the problems that were elicited in the first step, namely that of integrating the respective information systems. We did so by

Figure 8. Data-flow diagram of receiving goods (excerpt)

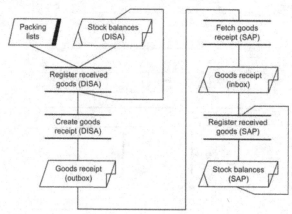

Figure 9. Partial interaction model (top) and collaboration diagram (bottom)

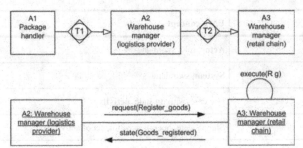

developing interaction models to bring the communicative structure to the surface. A simple example is shown in Figure 9 (top) concerning the inconsistency issue. We thereby identified the respective warehouse managers as the actors who are responsible to negotiate and control the synchronization of the warehouses.

In the third step, we used language mapping to create initial UML models for the design of an appropriate information system support. Figure 9 (bottom) shows the part of the collaboration diagram for transaction T2: Register goods. The phases "promise" and "accept" can be omitted as they are provided for in a framework contract. In the light of this model, we were able to assess that the "state" phase is not implemented in the current system. As a consequence, a failure in receiving the update file cannot be recognized by the sender and the file is not resent.

The Language-Mapping Experiment

In order to check the plausibility of the language-mapping described in Section 3 and to get additional insights, we carried out an experiment. We provided eight master students in their final year with four DEMO models of a simple order processing. From January 28 to February 4, 2005, they were supposed to express all information contained in the DEMO models with the help of an arbitrary selection of UML diagrams without any knowledge of the mapping framework. The resulting models were to be complemented by a questionnaire consisting of three parts: a table specifying the concept mapping, a graph detailing the relations between DEMO and UML diagrams, and some general questions regarding the mapping process. The results of concept and diagram mappings are shown in Tables 1 and 2.

Concerning fact diagram and business process diagram, the empirical results coincide completely with the proposed language mapping. The action diagram has been translated into an activity diagram by most participants, whereas our conceptual approach suggested a statechart diagram here. But this can also be counted as an agreement because the activity diagram is a special case of a statechart diagram.

The case of the interaction diagram is more involved. The participants of the experiment considered the use case diagram as the most appropriate counterpart. The answers to part three of the questionnaire suggest that this choice was motivated by the fact that use case diagrams are the only ones in UML that make explicit reference to actors. But empirical studies such as Maij, Toussaint, Kalshoven, Poerschke, and Zwetsloot-Schonk (2002) found that the mapping from DEMO to use cases is not straightforward. But nevertheless, this indicates that it is worthwhile to extend the framework to use cases.

Table 1. Concept mapping (summary)

DEMO concept	UML concept
Actor	**Actor**, role, swimlane
System	**System**, swimlane
Transaction	Use case, activity state, **activity**
Transaction phase (O, E, R)	Signal, state, operation, actor, set of activities
Communicative action	**Actor-use case association**, activity
Objective action	**Activty**, state
State	Guard, initial state, **state**, activity, initial & final state
Wait for state (action diagram)	Activity state, synchronisation, **state**, activity
Selection ( )	Decision diamond
Causal relation	Decision diamond , **transition**, (no counterpart)
Optional causal relation	**Decision diamond**, guard, (no counterpart)
Conditional relation	**Decision diamond** , (no counterpart)
Initiation disk	**Initial state**, transition
Category	Object, **class**
Fact type (unary, binary, ternary)	Class, association, qualifier, (no counterpart)

Table 2. Diagram mapping

DEMO diagram	UML diagram(s)
Fact Diagram	**Class Diagram (4)** Object Diagram (1) Both (1) No mapping (2)
Interaction Diagram	**Use Case Diagram (5)** Collaboration Diagram + Sequence Diagram (1) Use Case Diagram + Sequence Diagram (1) Use Case Diagram + Sequence Diagram (1)

Table 2. continued

	Activity Diagram (5)
Business Process Diagram	Use Case Diagram (1)
	Both (1)
	Sequence Diagram (1)
	Activity Diagram (6)
Action Diagram	Sequence Diagram (1)
	Statechart Diagram (1)

CONCLUSION

The purpose of this chapter is to suggest one way of mediating between the action and reaction views by providing a mapping between their associated languages, DEMO and UML. This is done by mapping their respective concepts, and eventually transforming diagrams of the former into corresponding ones of the latter. These two languages represent completely different paradigms: DEMO is an approach that is deeply rooted in linguistics and the study of human communication, while UML has many of its roots in computer science and the study of software artefacts (though by far not all). It is therefore surprising that a language mapping can be undertaken at all. It should be noted, though, that we have chosen from the set of all language-action approaches the one that best facilitates an integration with UML. Other languages of the action view might prove to be less suitable. Nevertheless, we hope that our work can contribute to narrowing the gap between organizational modeling and the design of information systems.

REFERENCES

Austin, J. L. (1962). *How to do things with words*. Oxford: Oxford University Press.

Caplat, G., & Sourrouille, J. L. (2003). Considerations about model mapping. In J. Bezivin & J. Gogolla (Eds.), *Proceedings of the Workshop in Software Model Engineering WiSME@UML 2003*. Retrieved from http://www.metamodel.com/wisme-2003/18.pdf

Denning, P. J., & Medina-Mora, R. (1995). Completing the loops. *Interfaces, 25*(3), 42-57.

Dietz, J. L. G. (1999). Understanding and modeling business processes with DEMO. In J. Akoka, M. Bouzeghoub, I. Comyn-Wattiau, & E. Métais (Eds.), *Proceedings of the 18th International Conference on Conceptual Modeling ER '99* (pp. 188-202). Berlin: Springer.

Dietz, J. L. G., & Habing, N. (2004). The notion of business process revisited. In R. Meersman & Z. Tari (Eds.), *Proceedings of the OTM Confederated International Conferences, CoopIS, DOA, and ODBASE* (pp. 85-100). Berlin: Springer.

Dignum, F., & Weigand, H. (1995). Modelling communication between cooperative systems. In J. Iivari, K. Lyytinen, & M. Rossi (Eds.), *Proceedings of the 7th International Conference on Advanced Information Systems Engineering CAiSE '95* (pp. 140-153). Berlin: Springer.

Evans, A., Maskeri, G., Sammut, P., & Willans, J. S. (2003). Building families of languages for model-driven system development. In J. Bezivin & M. Gogolla M, (Eds.), *Proceed-*

ings of the Workshop in Software Model Engineering WiSME@UML 2003. Retrieved from http://www.metamodel.com/wisme-2003/ 06.pdf

Goldkuhl, G. (1996). Generic business frameworks and action modelling. In F. Dignum, J. Dietz, E. Verharen, & H. Weigand (Eds.), *Proceedings of the First International Workshop on Communication Modeling.* Electronic Workshops in Computing. Berlin: Springer.

Goldkuhl, G., & Lind, M. (2004). The generics of business interaction — emphasizing dynamic features through the BAT model. In M. Aakhus & M. Lind (Eds.), *Proceedings of the 9th International Working Conference on the Language-Action Perspective on Communication Modelling LAP 2004* (pp. 1-26). New Brunswick, NJ: Rutgers University.

Goldkuhl, G., & Röstlinger, A. (1993). Joint elicitation of problems: An important aspect of change analysis. In D. Avison, J. Kendall, & J. DeGross (Eds.), *Human, organizational, and social dimensions of information systems development.* Amsterdam, The Netherlands: North-Holland.

Habermas, J. (1984). *The theory of communicative action 1, Reason and the rationalization of society.* Boston: Beacon Press.

Hulstijn, J., Dignum, F., & Dastani, M. (2004). Coherence constraints for agent interaction. In R. Mv. Eijk, M. P. Huget, & F. Dignum, (Eds.), *Proceedings of the Workshop on Agent Communication AAMAS 2004* (pp. 134-152). Berlin: Springer.

Johannesson, P. (1995). Representation and communication: A speech act based approach to information systems design. *Information Systems, 20*(4), 291-303.

Kethers, S., & Schoop, M. (2000). Reassessment of the action workflow approach: Empirical results. In M. Schoop, & C. Quix (Eds.), *Proceedings of the Fifth International Workshop on the Language-Action Perspective on Communication Modelling LAP 2000* (pp. 151-169). RWTH Aachen University.

Lehtinen, E., & Lyytinen, K. (1986). An action based model of information systems. *Information Systems, 11*(4), 299-317.

Liu, K., Sun, L., Barjis, J., & Dietz, J. L. G. (2003). Modelling dynamic behaviour of business organisations - extension of DEMO from a semiotic perspective. *Knowledge-Based Systems, 16*(2), 101-111.

Lodder, A. R., & Herczog, A. (1995). DiaLaw: A dialogical framework for modelling legal reasoning. In *Proceedings of the 5th International Conference on Artificial Intelligence and Law* (pp. 146-155). New York: ACM.

Maij, E., Toussaint, P. J., Kalshoven, M., Poerschke, M., & Zwetsloot-Schonk, J. H. M. (2002). Use cases and DEMO: Aligning functional features of ICT-infrastructure to business processes. *International Journal of Medical Informatics, 65*(3), 179-191

Medina-Mora, R., Winograd, T., Flores, R., & Flores, F. (1992). The action workflow approach to workflow management technology. In J. Turner & R. Kraut (Eds.), *Proceedings of the Conference on Computer-Supported Cooperative Work CSCW'92* (pp. 281-288). New York: ACM.

Miller, J., & Mukerji, J. (2003). *MDA guide* (Version 1.0.1). Needham, MA: OMG. Retrieved from http://www.omg.org/docs/omg/03-06-01.pdf

OMG. (2003). *Unified modeling language specification* (Version 1.5). Needham, MA: OMG. Retrieved from http://www.omg.org/docs/formal/03-03-01.pdf

OMG. (2004). *Enterprise collaboration architecture specification* (Version 1.0). Needham, MA: OMG. Retrieved from http://www.uml.org

Reijswoud, V. E. v. (1996). *The structure of business communication: Theory, model and application*. PhD thesis, TU Delft, The Netherlands.

Reijswoud, V. E. v., & Dietz, J. L. G. (1999). *DEMO modelling handbook*. TU Delft, The Netherlands. Retrieved from http://www.demo.nl/documents/handbook.pdf

Searle, J. R. (1969). *Speech acts, an essay in the philosophy of language*. London: Cambridge University Press.

Winograd, T., & Flores, F. (1986). *Understanding computers and cognition: A new foundation for design*. Norwood, NJ: Ablex.

Chapter VIII

Using UML Notation for Modeling Business Interaction

Sandra Haraldson, University College of Borås, Sweden

Mikael Lind, University College of Borås, Sweden

Jan Olausson, University College of Borås, Sweden

ABSTRACT

Business modeling is concerned with asking questions and giving answers to these questions. In systems development, different types of diagrams, notational rules, are used to document answers and to give inspiration to new questions. Popular notations used today are diagrams, such as use case diagrams and activity diagrams, within the unified modeling language (UML). UML is claimed to be methodology-independent. Such a claim means that there is a need for theories to guide the analyst to direct attention towards desired aspects. This chapter deals with the issue of how business interaction and its support by information systems could be modeled by modeling techniques put forward in UML. A conceptual analysis has been performed that reveals that it is possible, and there is a need to use UML together with the proposed theories in order to arrive at an intentional and conscious design. The analysis has been structured around the concepts of action, actor, and business process. The analysis shows that some basic foundations could be covered in the chosen diagrams, but that there is also a need to complement those diagrams with richer properties concerning all these concepts.

INTRODUCTION

When developing information systems, it is common to begin with some sort of business modeling in order to get an understanding of the business context in which new systems are to be used (e.g., Bubenko & Kirikova, 1999; Jacobson, Ericsson, & Jacobson, 1995). It is considerably less common to make explicit use of the results of such modeling when defining system requirements. Information systems are used to perform and support business actions and therefore, requirements ought to be derived explicitly from business models if the information system is to contribute to the effectiveness of the business and organizations' interaction with each other.

The purpose of business modeling is to generate models of the business under consideration. To generate the models, the modeler needs to gather information about the business, and therefore we can say that business modeling is about asking and answering questions. The concept of a model implies a simplified description of an object, hence, a business model is a simplified description of a business that illustrates different aspects relevant for the purpose of the model.

One purpose of using models (diagrams) in the process of business modeling is to document the answers to the questions. Different types of models are used to document the answers depending on the desired aspects that are focused. Documented answers are important sources of inspiration when deriving new questions. In this context, it is important to find arguments of what questions to put forward in order to capture the desired aspects. Such arguments can be found in theories. A theory contains concepts and categories with clear interrelations. It is thus necessary that there exist modeling primitives in the business models for capturing the concepts and categories focused in the theory.

Of course, there are approaches to information systems development (ISD) that show awareness of the connection between business and information systems (e.g. Jacobson et al., 1995), awareness in the sense that they make use of conceptual business modeling when defining requirements concerning the informational content of a system, as well as deriving the places where support from information systems is needed from the identified business tasks. One thing they seem to miss is that the intentional/social actions forming business tasks are also crucial when deciding appropriate information content as well as designing user interfaces. A system that is unclear about the business actions it is able to support and maintain information about is most likely unusable.

A systems development method could be seen as a set of guidelines to achieve certain goals (Goldkuhl, Lind, & Seigerroth, 1998). Methods advocate modeling techniques consisting of procedure, notation, and concepts. The notation helps the modeler in directing attention towards the desired aspects. A key question is, of course, about knowing what aspects to address in a certain development situation. There is thus a need for theories that help in directing such attention (c.f. Dietz, Goldkuhl, Lind, & Reijswoud, 1998; Lind & Goldkuhl, 1997).

The reason for businesses to exist is to contribute with value to other business parties. An important starting point in business modeling is therefore the interaction performed between business parties. Through such interaction, expectations are created and fulfilled between the business parties and thereby, requirements on more "internal" organizational processes can be determined. Frameworks for dyadic business interaction have been presented by a number of scholars (c.f. Ahlström, 2000; Dietz, 1999; Goldkuhl, 1998; Medina-Mora, Winograd, Flores, & Flores, 1992; Schmidt & Lindemann, 1998; Weigand & van den Heuvel, 1998).

One dominant modeling technique used within different systems development methods is the unified modeling language (UML) (c.f., e.g., Kruchten, 2000). "One characteristic of UML — in fact, the one that enables the widespread industry support that the language enjoys — is that it is methodology-independent. Regardless of the methodology that you use to perform your analysis and design, you can use UML to express the results" (OMG, 2006). The purpose of this chapter is to analyze the possibilities to use certain diagrams of UML as a way to document answers and direct attention towards desired aspects brought forward in theories of business interaction. The research question dealt with in this chapter is *how business interaction and its support by information systems could be modeled by different modeling techniques.*

Due to the limited space, we focus on business interaction situations and the role of information systems in these situations. We also delimit ourselves to exemplify with use case diagrams and activity diagrams as notational rules within UML. The applied research method is a conceptual analysis of (1) concepts found in the theory used for studying business interaction and information systems used in such context, and (2) to map these concepts to the concepts revealed in parts of UML (use case diagrams and activity diagrams).

The chapter is structured as follows. Following this introduction, we will introduce theories to be used for directing attention towards business interaction and its support by information systems. After that section, we will introduce our understanding of the used parts in UML: use case diagrams and activity diagrams as modeling techniques. The analysis will compare important aspects of the proposed theories and of the UML. In the end of the chapter, we will bring forward some highlights from the study and propose some issues for further research.

THEORY ABOUT BUSINESS INTERACTION AND INFORMATION SYSTEMS

The theory used in this chapter for paying attention to essentials in business interaction and information systems has its foundations in socioinstrumental pragmatism (SIP) in which socioinstrumental action is seen as the basic unit of analysis. This section is therefore introduced with a discussion of socioinstrumental action as the basic unit of analysis. Following this discussion, a theory of business interaction, which has been applied in many business development cases, will be brought forward. Then there will be a discussion of how information systems can be interpreted given such a basic unit of analysis.

The Notion of Socioinstrumental Action

The basic concept of socioinstrumental action is action (Goldkuhl & Röstlinger, 2002). An action is a purposeful and meaningful behavior of a human being. A human being intervenes in the world in order to create some differences. An important distinction is made between the result and the effects of the action (von Wright, 1971). The action result lies within the range of the actor and the action effects may arise as consequences outside the control of the actor. An action is performed in the present based on a history and aims at the future (Goldkuhl & Röstlinger, 2002). A social action is an action oriented towards other persons (Weber, 1978). The action can be a communicative act, for example, someone saying something to another person, or material. Material actions count as social actions if they are directed to other persons (Goldkuhl, 2001; Goldkuhl & Röstlinger, 2002). Actor relationships between the intervening actor and the recipient are established through social actions (Habermas, 1984).

An organization consists of humans, artifacts and other resources, and actions. Humans (often supported by artifacts) perform actions in the name of the organization (Ahrne, 1994; Taylor, 1993). Actions are performed within the organization — internal acts — and there are also external acts towards other organizations (e.g., customers or suppliers). Humans act in order to achieve ends (von Wright, 1971). Human action often aims at making material changes. Humans do however, not only act in the material world: they also act communicatively towards other humans. Austin (1962) and Searle (1969) mean that to communicate is also to act. Human action is about making a difference, where such difference can have impact in the social world as well as in the material world.

A generic model of social action, including both communicative and material acts, is presented by Goldkuhl (2001) and Goldkuhl and Röstlinger (2002). For example, an order from a customer to a supplier is a communicative act. The delivery of goods from the supplier to the customer is a material act. Each of these actions is performed by one business party (an "interventionist") addressed to the other party (the recipient). Since they are actions directed from one actor towards another actor, they must both be considered as social actions. Language is not the only medium for interacting with other people. The delivery of a product to a customer is not only to be seen as a change of place of some material stuff. In this context, it must also be considered as a fulfillment of a request and a promise made earlier. Actions are often multifunctional. One example of multifunctionality is that a customer order both represents a *request* to the supplier to deliver something and a *commitment* of paying for the delivery. There also exists a duality of actions. The performer of an act (in an organizational context) both acts on behalf of himself/herself, and on behalf of the organization that the performer represents. Further, acts are multiconsequential. This means that a certain act can trigger several acts. Since there exists a duality of acts and since these are multiconsequential, one can distinguish between interorganizational acts, that is, acts directed towards a party in another organization, and intraorganizational acts, acts directed towards somebody in the same organization.

Understanding Business Interaction

An organization's existence is determined by its capability to contribute with value to its customers. A business means that agents, acting on behalf of the organization (c.f Ahrne, 1994), perform actions oriented towards somebody else (Goldkuhl & Röstlinger, 2002). In a business interaction, two roles can be distinguished: supplier and customer. Based on communicative (Habermas, 1984) and language/action theories (Searle, 1969), it can be found that a business interaction sequence involves establishing and realizing expectations between the two parties.

Frameworks for dyadic business interaction have been presented by a number of scholars: confer for example, Ahlström (2000) for an overview of some frameworks. A well-known reference model for electronic markets has been presented by Schmidt and Lindemann (1998). Within the language/action (L/A) tradition, there are several business interaction frameworks: see for example Dietz (1999), Goldkuhl (1998), Weigand and van den Heuvel (1998), and Medina-Mora et al. (1992); all building on the speech act insights by Searle (1969). These L/A approaches are important since they emphasize actions, communication, and interactions in the relations between customer and supplier.

In the BAT model (Goldkuhl & Lind, 2004), this business interaction sequence is divided into a number of different communicative and material exchanges. These are exchanges of proposals, commitments, fulfillments, as well as assessments (c.f. Figure 1). These exchanges constitute a business transaction. These exchanges are constituted of interchanges in patterns of initiatives and responses where each response also serves as an initiative for another response (Linell, 1998; Schiffrin, 1994).

The BAT model is a framework describing generic business interaction logic (Goldkuhl, 1998). The basis is about one party having a capability (= supplier) and another party lacking this capability (= customer). These capabilities are developing (on each side) during business interaction. BAT describes interaction between particular actors as well as interaction when expressing a general interest aimed at potential customers/suppliers (Goldkuhl & Lind, 2004). Two levels of business interaction are thus distinguished; the market level and the dyadic level (see Figure 1). On the market level, suppliers and customers search for knowledge and contacts concerning the corresponding party. On this level, there is also an exposure of a supplier's capability towards a market of customers, and vice versa. The interaction on this level is, according to BAT, driven by a *general business interest* of both suppliers and customers.

Figure 1. Levels of business interaction (Goldkuhl & Lind, 2004)

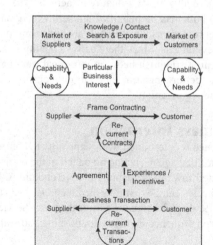

Figure 2. The constituents of frame contracting (BAT frame contracting transaction model, Goldkuhl & Lind, 2004)

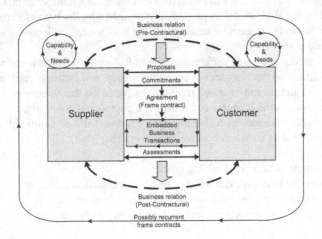

When a contact is established between a particular supplier and a particular customer, the general business interest is turned into a particular business interest. The business interaction moves to the dyadic level. On this level, there is a distinction made between frame contracting and business transaction (see Figure 2 and Figure 3). Sometimes frame contracts govern business transactions. Other times, business transactions are instead governed by separate (single) transaction orders and no frame contract exists.

Figure 2 shows that frame contracting consists of two phases of exchange prior to recurrent business transactions (covered in Figure 3), and a phase of assessment after the

Figure 3. The constituents of the business transaction (BAT business transaction model, Goldkuhl & Lind, 2004)

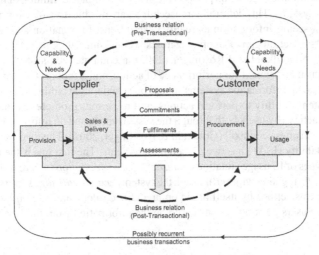

realization of these business transactions. The frame contract agreed upon in the commitment phase of frame contracting thus governs the realization of business transactions.

From Figures 1, 2, and 3, it can be derived that there are a number of phases of interaction covered by the BAT model. A phase is distinguished by the type of exchange made between the parties in the business interaction. In the BAT model, both communicative and material exchanges are acknowledged.

The BAT model proposes different aspects of *dynamic* business interaction. This concerns the continuous development of capability, needs, and business relations, but also recurrent frame contracts and business transactions based on the assessments made. The basic unit of analysis is the business act, which is a component consisting of action pairs, exchanges, business transactions and transaction groups (Lind & Goldkuhl, 2003). The model is characterized as a comprehensive framework that (ibid):

- Views business action as a building block,
- Emphasizes the exchange character of business interaction and
- Adopts a symmetric view on business parties and their interaction,
- Acknowledges communicative, material, and financial interaction.

The BAT model is a generic framework for business dyads to be understood as a pragmatic instrument. The scope of the model is to be used for evaluation, modeling, and design of business interaction (ibid).

Understanding Information Systems

Information systems are closely related to human action. Such social and organizational issues are handled within linguistic (Dietz & Widdershoven, 1992; Goldkuhl & Lyytinen, 1982; Winograd & Flores, 1986) and semiotic perspectives (Stamper, 2000) for understanding information systems. Lyytinen (1981) claims that a substantial part of a practice is the business language, which includes vocabulary, as well as rules for communicative action.

Goldkuhl (1995) bases his view on information systems on a communicative action perspective. This view is based upon, but transcends, the notion of e-message proposed by Langefors. "A communicative action perspective gives an alternate definition of information and information systems. This definition transcends a narrow objectivistic view of information; that is, just seeing information as reality descriptions. Information and information systems are parts of action games in organizations" (Goldkuhl, 1995, p. 77).

According to Goldkuhl and Röstlinger (2002), a computerized system is an action system. It is both an instrument for performance of action, and a support tool for humans to perform their actions. Information systems should be actable. IS actability is defined as "an information system's ability to perform actions, and to permit, promote and facilitate the performance of actions by users both through the system and based on information from the system, in some business context" (Goldkuhl & Röstlinger, 2002). The theory of information systems actability (ISAT) has two essential ingredients. The first one is the distinction between three types of IS usage situations: *interactive usage situation* (where users perform actions interactively together with and through the system), *automatic usage situations* (where the system performs actions by itself based on predefined rules), and *consequential usage situations* (where users perform actions based on the information from the system).

Sjöström and Goldkuhl (2002) have further related these different usage situations to different types of actions. Sjöström and Goldkuhl (2002) claim the need for focusing on social actions and the action relationships between the involved actors instead of focusing on usage situations. Thereby, the focus is aimed towards human-to-human communication in which the IT-system takes part. The different types of actions that Sjöström and Goldkuhl (2002) acknowledge in this context are *interactive action*, *automatic action,* and *consequential action*.

The second ingredient is the interpretation of an IS as consisting of (Goldkuhl & Röstlinger, 2002) an *action potential* (a predefined and regulated repertoire of actions), *actions* performed through and by the system, an *action memory* (a memory of earlier performed actions including prerequisites for actions), and *messages* and *documents* (where some documents are action media for user's interactive actions).

UML as a Modeling Language

The UML first started as an effort by Booch and Rumbaugh, in 1994, to combine their two methods: the Booch and OMT methods. The effort was therefore not only to create a common notation, and the first public draft of what today is the UML was presented as the unified method. They were soon joined by Ivar Jacobson, the creator of the objectory method at Rational Corporation. As a group, the three persons behind UML (i.e., Booch, Rumbaugh, and Jacobson) came to be known as the three amigos. It was at this point that they decided to focus on a common diagramming notation — the UML — rather than on a common method. "The Unified Modeling Language is a visual language for specifying, constructing and documenting the artifacts of systems" Larman (2005). In the definition, the word *visual* is a key point: the UML is the de facto standard *diagramming notation* for drawing or presenting pictures (with some text) related to software design, primarily that of OO software. The latest version of UML (2.0) is documented in OMG (2005).

The UML vocabulary is built upon three foundations: elements, relations, and diagrams. Elements are abstractions and the most important components in a model. Relations hold the elements together and in the diagrams, interesting collections of elements are gathered. There are four different types of elements in UML; structural, behavioral, grouped, and commented elements. In this section, the first two will be described. Structural elements can be compared to nouns in linguistics. They are static and often represent conceptual or physical elements. Six different kinds of *structural elements* can be found in UML; classes, interfaces, collaborations, use cases, components, and nodes. *Behavioral elements* can be compared to verbs in linguistics. Contrary to structural elements they are dynamic and represent different conducts in time and space. These behaviors are the most fundamental elements that are part of a UML model. They are often connected to different structural elements of classes and objects. UML consists of two behavioral elements; interaction and state machine. A diagram is a depiction of several different elements, often created to show a system from different perspectives. Theoretically, one diagram can contain a countless amount of combinations of elements and relations, but practically, they are limited to the nine most common combinations such as the class diagram, the object diagram, the use case diagram, the sequence diagram, the collaboration diagram, the state diagram, the activity diagram, the component diagram, and the realization diagram.

A conceptual understanding is important when choosing a modeling language because the concepts that are used also imply that a certain meaning is adopted. All modeling languages are building upon and influenced by some kind of perspective, included in the different modeling elements. Therefore, we list some of the most central UML concepts that constitute the two diagrams in focus (i.e., activity diagram and use case diagram) that we identified as relevant to focus more closely in this study. In this study, we are interested in modeling what the descriptions of UML notation labels behavioral modeling. In the following sections, we describe *use case diagrams* and *activity diagrams* in short, together with concepts identified as central for each type of diagram.

Use Cases

The idea of employing use cases to describe functional requirements was introduced in 1986 by Ivar Jacobson (one of the main contributors to UML). The idea of use cases was seminal and widely appreciated. Although many have made contributions to the subject, arguably the most influential and coherent next step in defining what use cases are and how to write them came from Alistair Cockburn, based on his earlier work and writings from 1992 onwards.

According to Larman (2005), use case models and use case diagrams are frequently mixed up, and he acknowledges that use cases are primarily textual documents and not diagrams. Therefore, use case modeling is primarily an act of writing text, and use case modeling as an act of drawing diagrams is only secondary. Nevertheless, use cases as text documents are of minor interests in this study and the focus is on use cases as diagrams. A use case diagram could be used as a complement to a use case model in order to show the names of use cases and actors, and their relationships. The use case diagram represents a context diagram of a system and its environment. Use cases (both as written text and drawn diagrams) could be seen as a tool for showing related success or failure scenarios that describe an actor using a system to support a goal. Larman (2005) points out that use cases are of value because they emphasize the user goals and perspective.

Diagram Description

As mentioned above, UML provides the use case diagrams notation to illustrate names of use cases and actors, and the relationships between them. According to Larman (2005), a use case diagram provides a succinct visual context diagram for the system, and it illustrates the external actors and how they use the system. Moreover, Larman (2005) acknowledges that, as a contextual diagram, it shows the system boundaries, describing what lies outside and what inside, and how the system is used. Larman (2005) also points out that it serves as a communicative tool that summarizes the behavior of a system and its actors, and that the diagram should be created in connection with an actor-goal list.

A use case shows *what* a system does, and not *how* it is done. A use case defines the behavior of a system (or parts of it), and it gives a description of a number of activities that result in a measurable outcome for the user. A use case often consists of a main flow and a series of alternative flows that point out things that could go wrong or valid alternatives besides the main flow. Use cases have proven to be efficient in testing and user documentation and to facilitate requirements engineering. A use case diagram contains one or more use cases, actors, and their relations. In practice, this implies the modeling of the context where certain behavior is valid, or those requirements needed for certain behavior to be completed. It is also possible to place comments and include limitations in the diagrams. As mentioned above, it is possible to employ use case diagrams in two areas: system context or system requirements. Modeling a system context implies drawing a rectangle around the system and identifying the different actors that are found within and outside the system boundaries. The diagram is used to state which roles the different actors are playing. Modeling system requirements implies a definition of the purpose of the system, that is, what the system is intended to do independent of how it should be performed. The diagram is used to state the system's behavior as it appears to an outside observer.

Activity Diagrams
Diagram Description
According to Larman (2005), the semantics of activity diagrams are loosely based on Petri nets, an important computational theory in computer science. A UML activity diagram shows sequential and parallel activities in a process. They are useful for modeling business processes, workflows, data flows, and complex algorithms.

A UML activity diagram gives a rich notation to show sequences of activities, including parallel activities. According to Larman (2005), activity diagrams might be applied to any perspective or purpose, but they are popular for visualizing business workflows and processes, and use cases. Furthermore, Larman (2005) states that UML activity diagrams are highly suitable for business process modeling. Activity diagrams can also be complemented by data flow models.

Larman (2005) acknowledges a few guidelines that have emerged in activity modeling, and these include the following statements: This technique proves most valuable for very complex processes, usually involving many parties. Use case text suffices for simple processes. If modeling a business process, take advantage of the "rake" notation and sub-activity diagrams.

Central Concepts
An actor in UML is seen as something with behavior, and the term is used synonymously with that of a role. An actor could be a person, a computer system, or an organization. The notion of action in use cases has a more detailed definition. An actor in use cases is anything with behavior, including the system under discussion (SuD) itself when it calls upon the services of other systems. Primary and supporting actors will appear in the action steps of the use case text. Actors are roles played not only by people, but also by organizations, software, and machines. According to Larman (2005), three kinds of external actors could be identified in relation to the SuD: (1) Primary actor – has user goals fulfilled through using services of the SuD, and this actor is essential to identify in order to find the user goals that drives the use cases. (2) Supporting actor – provides a service (for example information) to the SuD. The automated payment authorization service is one example. The supporting actor is often a computer system, but could also be an organization or a person. This second actor is important to identify to clarify external interfaces and protocols. (3) Offstage actor – is the third type of actor. This type of actor has an interest in the behavior of the use case, but is not primary or supporting. A government tax agency could serve as an example of an offstage actor, and this third actor is important to ensure that all necessary interests are identified and satisfied. Offstage actor interests are sometimes subtle or easy to miss unless these actors are explicitly named. An actor is seen as the user in use cases, and the term is used synonymously with that of a role, where a role is the behavior of something that

participates in a given situation (Strand, 2001). Behavior is visible action effects, including possible outcomes (Strand, 2001).

In activity diagrams there is a distinction between two types of states; activity and action (Strand, 2001). It is not possible to divide an action, and it will be completed irrespective of what might happen outside this specific action. On the contrary, activities can be divided into further action diagrams in order to reach a greater richness of detail. This means that an activity could be regarded as a collection of actions.

A scenario is a specific sequence of actions and interactions between actors and the system; it is also called a use case instance. It is one particular story of using a system, or one path through the use case, for example, the scenario of successfully purchasing items with cash, or the scenario of failing to purchase items because of a credit payment denial.

In the UML notation, you can model sequential actions, which implies that one action is followed by another action, and so on. In UML these are called transitions, and they are modeled as lines drawn to the connection line between different activities.

ANALYSIS: THEORY-INSPIRED MODELING WITH UML NOTATION

In the section "Theory about business interaction and information systems," we identified a number of core concepts essential to include in a model according to the theories used as a base for this study. This collection of core concepts constitutes the essential business elements (i.e., the essential modeling aspects). In this section, we analyze the possibility to model these concepts with UML. This means that we determine whether the core concepts identified from the theory also are present in the UML language. However, the question is not only to identify the concepts in UML and the possibility to use them in modeling, it is also essential that we analyze the meaning of each concept.

Table 1. Concepts related to action

Concept	**Theories:** SIP, BAT, ISAT	**Modeling tools:** Use case and activity diagrams
Action	Main concept Different characteristics (communicative, material, social)	Important concept
Action result	X	-
Initiative	X	= first part of interaction
Response	X	= second part of interaction
Interactive action	X (in relation to IS)	Described in use case but not explicit
Automatic action	X (in relation to IS)	Described in use case but not explicit
Consequential action	X (in relation to IS)	Described in use case but not explicit

Table 2. Concepts related to the actor

Concept	**Theories:** SIP, BAT, ISAT	**Modeling tools:** Use case and activity diagrams
Actor	X	X Different characteristics (primary, supporting, offstage)
Agent	X	-
Actor relationships	X	-
Organization	Note: Different characteristics (supplier, customer)	X
User	X	X
Role	X	X

In our conception of use cases and activity diagrams as modeling tools (notation), the two most dominating concepts, according to our theoretical lenses, are *action* (see Table 1) and *actor* (see Table 2). Founded in action as the basic unit of analysis, we also derive more action-oriented holistic concepts that are related to *business processes* (see Table 3). Those basic concepts are also core categories brought forward in theory. In this section, we will discuss these concepts, differences, and similarities in order to create an understanding for the benefit of combining a modeling language such as UML (see section UML as a modeling language) with theories such as the ones presented previously (see section "Theory about business interaction and information systems") in a theory-inspired modeling situation with the two diagrams put forward in UML.

We use the tables (see Table 1, 2, and 3) to relate concepts in the used theories and UML. Each table covers each of the core concepts mentioned above. The first column in the tables shows the concept, the second column marks the existence in used theories, and the third marks the existence in UML. The existence is marked with an X and the table also contains comments. Table 1 shows concepts and categories related to the core concept of action.

The notion of *action* is the basic unit of analysis in both the theories and in the modeling tools. The conception of action does, however, differ. In the theories, there is a distinction made between the *action result* and the *action effect*. The action result is under the control of the performing actor, but not the effect, whereas this distinction is not made in UML. In UML it is possible to illustrate different states of an object, but there is no distinction made in relation to an actor's control.

When an actor acts, it can either be an *initiative* for another actor to act or a *response* to a previous action. Use cases are in-depth descriptions of the possible actions in a system. We can see benefits in categorizing these actions in the three categories, *interactive, automatic, and consequential actions,* in order to broaden the understanding of the information systems use. In the theories, one can see that the properties of an action that are important for making abstractions are much more comprehensive as compared to what the modeling tools put forward.

Table 3. Concepts related to a business process

Concept	Theories: SIP, BAT, ISAT	Modeling tool: Use case and activity diagrams
Action patterns	X	X (transitions as one kind of concept binding several actions together)
Exchange	Different characteristics (communicative, material) as well as different types (proposal, commitment, fulfillment, assessment)	-
Business transaction	X	Workflow/process
Action potential	X (in relation to IS)	X
Action memory	X (in relation to IS)	-
System	X	X
Environment	X (Context)	X

Let us move further in the analysis by concentrating on the next core concept; the one who performs the actions—the actor. Table 2 shows the concepts that are related to the actor.

In UML, all objects using a system (or the system under discussion), that is, the *user*, could be regarded as an *actor*. There is no distinction between human and nonhuman actors: instead an actor is defined by its role. Actor relationships in UML do not exclusively imply relations between human actors, which was the intention with this concept. Nevertheless, it could be argued that it is possible to illustrate indirect relations between human actors if combining several use cases in one. In the communication theories presented, there is a distinction between human actors and other kinds of actors. Humans are actors, but not the only kind of actor. *Organizations* are conceived to be actors in both the theory and in the modeling tool. Organizations can, however, not act by themselves. They must act through their *agents*. Employees of an organization are agents of that organization. These human agents are acting on behalf of the organization. Humans are, however, not the only agents. Different artifacts, as for example IT systems, can be given *roles* as agents performing organizational actions. Actions to be performed by such agents have, however, been specified by human agents. Whenever two actors interact, the interaction creates a *relationship* between the actors. In the theories one can see that the notion of an actor goes beyond the user concept. We believe that it is important to conceive the different dimensions and abstractions of actor in order to achieve a contextual understanding of action performed by and with an information system.

Let us now move further in the analysis by concentrating on the next core concept: the more holistic one covering several interrelated actions–the business process. Table 3 shows different concepts that group actions together into what we have chosen to call a business process.

Use cases depict which actions a *system* is able to perform and not how they are performed, and for that reason it is hard to visualize the process in this diagram. In activity diagrams, however, sequences of actions (as a kind of workflow/process) can be traced that, according to us, can be regarded as a process. A business process is, according to many scholars, to be conceived as a collection of activities that produce value to some other party. The notion of business process can, however, vary a lot (c.f., e.g., Keen & Knapp, 1996). An organization interacts with outside actors on whom they depend. It serves clients with products, and it is served by suppliers providing preproducts. An organization ceases to exist if it cannot serve other parts in the society. Communication plays an important role in an organization's *interaction* with its *environment*. According to BAT, business agreements are developed and established through communication. Mutual commitments are created and resolved in international *patterns of action*. Such commitments must be forwarded into the organization and remembered for future actions (e.g., for fulfillment of the *business transaction*), this is the organization's *action memory*. In UML, the collection of use cases could be seen as the system's action repertoire (i.e., the *action potential*), because it holds the different actions (with variations in behavior) that a system is able to perform. IT systems play roles in the organization's communication with outside actors. Important functions of IT systems could, for example, be keeping track of made proposals and commitments in the *exchanges* constituting the business transaction.

There is a technological base for IT systems providing hardware and software for executing rule-governed artificial behavior. This rule-governed behavior implies identification and specification of predefined communicative actions (action potential) to be performed with support of the IT system. These communicative actions of the IT system have impact on the actions performed by humans within and outside the organization. Some actions (in interactive use situations) are performed by humans and IT systems together. These actions are coproduced by the human and artificial agents. The different agents have, of course, distinct roles in such a cooperation based on their respective human and artificial character. Concerning the concept of business process, it can be seen that the theories provide a wider variety of aspects as compared to the modeling tools, as well as thorough coordinative dimensions of business processes, which needs to be taken into consideration when constructing meaningful holistic concepts founded in the notion of action.

Modeling business interaction demands diagrams that can document the important aspects that the modeler wants to elicit. Therefore, it is important that the notation used in the diagrams and the theories inspiring the modeling harmonize. The analysis shows that it is possible to use UML together with the used theories, but that there is a need for a richer notation revealing more comprehensive dimensions for all the core concepts (action, actor, and business process) brought forward in this analysis.

CONCLUSION

From our theoretical analysis, we can see that it is possible to use UML (use case and action diagrams) to model business interactions. Business modeling is about asking questions and giving answers. Theories are instruments for directing attention towards desired aspects of an organization, and methods are normative instruments for capturing the answers. In this chapter, we have shown the possibilities and benefits of combining the chosen theories and the UML notation in business modeling situations.

In this chapter, we have looked at modeling business interaction by using some parts of the UML notation. The theory used to understand the constituents of business interaction has its foundation in the notion of social action. The analysis, in which the possibility to represent important business interaction concepts by chosen UML diagrams was studied, has intentionally been structured based on essential concepts in the theory. These concepts have been *action, actor,* and *business process*. In order to extract relevant knowledge concerning business interaction, we find that it is necessary that these concepts can be represented in the chosen diagrams. Without making use of a solid theoretical foundation we might still be able to extract relevant knowledge, but it would imply that business modeling is rather driven by chance (c.f. Cronholm & Goldkuhl, 2002; Olausson & Lind, 2005). We claim that we cannot afford such an approach when using different types of diagrams, and since UML is claimed to be methodology-independent, the use of UML modeling techniques must be complemented by theory-inspired arguments of why we focus certain aspects in a business modeling situation. The modeling situation must be driven by the modeler's intentions and consciousness.

In some respect, we have found in the analysis that the studied diagrams do, however, *not* provide a sufficiently rich notation. In order to arrive at relevant business models, it is important that the diagrams in which the models are expressed support the theories used for gathering information about the business in design. In order to capture relevant knowledge of business interaction situations, we therefore propose that the studied diagrams should be complemented by:

1.   A richer action concept
2.   A distinction between the action performed by an IS and the actor on whose behalf it is acting
3.   More comprehensive dimensions of business processes covering both transformation and coordination

In this chapter, we used use cases and action diagrams in order to show the benefits of a theory-inspired way of working. The theories do also include concepts not used in the diagrams, so it would be interesting to look upon other parts of UML in order to get a full understanding of how UML can be used to capture all relevant aspects for modeling business interaction. For further research, we also propose an empirical study using the UML notation when applying the proposed theories. Related work in this area has been done by Ågerfalk and Eriksson (2004) and Rittgen (2006). They have suggested different constructive approaches to derive UML models based on language/action models.

REFERENCES

Ågerfalk, P. J., & Eriksson, O. (2004). Action-oriented conceptual modeling. *European Journal of Information Systems, 13*(1), 80-92.

Ahlström, M. (2000). *Offset management for large systems—A multibusiness marketing activity.* PhD dissertation, Dept of Management and Economics, Linköping University.

Ahrne, G. (1994). *Social organizations. Interaction inside, outside and between organization.* London: Sage.

Austin, J. L. (1962). *How to do things with words.* Oxford: Oxford University Press.

Bubenko, J . A. Jr., & Kirikova, M. (1999). Improving the quality of requirements specifications by enterprise modeling. In A. G. Nilsson, et al. (Eds.), *Perspectives on business modeling: Understanding and changing organisations.* Heidelberg: Springer Verlag.

Cronholm, S., & Goldkuhl, G. (2002, September 12-14). *Actable information systems — Quality ideals put into practice*. Paper presented at the Eleventh Conference On Information Systems (ISD 2002), Riga, Latvia.

Dietz, J. L. G. (1999). Understanding and modeling business processes with DEMO. In *Proceedings of the 18th International Conference on Conceptual Modeling (ER'99)*, (LNCS). Berlin, Germany: Springer.

Dietz, J. L.G., Goldkuhl, G., Lind, M., & Reijswoud, V. E. (1998, June 25). The communicative action paradigm for business modeling — A research agenda. In *Proceedings of the third LAP Conference on The Language Action Perspective on Communication Modeling*, Märsta, Sweden.

Dietz, J. L. G., & Widdershoven, G. A. M. (1992). A comparison of the linguistic theories of Searle and Habermas as a basis for communication support systems. In *Linguistic instruments in knowledge engineering* (pp. 121-130). New York: North-Holland.

Goldkuhl, G. (1995). Information as action and communication. In B. Dahlbom (Ed.), *The infological equation — essays in honor of Börje Langefors*. Göteborg University.

Goldkuhl, G. (1998). *The six phases of business processes — business communication and the exchange of value*. Accepted to the 12th Biennial ITS (ITS'98) Conference — Beyond Convergence, Stockholm.

Goldkuhl, G. (2001). Communicative vs. material actions: Instrumentality, sociality, and comprehensibility. In *Proceedings of the 6th International Workshop on the Language Action Perspective (LAP2001)*, RWTH, Aachen.

Goldkuhl, G., & Lind, M. (2004). The generics of business interaction — Emphasizing dynamic features through the BAT model. In *Proceedings of the 9th International Working Conference on the Language-Action Perspective on Communication Modeling*, Rutgers University, The State University of New Jersey, New Brunswick.

Goldkuhl, G., Lind, M., & Seigerroth, U. (1998). Method integration as a learning process. In N. Jayaratna, B. Fitzgerald, T. Wood-Harper, & J. M. Larrasquet (Eds.), *Training and education of methodology practitioners and researchers*. London: Springer-Verlag.

Goldkuhl, G., & Lyytinen, K. (1982). A language action view of information systems. In *Proceedings of the 3rd International Conference on Information Systems,* Ann Arbor, MI.

Goldkuhl, G., & Röstlinger, A. (2002). Towards an integral understanding of organisations and information systems: Convergence of three theories. In *Proceedings of the 5th International Workshop on Organisational Semiotics*, Delft, The Netherlands.

Habermas, J. (1984). *The theory of communicative action 1*. Boston: Beacon Press.

Jacobson, I., Ericsson, M., & Jacobson, A. (1995). *The object advantage — business process reengineering with object technology*. Boston: ACM Press.

Keen, P. G. W., & Knapp E. M. (1996). *Every manager's guide to business processes — A glossary of key terms & concepts for today's business leader*. Boston: Harvard Business School Press.

Kruchten, P. (2000). *The rational unified process — An introduction* (2nd ed.). Boston: Addison Wesley

Larman, G. (2005). *Applying UML and patterns: An introduction to object-oriented analysis and design and iterative development*. Westford, MA: Courier.

Lind, M., & Goldkuhl, G. (1997). Reconstruction of different business processes — a theory and method driven analysis. In F. Dignum & J. Dietz (Eds.), *The language/action perspective. Proceedings of the Second International Workshop on Communication Modeling,* Eindhoven University of Technology, The Netherlands.

Lind, M., & Goldkuhl, G. (2003). The constituents of business interaction — Generic layered patterns. *Data & Knowledge Engineering, 47*(3), 299-40.

Linell, P.(1998). *Approaching dialogue. Talk, interaction, and contexts in dialogical perspectives.* Amsterdam, The Netherlands: John Benjamins Publishers.

Lyytinen, K. (1981). *Language oriented development of information systems – Methodological and theoretical foundations.* Licentiate thesis, University of Jyväskylä

Medina-Mora, R., Winograd, T., Flores, R., & Flores, F. (1992). The action workflow approach to workflow management technology. In J. Turner & R. Kraut (Eds.), *Proceedings of the Conference on Computer-Supported Cooperative Work (CSCW'92).* New York: ACM Press.

Olausson, J., & Lind, M. (2005, August 15-27). *Modeling assignments.* Accepted to the 14th Conference on Information Systems Development, Karlstad University, Sweden.

OMG. (2005). *Unified modeling language: Superstructure* (Version 2.0). Retrieved from http://www.omg.org/cgi-bin/apps/doc?formal/05-07-04.pdf

OMG. (2006). *Introduction to OMG's UML.* Retrieved January 01, 2006, from http://www. omg.org/gettingstarted/what_is_uml.htm

Rittgen, P. (2006). A language-mapping approach to action-oriented development of information aystems. *European Journal of Information Systems, 15*(1).

Schiffrin, D. (1994). *Approaches to discourse.* Oxford: Blackwell.

Schmidt, B. F., & Lindemann, M. A. (1998). Elements of a reference model for electronic markets. In E. Sprague (Eds.), *Proceedings of the 31st Hawaii International Conference on System Science (HICSS'98).*

Searle, J. R. (1969). Speech acts. *An essay in the philosophy of language.* London: Cambridge University Press.

Sjöström, J., & Goldkuhl, G. (2002). *Information systems as instruments for communication — Refining the actability concept.* Accepted to the 5th International Workshop on Organisational Semiotics, Delft, The Netherlands.

Stamper, R. (2000). Organisational semiotics: Informatics without the computer? In K. Liu, R. J. Clarke, P. B. Andersen, & R. K. Stamper (Eds.), *Information, organisation and technology: Studies in organisational semiotics.* Norwell: Kluwer Academic Publishers.

Strand, L. (2001). *UML & RUP — Att lyckas med OO-projekt.* Decendo, Stockholm, Sweden.

Taylor, J. R. (1993). *Rethinking the theory of organizational communication: How to read an organisation.* Norwood, NJ: Ablex.

von Wright, G. H. (1971). *Explanation and understanding.* London: Rouledge & Kegan Paul.

Weber, M. (1978). *Economy and society.* Berkeley: University of California Press.

Weigand, H., & van den Heuvel, W-J. (1998). Metapatterns for electronic commerce transactions based on FLBC. In *Proceedings of the 31st Annual Hawaii International Conference on System Sciences* (pp. 261-270).

Winograd, T., & Flores, F. (1986). *Understanding computers and cognition: A new foundation for design.* Norwood, NJ: Ablex.

Section IV

Applying UML
in Enterprise Modeling

Chapter IX

Using UML for Reference Modeling

Peter Fettke, Institute for Information Systems (IWi) at the German Research
Center for Artificial Intelligence (DFKI), Germany

Peter Loos, Institute for Information Systems (IWi) at the German Research
Center for Artificial Intelligence (DFKI), Germany

Jörg Zwicker, Institute for Information Systems (IWi) at the German Research
Center for Artificial Intelligence (DFKI), Germany

ABSTRACT

Within the information systems field, information modeling is a vital instrument to develop information systems. However, the modeling process is often resource consuming and faulty. As a way to overcome these failures and to improve and to accelerate the development of enterprise-specific models, the concept of reference modeling has been introduced. A reference model is a conceptual framework, and may be used as a blueprint for information systems development. Yet little research has been undertaken on using unified modeling language (UML) for reference modeling. In this paper, we analyze potentials and limitations of using UML for reference modeling. Our investigation is based on the framework for research on conceptual modeling proposed by Wand and Weber. The framework comprises four elements: reference modeling languages, reference modeling methods, reference models, and reference modeling context. Each framework element is discussed with respect to possible applications and limitations of UML for reference modeling. As well, we illustrate further research opportunities.

INTRODUCTION

Within the information systems field, information modeling is a vital instrument to develop information systems (Frank, 1999; Mylopoulos, 1998; Scheer & Hars, 1992; Wand & Weber, 2002). However, the modeling process is often resource consuming and faulty. As a way to overcome these failures and to improve and to accelerate the development of enterprise-specific models, the concept of reference modeling has been introduced (Mertins & Bernus, 1998; Mišic & Zhao, 2000; Scheer & Nüttgens, 2000).

Reference modeling addresses the whole enterprise from perspectives that are relevant for business engineering, business process management, and information systems analysis and design (Becker, Kugeler, & Rosemann, 2003; Rosemann, 2003a, b). Application fields comprise strategic and organizational issues as well as the design of information systems for multitude business fields within an enterprise. Besides the construction of concrete reference models, a challenge of reference modeling research is the development of comprehensive techniques for the construction and application of reference models. This encompasses the development of language basic and methodical procedures for model's construction and application, as well as construction of approaches to fulfill specific requirements for tool support.

To explicitly represent a reference model, a modeling language is utilized. In theory and practice, a standardized language for reference modeling has not been established (Fettke & Loos, 2004). Yet little research has been undertaken on using Unified Modeling Language (UML) for reference modeling. The objective of this chapter is to analyze potentials and limitations of using UML for reference modeling. This study is of both practical and theoretical relevance. From a practical point of view, UML is a well-known, general-purpose, tool-supported, process-independent, and industry-standardized modeling language for visualizing, describing, specifying, and documenting information system artifacts (Fettke, 2005, p. 2921). Using UML for reference (enterprise) modeling supports strategic and organizational issues that go beyond the design of information systems. Hence, an analysis of UML for reference modeling can give some useful and interesting insights.

Beside the practical relevance, this study is of importance for the theory of enterprise modeling in general, and for the theory of reference modeling in particular. The limitations of using UML for reference modeling show gaps and areas of improvements. The results of the investigation represent a meaningful basis for the enhancement of reference modeling with their methods, tools and so forth, on the one hand, and the UML for supporting reference modeling on the other hand. Therefore, the study can stimulate the scientific progress of reference modeling and UML design.

The chapter unfolds as follows: After this introduction, the study's theoretical background is discussed. Based on the framework for research on conceptual modeling proposed by Wand and Weber (Wand & Weber, 2002), section three analyzes UML-based reference modeling from the view of reference modeling languages, reference modeling methods, reference models, and reference modeling context. An example for UML-based reference modeling is given in Section four. Potentials and limitations of this approach are explored in Section five. Finally, conclusions and limitations of this study are discussed. Also, we point to some further research directions.

THEORETICAL BACKGROUND
Unified Modeling Language

In 1994, Grady Booch, Jim Rumbaugh, and Ivar Jacobson joined together to unify the plethora of existing object-oriented systems engineering approaches at semantics and notation level (Booch, 2002; Fowler, 2004; Rumbaugh, Jacobson, & Booch, 1998). Their effort leads to the unified modeling language (UML), a well-known, general-purpose, tool-supported, process-independent, and industry-standardized modeling language for visualizing, describing, specifying, and documenting system artifacts.

UML is applicable to software and nonsoftware domains, including software architecture (Medvidovic, Rosenblum, Redmiles, & Robbins, 2002), real-time and embedded systems (Douglass, 1998), business applications (Eriksson & Penker, 2000), manufacturing systems (Bruccoleri, Dieaga, & Perrone, 2003), electronic commerce systems (Saleh, 2002), data warehousing (Dolk, 2000), bioinformatics (Bornberg-Bauer & Paton, 2002), and others. The language uses multiple views to specify system's structure and behavior. The recent version UML 2.0 supports 13 different diagram types. Table 1 provides an overview of the main concepts of each diagram. For a description of all semantics, see Fowler (2004), OMG (2003b, 2004), and Rumbaugh et al. (1998).

There is a great deal of terminological confusion in the modeling literature. It can be distinguished between an abstract syntax and a concrete syntax or notation of a language. While the abstract syntax specifies conceptual relationships between the constructs of the language, the concrete notation defines symbols representing the abstract constructs. In contrast, a modeling method provides procedures by which a language can be used. A consistent and suited set of modeling methods is called a methodology. The UML specification provides an abstract syntax and a concrete notation for all UML diagrams, as well

Table 1. UML diagram types

Focus	Diagram	Purpose
Static diagrams	Class	Data and behavior structure
	Object	Example configuration of instances
	Package	Structuring of models
	Composite structure	Structure and interaction between architecture components
Dynamic diagrams	Use case	User interaction with system
	State machine	Change events during object's lifetime
	Activity	Procedural and parallel behavior
	Sequence	Interaction between objects emphasizing sequences
	Communication	Interaction between objects emphasizing communication
	Interaction overview	Interplay of interactions between objects
	Timing	Interaction between objects emphasizing time
Implementation diagrams	Component	Structure and connections of components
	Deployment	Deployment of components to system nodes

as an informal description of the constructs' semantics. A modeling method or a modeling methodology is not defined by the UML standard. Hence, the language is process-neutral, and can be used with different software development processes.

The specification of the UML is publicly available and maintained by the Object Management Group (OMG). OMG's standardization process is formalized and consists of several proposal, revision, and final implementation activities (Kobryn, 1999, p. 31f.). Modeling tools supporting the development of UML diagrams are available from a number of commercial vendors and the open source community (OMG, 2005a, 2005b; Robbins & Redmiles, 2000).

Reference Modeling

A reference model is a model representing a class of domains (Fettke & Loos, 2003a). It is a conceptual framework that could be used as the blueprint for information system development. Reference models are also called universal models, generic models, or model patterns. To use reference models, they must be adapted to the requirements of a specific enterprise. We refer to such an adapted model as an application model.

Fields of application of reference modeling address all levels and business fields of enterprises. The current spread of applications arise from the objectives resp. fields of application of existing reference models, although not all possible fields of application must be covered thereby. Within literature, numerous reference models are proposed. These refer to whole institutions (e.g., for industrial enterprises, Kruse, Hars, Heib, & Scheer, 1993; Scheer, 1994; Scheer & Hars, 1992), specific business functions (e.g., for inventory management, Schwegmann, 1999, or for supply chain management, Huan, Sheoran, & Wang, 2004; Stephens, 2001; Supply-Chain Council Inc., 2005), specific business objects (e.g., for life insurance, Rüffer, 1999, or for branch business, Gerber & Mai, 2002) of enterprises. Aside, reference models supporting domain-independent problems have been developed, for example, for data modeling (Hay, 1996) or the selection, introduction, or customization of off-the-shelf software (Rosemann, 2003b). Available reference models address the strategy, process resp. organization, as well as the system level of enterprises with different extent, whereas a strict classification of the reference models is not possible.

Adopting the well-established framework of Wand and Weber (2002) for conceptual modeling, we conceptualize the field of reference modeling using four perspectives (cf. Figure 1 and Fettke & Loos, 2004):

*   **Reference modeling languages:** A reference modeling language provides a set of constructs and rules that show how to combine the constructs to model real-world domains, for example, event-driven process chains (EPC) (Aalst van der, 1999), entity-relationship model (ERM), (Chen, 1976), or the unified modeling language (UML) (Rumbaugh et al., 1998).
*   **Reference modeling methods:** A modeling method provides procedures by which a language can be used, for example, the Unified Software Development Process (USDP) (Jacobson, Booch, & Rumbaugh, 1998).
*   **Reference models:** A reference model is a model representing a class of domains, for example, a reference model for production planning and control systems. It is a conceptual framework or blueprint for system development.
*   **Context:** Each modeling process is embedded in a specific context setting that comprises technical, economic, social, and other factors, for example, tools used for

reference modeling (Becker, Algermissen, Delfmann, & Niehaves, 2004) or markup languages for reference models (Mendling & Nüttgens, 2004) constitute particular technical factors.

The presented, adopted framework is used to structure the examination of UML-based reference modeling in the following section.

Related Research Fields

Reference modeling research is related to several other research fields that are discussed next.

Patterns

Within computer sciences, the notion of design patterns was born at the end of the 1980s. Design patterns are "proven solutions to recurring design problems" (Coplien, 2000, p. 1604) (see also Coad, 1992; Fowler, 2003b; Gamma, 1992; Schmidt, Fayad, & Johnson, 1996). So far, pattern-oriented design is well-recognized in science and practice (Fowler, 1998; Gamma, Helm, Johnson, & Vlissides, 1995).

Within literature, numerous pattern types are documented (for instance Coplien & Schmidt, 1995; Harrison, Foote, & Rohnert, 1999; Martin, Riehle, & Buschmann, 1998; Vlissides, Coplien, & Kerth, 1995) (see for examples of pattern catalogs Buschmann & Meunier, 1995; Fowler, 2003a; Rising, 2000; Tichy, 1997; Zimmer, 1995). To categorize known patterns, several characteristics are proposed. A possible systematization of well-known pattern concepts regarding the phase of software developments is outlined in Table 2.

Furthermore within literature, additional pattern types are mentioned that are not considered by the preceding systematic, for example, process patterns (Ambler, 1998, 1999, 2000; Ambler & Constantine, 2000a, 2000b; Zapf & Heinzl, 2000), organizational patterns (Coplien & Harrison, 2004), meta-patterns (Pree, 1995), and anti-patterns (Brown, Malveau, McCormick III, & Mowbray, 1998; Brown, McCormick III, & Thomas, 1999, 2000).

Generally, patterns are small solutions for modeling problems. To improve the efficiency of the pattern approach, the focus of contribution can be seen in the development

Figure 1. Reference modeling framework (Based on Wand & Weber, 2002)

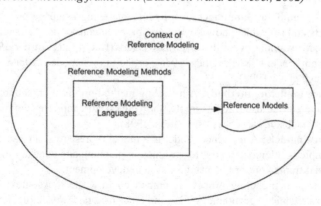

Table 2. Systematization of patterns

Phase	Pattern
Requirements definition	*Business patterns*: These patterns explicitly describe business structures and processes. They provide solutions for the conceptual design of software systems. (Braga, Germano, & Masiero, 1998; Broy, Denert, Renzel, & Schmidt, 1997; Carey, Carlson, & Graser, 2000; Coad, Lefebvre, & De Luca, 1999; Coad, North, & Mayfield, 1997, pp. 433-456; Eriksson & Penker, 2000; Fowler, 1997; Hay, 1996; Hellenack, 1997; Kilov & Simmonds, 1996)
Design specification	*Design patterns*: Solutions for design problems of software systems are addressed by design patterns (Gamma et al., 1995). *Architecture patterns*: These patterns do not describe a small design problem, but the basic setup and structure of a system (Buschmann, Meunier, Rohnert, Sommerlad, & Stal, 1996; Schmidt, Stal, Rohnert, & Buschmann, 2000).
Implementation description	*Idioms*: Technical aspects of implementation of software systems are described by idioms that are aligned to certain implementation languages (Beck, 1997, 1998).

of pattern languages. A pattern language is a collection of patterns for a special domain wherein numerous relations between the patterns are documented. First pattern languages were developed for technical domains (Buschmann et al., 1996).

The basic idea of design patterns is already compared with reference modeling in the information system discipline (Schwegmann, 1999; Speck, 2001, pp. 228-246). Considering the aforementioned pattern types, it could be reasoned that some of the patterns have similarities to reference models. Especially the objectives of business patterns and reference models are quite similar because both document reasonable modeling know-how on a conceptual level.

Despite the similarities and differences between patterns and reference models in general, both approaches possess a different history and culture and they are, therefore, not comprehensively comparable: Within the pattern community, approaches and criteria to find patterns are more or less applied ("pattern mining," in Rising, 1998). Such approaches are not common in the reference modeling domain. For example, it is a common view that patterns document recurring modeling solutions, whereas three or more experiences with using this solution are necessary before calling them a pattern (N.N., 1998). Within reference modeling, reference models are not necessarily proven solutions. Often they are comprehensive models that can be designed from scratch using a procedure model. In this way, the modeling content is mostly given by the intended future application domain. Nevertheless, reference models are not only designed within sciences. There are also reference models designed by practitioners. However, most of these models are not published because they represent competition-relevant know-how of organizations. In contrast, within the pattern community, patterns are explicitly used to share modeling knowledge (Fowler, 2003b).

The aforementioned examples show differences between research lines in reference modeling and patterns. Both fields have established their autonomy as research fields with some intersections. Despite of possible similar aspects, reference modeling and patterns are different research fields with partly differing application fields.

Model Driven Architecture

To provide a consistent view for software development, the Object Management Group promotes the framework standard model driven architecture (MDA) since 2000 (Fettke & Loos, 2003b; Mellor, Scott, Uhl, & Weise, 2002; OMG, 2000, 2001a, 2001b, 2003a). Thus, an approach for developing software shall be established that comprises the implementation, the analysis, as well as the design of systems. The standard promotes modeling through the whole system's life cycle, and aims at automated generation of technology-dependent system specifications (Frankel, 2003). The basic concepts of MDA are (Kleppe, Warmer, & Bast, 2003, pp. 15-31, 83-106):

- **Models:** Within MDA, a platform independent model (PIM) and a platform apecific model (PSM) is distinguished. Compared to a PSM, a PIM represents the modelled object without any relation to a specific technology.
- **Modeling language:** Both the PIM and the PSM are represented using a modeling language. MDA prefers languages with a well-defined syntax and semantic for the automated interpretation of the models. Hence, the UML can be used as modeling language, whereas the MDA is also open for other languages. Nevertheless, the OMG proposed UML as preferred language.
- **Transformation definition:** A PSM shall be created automatically by applying a designed PIM. Such transformations are realized by transformation tools using transformation definitions. These definitions describe how language constructs of a PIM can be mapped to language constructs of a PSM.

The overall process of developing an information system using MDA is similar to a classical development process. The important difference is the automatic transformation between analysis, design, and implementation. Furthermore, iterations of the development process should begin at the analysis phase. This can avoid inconsistent and outdated system artefacts of early phases.

A main idea of the MDA approach is to describe application domains independently of specific technology. Within the information systems discipline, this is not new. In particular, the field of reference modeling has a similar goal. As documented within the following section, reference models exist for several application domains. These models can be applied as PIM. Moreover, known reference modeling methods foster the design of model transformation processes within the MDA. Both interrelationships show potentials for a mutual support of the disciplines.

UML-BASED REFERENCE MODELING
Reference Modeling Language

Modeling languages are utilized to represent reference models. A standardized language for reference modeling has not been established in theory and practice (Taylor & Probst, 2003), although a tendency to the standardization of used language concepts is obvious. Current contributions usually use well-known and established modeling languages. Concepts are used that can be classified to different language families, like, for example, data modeling, process modeling, and object-oriented modeling. Extensions and adaptations of these languages are discussed, which raises the claim to fulfill special requirements of reference modeling.

Requirements on modeling languages move in the spread of theoretical precision and pragmatic usability (Frank, 1998, 2002; Paige, Ostroff, & Brooke, 2000). Often, models are represented using languages without formal semantics and only limited well-defined syntax. This situation is very critical from the viewpoint of models' application, although, semiformal languages are occasionally ascribed a higher acceptance, understandability, and usability.

The standardization of the UML in terms of their syntactic and semantic specification forwards the use of this language in the scope of modeling. Using UML for reference modeling provides a basis for the construction and application of reference models. The adaptation of UML-based reference models in order to form application models does not influence the language. Thus, the application models are also represented in UML. Because UML is the de facto standard for object-oriented analysis and design, the implementation of information systems is accelerated. In addition, this is promoted by a huge number of available tools supporting the development of UML diagrams (Fettke, 2005).

Using UML for reference modeling does not only improve the system's development process, also the communication about the reference models between different stakeholders is facilitated. This aspect is particularly necessary in nonsoftware domains where the development of an information system is not strived (cf. Section 2). Because the UML is well-known and widely disseminated, it is easier to exchange the models and to communicate between different persons. For this, the specification forms the common basis for interpreting and understanding the models.

Following, the consideration of specific requirements of reference modeling is analyzed. In recent publications, concepts such as multiperspective modeling, management of variants, and reusability are discussed that prove to be useful for reference modeling (Becker, Delfmann, Dreiling, Knackstedt, & Kuropka, 2004; Dreiling, Rosemann, Aalst van der, Sadiq, & Khan, 2005; Rosemann & Shanks, 2001):

- **Multiperspective modeling:** The analysis and representation of enterprises from different perspectives is a vital modeling concept. Model perspectives can be construed regarding several demarcation criteria. Basically, perspectives can be distinguished either based on analytical characteristics or based on subjective needs. Subjective needs are expressed in terms of perceptions, presuppositions, and preferences of modelers or model users (Frank, 2002). The benefit of using multiperspective modeling for reference modeling has been emphasized for some time. Reference modeling considers enterprises from different perspectives. Interdisciplinary orientation results from requirements of different stakeholders during the application of a reference model. For example, application projects of reference models can influence the strategy level, process or organization level, and system level within an enterprise. Participating actors or roles possess different experience knowledge and have different needs while designing and representing reference models. In the scope of UML-based reference modeling, multiperspective modeling can be realized using the available UML diagram types and modeling on different abstraction levels. Using different diagram types for representing a modeling domain facilitates different views (structural, dynamical, and implementation view). Thus, different constellations of one or more UML diagrams constitute different perspectives. In addition, modeling on several abstraction levels satisfies different information needs. The following three examples shall emphasize both preceding approaches: (1) Different perspectives could result from a global or strategic point of view. On the one hand, the entire reference model is to be depicted from one perspective; for example, using one UML class diagram to describe the entire structure. On the other hand, further perspectives could describe only views on single parts of the reference model that are relevant for different stakeholders; for example, using several UML class diagrams to represent parts of the overall model, completed with other diagram types depicting different views. (2) In regard to the description of processes, different requirements on granularity can exist. While an end user is primarily interested in the functions and their execution sequence, the process description has to be described more precisely for the software development. The different granularity can be realized modeling different detail levels. Additionally, in some UML diagram types it is possible to package constructs; for example, decomposing of activities in subactivities and indicating subactivity diagrams within a UML activity diagram. (3) Different requirements of representation could also exist on system level, for example, architectures can be described at build-time and run-time using pertinent UML diagram types.

- **Management of variants:** Management of variants facilitates the systematic utilization of alternative configurations of business systems. The industrial management of variants of product components is a vital instrument in order to control the complexity in production processes. As bill of materials is used to specify complex technical products, models and model variants can be used to describe a modeling domain. While model perspectives offer different views on a particular issue, model variants represent different issues that are similar or comparable regarding a particular viewpoint. So, model variants represent possible configurations for certain issues. Possible configurations are not partitioned in several, conceptually independent models, but are described in one model, and are indicated as variants. For the management of variants, more or less elaborated concepts for several modeling languages are suggested. In the scope of object-oriented modeling languages, especially UML, the use of inheritance mechanism and parameterizations are proposed (Schlagheck, 2000, pp. 74-76; Schwegmann, 1999, pp. 140-165, 173). While the inheritance is a concept of the object-oriented paradigm, the parameterization has no reference to concepts of object-orientation. Using these techniques, variants can be documented as follows: Within a structural view, the inheritance can be used to represent variants of classes for different application contexts. The variant-dependent existence of classes, attributes, methods, and relationships can be depicted by parameters that express the characteristics of correspondent variants. Within dynamic models, variants can primarily be documented using parameters. For example, using a UML activity diagram, it is possible that certain functions within a business process can be dropped out depending on a chosen business strategy. These functions or the partly process are indicated by a correspondent parameter. More challenging concepts for the representation of variants are tightly connected to the following concepts of reuse and adaptation of reference models.

- **Reusability and adaptation:** A central theme of reference modeling is the reusability of models in different contexts as well as for different purposes. This is a substantial concept for resource-saving. The simplest case of reusing is to manually copy the reference model. Limitations regarding the model adaptation do not exist in this case, although problematic redundancies and inconsistencies between the different models arise. For example, if a process alteration within the reference model is proposed, it has to be guaranteed that the changes are available in all applications of the reference model. To support the reuse and adaptation of models, a number of more powerful concepts have been proposed. Vom Brocke describes a wide spread of concepts that can be adopted for the UML (vom Brocke, 2003, pp. 259-319):

- *Configuration* allows reusing existing models based on a defined scope of configuration. For example, dependent on parameters of a certain business strategy alternative, configurations of business processes can be defined. Proposals for the corresponding preparation of language constructs are discussed by Remme and Schütte. Independently from object-orientation, Remme proposes placeholders for model elements that have to be instantiated with certain characteristics during the model's application (Remme, 1997). The realization of placeholders is easy to adopt in UML diagrams by indicating corresponding constructs, for example, using stereotypes that refer to the necessity of instantiation of elements. Schütte discusses build-time-operators for process and data models that allow foreseen manipulations of the model using parameters, like enterprise-specific characteristics (Schütte, 1998, pp. 244-276). As first approaches using annotations and stereotypes for constructs in UML class and activity diagrams show, the concept of build-time-operators can easily be adopted for UML, for example, Schlagheck (2000) and Tzouvaras (2003).

- *Aggregation* allows assembling of several model building blocks into one larger model component. Using UML, this is not a special challenge. The only prerequisite is that the building blocks have to be designed in one diagram type in order to join the model constructs at correspondent interfaces. For example, the application of reference models along the supply-chain can initiate the composition of a process model using two partly models that represent, on the one hand, an industrial enterprise, on the other, a commercial enterprise.

- *Specialization* allows a selective use of a general reference model for a specific context. For this purpose, the object-oriented concept of inheritance finds its equivalences within the UML. The inheritance facilitates the specialization of model contents in structure diagrams like UML class and package diagram. Thus, different application contexts or purposes of the model, represented by the model constructs, can be depicted as specializations. For example, a reference model for commerce can be restricted to the commerce of digital products (Luxem, 2000).

- *Instantiation* allows extending a reference model at certain spots ("hotspots"). Indications refer to the spots within the model. During the application of the model, the model has to be extended at the spots to fulfill requirements regarding the concrete application context. For realizing instantiation, requirements that have to be addressed by the modeling language are the indication of the spots and the facilitation of extensions' embedding at the spots. The indication of the spots can be realized using placeholder, as mentioned at the configuration. Using UML, correspondent model constructs can be indicated using stereotypes that mark the spot. While instantiating the model, extensions in the UML diagrams can easily be realized by refining the model at the spot. For example, it is possible to describe a business process for order processing, in general, using a UML activity diagram, and indicate a spot for the payment. At the use of this process, it is instantiated using a special system of payment.

○   With the *construction of analogies,* a specific aspect of a reference model is reused. Within software engineering, the pattern-oriented design refers to the potentials of systematic usage of analogy relations in construction processes (Fowler, 1997; Gamma et al., 1995). The patterns document experiences during constructions that can be applied in similar construction processes (cf. Section 2). The notion of the construction of analogies can be transferred to the application of reference models. With this, modeling languages do not have to fulfill special requirements. Moreover, with the construction of analogies, only characteristics of a reference model are reused in different contexts. For example, a process for the occupancy planning of machines in an industrial enterprise can also be used for the occupancy planning of operating rooms in a hospital.

Considering the support of multiperspective modeling, management of variants, and reuse, as well as adaptation of models by the UML, it becomes obvious that UML does not have any language integrated approaches in terms of specific constructs or procedural models for realizing these concepts. All approaches mentioned before are only interpretations of existing UML concepts, as well as proposed extensions or adaptations of the UML. Language-integrated approaches, based on UML's specification, would promote the holistic support of these concepts that are not only useful for reference modeling, but also for information modeling in general. Establishing extensions and adaptations that are not based on the specification resp. metamodel of the UML are not supported by tools, and their semantic and syntactic definition has to be specified.

Furthermore, a comprehensive evaluation of the described approaches does not exist. The sufficiency, feasibility, and applicability have to be analyzed to guarantee an appropriate qualification of these approaches to fulfill corresponding requirements of reference modeling.

Reference Modeling Methods

Reference modeling can be conceptually divided into two processes (cf. Figure 2). On the one hand, a reference model is designed within the scope of the construction process. On the other hand, a reference model is reused within the scope of the application process. Both processes are always temporally separated and normally disassociated regarding organization and human resources. The conceptual separation is a prerequisite for reusing reference models in different contexts, but requires a careful coordination of both processes.

Applying this separation within UML-based reference modeling, the UML is, on the one hand, embedded in the construction process as modeling language for constructing the reference models and, on the other hand, the UML has a considerable influence on the application of the models. On closer examination, the impact of the UML on the single processes has to be differentiated in regard to their partly activities. Referring to the construction process, the following activities can be distinguished:

1.   **Problem definition:** In this phase, two main activities can be distinguished. First of all, the purpose and domain of the reference model has to be specified in detail. This forms the basis and determines the concepts for the subsequent model development.

Figure 2. Processes of reference modeling

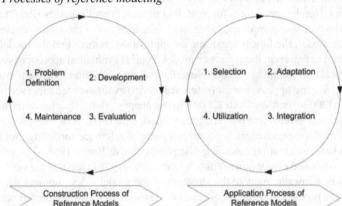

The second activity is the constitution of the modeling language for representing the reference model as well as the specification of modeling guidelines (Schütte, 1998). Thus, UML-based reference modeling implies the constitution of UML as modeling language in this phase. In the sense of method engineering (Dietzsch, 2002), necessary adaptations of the UML's language constructs for the model construction have to be elaborated. UML's extension mechanism in terms of the heavyweight extension supported by Meta-Object Facility (MOF), a language for specifying, constructing, and managing metamodels (OMG, 2002) like the UML metamodel, or stereotypes as lightweight user extension (Fettke, 2005, p. 2925) can be used. Further extension mechanism like constraint expressions by Object Constraint Language (OCL), a language for describing expressions on UML models (OMG, 2003c), or tagged values by attaching additional information to model elements, are not considered here. They are the object of the actual design of the reference model.

2. **Development:** For the defined problem and the delimited and isolated domain, a model is to be developed using the determined modeling language. Often, available enterprise-specific models (inductive procedure) or theoretical presumptions (deductive procedure) are starting points of the development. Beside these vital procedure approaches, further procedures are possible. A result of the development is the description of all modeling views and variants as well as the references between the single models. In UML-based reference modeling, parts or the whole reference model are represented using UML. With dependence on the content and objective of the reference model, several diagram types can be used. These enable different views on reference models that follow the focuses and purposes of the diagram types depicted in Table 1. Implementation diagrams play a subordinated role for representing the reference models because of their relation to the concrete application context and an instance of the reference model. Nevertheless, implementation diagrams can also be used to represent a universal model of an allocation of information system components within an abstract system landscape.

3. **Evaluation:** It is an important factor of reference modeling to guarantee a certain quality of reference models (Fettke & Loos, 2003c). The evaluation should not exclusively

be performed after the completion of the model, but also during the development of the model. Hereby, guidelines for modeling support model's quality (Schütte, 1998). The evaluation also comprises, for example, the analysis of the effects caused by the reference model, the fitness regarding an application context, and the modeling language used to represent the reference model. Typical evaluation approaches comprise economical and technical aspects. Nevertheless, no evaluation method is commonly accepted. Several approaches for (reference model) evaluation are surveyed by Fettke and Loos (2003c) and Van Belle (2003). In this chapter, the evaluation of the modeling language used to represent the reference models, here UML, is of interest. The evaluation of modeling grammars is no special issue of reference modeling, but a matter of the whole information modeling discipline (Siau & Rossi, 1998). For example, a metamodel-based evaluation (Fettke & Loos, 2003c, p. 84) focuses the syntactic correctness or allows to analyze the structure of the model's development process and application process. A metamodel-based evaluation of UML-based reference models can be realized using the UML metamodel specified by the OMG. Further approaches use an ontology-based evaluation where the ontological correctness of modeling grammars is analyzed (e.g., Opdahl & Henderson-Sellers, 2002).

4.   **Maintenance:** During the use of reference models, experiences are gained that possibly require model corrections or improvements. Several reasons for maintenance activities can be stated: Modeling errors are identified in terms of errors regarding the application of the chosen modeling language or errors regarding the reproduction of the content. Further reasons can be identified where no errors cause maintenance activities. On the one hand, there are necessary adaptations of the represented content, if new requirements from the view of the application arise. On the other hand, besides the content of the reference model, the modeling language can even cause maintenance activities. Although the UML in the scope of UML-based reference modeling is determined at the beginning of the model construction and all necessary extensions and adaptations of the language are specified, experiences associated with the language's appropriateness can be gained: So, during the application of the reference model, it could be noticed that the UML and their diagram types are not suitable to represent the content (e.g., the UML's expression mightiness is not appropriate or alternatively required views on the content cannot be represented using UML). Independent from the suitability for representing the content, further maintenance activities can even be caused by the language (e.g., alterations of the UML (new versions) and changes in the metamodel, or model constructs provide no sufficient possibility for adapting the model). Language-caused maintenance can result in the following possible activities: (1) revising the model based on revised modeling constructs or newly introduced UML extensions, (2) adapting required views on the content realized by replacing model parts or introducing additional modeling languages beside the UML, (3) a complete reconstruction of the reference model in a new language. The latter case abandons the scope of maintenance of a reference model and initiates a new construction process.

Referring to the application of a reference model, the following activities are necessary:

1.   **Selection:** First of all, an appropriate reference model is to be selected from existing reference models. For this purpose, reference model catalogs can be used, for example,

Fettke, Loos, and Zwicker (2005). Such catalogs offer a comprehensive directory of existing reference models and allow a systematic access to the models. To support UML-based reference modeling, a systematization of UML-based reference models is necessary (cf. following section). A catalog of UML-based reference models classifies only models that use UML besides possible further languages.

2.   **Adaptation:** An appropriate reference model has to be adapted to the specifics of an individual enterprise. Within UML-based reference modeling, the adapting concepts depicted in the preceding section can be used to generate an individual application model from the reference model.

3.   **Integration:** If more than one model is used during the application process, several models have to be integrated. On the one hand, it is possible that a reference model has to be integrated with an already existing enterprise-specific model. Thereby, it is necessary to resolve redundancies. On the other hand, it is also possible that several reference models are used that must be assembled. With this, the single models have to be aggregated to one comprehensive reference model. All necessary integrations in this phase arise from requirements to the languages in which the integrating models are represented. If the models were not designed in the same modeling language, models' transformations in a unique language have to be done to enable the model integration. The use of standardized and broad-disseminated languages like UML is of huge advantage. Integrations of UML-based models that follow the same standardization version can be done based on the correspondent metamodel of the UML. The transformation of models that are not constructed in UML or which differ in UML versions can only be realized using transformation definitions based on standardized syntactic and semantic specification of the language.

4.   **Utilization:** The customized and integrated reference model is now ready for use. The question that arises in this phase is how the reference model can be used for the fundamental problem. The application of models is here promoted by tool support of UML. Moreover, the well-defined syntax and semantics facilitates the mechanical application of the reference models. For example, using UML to represent and apply reference models promotes the model driven architecture (MDA) approach (cf. Section 2). MDA prefer modeling languages with a well-defined syntax and semantics for the automated interpretation of the models. Using UML for reference modeling makes it possible to apply the reference models within the scope of MDA. After an adaptation of the reference models to create specific application models, an automated implementation can be realized. Nevertheless, for a manual use of reference models, the acceptance by a broad group of stakeholders is guaranteed, because UML is well-known and industry-standardized.

Reference Models

Within the literature, numerous more or less elaborated reference models are proposed (Fettke et al., 2005). To offer a comprehensive directory of existing reference models and to allow a systematic access to the models, reference model catalogs can be used. Such catalogs are of both practical and theoretical importance. From a practical viewpoint, the selection of an appropriate reference model is complicated. One presumption of reusing a reference model is to know its availability, its application domain, its potentials and limitations, and so forth. An appropriate model catalog can offer such information. Thus, this instrument fosters a rational and systematic model selection process, as mentioned in the preceding section.

Beside the practical relevance, catalogs of reference models are of importance for the theory of enterprise modeling in general, and for the theory of reference modeling in particular. Catalogs of existing reference models can show varieties, gaps and areas of improvements. Reference model catalogs with a huge number of existing models represent a meaningful basis for new and advanced reference models. Even if existing reference models do not take into account in conjunction with the development of a new reference model, at least the scope of already developed reference models should be made clear by such a catalog afterwards. Therefore, a catalog of reference models stimulates the scientific progress of reference modeling.

The table found in the Appendix of this paper represents a catalog of UML-based reference models. For the purpose of brevity, the amount is restricted to 11 reference models. The classification of models within a catalog can be done using numerous describing criteria (See Fettke et al., 2005 for a more detailed catalog of process reference models). The criteria used in this study exemplify typical reference model characteristics:

- **Identification:** The identification of reference models is made by running numbers and reference model names. References, wherein the reference models are described, are also specified (primary literature). This information is completed with additional references (secondary literature) wherein certain reference model properties are explained. The specification of secondary literature particularly supports to provide information about limited accessible reference models.

- **Construction:** The following criteria address the construction of UML-based reference models:
  - ○ **Domain:** The domain describes the intended field of the reference model's application from perspective of the person(s) or institution responsible for developing the reference model.
  - ○ **Modeling language(s):** The language criteria state the modeling language(s) used to represent the reference model. To address the consideration and classification of UML-based reference models, UML diagram types are particularly specified. Further modeling languages are additionally described.
  - ○ **Construction method:** This criterion states the modeling concept used by the responsible person(s) or institution for developing the reference model.
  - ○ **Evaluation:** This criterion describes the used methods for evaluating the reference model by the person(s) or institution responsible for developing the reference model or by third parties. Evaluation methods are only considered if they are explicitly intended for model evaluation by the evaluator. Besides the method, it is stated whether the result of performed evaluation is intersubjective verifiable.

- **Application:** The following criteria address the application of the reference models:
  - ○ **Access:** This criterion specifies the accessibility to the reference model by third parties. If the reference model is completely obtainable over usual ways of librarianship, the access is classified as "open." The access is "closed" if the responsible person(s) or institution provides no possibility for using and recognizing the reference model by third parties. If the access is neither open nor closed, the access is classified as "limited." This is the case, for example, if the reference model can be purchased as stand-alone product, or if it is accessible

over an internet server that does not belong to official librarianship. If the access to the reference model is closed, the information of all aforementioned and following criteria is based on statements from the specified primary and secondary literature.

○   **Tool support:** This criterion describes whether the reference model can be automatically used by a software tool or whether the reference model is only available in paper or digital copy.

○   **Application method(s):** This criterion describes the known method respectively concept for applying the reference model.

○   **Reuse and customization:** This criterion lists mechanisms that are proposed for reusing and customizing of model elements in the scope of the model's application.

○   **Use case(s):** The use case(s) describes how often the reference model was applied to construct an application model. This is also a way of evaluating: similar to case studies, but independently realized. The real application projects are not construed as ex ante evaluating studies, rather than the project results are used as ex post evaluation.

Using these criteria, UML-based reference models can be classified. Most of the publicly available UML-based reference models were developed in science. In spite of this, it can be suspected that UML-based reference models can be found in the reality of enterprise modeling. Nevertheless, the survey and classification illustrates some lacks that restrict the applicability of the models. A general but important fact is the restricted access to some reference models. This fact is plausible in regard to reference models developed within practice; however, the limitation of reference models from science is inappropriate. Moreover, all of the analyzed reference models with their origin in science do not possess tool support tailored for the concrete reference model. From the view of reference modeling objectives, the propagation and application of the models is prohibited by the lack of access and missing tool support. From a methodical point of view, the lack of evaluations, reference model-based application methods, and integrated concepts for reusing and adapting of some of the reference models does not promote their applicability. Further restrictions arise from the languages used to represent the reference models. In spite of the possibilities for modeling and representing different aspects provided by the several UML diagram types, some reference models additionally use further modeling languages. This fact complicates an integrated tool support for the overall reference model, and restricts the language-integrated representation of the reference model.

Table 3 summaries the usage of UML diagrams over the 11 reference models of the exemplary reference model catalog: All reference models use UML class diagrams. Additionally, four of them also use package diagrams, three use activity diagrams, two use case diagrams, and in one case, a state machine diagram is used. Following Table 1, all reference models cover at least the static view on the model content by using class and package diagrams. Six of them additionally represent dynamic aspects in terms of use case, activity and state machine diagrams. Therewith, the latter forms the process view on the represented model object. Figure 3 illustrates the usage of the several diagrams.

The usage of only five UML diagram types cannot be explained free of doubt. The concentration on the class diagram is a consequence of the necessity to represent the structural perspective of the model. Within UML, the class diagram is the mostly used diagram type.

Table 3. Summary of UML diagram usage

Focus	Diagram	Number of reference models	Number of reference models within the focus	Number of reference models within the focus using further languages
Static	Class	11	11	5
	Package	4		
Dynamic	Activity	3	5	1
	case	2		
	State machine	1		

Figure 3. Depiction of UML diagram usage

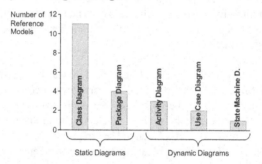

The package diagram is applied to further structure the contents of the reference models. All additionally used UML diagram types serve to represent process knowledge on a general and universal view.

Five of the entire 11 reference models additionally use further languages. In particular, modeling languages to model the process view are used: the Event-driven Process Chain (EPC), process hierarchy-diagrams and MEMO-OrgML. In one case, the Entity-relationship Model (ERM), function trees and further proprietary languages and diagrams are used. The reason for using additional languages and diagrams beside the UML diagrams can probably be seen, from the view of the reference models designer, as a lack of appropriate support to represent certain model content by using UML. Considering Table 4, it becomes obvious that most of the reference model that apply only static UML diagrams additionally use further languages, especially languages that can be classified to languages for process modeling. Following this argumentation, the capabilities of UML seem not appropriate for the modelers for representing process knowledge.

Context

All reference modeling processes are embedded in a particular context setting that comprises technical, economic, social, and other factors. UML as reference modeling language does not only represent a direct perspective of reference modeling (as reference modeling

Table 4. Summary of the usage of further languages

	Number of reference models with using further static languages	Number of reference models using further dynamic languages	Number of reference models using further static and dynamic languages	Total
Reference models with only static UML diagrams	0	4	0	4
Reference models with only dynamic UML diagrams	0	0	0	0
Reference models with static and dynamic UML diagrams	1	0	0	1
Total	1	4	0	5

language), but also influences contextual issues. In this chapter, the technical factor of tools used for reference modeling shall be considered in particular.

Modeling tools are software systems that support the construction and application of information models. Basically, it is desired that all aforementioned concepts regarding the realization of reference modeling are supported by modeling tools: though existing tools do not offer comprehensive functionalities for reference modeling. Nevertheless, modeling tools supporting the development of UML models are available from a number of vendors and the open source community (Fettke, 2005, p. 2921). To realize reference modeling, the responsible persons can use existing modeling tools. The lack of support of reference modeling functionalities has to be addressed by tool vendors. The development of required concepts and approaches as well as the verification of their feasibility is the task of the research community.

Currently, reference modeling tools supporting distributed modeling are discussed (vom Brocke, 2003). With these tools, the communication between the vendors resp. constructors of reference models and the users shall be improved. Besides basic modeling functionalities, these tools should provide further functionalities in order to be usable as virtual engineering communities (VEC) (Fettke & Loos, 2003d) . The use of such tools is predestinated in the scope of UML-based reference modeling. The well-defined standardization of the UML provides the common communication basis between different stakeholders in reference modeling projects, and enables uncomplicated model exchanges.

A VEC provides the following functionalities in detail:

- **Construction of reference models:** First of all, a VEC provides basic functionalities for developing, modifying, and deleting of reference models, as well as for the graphical representation of models. All persons of a reference modeling project can participate in the construction and application of reference models.
- **Supply and demand of reference models:** In the VEC, the existing offer of reference models is stored and can be retrieved. Persons who demand reference models can also formulate special requests for reference models.

- **Tender:** Invitations for developing reference models for certain domains enable efficient coordination of suppliers and persons who demand for reference models. The development of a reference model can directly be coordinated for a certain demand and does not need to be developed for the anonymous market.
- **Forum:** By means of a conventional forum, users of the VEC can exchange general information, hold discussions about the construction and use of reference models, as well as discuss further problems of reference modeling.
- **Personalization:** A user of the VEC can adapt the functionality and user interface of the tool to his/her special needs. For example, single users could be interested only in process reference models. The filtering of such models can be realized by specifying process modeling languages used to represent the reference model's processes; for example, using UML, the behavior diagrams have to be specified.
- **Project management:** The VEC can also be used as a platform for project management in cross-enterprise organizations. This enables an efficient planning and controlling of construction and application processes within the reference modeling.

Considering VEC in the scope of UML-based reference modeling, the UML has only a secondary influence on the tender, forum, personalization, and project management. For example, the tender can focus on the invitation to develop UML-based reference models. Within the forum, special issues regarding the application of UML in reference modeling could be discussed. The personalization could be done using special aspects provided by the UML. And finally, the project management could address special tasks that have to be implemented, if the UML is used for reference modeling; for example, using an extension mechanism to adapt the UML to fulfill special requirements for a certain reference model. However, for UML-based reference modeling, the construction and the supply as well as demand functionalities can directly be aligned to UML as language for modeling, representing, and exchanging reference models. As mentioned before, the UML provides the common communication and modeling basis between different stakeholders in reference modeling projects, and enables model exchanges.

Technical implementations of construction and the supply as well as demand functionalities for the VEC can utilize the mentioned advantages. Typical requirements and aspects of realizing tools in general are discussed within the literature (Fettke, Loos, & Pastor, 2004; Hofstedeter & Verhoef, 1996). The lower bound of functionalities is defined by graphical editors and a central database for the models. Yet the upper bound of an effective support is not obvious. For example, the following aspects are discussed:

- **Meta-case tools:** To reduce costs and to increase flexibility of modeling, the development of metacase tools is challenging. Such tools are independent of a certain modeling approach, and the modeling concepts can be influenced within defined ranges (Fettke et al., 2004). The use of such tools decouples the construction and application of reference models from the used modeling and representation language. So, the metamodel of the UML could be defined within a metacase tool for realizing a UML-based reference model. This has advantages because additional languages, which are possibly necessary within the reference modeling, could also be defined without introducing an additional tool. Alterations of the UML by the OMG do not initiate a change of the tool, but can be implemented in the meta-case tool by adaptation of the UML metamodel.

- **Distributed tools:** Often, more than one person is involved in model construction. Thus, concepts for distributed modeling are proposed (Ram & Ramesh, 1998; vom Brocke, 2003). These concepts support the communication between spatial-distributed modelers, in particular. Efficient exchange formats are needed in order to transfer reference models between different modelers and the distributed-tool environments. For this purpose, the advantage of the standardization of the UML can be utilized. The distributed tools or modelers could communicate among each other directly using the UML models. The specified and standardized UML metamodel guarantee the common understanding of the communication contents. Because the communication is not restricted to the construction and application of the models, the realization of a marketplace for reference models can also profit from this approach.
- **Reuse:** If a reference model is reused in fact, it can be manually copied in the simplest case. The disadvantages of this solution, like missing alteration service and uncontrolled redundancies, are obvious. First technical concepts to overcome this problems are introduced by vom Brocke (vom Brocke, 2003, pp. 235-258). His approach necessitates defining reference model components that can be identified by a unique signature. These components can then be integrated at run-time by physical referencing. This approach is obviously not limited to a special modeling language. Therefore, it can be adopted in UML-based reference modeling. The technical implementation of this approach would, therefore, support the application of reference models using UML.

Example

To come to a deeper understanding of UML-based reference modeling, a particular reference model is described in more detail. For this purpose Schwegmann's reference model is selected and described next (Schwegmann, 1999, pp. 185-223).

Schwegmann designs a reference model for inventory management using a self-developed procedure. Besides a part for developing object-oriented reference models, the procedure model comprises also a second part for constructing specific application models using the reference model. Schwegmann's reference model consists of a basic model *storage system* and five extension models to the basic model. The extension of the basic model using model specialization is one of the possibilities to represent variants of the reference model and to promote reusing the model content. Further approaches are realized within the models using a special mechanism for representing model variants.

Figure 4 shows an extract of the class model of the basic model *storage system*. A detailed description of the model is given by Schwegmann (1999, pp. 191-194). The model illustrates some interesting particularities. On the one hand, it points up the abstraction of the model content from concrete application contexts. On the other hand, it shows the integration of mechanism for the management of variants to promote reusing and customizing of the model. The illustrated presentation of variants using variants container and model specialization are based on inheritance concepts of the object-oriented paradigm. Additionally, Schwegmann uses explicit parameterization of model constructs, as can be seen at some associations, attributes, and methods.

Figure 5 presents an extract of the reference model's basic process model. For modeling the dynamic view within the model, the event-driven process Chain (EPC), is used. As with the class model, the process model also integrates a mechanism for the management of variants. Therefore, several paths in the process model are annotated with particular configuration parameters.

*Figure 4. Extract of the class model **storage system** (Adapted from Schwegmann, 1999, p. 183)*

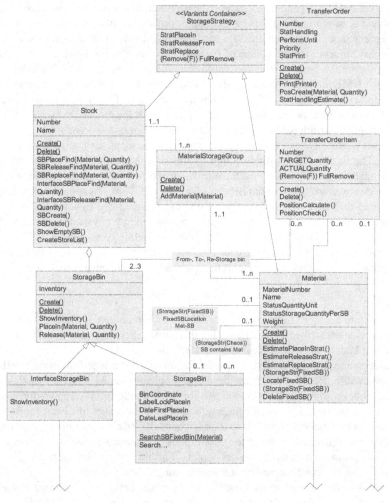

Potentials and Limitations

UML is a vital instrument for reference modeling. Special capabilities of this language make useful contributions for challenges of reference modeling. Besides several potentials, limitations arise that do not put the applicability into question, but restrict the conditions of using UML for reference modeling. Table 2 summarizes the potentials and limitations of UML-based reference modeling.

Many of the depicted potentials and limitations do not only refer to reference modeling in particular, but rather to information modeling in general. Nevertheless, they promote or limit the reference modeling thereby. While the listed potentials illustrate the applicabil-

Figure 5. Extract of the process model find storage bin place-in (adapted from Schwegmann, 1999, p. 199)

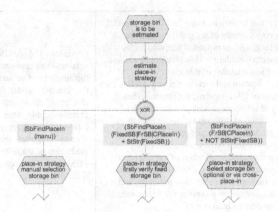

ity and usefulness of the UML as reference modeling language, some limitations point to further research demands.

CONCLUSION AND FURTHER RESEARCH

Within the Information Systems field, reference modeling is known for many years. Despite the relevance of an appropriate reference modeling language, yet little research has been done on using unified modeling language (UML) for reference modeling. In this paper, we discuss the potentials and limitations of UML-based reference modeling. Our analysis unfolds along a reference modeling framework based on the Wand and Weber framework for conceptual modeling. We demonstrate the applicability and usefulness of using UML for reference modeling by analyzing the framework elements: reference modeling languages,

Table 5. Potentials and limitations of UML-based reference modeling

	Potential	Limitation
Reference modeling languages	- UML's well-defined syntax and semantics promotes the construction and application of reference models - Availability of several UML diagram types and the support of different-granular modeling facilitate multiperspective modeling and representation of different views (structure, process and implementation view) - Proposed adaptations of UML elements like placeholders and build-time-operators, as well as some capabilities of the UML like the inheritance, support the management of variants and reusing as well as adapting of reference models	- UML does not have language-integrated approaches (constructs, procedure models) for managing perspectives, variants, and for reusing and adapting of models - lack of experiences regarding feasibility, applicability, sufficiency using existing approaches for multiperspective modeling, management of variants, and reusing and adapting of models

Table 5. continued

Reference modeling methods	- Extension mechanism to adapt the UML to special modeling requirements of the domain (domain modeling language) or proposed adaptations for multiperspective modeling, management of variants, and reusing and adapting of models - UML specification and metamodel as guideline for development of UML models, for language-based evaluation of reference models, for metamodel-based integration of different reference models or reference models with existing application models - UML's well-defined syntax and semantics promotes mechanical application of the reference model, for example, promotes the MDA approach - The wide dissemination, the high publicity, and the existing standardization promotes the acceptance of the UML models by human user	- Alterations of the UML (new versions) and changes in the metamodel can initiate revisions of the reference model, for example, changes of the introduced language extensions; adaptation of the reference model, regarding the changed language constructs; new evaluation of the reference model - UML's size and complexity arise difficulties in writing and reading diagrams
Reference models	- Availability of UML-based reference models for different domains	The applicability of models is restricted due to several lacks of existing models: - Limited or closed access to the model - Lack of comprehensive evaluation based on defined evaluation methods - Lack of appropriate application methods - Lack of reference model-based tool support - Lack of integrated reuse and customization concepts - Unspecified UML version used to represent the reference model - Representation of the reference models using additional modeling languages beside UML (possible solution are meta-case tools, cf. tool support)
Reference modeling context (tool support)	- Availability of UML tools - UML specification and metamodel provides a basis for tool communication and model exchange, in particular for distributed tool environments - UML metamodel supports using metacase-tools that counteract changes of tools due to alternations of UML facilitates the use of additional languages besides UML within the same tool environment	- Existing tools does not offer comprehensive functionalities especially for reference modeling - Alterations of the UML (new version) and changes in the metamodel requires the adaptations of existing tools or the introduction of new tools as well as the adaptation of possible reference modeling specific functionalities to support the new standard

reference modeling methods, reference models, and reference modeling context with respect to possible applications and limitations of UML. The results demonstrate numerous advantages of UML as a reference modeling language. To sum up, these are the standardization of the UML in terms of their metamodel and well-defined syntax and semantics, the availability of several diagram types, the extensibility and adaptability of language constructs, and the disseminated tool support. The depicted potentials certify the qualification and applicability of UML for reference modeling.

Despite the positive influence of UML on the construction and application of reference models, some limitations are identified that restrict the use of UML for reference modeling. Although almost everyone acknowledges the practical benefits of a standardized modeling language, e.g. protection of investments in technology, easier model exchange and reuse, better professional training (Frank, 1997, p. 13), there are important opportunities that have to be challenged. UML's size (UML 2 has approximately 1000+ pages) and complexity is overwhelming compared with other languages (Siau & Cao, 2001): therefore, users have difficulties in writing and reading diagrams (Agarwal & Sinha, 2003; Laitenberger, Atkinson, Schlich, & Emam, 2000) and tool vendors have problems to fully support the UML standard. Furthermore, the maintenance of the standard is very expensive and error-prone, for example, Fuentes, Quintana, Llorens, Génova, and Prieto-Díaz (2003) identified several hundred errors in UML's metamodel. Other authors criticize UML for its semantics inconsistency, construct ambiguity, notation inadequacy, and cognitive misdirection (Champeaux, 2003; Frank, 1998; Henderson-Sellers, 2002; McLeod, Halpin, Kangassalo, & Siau, 2001; Shen & Siau, 2003; Thomas, 2002; Wang, 2001). Besides these general challenges, the UML and the existing tool support do not comprehensively include concepts and functionalities to specifically fulfill requirements of reference modeling. Though this is not an objective of the UML, it is a challenge for research to develop concepts for UML-based reference modeling. Despite of first proposed approaches to overcome these restrictions, considerably more work is necessary for determining reference modeling-related requirements and realization concepts. Finally, the application of existing UML-based reference models seems to be restricted due to some deficits of reference models. To overcome these failures and to improve and to accelerate the development of enterprise-specific models, the existing reference models have to be refined, and new models for a wide covering of application domains should be constructed.

REFERENCES

Aalst van der, W. M. P. (1999). Formalization and verification of event-driven process chains. *Information and Software Technology, 41*(10), 639-650.

Agarwal, R., & Sinha, A. P. (2003). Object-oriented modeling with UML: A study of developers' perceptions. *Communications of the ACM, 46*(9), 248-256.

Ambler, S. W. (1998). *Process patterns — Building large-scale systems using object technology*. Cambridge: Cambridge University Press.

Ambler, S. W. (1999). *More process patterns — Delivering large-scale systems using object technology*. Cambridge: Cambridge University Press.

Ambler, S. W. (2000). *The unified process elaboration phase — Best practices in implementing the UP*. Lawrence, KS: R&D Books.

Ambler, S. W., & Constantine, L. L. (2000a). *The unified process construction phase — Best practices for completing the unified process*. Lawrence, KS: CMP Books.

Ambler, S. W., & Constantine, L. L. (2000b). *The unified process inception phase — Best practices for completing the unified process*. Lawrence, KS: CMP Books.

Beck, K. (1997). *Smalltalk best practice patterns*. Upper Saddle River, NJ: Prentice Hall PTR.

Beck, K. (1998). *Kent Beck's guide to better smalltalk — A sorted collection*. Cambridge: Cambridge University Press.

Becker, J., Algermissen, L., Delfmann, P., & Niehaves, B. (2004). A Web-based platform for the design of administrational reference process models. In X. Zhou, S. Su, M. P. Papazoglou, M. E. Orlowska, & K. G. Jeffery (Eds.), *Web information systems — WISE 2004: 5th International Conference on Web Information Systems Engineering* (LNCS 3306, pp. 159-168). Berlin: Springer.

Becker, J., Delfmann, P., Dreiling, A., Knackstedt, R., & Kuropka, D. (2004). *Configurative process modeling — Outlining an approach to increased business process model usability*. Paper presented at the Information Resources Management Association Conference (IRMA), New Orleans.

Becker, J., Kugeler, M., & Rosemann, M. (Eds.). (2003). *Process management*. Berlin: Springer.

Booch, G. (2002). Growing the UML. *Software and Systems Modeling, 1*, 157-160.

Bornberg-Bauer, E., & Paton, N. W. (2002). Conceptual data modelling for bioinformatics. *Briefings in Bioinformatics, 3*(2), 165-180.

Braga, R. T. V., Germano, F. S. R., & Masiero, P. C. (1998). *A family of patterns for business resource management*. Retrieved November 14, 2002, from http://jerry.cs.uiuc.edu/plopd4-submissions/P05.pdf

Brown, W. J., Malveau, R. C., McCormick III, H. W., & Mowbray, T. J. (1998). *Antipatterns — Refactoring software, architectures, and projects in crisis*. New York: John Wiley & Sons.

Brown, W. J., McCormick III, H. W., & Thomas, S. W. (1999). *Antipatterns and patterns in software configuration management*. New York: Wiley Computer.

Brown, W. J., McCormick III, H. W., & Thomas, S. W. (2000). *Antipatterns in project management*. New York: Wiley Computer.

Broy, M., Denert, E., Renzel, K., & Schmidt, M. (Eds.). (1997). *Software architectures and design patterns in business applications. Report TUM-I9746*. München: Technische Universität München.

Bruccoleri, M., Dieaga, S. N. L., & Perrone, G. (2003). An object-oriented approach for flexible manufacturing control systems analysis and design using the unified modeling language. *The International Journal of Flexible Manufacturing Systems, 15*(3), 195-216.

Buschmann, F., & Meunier, R. (1995). A system of patterns. In D. C. Schmidt (Ed.), *Pattern languages of program design* (pp. 325-343). Reading, MA: Addison-Wesley.

Buschmann, F., Meunier, R., Rohnert, H., Sommerlad, P., & Stal, M. (1996). *Pattern-oriented software architecture — A system of patterns*. Chichester: John Wiley & Sons.

Carey, J., Carlson, B., & Graser, T. (2000). *San Francisco design patterns — Blueprints for business software*. Reading, MA: Addison-Wesley.

Champeaux, D. d. (2003). Extending and shrinking UML. *Communications of the ACM, 46*(3), 11-12.

Chen, P. P. S. (1976). The entity-relationship odel — Toward a unified view of data. *ACM Transactions on Database Systems, 1*(1), 9-36.

Coad, P. (1992). Object-oriented patterns. *Communications of the ACM, 35*(9), 152-159.

Coad, P., Lefebvre, E., & De Luca, J. (1999). *Java modeling in color with UML — Enterprise components and process*. Upper Saddle River, NJ: Prentice-Hall.

Coad, P., North, D., & Mayfield, M. (1997). *Object models — Strategies, patterns, and applications* (2nd ed.). Upper Saddle River, NJ: Yourdon.

Coplien, J. O. (2000). Software design patterns. In D. Hemmendinger (Ed.), *Encyclopedia of computer science* (4th ed., pp. 1604-1606). London; New York: Nature Publishing Group, Grove's Dictionaries.

Coplien, J. O., & Harrison, N. B. (2004). *Organizational patterns of agile software development*: Upper Saddle River, NJ: Prentice Hall PTR.

Coplien, J. O., & Schmidt, D. C. (1995). *Pattern languages of program design*. Reading, MA: Addison-Wesley.

Dietzsch, A. (2002). Adapting the UML to business modelling's needs — Experiences in situational method engineering. In J. M. Jézéquel, H. Hussmann, & S. Cook (Eds.), *UML 2002* (LNCS 2460, pp. 73-83). Berlin, Heidelberg: Springer.

Dolk, D. R. (2000). Integrated model management in the data warehouse era. *European Journal of Operational Research, 122*(2), 199-218.

Douglass, B. P. (1998). *Real-time UML: Developing efficient objects for embedded systems*. Reading, MA: Addison-Wesley.

Dreiling, A., Rosemann, M., Aalst van der, W. M. P., Sadiq, W., & Khan, S. (2005). Model-driven process configuration of enterprise systems. In O. K. Ferstl, E. J. Sinz, S. Eckert, & T. Isselhorst (Eds.), *Wirtschaftsinformatik 2005 — eEconomy, eGovernment, eSociety* (pp. 687-706). Heidelberg: Physica.

Eriksson, H. E., & Penker, M. (2000). *Business modeling with UML — Business patterns at work*. New York: John Wiley & Sons.

Fettke, P. (2005). Unified modeling language. In M. Khosrow-Pour (Ed.), *Encyclopedia of Information Science and Technology* (Vol. I-V, pp. 2921-2928). Hershey PA: Idea Group Reference.

Fettke, P., & Loos, P. (2003a). Classification of reference models — A methodology and its application. *Information Systems and e-Business Management, 1*(1), 35-53.

Fettke, P., & Loos, P. (2003b). Model driven architecture (MDA). *Wirtschaftsinformatik, 45*(5), 555-559.

Fettke, P., & Loos, P. (2003c, October 13). Multiperspective evaluation of reference models — Towards a framework. In M. A. Jeusfeld & Ó. Pastor (Eds.), *Conceptual modeling for novel application domains — ER 2003 Workshops ECOMO, IWCMQ, AOIS, and XSDM,* Chicago (pp. 80-91). Berlin: Springer.

Fettke, P., & Loos, P. (2003d). *Specifying business components in virtual engineering communities*. Paper presented at the 9th Americas Conference on Information Systems (AMCIS), Tampa, FL.

Fettke, P., & Loos, P. (2004). Referenzmodellierungsforschung. *Wirtschaftsinformatik, 46*(5), 331-340.

Fettke, P., Loos, P., & Pastor, K. (2004, March 9-11). GenGraph: A multigrammar and multiperspective business modeling tool — Overview on conceptualization and implementation. In M. Rebstock (Ed.), *Modellierung betrieblicher Informationssysteme — MobIS 2004 — Proceedings of the MobIS 2004 in conjunction with the Multikonferenz Wirtschaftsinformatik (MKWI 2004),* Essen, Germany (pp. 79-90). Bonn.

Fettke, P., Loos, P., & Zwicker, J. (2005, September 5). Business process reference models: Survey and classification. In E. Kindler & M. Nüttgens (Eds.), *Business process reference models. Proceedings of the workshop on Business Process Reference Models (BPRM 2005), Satellite Workshop of the 3rd International Conference on Business Process Management (BPM)*, Nancy, France (pp. 1-15).

Fowler, M. (1997). *Analysis patterns: Reusable object models*. Menlo Park, CA: Addison-Wesley.

Fowler, M. (1998). Software patterns. In S. Zamir (Ed.), *Handbook of object technology* (pp. 36-31, 36-38). Boca Raton: CRC Press.

Fowler, M. (2003a). *Catalog of patterns of enterprise application architecture*. Retrieved February 11, 2005, from http://www.martinfowlder.com/eaa/Catalog/

Fowler, M. (2003b). Patterns. *IEEE Software, 20*(2), 56-57.

Fowler, M. (2004). *UML distilled — A brief guide to the standard object modeling language* (3rd ed.). Boston: Addison-Wesley.

Frank, U. (1997). *Towards a standardization of object-oriented modelling languages?* (No. 3). Koblenz, Germany: Institut für Wirtschaftsinformatik der Universität Koblenz Landau.

Frank, U. (1998). Object-oriented modelling languages: State of the art and open research questions. In M. Schader & A. Korthaus (Eds.), *The unified modeling language: Technical aspects and applications* (pp. 14-31). Heidelberg: Physica.

Frank, U. (1999, August 13-15). *Conceptual modeling as the core of the information systems discipline — Perspectives and epistemological challenges*. Paper presented at the 5th Americas Conference on Information Systems (AMCIS 1999), Milwaukee, Wisconsin.

Frank, U. (2002). *Multiperspective enterprise modeling (MEMO) — Conceptual framework and modeling languages*. Paper presented at the 35th Hawaii International Conference on Systems Science (CD-ROM).

Frankel, D. S. (2003). *Model driven architecture: Applying MDA to enterprise computing*. Indianapolis: Wiley.

Fuentes, J. M., Quintana, V., Llorens, J., Génova, G., & Prieto-Díaz, R. (2003). Errors in the UML metamodel? *ACM SIGSOFT Software Engineering Notes, 28*(6), 1-13.

Gamma, E. (1992). *Objektorientierte Software-Entwicklung am Beispiel von ET++ - Design-Muster, Klassenbibliothek, Werkzeuge*. Berlin et al.: Springer.

Gamma, E., Helm, R., Johnson, R., & Vlissides, J. (1995). *Design patterns — Elements of reusable object-oriented software*. Reading, MA: Addison-Wesley.

Gerber, S., & Mai, A. (2002). Ein Referenzmodell für das Filialgeschäft von Banken als betriebliche Wissensplattform. In J. Becker & R. Knackstedt (Eds.), *Wissensmanagement mit Referenzmodellen: Konzepte für die Anwendungssystem- und Organisationsgestaltung* (pp. 195-206). Heidelberg: Physica-Verlag.

Harrison, N., Foote, B., & Rohnert, H. (1999). *Pattern languages of program design 4*. Reading, MA: Addison-Wesley.

Hay, D. C. (1996). *Data model patterns — Conventions of thought*. New York: Dorset House.

Hellenack, L. J. (1997, January). Object-oriented business patterns — Forming a foundation for business development and implementation efforts. *Object Magazine, 70*, 23-30.

Henderson-Sellers, B. (2002). The use of subtypes and stereotypes in the UML model. *Journal of Database Management, 13*(2), 43-50.

Hofstedeter, A. H. M., & Verhoef, T. F. (1996). MetaCASE: Is the game worth the candle? *Information Systems Journal, 6*(1), 41-68.

Huan, S. H., Sheoran, S. K., & Wang, G. (2004). A review and analysis of supply chain operations reference (SCOR) model. *Supply Chain Management — An International Journal, 9*(1), 23-29.

Jacobson, I., Booch, G., & Rumbaugh, J. (1998). *The unified software development process.* Reading, MA: Addison-Wesley.

Kilov, H., & Simmonds, I. D. (1996). Business patterns: Reusable abstract constructs for business specification. In J. C. Pomerol (Ed.), *Implementing Systems for Supporting Management Decisions — Concepts, methods and experiences* (pp. 225-248). London: Chapman & Hall.

Kleppe, A., Warmer, J., & Bast, W. (2003). *MDA explained: The model driven architecture: Practice and promise.* Boston: Addison-Wesley.

Kobryn, C. (1999). UML 2001: A standardization odyssey. *Communications of the ACM, 42*(10), 29-37.

Kruse, C., Hars, A., Heib, R., & Scheer, A. W. (1993). Ways of utilizing reference models for data engineering in CIM. *International Journal of Flexible Automation and Integrated Manufacturing, 1*(1), 47-58.

Laitenberger, O., Atkinson, C., Schlich, M., & Emam, K. E. (2000). An experimental comparison of reading techniques for defect detection in UML design documents. *The Journal of Systems and Software, 53*(2), 183-204.

Luxem, R. (2000). *The impact of trading digital products on retail information systems.* Paper presented at the Proceedings of the 33rd Hawaii International Conference on System Sciences, Maui.

Martin, R. C., Riehle, D., & Buschmann, F. (1998). *Pattern languages of program design 3.* Reading, MA: Addison-Wesley.

McLeod, G., Halpin, T., Kangassalo, H., & Siau, K. (2001). *UML: A critical evaluation and suggested future.* Paper presented at the 34th Hawaii International Conference on System Sciences.

Medvidovic, N., Rosenblum, D. S., Redmiles, D. F., & Robbins, J. E. (2002). Modeling software architectures in the unified modeling language. *ACM Transactions on Software Engineering and Methodology, 11*(1), 2-57.

Mellor, S. J., Scott, K., Uhl, A., & Weise, D. (2002, September 2). Model-driven architecture. In Z. Bellahsene (Ed.), *Advances in Object-Oriented Information Systems, OOIS 2002 Workshops,* Montpellier, France (pp. 290-297). Berlin: Springer.

Mendling, J., & Nüttgens, M. (2004). XML-based reference modelling: Foundations of an EPC Markup Language. In J. Becker & P. Delfmann (Eds.), *Referenzmodellierung — Grundlagen, Techniken und domänenbezogene Anwendung* (pp. 51-72). Berlin et al.: Springer.

Mertins, K., & Bernus, P. (1998). Reference models. In G. Schmidt (Ed.), *Handbook on architectures of information systems* (pp. 615-617). Berlin: Springer.

Mišic, V. B., & Zhao, J. L. (2000, October 9-12). Evaluating the quality of reference models. In V. C. Storey (Ed.), *Conceptual Modeling — ER 2000 — 19th International Conference on Conceptual Modeling,* Salt Lake City, Utah (pp. 484-498). Berlin: Springer.

Mylopoulos, J. (1998). Information modeling in the time of the revolution. *Information Systems, 23*(3/4), 127-155.

N.N. (1998). *The software patterns criteria: Proposed definitions for evaluating software pattern quality*. Retrieved in 2005, from http://www.antipatterns.com/whatispattern/

OMG. (2000, November 27). *Model driven architecture*. White Paper, Draft 3.2. Object Managment Group.

OMG. (2001a, November). *Developing in OMG's Model-Driven Architecture* — Object Management Group White Paper, Revision 2.6. Object Management Group.

OMG. (2001b). *Model driven architecture (MDA)* (No. document number ormsc/2001-07-01): Object Management Group.

OMG. (2002). *Meta object facility (MOF) specification, 1.4* (No. formal/02-04-04). Needham, MA: Object Management Group.

OMG. (2003a). *MDA Guide Version 1.0.1* (No. document number: omg/2003-06-01): Object Management Group.

OMG. (2003b). *UML 2.0 Infrastructure Specification* (Final adopted specification No. ptc/03-09-15). Needham, MA: Object Management Group.

OMG. (2003c). *UML 2.0 OCL Specification* (Final adopted specification No. ptc/03-10-14). Needham, MA: Object Management Group.

OMG. (2004). *UML 2.0 Superstructure Specification* (FTF convenience document No. ptc/04-10-02). Needham, MA: Object Management Group.

OMG. (2005a). *OMG's List Of UML 2.0 Tools*. Retrieved July 5, 2005, from http://www.uml.org#Links-UML2Tools

OMG. (2005b). *Other Links Of UML Tools (1.X And 2.0)*. Retrieved July 5, 2005, from http://www.uml.org/#Links-Tools

Opdahl, A. L., & Henderson-Sellers, B. (2002). Ontological evaluation of the UML using the Buge-Wand-Weber model. *Software and Systems Modeling, 1*(1), 43-67.

Paige, R. F., Ostroff, J. S., & Brooke, P. J. (2000). Principles for modeling language design. *Information & Software Technology, 42*(10), 665-675.

Pree, W. (1995). *Design patterns for object-oriented software development*. Wokingham: Addision-Wesley.

Ram, S., & Ramesh, V. (1998). Collaborative conceptual schema design: A process model and prototype system. *ACM Transactions on Information Systems, 16*(4), 347-371.

Remme, M. (1997). *Konstruktion von Geschäftsprozessen: ein modellgestützter Ansatz durch Montage generischer Prozesspartikel*. Wiesbaden: Gabler.

Rising, L. (1998). Pattern mining. In S. Zamir (Ed.), *Handbook of object technology* (pp. 38-31, 38-39). Boca Raton: CRC Press.

Rising, L. (2000). *The pattern almanac 2000*. Boston: Addison-Wesley.

Robbins, J. E., & Redmiles, D. F. (2000). Cognitive support, UML adherence, and XMI interchange in Argo/UML. *Information and Software Technology, 42*(2), 79-89.

Rosemann, M. (2003a). Application reference models and building blocks for management and control (ERP Systems). In P. Bernus, L. Nemes, & G. Schmidt (Eds.), *Handbook of enterprise aArchitecture* (pp. 595-615). Berlin: Springer.

Rosemann, M. (2003b). Using reference models within the enterprise resource planning lifecycle. *Australian Accounting Review, 10*(3), 19-30.

Rosemann, M., & Shanks, G. G. (2001, December 4-7). *Extension and Configuration of Reference Models for Enterprise Resource Planning Systems*. Paper presented at the 12th Australasian Conference on Information Systems (ACIS 2001), Coffs Harbour.

Rüffer, T. (1999, October 14-15). Referenzgeschäftsprozeßmodellierung eines Lebensversicherungsunternehmens. *Modellierung betrieblicher Informationssysteme — Proceedings der MobIS-Fachtagung, Universität Bamberg* (pp. 86-107). Bamberg.

Rumbaugh, J., Jacobson, I., & Booch, G. (1998). *The Unified Modeling Language reference manual*. Reading, MA: Addison-Wesley.

Saleh, K. (2002). Documenting electronic commerce systems and software using the unified modeling language. *Information and Software Technology, 44*(5), 303-311.

Scheer, A. W. (1994). *Business process engineering — Reference models for industrial enterprises* (2nd ed.). Berlin: Springer.

Scheer, A. W., & Hars, A. (1992). Extending data modeling to cover the whole enterprise. *Communications of the ACM, 35*(9), 166-172.

Scheer, A. W., & Nüttgens, M. (2000). ARIS architecture and reference models for business process management. In A. Oberweis (Ed.), *Business process management — Models, techniques, and empirical studies* (pp. 376-389). Berlin: Springer.

Schlagheck, B. (2000). *Objektorientierte Referenzmodelle für das Prozess- und Projektcontrolling - Grundlagen - Konstruktion - Anwendungsmöglichkeiten*. Wiesbaden: DUV.

Schmidt, D., Stal, M., Rohnert, H., & Buschmann, F. (2000). *Pattern-oriented software architecture — Patterns for concurrent and networked objects*. Chichester, UK: John Wiley & Sons.

Schmidt, D. C., Fayad, M., & Johnson, R. (1996). Software patterns. *Communications of the ACM, 39*(10), 36-39.

Schütte, R. (1998). *Grundsätze ordnungsmäßiger Referenzmodellierung: Konstruktion konfigurations- und anpassungsorientierter Modelle*. Wiesbaden: Gabler.

Schwegmann, A. (1999). *Objektorientierte Referenzmodellierung — Theoretische Grundlagen und praktische Anwendung*. Wiesbaden: DUV.

Shen, Z., & Siau, K. (2003). *An empirical evaluation of UML notational elements using a concept mapping approach*. Paper presented at the International Conference on Information Systems (ICIS), Seattle, Washington.

Siau, K., & Cao, Q. (2001). Unified Modeling Language (UML) — A complexity analysis. *Journal of Database Management, 12*(1), 26-34.

Siau, K., & Rossi, M. (1998). *Evaluating of information modeling methods — A review*. Paper presented at the 31st Hawaii International Conference on Systems Science (HICSS '98).

Speck, M. C. (2001). *Geschäftsprozessorientierte Datenmodellierung - Referenz-Vorgehensmodell zur fachkonzeptionellen Modellierung von Informationsstrukturen*. Münster: Logos.

Stephens, S. (2001). The supply chain council and the supply chain operations reference model. *Supply Chain Management, 1*(1), 9-13.

Supply-Chain Council Inc. (2005). *Supply-chain operations reference-model: SCOR Version 7.0 Overview*. Retrieved from http://www.supply-chain.org

Taylor, C., & Probst, C. (2003, September 29-October 2). Business Process Reference Model Languages: Experiences from BPI projects. In K. R. Dittrich, W. König, A. Oberweis, K. Rannenberg, & W. Whalster (Eds.), *INFORMATIK 2003 - Innovative Informatikanwendungen, Band 1, Beiträge der 33. Jahrestagung der Gesellschaft für Informatik e.V. (GI), Frankfurt am Main* (Vol. 34, pp. 259-263). Frankfurt am Main: Gesellschaft für Informatik.

Thomas, D. (2002). UML — Unified or universal modeling language? *Journal of Object Technology, 2*(1), 7-12.

Tichy, W. F. (1997). *A catalogue of general-purpose software design patterns*. Paper presented at the Technology of Object-Oriented Languages and Systems (TOOLS), Santa Barbara, CA.

Tzouvaras, A. (2003). *Referenzmodellierung für Buchverlage: Prozess- und Klassenmodelle für den Leistungsprozess*. Göttingen: Cuvillier.

Van Belle, J. P. W. G. D. (2003). *A framework for the analysis and evaluation of enterprise models*. Unpublished doctoral thesis, University of Cape Town, Cape Town, South Africa.

Vlissides, J. M., Coplien, J. O., & Kerth, N. L. (1995). *Pattern languages of program design 2*. Reading, MA: Addison-Wesley.

vom Brocke, J. (2003). *Referenzmodellierung: Gestaltung und Verteilung von Konstruktionsprozessen*. Berlin: Logos.

Wand, Y., & Weber, R. (2002). Research commentary: Information systems and conceptual modeling — A research agenda. *Information Systems Research, 13*(4), 363-377.

Wang, S. (2001). *Experiences with the Unified Modeling Language (UML)*. Paper presented at the 7th Americas Conference on Information Systems (AMCIS) 2001.

Zapf, M., & Heinzl, A. (2000). Evaluation of generic process design patterns: An experimental study. In A. Oberweis (Ed.), *Business Process Management — Models, Techniques, and Empirical Studies* (pp. 83-98). Berlin: Springer.

Zimmer, W. (1995). Relationships between design patterns. In D. C. Schmidt (Ed.), *Pattern Languages of Program Design* (pp. 345-364). Reading, MA: Addison-Wesley.

Identification				Construction			
				Modeling Language(s)		Construction Method	Evaluation / Inter-subjective Verifiable
No.	Name	Primary Literature [Secondary Literature]	Domain	UML Diagram(s)	Further Language(s)		
1	Frank's Reference Model	(Frank, 2000, 2001, 2002)	Internet Platform for Commerce	Class Diagram	MEMO-OrgML	n.S.	Prototype, Critical Argumentation / Partly
2	Herrmann's Reference Model	(Herrmann, 2002)	Reliability Requirements for Business Processes	Class Diagram, Package Diagram, Activity Diagram, State Machine Diagram	-	Schütte's Procedure Model	n.S.
3	Insurance Architecture (VAA)	(GDV (Ed.))	Insurer	Class Diagram, Use Case Diagram	ERM, Function Tree, Further Proprietary Diagrams and Verbal Descriptions	n.S.	n.S.
4	IOOP Reference Model (Object-oriented Derivation of the "Aachener PPS"-Model)	(Kees, 1998)	Production, Planning and Control Systems	Class Diagram	-	Derivative Method (Using Existing Models)	Prototyp and Case Studie / Partly
5	OMG Common Warehouse Metamodel (CWM)	(OMG, 2003a) [(Melchert, Schwinn, & Herrmann, 2003)]	Data Warehousing	Class Diagram, Package Diagram	-	n.S.	n.S.
6	Pumpe's Reference Model	(Pumpe, 2000)	Seaport Container Terminal	Class Diagram	EPC	Empirical	Ad Hoc Evaluation / Partly
7	Reference Model of Gerber/Mai	(Gerber & Mai, 2002)	Branch Business of Banks	Class Diagram	Process Hierarchy-Diagrams	n.S.	n.S.
8	Schaich's Reference Model	(Schaich, 2000)	Production Machinery	Class Diagram, Package Diagram, Use Case Diagram	-	Balzert's Object-oriented Analysis (OOA)	Exemplary Application
9	Schlagheck's Reference Model	(Schlagheck, 2000)	Controlling	Class Diagram, Activity Diagram		Procedure Model	Prototype / Partly
10	Schwegmann's Reference Model	(Schwegmann, 1999)	Inventory Management	Class Diagram	EPC (Extensions for Variants)	Procedure Model	Ad Hoc Evaluation / Partly
11	Tzouvaras's Reference Model	(Schumann & Tzouvaras, 2003; Tzouvaras, 2003) [(Tzouvaras & Hess, 2002; Tzouvaras, Schumann, & Hess, 2002)]	Service Processes at Book Publishers	Class Diagram, Package Diagram, Activity Diagram	-	Procedure Model	Two Case Studies / Partly

n.S. - no statement

Application					
No.	Access	Tool Support	Application Method(s)	Reuse and Customization	Use Case(s) / Inter-subjective Verifiable
1	Limited	n.S.	n.S.	n.S.	n.S.
2	Open	n.S.	n.S.	n.S.	0 (Herrmann, 2002, p. 200) / No
3	Limited	Yes	n.S.	n.S.	n.S.
4	Open	No	n.S.	n.S.	Real Application / No
5	Open	No	n.S.	n.S.	Real Application (Melchert, Schwinn, & Herrmann, 2003) / Partly
6	Open	No	n.S.	n.S.	n.S.
7	Closed	Yes	n.S.	n.S.	n.S.
8	Open	n.S.	n.S.	n.S.	n.S.
9	Open	No	Procedure Model	Model Specialization, Build-Time-Operators	n.S.
10	Open	No	Procedure Model	Model Specialization, Parameterization, Build-Time-Operators	n.S.
11	Open	No	n.S.	Build-Time-Operators	n.S.

n.S. - no statement

Chapter X

Modeling the Resource Perspective of Business Processes by UML Activity Diagram and Object Petri Net

Kamyar Sarshar, Institute for Information Systems (IWi) at the German Research Center for Artificial Intelligence (DFKI), Germany

Peter Loos, Institute for Information Systems (IWi) at the German Research Center for Artificial Intelligence (DFKI), Germany

ABSTRACT

Given that business processes are performed in an organizational context, it is essential that process-modeling notations provide proper mechanisms to represent the resources perspective of business processes. After relating the resource perspective within a framework to other business process perspectives and discussing the life cycle resource models undergo, this contribution introduces the UML 2.0 activity diagrams as well as object Petri nets regarding their approach to model the resource perspective of business processes. Afterwards, the application of the notations is illustrated by a real-life process of the health-care domain. The following comparison of the notations indicates the benefits and the limitations of both notations.

INTRODUCTION

Business processes are market-centered representations of organizational activities toward the satisfaction of specific customer needs (Becker, Dreiling, Holten, & Ribbert, 2003; Georgakopoulos, Hornick, & Sheth, 1995; Scheer, 1998). The aspect of business process modeling that has been deeply investigated is the representation of the control-flow. The control-flow describes the execution order of tasks through constructors that permit the flow of execution control (Kiepuszewski, ter Hofstede, & van der Aals, 2001). Investigation on the control-flow perspective has recently gained maturity by the identification and formal definition of a set of patterns that can be used for the evaluation of process modeling notations (Russell, ter Hofstede, Edmond, & van der Aalst, 2004; van der Aalst, ter Hofstede, Kiepuszewski, & Barros, 2003). Dumas and Hofstede have investigated the strengths and limitations of UML 2.0 activity diagrams for business process modeling regarding the control-flow perspective by examining their ability to represent those patterns (2001).

While investigations on the control-flow have gained substantial interest, the resource perspective that deals with the involvement of human and nonhuman activity performers in the execution of tasks has received significantly less attention (Basu & Kumar, 2002). But given that business processes are performed in an organizational context, it is essential that notations applied to business process modeling provide proper mechanisms to represent the structure of the resource perspective, as well as to offer adequate mechanisms to allocate tasks to the resources responsible for their execution.

Within this chapter, we investigate UML 2.0 activity diagrams capabilities to model the resource perspective of business processes. Since the UML activity diagram has been closely related to the concept of Petri nets, our contribution compares them with the Petri net formalism. We have chosen the object Petri net that has emerged to combine Petri nets with the object-oriented paradigm (Valk, 2004). It allows the definition of tokens again as Petri nets, and has already been applied to process modeling by a number of contributions (Moldt & Valk, 2000; Valk, 1998; van der Aalst, Moldt, Valk, & Wienberg, 1999). To demonstrate the application of both notations in terms of resource modeling, we will model real-life processes of the health-care domain.

The reminder of this chapter is as follows: the section after this introduction will introduce a conceptual framework for business process modeling, and puts the resources perspective and its application in the broader view of a business processes life cycle. Additionally, the section defines a number of relevant terms that are not used consistently within the literature. In Section 3, we introduce the UML 2.0 activity diagrams and discuss their approach to resource modeling. Section 4, accordingly, introduces the object Petri nets. Section 5 presents the application of the notations by a real-life health-care process. Section 6 presents a comparison of the two notations. The final section concludes with a brief summary and suggestions for future fields of work.

RESOURCE PERSPECTIVE OF BUSINESS PROCESSES

Conceptual Framework

A common way of dealing with the complexity of business processes is to define distinctive *perspectives*, clarify the contents of each perspective, and describe within a framework

Figure 1. Different perspectives on a business process (Adapted from van der Aalst & van Hee, 2002)

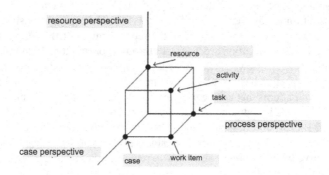

how these perspectives interrelate to each other (Scheer, 1998). The main perspectives of business processes, which are often referred to in the literature, are the *case perspective*, the *control-flow perspective* (also called process perspective or routing), and the *resource perspective* (van der Aalst & van Hee, 2002). Figure 1 illustrates these perspectives within a common framework that will be introduced in greater detail in the following.

The *case perspective* deals with the object that is transformed by the business process execution. Registration forms at the university administration, raw materials in the car production, or hospital patients can be regarded as cases. A case is represented by a set of attributes that are transformed by the execution of *tasks*. Tasks are atomic units of work that can be performed manually, automatically, or semiautomatically. A *work item* is defined as the combination of a specific case and a task that has to be carried out upon it. This is illustrated in Figure 1 at the conjunction of the control-flow and case perspective. The *control-flow perspective*, however, specifies the order in which tasks have to be carried out upon cases to achieve a desired outcome. Basically, the control-flow perspective consists of sequential, parallel, selective, and iterative execution of tasks. In contrast to the first two perspectives, which specify what is to be done, the *resource perspective* indicates who is responsible for doing it. In this sense, a resource is an entity (human or technical) that has the ability to perform a task upon a specific case. Even though some authors give broader definitions of resources (van der Aalst, Kumar, & Verbeek, 2003), we focus on resources with the ability to actively contribute to the process execution, and neglect passive resource like physical material, information, or rooms. The term *activity* is used for work items, as soon as it becomes clear which resource has the responsibility for its performance. This is illustrated in Figure 1 at the conjunction of the control-flow, the case, and the resource perspective. In other words, as soon as a work item is allocated to a resource and is just about to be carried out, it becomes an activity. This clarifies the difference between tasks as generic pieces of work and activities as their current performance upon a specific case.

Resources are classified into *resource classes* to simplify their allocation to tasks. The classification of resources is often based on qualification or function. A qualification-based classification distinguishes between resources based on a defined set of skills, also referred to as a *role*. For instance *Administrator*, *Executive*, *Counterstaff*, or *Doctor* are roles that include a set of qualification. Additionally, resources might be classified upon functions of an organization. Functions are *Production*, *Marketing*, *Sales*, or *Customer service*, reflecting different departments of an organization and leading to *organizational units*. For an accurate classification of resources, it might be useful to allocate each resource to more than one class. Within the two possible classifications mentioned above, a person can belong to an organizational unit, and within that unit fill a specific role.

Resource Perspective within the Business Process Life Cycle

A business process life cycle reflects the idea to design, implements and continuously improves the performance of business processes by permanently monitoring and analyzing the running instance and plan, and improves future process types (Scheer, 1998). Zur Muehlen (2004) extends prior business process life cycles (Galler & Scheer, 1995; Heilmann, 1996) to the resources perspective, as illustrated in Figure 2.

Figure 2. The resource perspective combined with the business process life cycle (Adapted from zur Muehlen, 2004)

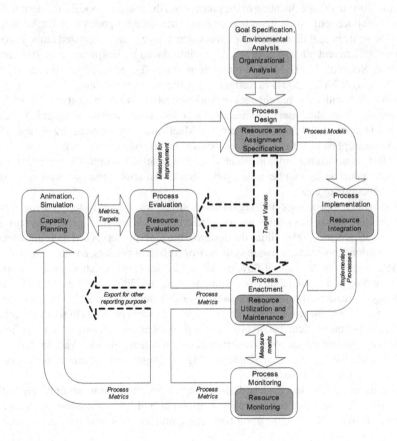

The life cycle starts with the analysis of organization goals, the environment of the future process as well as the organizational structure, and rules on how to allocate work items to resources. The information gathered at this early analysis stage is used for the purposes of the *design phase*. Regarding these two phases Weske et al. (Weske, Goesmann, Holten, & Striemer, 1999) introduce a reference model on how to survey and design proper process models for an organization. The overall objective of the design phase is to adequately describe the structure of the control-flow and the resource perspective, as well as to define responsibilities for the execution of each task by allocating them to appropriate resources. The modeling of the control-flow includes the specification of the logical order in which tasks have to be performed. The resources model reflects different resource classes and illustrates how they are interrelated to each other. Metaresource models that could be the starting point for the resource modeling have been proposed, among others, by van der Aalst et al. (van der Aalst, Verbeek, & Kumar, 2001), Winter and Ebert (1996), Cheng (1999) and Scheer (2001).

As long as a single or several units of human resources within an organization are considered, the resource model is basically represented by a hierarchy of leaders and subordinates and is modeled by the organizational charts. However, alternative organizational models are the matrix of the network organization that might be applied in an interorganizational context (Picot, Reichwald, & Wigand, 2001).

In addition to the specification of the process and the resource models, the design phase involves the allocation of work items to resources. The allocation policy used for this purpose reflects the strategy that determines how work items have to be distributed among process participants. Different allocation strategies are introduced by Hoffmann et al. (Hoffmann, Löffeler, & Schmidt, 1999). Momotko and Subieta (2002) and Governatori et al. (Governatori, Rotolo, & Sadiq, 2004) investigate dynamic allocation strategies, and suggest an approach to deal with dynamic changes of work allocation. While in most cases work items are assigned to individual users, Domingos et al. (Domingos, Martins, Preguiça, & Duarte, 1999) and Dourish et al. (Dourish, Holmes, A. MacLean, Marqvardsen, & Zbyslaw, 1996) propose a concept on how to assign work items to teams. Baggio et al. (Baggio, Wainer, & Ellis, 2004) argue that the order in which cases are handled by a process participant has a significant impact on the number of late jobs. They also discuss some issues on how to deal with the execution of cases.

The modeled processes and organization structures are ready to enter the process implementation phase, where they are integrated into workflow management systems (zur Muehlen & Rosemann, 2004). Since the design of business processes and their implementation is often done by diverse software systems from different vendors, an interchange format being able to represent the control-flow as well as the resource perspective becomes a critical issue. Mendling et al. (Mendling, Neumann, & Nüttgens, 2004) compare 15 XML-based interchange formats for business processes regarding their metamodels. The comparison indicates that except for two formats, all others provide some concepts to represent roles as an abstraction of the participants involved in the process execution. However, these formats are short of representing the resource structure as a distinctive model. Van der Aalst et al. (2001) extends the XRL (exchangeable routing language) with entities representing the resource perspective of a process.

The importance of the models designed at the design phase is not only due to their application at run-time, but they are already useful at build-time for adjustments through simulation. Desel and Erwin (2000) point out the importance of a formal syntax and semantics of process models, since otherwise they would not be properly executable by a simulation engine. Domains for the simulation regarding resources allocation might be, for example, manufacturing plants (Czarnecki, Schroer, & Rahman, 1997) or hospitals (Pitt, 1997).

The later phases of the life cycle include enactment and evaluation. The enactment phase stands for the instantiation of models, and involves the notification of human and technical resources specified for performing work items. While the process enactment is running, the monitoring takes place in order to measure the performance of process enactment by collecting data on metrics, such as the length of work queues, the idle time of resources, or the wait time of pending activities. Castellanos et al. (Castellanos, Casati, Dayal, & Shan, 2004) present a set of concepts that enables data mining techniques to business process execution to analyze and predict metrics of interest. Results from this evaluation might be used for planning the capacity of resources, or for finding indications on how to reorganize the resources, or provide trainings to improve the skills of process participants.

UML ACTIVITY DIAGRAMS
Activity Diagram Foundations

UML 2.0 comprises 13 diagrams that specify different aspects of a system. This chapter will deal with the UML 2.0 activity diagram as one of the behavioral diagrams of UML 2.0 in the way introduced in Object Management Group (2004). Within UML 1.x, the activity diagram was seen as a special form of the state diagram. But since the semantics of the underlying state machine restricted the use of activity diagrams, this tie has been removed in UML 2.0. Consequently, they went through a major revision that has significantly extended their expressiveness.

The core elements of activity diagrams are illustrated in Figure 3 and will be introduced briefly. Basically, an activity diagram consists of nodes and edges. The nodes can be categorized into action nodes, control nodes, and object nodes. Activities consist of actions nodes that represent atomic pieces of work insofar as they may not be decomposed further. In that sense, the term *action* corresponds to the term *task* in the way introduced in Section 2. However, an *activity* has been introduced as a work item allocated to a resource that is obviously different from the meaning of this term in context of activity diagrams. An action executes when all control and data inputs needed are satisfied, and provides control and data to other actions after they have been completed. The send signal action can activate and accept event action. If the accept event action has no incoming edge, it can start as soon as the event occurs. Control nodes route control and data through an activity diagram. The flow in an activity diagram starts at initial nodes. As soon as an initial node starts, it receives control and passes it immediately along its outgoing edges. Decision nodes choose between outgoing flows. Usually outgoing edges from a decision node have guards that determine at run-time which edge has to be followed. Merge nodes bring together multiple flows by passing control and data token arrived at their incoming edges to outgoing edges. The fork node is applied to split the flow into multiple concurrent flows by duplicating control and data arriving at a fork across all outgoing edges. These multiple flows can be synchronized again by a join node where data and control must be available at all incoming edges before they can be passed to the outgoing edge. The use of activity final nodes or flow final nodes is dependent on whether the whole activity has to be terminated or just the flow at one edge. Object nodes indicate an instance of a particular classifier and have a variety of applications.

Figure 3. Core elements of UML activity diagrams

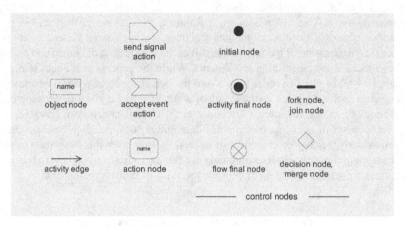

An object node can hold a single or multiple token, while their "upper bound" indicates the maximum number of tokens they may contain. For an in-depth introduction of these elements we refer to OMG document (Object Management Group, 2004) as well as to Bock (2003-2005), Fowler (2004), and Schnieders, Puhlmann, and Weske (2004).

One of the major changes of UML 2.0 activity diagrams is the integration of control and data by a "Petri-like semantics" (Object Management Group, 2004). In particular, activity diagrams follow the traditional use of undistinguishable (black) tokens as a representation of control flow, and use colored tokens for representing data flow at run-time. While control tokens regulate when successive actions are able to start through passing control to flow edges, data tokens transport input and output data of actions by passing object flow edges.

Figure 4. Activity diagram example for a catheter investigation

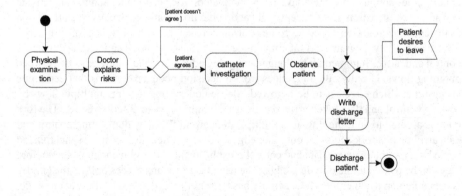

However, in contrast to the Petri nets, tokens of activity diagrams are used for a textual description of the semantics of the elements, and are neither used explicitly for modeling purposes nor as a vehicle for formalizing the semantics of activity diagram elements. Another difference between the two notations is that Petri nets represent basically closed systems where all changes occur due to firing of transitions within the system rather then through events in the system environment. In contrast, activity diagrams are open systems, capable of being reactive to their environment by responding to external events. This is one reason why activity diagrams are seen as well-suited, not only for specifying dynamic aspects of the implementation level of a software system, but also to express high-level specification of business processes (Eshuis & Wieringa, 2003). Figure 4 illustrates the application of the activity diagram where the event *patient desires to leave* influences the execution of the process and leads to the discharge of the patient.

Modeling the Resource Perspective by Activity Diagrams

Activity diagrams use partitions to represent groups of nodes and edges that have common characteristics. Depending on whether activity diagrams are applied for design specification for software implementation or for a height-level specification of business processes, partitions can have different applications. In the context of business process modeling, partitions often correspond to organizational units (Object Management Group, 2004). The swimlane notation of partitions divide process models graphically into distinctive areas of parallel vertical or horizontal lines, with a box at one end labeling the name of the partition. Swimlanes have no impact on the token flow of the model, and are just used to indicate what or who is responsible for the execution of actions grouped by the partition.

A simple form of applying partitions to business process modeling is to locate, horizontally or vertically, side-by-side, all resources involved in their execution. The allocation of business process tasks (activity diagram actions) to resources is achieved by locating them according swimlanes. This would be sufficient to illustrate which units are generally involved in the process execution, and which part of the process they are dealing with. Although this approach is straight forward, it is inappropriate to represent the resource perspective of a business process, since it is lacking in illustrating the organizational structure of the units involved in the process execution. With a side-by-side representation of partitions, it remains unclear whether the units are at the same organizational level; whether some of them belong to a higher-level unit within the hierarchy or others to a lower one. As a result, partitions of the UML activity diagrams can be structured in order to represent the relation between the units. One way of structuring partitions is to divide them into subpartitions. By using subpartitions, the hierarchy of units within an organization can be expressed appropriately. Partitions and subpartitions can directly correspond to equivalent organizational units illustrated through an organization chart. This leads to a reasonable representation of the resource perspective of business processes for hierarchically organized companies. However, not all companies have a hierarchical organization. In order to expand the expressiveness of partitions, the UML activity diagrams also include the possibility for multidimensional partitions that are useful to express matrix organizations. For example, an organization may have one dimension for the locations where a company runs its plants, while the other dimension corresponds to equivalent organizational units within each plant.

But the use of swimlanes is just one possible notation to allocate tasks to partitions. In some modeling situations, using swimlanes may not be practicable. An alternate notation is to add the partition name to the action name, as shown in Figure 5. Double colon within the partition name indicates partition hierarchy, where the later partitions are nested in the partitions coming earlier in the name. Comma-delimited partition stands for multidimensional partition name, expressing that the node is contained in more then one partition.

Whenever actions are to occur outside the primary concern of a model, an activity diagram partition can be labeled with the keyword «external». For instance, an external partition can be used to represent the parts of a business process dealing with the customer or the supplier of a company. In these situations, a partition labeled by «external» indicates that even if it is located next to other partitions, it does not have to be interpreted as another organizational unit. The keyword «external» can also be added to the name of some actions

Figure 5. Alternative use of partitions within activity diagrams

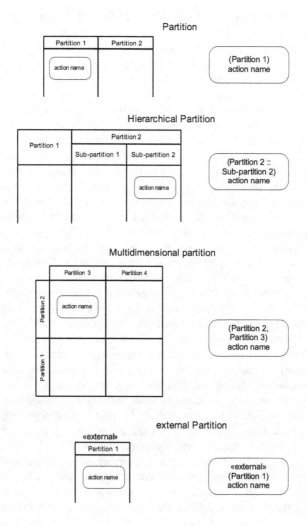

within a swimlane to express that out of all other actions, these are not performed by the unit. Figure 5 illustrates alternative approaches to representing partitions within activity diagrams.

OBJECT PETRI NET
Object Petri Net Foundations

Petri net is a generic term for a number of modeling techniques, graphical representations, and notational conventions that are all based on the concept of net formalism introduced by Carl Adam Petri (Petri, 1962). Since their introduction, Petri nets have been extensively investigated within the scientific community, whereby different extensions and applications were introduced (Reisig & Rozenberg, 1998). The most basic idea of the Petri nets is the concept of local state and local action. A local action is generally influenced by a set of local states only. The convention for the graphical notation is to represent states (also called places) by circles, and actions (also called transitions) by boxes. Places and transitions are connected by directed arcs that always run from a place to a transition, or from a transition to a place. This leads to the following definition for Petri nets (Petri, 1996):

Definition 1. A Petri net is a triple (P, T, F):

- P is a finite set of places,
- T is a finite set of transitions (P ∩ T = ∅),
- F ⊆ (P × T) ∪ (T × P) is a set of arcs (flow relation)

A significant difference between Petri net types is their token concept. Within elementary Petri nets, undistinguishable black tokens represent the availability of states, while at high-level Petri nets, tokens are data structures that are transformed by transitions. Van der Aalst (1998) proposes an interpretation of Petri nets elements for modeling business processes where tasks are modeled by transitions, conditions by places, and the process case

Figure 6. Business process interpretation of elementary Petri nets (Adapted form van der Aalst, 1998)

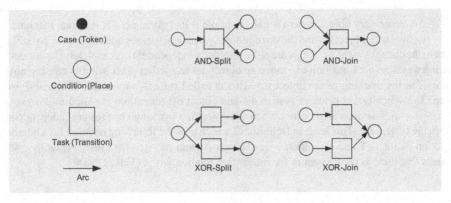

by token. The control-flow perspective is represented by the appropriate structure of places and transitions. These elements are illustrated in Figure 6.

Even though the use of structured tokens permits the representation of more complex systems, they still remain passive and have no dynamic behavior. With the emergence of object-orientation, some research has been conducted to combine Petri net models with the object-oriented paradigm (Girault & Valk, 2003). The object Petri net is one of these approaches that add dynamic behavior to tokens by defining them as Petri nets again (Valk, 2004). The approach has its origins in works describing the execution of task systems in systems of functional units (Jessen & Valk, 1987; Valk, 1987; Valk, 1991). Later, the formalism was generalized to *elementary object nets (EOS)* (Valk, 1996, 1998), whereby one or more so-called object nets move through a system net as ordinary tokens. System and object nets are roles within each level of modeling. In other words, while a Petri net is a system net at a level containing object nets as token, it can be the object net of another Petri net in a lower hierarchy.

A central characteristic of the approach is the distinction between reference and value semantics. The reference semantics restrict that all tokens within a system net have to refer to an identical object net (Valk, 1998). It has lead to the development of the *reference nets* (Kummer, 2002), and implemented by the *renew* tool (Kummer, Wienberg, Duvigneau, Schumacher, Köhler, Moldt, et al., 2004). The value semantics allows that object nets within a system net refer to independent object net copies. In contrast to the simple bimarking used by the reference semantics where the marking of the object Petri net consists of the marking of the object and the system net, the value semantics applied the p-marking (process marking) in order to execute consistently (Valk, 2001).

To introduce the use of object Petri net approach for workflow resource modeling and to keep the formal approach as simple as possible, we will focus on *unary EOS*. A unary EOS consists of only two levels: one system net and one object net, both being elementary net systems (EN systems) (Thiagarajan, 1987). The following definition introduced the elements of a unary EOS, as defined in Valk (1998)

Definition 2. A unary elementary object system is a tuple EOS = (SN,ON,ρ) where

- SN= (P,T,W,M_0) is an EN system with $|M_0|$ =1, called system net of EOS,
- ON = (B,E,F,m_0) is an EN system, called object net of EOS, and
- $\rho \subseteq T \times E$ is the interaction relation.

An elementary object system is called simple if its system net SN is a state machine.

Between the object net and the surrounding system net, various interactions are possible where the changes in the markings are either mutually independent or completely dependent. Firing a system net transition can move an object net to another place without causing any change in the marking of the object net. This is called *system-autonomous* or a *transport* step. The synchronous firing of system net and object net transitions is called *interaction*. An *object-autonomous* step occurs when the object net marking changes are independent from the system net. This leads to Definition 2 which uses the following notation for a binary relation ρ: for t∈T and e∈E let tρ:={e∈E|(t,e)∈ρ} and ρe:={t∈T|(t,e)∈ρ}. Then tρ = $\varnothing$ means that there is no element in the interaction relation with t (Valk, 1998).

Figure 7. Object Petri net example (Valk, 1998)

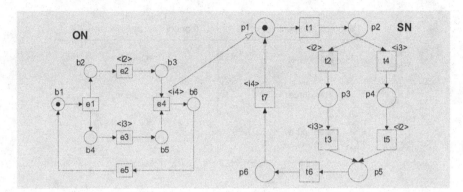

Definition 3. A bimarking of a unary elementary object system EOS = (SN,ON,ρ) is a pair (M, m) where M is a marking of the system net SN and m is a marking of the object net ON.

a. A transition t ∈ T is activated in a bimarking (M,m) of EOS if tρ = ∅ and t is activated in M. Then the follower bimarking (M′,m′) is defined by M →$_t$ M′ (w.r.t. SN) and m = m′. We write (M,m) →$_{[t,λ]}$ (M′,m′) in this case.
b. A pair [t, e] ∈ T × E is activated in a bimarking (M,m) of EOS if (t,e) ∈ ρ and t and e are activated in M and m, respectively. Then the follower bimarking (M′,m′) is defined by M →$_t$ M′ (w.r.t. SN) and m →$_e$ m′ (w.r.t. ON). We write (M,m) →$_{[t,e]}$ (M′,m′) in this case.
c. A transition e ∈ E is activated in a bimarking (M,m) of EOS if ρe = ∅ and e is activated in m. Then the follower bimarking (M′,m′) is defined by m →$_e$ m′ (w.r.t. ON) and M′ = M. We write (M,m) →$_{[λ,e]}$ (M′,m′) in this case.

Figure 7 gives an example of the three possible interaction relations between the system and object nets of object Petri nets (Valk, 1998).

The object net (ON) illustrated on the left is located at the place p1 of the system net (SN). The label <i$_n$> stands for the interaction relation ρ of definition 2. It synchronizes steps between the respective transitions of the object net and system net; a missing label indicates a mutually autonomous step. Since there is no such label at transition e1 and t1, an object autonomous step of the object net and a system autonomous step of the system net is possible. After these steps, object and system net have reached a point where interactions between the two levels at e2 and t2 as well as e3 and t4 are possible next steps.

Modeling the Resource Perspective by Object Petri Nets

One of the application domains of object Petri nets is workflow modeling. The idea of mapping the system net to the resource perspective, and the object nets to the control-flow perspective of a business process have been sketched by a minor case study of the

Figure 8. Business process interpretation of object Petri nets

	System net (resource perspective)	Object net (control-flow perspective)
● Token	Object net	Case
○ Place	Resource	Condition
▢ Transition	Relation btw. Resourcese	Task

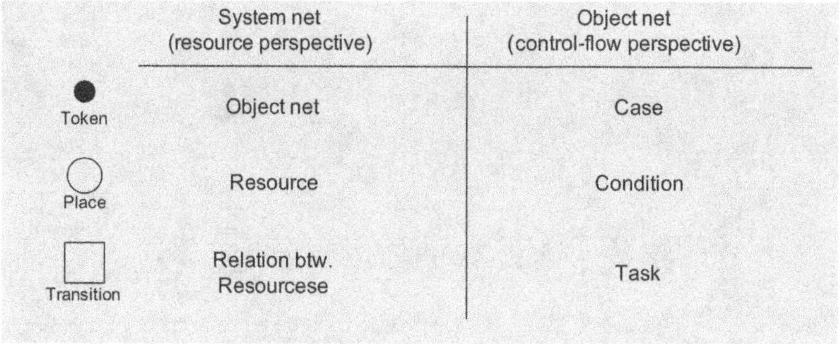

Dutch Justice department in Valk (2001). Van der Aalst generalizes the idea and introduces a conceptual framework for interorganizational workflow enactment by which different perspectives of workflows including control-flow, resource, data, task, and operation can be represented by the reference nets (van der Aalst et al., 1999). Based on these preliminary works, we introduce an approach of business process interpretation of object Petri nets. The elements of the object Petri net and their interpretation for representing these perspectives are illustrated in Figure 8.

A place of the system net represents a single resource, while the transitions stand for the relation between resources that pass a business process from one resource to another. Examples of such a relation would be *contract* or *delivery* relations between a company and its supplier or customers, or *referring* a patient from a general practitioner to a hospital. Tokens located at a system net place represent the control-flow of a business process. As long as a transition of the object net is not labeled for a synchronous step with the system net, the object is executed autonomously. In other words, tasks that execute by an autonomous step within a system net place are those that are allocated to the resource represented by the state. However, a synchronous step of the system and the object net passes the object net to a proceeding resource. The execution of a system net transition can also pass the process to another resource while it causes no changes in the process state. We call this a transportation step.

Figure 9 gives an example of applying object Petri nets to business process modeling. The illustrated business process includes three tasks: t_1, t_2, and t_3. t_1 is allocated to $unit_1$, t_2 to $unit_2$, and t_3 to $unit_3$. The system net illustrates these units and their interrelations. Since the process is initially located in $unit_1$, this resource is responsible for the autonomous execution of t_1. Afterwards, the synchronized execution of a_2 and u_{1_2} (<i1>) would pass the process to $units_2$ where task t_2 is executed by an autonomous step. Alternatively, the execution of a_3 and u_{1_3} (<i2>) passes the process to $units_3$ where t_3 is executed. The process returns to $unit_1$ by executing a_1 and u_{2_1} (u_{3_1}). By using the introduced occurrence sequence, the dynamic behavior of the business process, which includes the control-flow and the resource perspective, can be described formally as $[\lambda,t_1]$, $[u_{1\_2}, a_2]$, $[\lambda,t_2],[u_{2\_1},a_1]$ or alternatively as $[\lambda,t_1]$, $[u_{1\_3}, a_3]$, $[\lambda,t_3],[u_{3\_1},a_1]$.

The underlying semantics of the unary EOS allow copy tokens at the system net level, but because it applies the reference semantics, all copies refer to the same object net in-

Figure 9. Representing different business process perspectives by object Petri nets

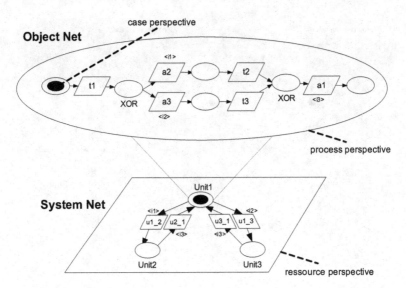

stance. For instance, if the above process included an AND instead of XOR, the concurrent execution of t_2 by unit$_2$ and t_3 by unit$_3$ would have an impact on the same process instance. However, in some situations it might be helpful to overcome this restriction and allow real copies of business process instances to be executed by distributed resources. This is the case when business processes are executed in a distributed environment of an interorganizational context, where the organizations have no permanent access to the same instance of the process at runtime. While the duplication of process instances represented by the token duplication at the system net level is not a challenge, merging copies of process instances is a delicate task. By executing parts of the business process through different resources, the state of each process instance changes independently. In order to avoid inconsistent joining of process instances, the value semantics and the p-marking of the object Petri net need to be applied. Informally described, the p-marking associates to every place of the system net a process of the object net that represents the execution history of the object net and defines the existence of a *least upper bound (lub)* as a condition for joining the object net instances. An example for a consistent joining of two process instances is given in Figure 10. The system net copies the object net from unit$_1$ to unit$_2$ and unit$_3$, where t_2 and t_3 are executed, leading to the process marking shown below. The next step is the consistent join of both instances by the two transitions labeled with <i2> that passes them to unit$_1$. For further details on the value-semantics of object Petri nets and their formal representation, we refer to Valk (2001, 2004).

Figure 10. Example of applying the value semantic of object Petri nets

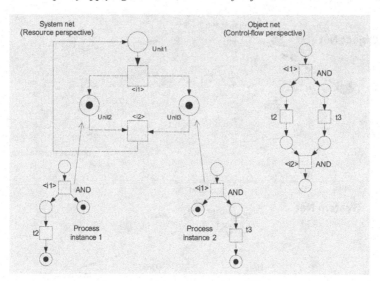

Application of the Notations

Following Figures 11 and 12 present a health-care process, in order to illustrate the application of both notations. For modeling the processes, we have used data collected at the cardiology of Mainz University Hospital (Sarshar, Dominitzki, Reichel, & Loos, 2005). The process expresses the treatment of patients who are sent by their general practitioner to the hospital for a cardiac catheter investigation. The investigation is undertaken to detect and treat narrowed heart arteries. It involves an x-ray screening at the catheter laboratory and usually a 1-2 day admission at the hospital.

To keep the models comparable, we designed the object Petri net version of the business process visually close to the activity diagram. The upper part of the object Petri net reflects the resource perspective by the system net mainly represented by the swimlanes of the activity diagrams. The lower part is the control-flow perspective. Synchronous transitions are labeled by $<i_n>$.

COMPARING THE NOTATIONS

After introducing and presenting the application of activity diagram and the object Petri net, in the following we compare the two notations, considering their approaches to modeling of the resource perspective of business processes. Basically, the process modeling notations are used to develop models at the design phase, which emphases an intuitive representation of the models. But the fact that the models undergo afterwards different stages

Figure 11. A health-care process represented by UML activity diagram

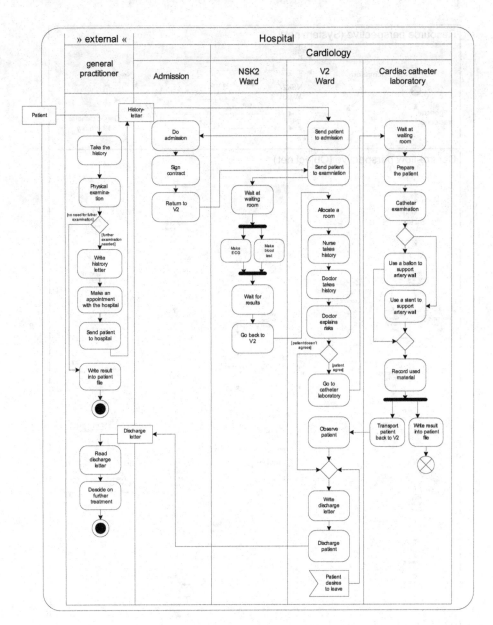

Figure 12. A health-care process represented by object Petri net

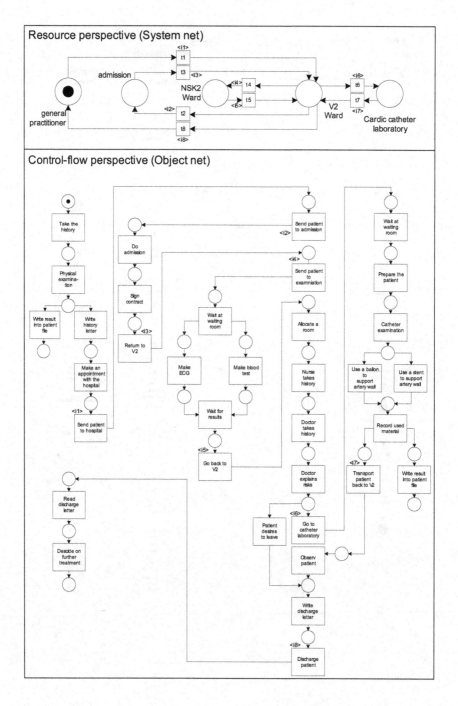

within their life cycle leads to some additional criteria. Our applied set of criteria is based on the framework and the business process life cycle introduced in Section 2.

Intuitive Representation of the Resource Perspective

As discussed in Section two, process-modeling notations are initially used at the design phase to develop models. Since the design stage often involves the cooperation with the end-user in order to evaluate the contents of the models, chosen notations have to be intuitively comprehended by people with little or no knowledge on modeling. The fact that already the formal semantics and the abstract representation of elementary Petri nets have been regarded as not intuitive for end-users (Green & Rosemann, 1999; Sarshar et al., 2005) leads to the presumption that this is also the case for object Petri nets. The models shown previously support this guess. The difficulty for end-users would probably be to comprehend the idea of the multilevel modeling, the independent and synchronous firing of transitions and that, depending on the modeling level (system or objects), places and transitions have to be interpreted differently, even if they are graphically represented similar at both levels. In contrast, the representation of the resource perspective through swimlanes is straight forward, and meets the requirement of an intuitive representation for end-users better than is the case with the object Petri net.

Representing Resources and their Relations

A further criterion for comparing the two notations is their expressiveness in modeling the resources and their relations. Activity diagrams offer partitions to represent resources involved in the execution of business processes, while object Petri nets use states of the system net for this matter. Hence, except for the «external» partition in activity diagrams, the notations are similar in representing resources. But the difference between the two notations is that swimlanes are used to represent only the resources involved in the execution of the business process tasks, and omit resources that are available, but not involved in the process execution. In other words, the swimlanes describe a business-process-specific view on the overall resource model. By using the object Petri nets, it is generally possible to give a holistic and process independent view of all existing resources by describing them with the system net, as often done by an organizational chart. In such an approach, the process specific parts of the system net would only be the labels indicating the synchronous firing of some transition within a specific process.

Another difference between the two notations is their applied concepts to express the relations between resources. The relation between organizational units or human resources within an organization is often defined by a hierarchy, or in some cases by a matrix, where the roles of leaders and subordinates are precisely defined. However, in a network organization, which can be used in an inter-organizational context, organizations do not interact based on a hierarchy, but on market-driven mechanisms like ordering and delivering goods and services. The swimlanes approach of the activity diagram is able to represent hierarchically organized resources (hierarchical partitions) and resources organized by a matrix (multidimensional partitions), but lacks modeling a network organization. Using the system net of an object Petri net to represent the resource perspective of a business process delivers enough flexibility to model different relations between resources including the network organization. This flexibility is rooted in the generic application of the system net transitions for mutual interrelation between resources. This approach extends the basically hierarchical view of activity diagram partitions to different kinds of interrelations that cause the passing of process execution responsibility to proceeding resources. In other words, using the system net for representing resources means not just to catch the static hierarchy of the organization, but also to indicate how a process is jointly executed by different resources beyond the hierarchy where, in fact, the hierarchy might not even play a major role. But despite this advantage, one has to keep in mind that system net can become very complex for nontrivial real-life situations. This is already obvious for the processes illustrated in Section 5. In reality, the cardiology consists of a lot more subunits that are all hierarchically related to each other. Considering all these subunits would have led to a complex system net that would suffer in terms of readability.

Allocation of Tasks to Resources

A further issue of modeling the resource perspective is the mechanism used for representing the allocation of tasks to resources. Both notations offer such a mechanism, even though they follow different approaches. The difference is illustrated by an example in Figure 13.

Using swimlanes, the activity allocation is done by locating tasks within according swimlanes. This is illustrated in Figure 13 for the activities *send patient to admission, do admission,* and *sign contract.* Object Petri nets, in contrast, do not present the allocation of each task to a resource, but illustrate the position within the process, where the responsibility is passed from one resource to another by a synchronous firing of system and object net transition. In Figure 13, the two transitions labeled by $<i_1>$ pass the process from *V2 ward* to *Admission* where both proceeding tasks are executed.

Figure 13. Different approaches to resource allocation to tasks

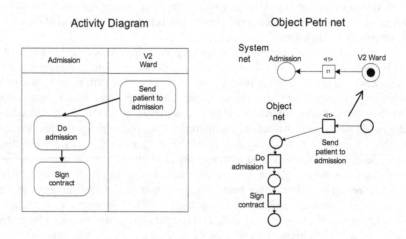

Supported by an XML-Format

Keeping in mind that modeling can be distributed to different modelers using different tools, the aspect of exchange format for business process models becomes crucial. The exchange format applied to business processes not only needs to be able to describe the control-flow perspective, but also needs to express their resource perspective, as well as to indicate the allocation of tasks to resources. The first choice for an interchange format for activity diagrams is the XML metadata interchange (XMI) (Object Management Group, 2005), which is basically an interchange format for metadata that are defined in terms of the metaobject facility (MOF). Accordingly, the Petri net markup language (PNML) (Billington, Christensen, van Hee, Kindler, Kummer, Petruc-ci, et al., 2003) as an XML-based interchange format for Petri nets should play the same role for object Petri nets. But in order to express an object Petri net, not only a Petri net alone has to be expressed, but also the interrelation between the transitions that need to be synchronously fired. Considering the variety of the existing and future Petri net types, PNML allows the definition of *Petri net types*. Hence, it has been extended to support the reference net semantics of the object Petri nets defined by the reference net and applied by the *renew* tool (Kummer et al., 2004). The characteristic of describing synchronously firing transitions has been included into reference nets by downlinks and uplinks. They have been implemented by the PNML definition as shown in Table 1.

Table 1. Interrelating transitions of object net and system net by PNML

Refence net chracteristic	Graphical-representation	PNML-representation

Uplink	uplink-name	`<transition id="...">`
		`<name>`
		`<text>...</text>`
		`</name>`
		`<uplink>`
		`<text>...</text>`
		`</uplink>`
		`</transition>`

Downlink	donwlink-name	`<transition id="...">`
		`<name>`
		`<text>...</text>`
		`</name>`
		`<downlink>`
		`<text>...</text>`
		`</downlink>`
		`</transition>`

Formal Semantics

The aspects discussed so far emphasize the graphical and textual representation of the models at the design phase. However, the design phase is not the end of business process modeling, but often a means for the proceeding stages in the life cycle. Some of these stages include formal analyses or evaluation of the models through simulation, as well as their implementation within an enterprise system, requiring a precise definition of the process semantic. A business process specified in terms of Petri nets has the great advantage to be unambiguous (van der Aalst, 1996): that makes them the preferred choice for analysis and simulation purposes. Accordingly, object Petri nets are well formalized. They have been investigated deeply on their formal characteristics (Köhler, 2003; Köhler & Rölke, 2005). This distinction between their reference and value semantics addresses relevant issues of central and distributed executions of business processes, and offers a formal solution for describing them. Additionally, they offer a formal approach to deal with multiple process instances, and indicate how to merge them consistently.

In contrast, the semantics of the activity diagram provided by the OMG is mainly text-based, which leads to ambiguities in understanding the semantics of them properly. A number of authors have undertaken major efforts to overcome this disadvantage by introducing a formal semantics for the notation. Approaches within the literature make use of use OCL (object constraint language) (Gogolla & Richters, 2002), FSP (finite state processes) (Rodrigues, 2000), pi-calculus (Dong & ShenSheg, 2003), and ASM (abstract state machine) (Hammer, Hanish, & Dillon, 1998; Ko, Lee, Noh, Cheol-Jung Yoo, & Chang, 2005) as well as Petri nets (Störrle, 2005). However, these approaches focus on the control-flow perspective, and neglect the involvement of resources within the execution of tasks.

Simulation engine

One major advantage of a formal notation is its ability to simulate represented process models. No simulation engine is known that supports the UML 2.0 activity diagrams including the partition notation. However, the *renew* tool (Kummer et al., 2004) is available for modeling and simulating the reference semantics of the object Petri nets formalized by the reference nets. Even though the tool is a prototype, it is well suited to demonstrating the instantiation and the execution of the models at run-time, including issues like deadlock detection, lead-time, and resource capacity considerations.

The comparison of the notations discussed above is summarized in Table 2.

CONCLUSION

The importance of business process modeling for the success of organizations has led to the development of a variety of modeling notations that can be applied to their design, analysis, and simulation. This contribution has introduced two notations, namely the UML activity diagram and the object Petri nets, and compared them with regard to their ability to represent the resource perspective of business process. Obviously, both notations have their strengths and limitations. While the strengths of the activity diagrams lie in their intuitive representation of the resource perspective by applying hierarchical and multidimensional swimlanes, and having a straightforward approach to allocate tasks to resources by locating them within swimlanes, the notation is limited in its expressiveness of the organizational structure and lacks formal semantics. In contrast, object Petri nets are well formalized,

Table 2. Summary of comparison

Criteria	UML activity diagram	Object Petri net
Intuitive representation of the resource perspective	Highly intuitive representation through the use of swimlanes	Less intuitive due to a multilevel modeling, synchronous firing of transitions, and representation of the elements
Representing resources and their relations	Resources are presented by partitions. The representation of their interrelations is limited matrix or hierarchies.	Resources are presented by system net state. The representation of their interrelations by system net transition is flexible and beyond formal organization structure. Models can become very complex.
Allocation of tasks to resources	Locating the task within the swimlane	Indicating where a process is passed to a proceeding resource
Supported by an XML-Format	XMI	PNML extended for reference net
Formal semantics	Different approaches for formalizing the control-flow perspective based on the textual semantics offered by OMG	Formalization of resources, tasks as well as their allocation and the dynamic behavior of the models during runtime
Simulation engine	-	Renew (Reference semantics)

consider central and distributed execution of process instances, and offer a formal approach to deal with inconsistencies. They are more flexible in representing the organization structure. However, they can be considered as not intuitive, and can become very complex for real-life processes.

Hence, one can conclude that both notations have complementary characteristics that should be combined to achieve an optimal solution for business process modeling. Such an approach can use the activity diagram as a front-end notation, preferably applied to capture relevant aspects of the reality in cooperation with end-users at the design stage, while the object Petri could serve to formalize the models for analysis, simulation, and implementation purposes for later stages. Such an integrated approach has been proposed, for instance, for a combined use of the event-driven process chain (EPC) (Keller, Nüttgens, & Scheer, 1992), and elementary Petri nets regarding the control-flow (Moldt & Rodenhagen, 2000). But since the transformation between semiformal and formal notations is a nontrivial task, further investigation is required on this issue in the future.

Another area for further investigation is the case perspective and its relations to the resource, as well as the control-flow of business processes. A common approach to business process cases is to model them as data structures manipulated by tasks. For many purposes, this is an accurate representation of a process case. But the approach implicitly assumes that the values of an attribute remain unchanged as long as no task is performed. This might be an oversimplification of the reality regarding domains like healthcare, where a patient can change his/her state spontaneously by developing a disease that needs to be treated immediately and, as a result, has an impact on the control-flow as well as on the resource perspective at runtime. Generally, these kinds of interrelations between the business process perspectives are not well understood and require more investigation in the future.

REFERENCES

Baggio, G., Wainer, J., & Ellis, C. (2004). *Applying scheduling techniques to minimize the number of late jobs in workflow systems.* Paper presented at the Proceedings of the 2004 ACM Symposium on Applied Computing, Nicosia, Cyprus.

Basu, A., & Kumar, A. (2002). Research commentary: Workflow management issues in e-business. *Information Systems Research, 13*(1), 1-14.

Becker, J., Dreiling, A., Holten, R., & Ribbert, M. (2003). Specifying information systems for business process integration — A management perspective. *Information Systems and E-Business Management, 1*(3), 231-263.

Billington, J., Christensen, S., van Hee, K., Kindler, E., Kummer, O., Petruc-ci, L., et al. (2003). *The Petri Net Markup Language: Concepts, technology, and tools.* Paper presented at the 24th International Conference on Application and Theory of Petri Nets ICATPN 2003, Eindhoven, The Netherlands.

Bock, C. (2003-2005). UML 2 activity and action models. 2(4), 43-53, part 2: Actions - 2(5), 41-56, part 3: Control nodes - 2(6), 7-23, part 4: Object nodes - 3(1), 27-41, part 5: Partitions - 3(7), 37-56, part 6: Structured Activities 4(4), 43-66. *Journal of Object Technology.*

Castellanos, M., Casati, F., Dayal, U., & Shan, M. C. (2004). A comprehensive and auto-mated approach to intelligent business processes execution analysis. *Distributed and Parallel Databases, 16*(3), 239-273.

Cheng, E. C. (1999). *An object-oriented organizational model to support dynamic role-based access control in electronic commerce applications.* Paper presented at the 32nd Annual Hawai'i International Conference on System Sciences (HICSS '99), Wailea.

Czarnecki, H., Schroer, B. J., & Rahman:, M. M. (1997). *Using simulation to schedule manufacturing resources.* Paper presented at the WSC '97, Proceedings of 1997 Winter Simulation Conference, Atlanta, GA.

Desel, J., & Erwin, T. (2000). *Modeling,Simulation and analysis of business processes.* Paper presented at the Business Process Management, Models, Techniques, and Empirical Studies.

Domingos, H. J., Martins, J. L., Preguiça, N. M., & Duarte, S. M. (1999). *A workflow architecture to manage mobile collaborative work.* Paper presented at the Encontro Português de Computação Móvel 1999 (EPCM '99), Tomar, Portugal.

Dong, Y., & ShenSheg, Z. (2003). *Using pi-calculus to formalize UML activity diagram for business process modeling.* Paper presented at the 10th IEEE International Conference and Workshop on the Engineering of Computer Based Systems (ECBS'03), Huntsville, AL.

Dourish, P., Holmes, J., MacLean, A., Marqvardsen, P., & Zbyslaw, A. (1996). *Freeflow: Mediating between representation and action in workflow systems.* Paper presented at the Proceedings of the 1996 Conference on Computer Supported Cooperative Work (CSCW'96), Boston.

Dumas, M., & Hofstede, A. H. (2001). *UML activity diagrams as a workflow specification language.* Paper presented at the UML 2001 — The Unified Modeling Language, Modeling Languages, Concepts, and Tools, 4th Inte. Conference, Toronto, Canada.

Eshuis, R., & Wieringa, R. (2003). *Comparing Petri net and activity diagram variants for workflow modelling - A quest for reactive Petri nets.* Paper presented at the Petri Net Technology for Communication-Based Systems.

Fowler, M. (2004). *UML distilled: A brief guide to the standard object modeling language; [covers through version 2.0 OMG UML standard]* (3rd ed.). Boston [u.a.]: Addison-Wesley.

Galler, J., & Scheer, A. W. (1995). Workflow-projekte: Vom Geschäftsprozeßmodell zur unternehmensspezifischen Workflow-Anwendung. *Information Management, 10*(1), 20-27.

Georgakopoulos, D., Hornick, M., & Sheth, A. (1995). An overview of workflow management: from process modeling to workflow automation infrastructure. *Distributed and Parallel Databases, 3*, 119-153.

Girault, C., & Valk, R. (2003). *Petri nets for systems engineering: A guide to modeling, verification, and applications.* Berlin: Springer.

Gogolla, M., & Richters, M.. (2002). Expressing UML class diagrams properties with OCL. In T. Clark & J. Warmer (Eds.), *Object modeling with the OCL* (2263 ed., pp. 85-114). Springer.

Governatori, G., Rotolo, A., & Sadiq, S. W. (2004). *A model of dynamic resource allocation in workflow systems.* Paper presented at the Database Technologies 2004, Proceedings of the 15th Australasian Database Conference, Dunedin, New Zealand.

Green, P., & Rosemann, M. (1999). *An ontological analysis of integrated process modelling.* Paper presented at the Advanced Information Systems Engineering, 11th International Conference CAiSE'99, Heidelberg, Germany.

Hammer, D. K., Hanish, A. A. R., & Dillon, T. S. (1998). Modeling behavior and dependability of object-oriented real-time systems. *Journal of Computer Systems Science and Engineering, 13*(3), 139-150.

Heilmann, H. (1996). Die Integration der Aufbauorganisation in Workflow-Management-Systeme. In H. Heilmann, L. J. Heinrich, & F. Roithmayr (Eds.), *Information engineering* (p. 147-165). München: Oldenbourg.

Hoffmann, M., Löffeler, T., & Y. Schmidt. (1999). Flexible Arbeitsverteilung mit Workflow-Management-Systemen. In T. Herrmann, A.-W. Scheer, & H. Weber (Eds.), *Verbesserung von Geschäftsprozessen mit Flexiblen Workflow-Management-Systemen* (pp. 135-159). Heidelberg: Physica.

Jessen, E., & Valk, R. (1987). *Rechensysteme: Grundlagen der Modellbildung.* Berlin: Springer.

Keller, G., Nüttgens, M., & Scheer, A. W. (1992). Semantische Prozeßmodellierung auf der Grundlage, Ereignisgesteuerter Prozeßketten (EPK). In A. W. Scheer (Ed.), *Veröffentlichungen des Instituts für Wirtschaftsinformatik* (Vol. 89). Saarbrücken.

Kiepuszewski, B., ter Hofstede, A. H. M., & van der Aals, W. M. P. (2001). *Fundamentals of control flow in workflows.*, [FIT-TR-2001-01]. Queensland University of Technology.

Ko, E.-J., Lee, S.-Y., Noh, H.-M., Cheol-Jung Yoo, & Chang, O.-B. (2005). *Workflow modeling based on extended activity diagram using ASM semantics.* Paper presented at the Computational Science and Its Applications — ICCSA 2005, Singapore.

Köhler, M. (2003). *Object Petri nets: Definitions, properties and related models.* [329]. Hamburg: University of Hamburg.

Köhler, M., & Rölke, H. (2005). *Reference and value semantics are equivalent for ordinary object Petri nets.* Paper presented at the Applications and Theory of Petri Nets 2005: 26th International Conference, ICATPN 2005, Miami, FL.

Kummer, O. (2002). *Referenznetze. Dissertation, Universität Hamburg, Fachbereich Informatik.*

Kummer, O., Wienberg, F., Duvigneau, M., Schumacher, J., Köhler, M., Moldt, D., et al. (2004). *An extensible editor and simulation engine for Petri nets: Renew.* Paper presented at the 25th International Conference on Application and Theory of Petri Nets (ICATPN 2004), Bologna, Italy.

Mendling, J., Neumann, G., & Nüttgens, M. (2004). *A comparison of XML interchange formats for business process modelling.* Paper presented at the EMISA 2004, Informationssysteme im E-Business und E-Government, Luxemburg.

Moldt, D., & Rodenhagen, J. (2000, November 13-14). Ereignisgesteuerte Prozeßketten und Petrinetze zur Modellierung von Workflows. In H. P. Giese (Ed.), *Visuelle Verhaltensmodellierung verteilter und nebenläufiger Software-Systeme. Workshop des Arbeitskreises, Grundlagen objektorientierter Modellierung (GROOM) der GI-Fachgruppe 2.1.9 (Objektorientierte Softwareentwicklung), Bericht Nr. 24/00-I* (pp. 57-63). Münster.

Moldt, D., & Valk, R. (2000). Objectoriented Petri nets in business process modeling. In W. M. P. van der Aalst, J. Desel, & A. Oberweis (Eds.), *Business process management, models, techniques, and empirical studies* (1806 ed., pp. 254-273). Berlin: Springer.

Momotko, M., & Subieta, K. (2002, September 8-11). *Dynamic changes in workflow participant assignment.* Paper presented at the 6th East-European Conference on Advances in Databases and Information Systems, ADBIS 2002, Bratislava, Slovakia.

Object Management Group (2004). *UML 2.0 superstructure specification.* Retrieved June 15, 2005, from http://www.omg.org/cgi-bin/doc?ptc/2004-10-02

Object Management Group (2005). *XML metadata interchange (XMI) specification.* Retrieved June 15, 2005, from http://www.omg.org/docs/formal/05-05-01.pdf

Petri, C. A. (1962). *Kommunikation mit Automaten.* Bonn: Dissertation, Universität Bonn.

Petri, C. A. (1996). Nets, time, and space. *Theoretical Computer Science, 153*(1-2), 3-48.

Picot, A., Reichwald, R., & Wigand, R. T. (2001). *Die grenzenlose Unternehmung: Information, Organisation und Management* (4th ed.). Wiesbaden: Gabler.

Pitt, M. (1997). *A generalised simulation system to support strategic resource planning in healthcare.* Paper presented at the WSC '97, Proceedings of 1997 Winter Simulation Conference, Atlanta, GA.

Reisig, W., & Rozenberg, G. (1998). *Lectures on Petri nets: Advances in Petri nets I: Basic models* (vol. 1). Berlin: Springer.

Rodrigues, R. W. S. (2000). *Formalising UML activity diagrams using finite state processes.* Paper presented at the UML 2000, Workshop on Dynamic Behaviour in UML Models: Semantics Questions, York, UK.

Russell, N., ter Hofstede, A. H. M., Edmond, D., & van der Aalst, W. M. P. (2004). *Workflow data patterns* [FIT-TR-2004-01]. Brisbane, Australia: Queensland University of Technology.

Sarshar, K., Dominitzki, P., & Loos, P. (2005). *Comparing the control-flow of EPC and Petri net from the end-user perspective - Statistical results of a laboratory experiment. Working papers of the Research Group Information Systems & Management* (http://www.isym.de), [25]. Mainz.

Sarshar, K., Dominitzki, P., Reichel, C., & Loos, P. (2005). *Krankenhausprozesse - Dokumentation erhobener Daten einer Feldstudie in einem Universitäts-Klinikum. Working Papers of the Research Group Information Systems & Management* (http://www.isym.de), [24]. Mainz.

Scheer, A.-W. (1998). *ARIS - Business process frameworks* (2nd ed.). Berlin [u.a.]: Springer.

Scheer, A.-W. (2001). *ARIS: Modellierungsmethoden, Metamodelle, Anwendungen* (4th ed.). Berlin: Springer.

Schnieders, A., Puhlmann, F., & Weske, M. (2004). *Process modeling techniques*, [01/2004]. Hasso-Plattner-Institut.

Störrle, H. (2005). Semantics and verification of data flow in UML 2.0 activities. *Electronic Notes in Theoretical Computer Science, 127*(4), 35-52.

Thiagarajan, P. S. (1987). Elementary net systems. In W. Brauer, W. Reisig, & R. G (Eds.), *Petri nets: Central models and their properties* (254 ed., pp. 26-59). Berlin: Springer.

Valk, R. (1987). *Nets in computer organization.* Paper presented at the Petri Nets: Applications and Relationships to Other Models of Concurrency, Advances in Petri Nets 1986, Proceedings of an Advanced Course, Bad Honnef.

Valk, R. (1991). *Modelling concurrency by task/flow EN systems.* Paper presented at the 3rd Workshop on Concurrency and Compositionality, Goslar, Germany.

Valk, R. (1996). *On processes of object Petri nets*, [FBI-HH-B-185/96]. Hamburg: University of Hamburg. Valk, R. (1998). *Petri nets as token objects - An introduction to elementary object nets.* Paper presented at the 19th International Conference on Application and Theory of Petri Nets, ICATPN'98, Lisbon, Portugal.

Valk, R. (2001). Concurrency in communicating object Petri nets. In G. A. Agha, F. De Cindio, & G. Rozenberg (Eds.), *Concurrent object-oriented programming and Petri nets, Advances in Petri nets* (vol. 2001, pp. 164-195). Berlin: Springer.

Valk, R. (2004). Object Petri nets - Using the nets-within-nets paradigm. In J. Desel, W. Reisig, & G. Rozenberg (Eds.), *Lectures on concurrency and Petri nets: Advances in Petri nets* (3098 ed., pp. 819-848): Springer-Verlag.

van der Aalst, W. M. P. (1996). *Three good reasons for using a Petri-net-based workflow management system.* Paper presented at the Proceedings of the International Working Conference on Information and Process Integration in Enterprises (IPIC'96), Cambridge, MA.

van der Aalst, W. M. P. (1998). The application of Petri nets to workflow management. *The Journal of Circuits, Systems and Computers, 8*(1), 21-661.

van der Aalst, W. M. P., Kumar, A., & Verbeek, H. M. W. (2003, March 9-12). *Organizational modeling in UML and XML in the context of workflow systems.* Paper presented at the Symposium on Applied Computing (SAC), Melbourne, FL.

van der Aalst, W. M. P., Moldt, D., Valk, R., & Wienberg, F. (1999). Enacting interorganizational workflow using nets in nets. In J. Becker, M. zur Mühlen, & M. Rosemann
(Eds.), *Workflow management '99* (pp. 117-136). Münster.

van der Aalst, W. M. P., ter Hofstede, A. H. M., Kiepuszewski, B., & Barros, A. P. (2003).
Workflow patterns. *Distributed and Parallel Databases, 14*(1), 5-51.

van der Aalst, W. M. P., & van Hee, K. (2002). *Workflow management: Models, methods,
and systems.* Cambridge, MA. [u.a.]: MIT Press.

van der Aalst, W. M. P., Verbeek, H. M. W., & Kumar, A. (2001). *Verification of XRL: An
XML-based workflow language.* Paper presented at the Proceedings of the 6th International Conference on CSCW in Design (CSCWD 2001).

Weske, M., Goesmann, T., Holten, R., & Striemer, R. (1999). *A reference model for workflow
application development processes.* Paper presented at the International Joint Conference
on Work Activities Coordination and Collaboration (WACC '99), San Francisco.

Winter, A., & Ebert, J. (1996). Ein Referenzschema zur Organisationsbeschreibung. In G.
Vossen & J. Becker (Eds.), *Geschäftsprozeßmodellierung und Workflow-Manage-
ment - Modelle, Methoden, Werkzeuge* (pp. 101-124). Bonn : International Thomson
Publishing.

zur Muehlen, M. (2004). Organizational management in workflow applications — Issues
and directions. *Information Technology and Management, 5*(4).

zur Muehlen, M., & Rosemann, M. (2004). *Multiparadigm process management.* Paper
presented at the 5th Workshop on Business Process Modeling, Development and Support (BPMDS 2004).

Section V
Quality and Consistency in Enterprise Modeling

Chapter XI

Merging and Outsourcing Information Systems with UML

Herman Balsters, University of Groningen, The Netherlands

ABSTRACT

Businesses can change their business structure by merging with other companies or, on the other end of the spectrum, by smoothly outsourcing some of their business processes to other more specialized parties. In this paper, we will concentrate on conceptual modelling of merging and outsourcing information systems. Merging of a collection of information systems will be defined as the construction of a global information system that contains exactly the functionality of the original collection of systems. Such global information systems are called federated information systems, when we wish to address the situation where the component systems are so-called legacy systems; that is, systems that are given beforehand and that are to interoperate in an integrated single framework in which the legacy systems are to maintain as much as possible their respective autonomy. Two major problems in constructing federated information systems concern achieving and maintaining consistency, and a uniform representation of the data on the global level of the federation. The process of creation of uniform representations of data is known as data extraction, whereas data reconciliation is concerned with resolving data inconsistencies. Outsourcing of an information system, on the other hand, will be defined as the handing over of part of the functionality of the original system to an outside party (the supplier). Such functionality typically involves one or more operations, where each operation satisfies certain input and output requirements. These requirements will be defined in terms of the ruling service level agreements (SLAs). We will provide a formal means to ensure that the outsourcing relationship between outsourcing party and supplier, determined by an SLA, satisfies specific correctness criteria. Formal specifications, as offered in this paper, can prove their value in the setup and evaluation of outsourcing contracts. We shall describe a uniform semantic framework for specification of both federated and outsourced information systems based on the UML/OCL data model. In particular, we will show that we can represent so-called exact views in UML/OCL, providing the means to capture the duality relation between federating and outsourcing.

INTRODUCTION

Businesses are, by nature, dynamic, and change continuously. Because of different economic prospects they grow in size and portfolio, or they have to reduce one of these aspects. There are several ways to accomplish growth or reduction. A smooth way may consist of hiring new employees or of outsourcing parts of one's noncore business processes to specialized parties in the market. More drastically, a company can merge its business with that of another business department, or even with that of another company. On the opposite side, a company can be forced to split its business into separate, independent business departments. The reason for such a merge or split may be of a different nature, for example, financial, organisational, or legal (Smith, Mitra, & Narasimhan, 1998). Merging is also known as *integrating*, and in this paper we will concentrate on integration as the result of *federating*. By federating we wish to address the situation where the component systems are so-called legacy systems; that is, systems that are given beforehand, and which are to interoperate in an integrated single framework in which the legacy systems are to maintain, as much as possible, their respective autonomy.

Splitting is also known as *unbundling*, and in this chapter we will concentrate on *outsourcing* as a particular aspect of unbundling. A variety of outsourcing models have been developed (Looff, 1995); outsourcing can range from having all the business processes (such as development, maintenance, and operations) performed by an outsourcing partner, up to having a contract with a partner performing only one single business task. Also, we find a growing interest in offshore outsourcing, where the bulk of processing is done in a low-cost country, with a small on-site staff at the customer's facility to handle the relationship management and coordination with the offshore parties.

The consultancy firm Forrester (2004) analyzed a number of large outsourcing ventures in the beginning of 2004; they found a European-wide trend towards large investments in outsourcing. Furthermore, the leading outsourcing category was that of infrastructure services. Second and third were the category of applications management and desktop outsourcing, and the category of outsourcing helpdesk and support services.

Whether expanding or shrinking, the process of changing one's business structure is very challenging, and necessarily addresses some critical issues. This is illustrated by the fact that in the special case of splitting, where business functions are handed over to independent third parties, more than 40% of outsourcing relationships fail to deliver the business value originally envisioned by the related parties (Gera, 2003). Due to reasons such as costs running higher than anticipated, poor service levels, and inadequate contract management, one can be faced with unsatisfactory outsourcing relationships and lack of flexibility (Sparrow, 2003).

In this chapter, we will concentrate on conceptual modelling of both federating and outsourcing information systems as particular aspects of integration and unbundling. Federating a collection of information systems will be defined as the construction of a global information system that contains exactly the functionality of the original collection of systems. Outsourcing of an information system, on the other hand, is defined as the handing over of part of the functionality of the original system to an outside party (the supplier).

Integration can be seen as having a certain duality relation with respect to unbundling, in the sense that integration deals with merging of existing component systems into one framework, while unbundling deals with splitting an existing system into a collection of autonomous components. In both cases, we are dealing with legacy systems with heterogeneous components with a large degree of autonomy. A major problem concerning federating and outsourcing of information systems that we will address in this paper is that of so-called *semantic heterogeneity* (Lenzerini, 2002; Sheth & Larson, 1990). Semantic heterogeneity refers to disagreement on (and differences in) meaning, interpretation, or intended use of related data. In both cases of merging and splitting, we have to convert data semantics and data formats from source systems to target systems. This conversion leads to a set of well-known problems-coined as data extraction and data reconciliation (Bouzeghoub & Lenzerini, 2001; Lenzerini, 2002)-that not only play a role in the data integration process, but also in the data unbundling process. Moreover, outsourcing of functionality of an information system usually involves one or more operations, where each operation satisfies certain input and output requirements. These requirements are typically defined in terms of the ruling service level agreements. In this paper, we describe a formal means to ensure that the outsourcing relationship between outsourcing party and supplier, determined by an SLA, satisfies specific correctness criteria. These correctness criteria will be defined in terms of consistency with respect to pre and postconditions pertaining to the outsourced operations. Formal specifications as offered in this paper can prove their value in the setup and evaluation of outsourcing contracts.

In Eriksson and Penker (2000), modelling business processes and information systems is seen as a valuable tool for business to understand the changes that will be caused by federating a collection of information systems, and also by outsourcing to outside suppliers. In Blaha and Premerlani (1998), UML has been advocated not only as a means to model a broad range of businesses and business applications, but also for the conceptual modelling of underlying information systems (such as databases). Though originally developed to model software systems, UML is also adequately suited for business modelling purposes. This is due to the fact that UML is equipped with a wide range of high-level modelling primitives in which one can capture complex requirements pertaining to data and processes occurring in many business applications. Moreover, the accompanying constraint language OCL (Demuth & Hussmann, 1999; Demuth, Hussmann, & Loecher, 2001; Warmer & Kleppe, 2003) provides UML with a wealth of additional possibilities to define business rules and business requirements. OCL is both a high-level language for modelling a wide range of (ad hoc) constraints, and is very detailed and precise as well. In Balsters (2003), it has been demonstrated that OCL has at least the same expressive power as the relational query language SQL, thus making OCL a very powerful language for specification of constraints, queries, and views. We will employ the UML/OCL language in this paper to model federating and outsourcing of information systems.

Our approach to constructing a federated information system from a collection of (semantically) heterogeneous component systems is based on the concept of *exact view* (Balsters & de Brock, 2004b) in the UML/OCL data model. In particular, we will show that a global federated information system constructed by exact views integrates component systems without any loss of constraint information (Balsters & de Brock, 2003ab; Balsters & de Brock, 2004b; Cali, Calvanese, De Giacomo, & Lenzerini, 2002; Miller, Haas, & Hernandez, 2000; Rahm & Bernstein, 2001; Spaccapietra, Parent, & Dupont, 1992). Using the concept of exact view, we will establish that only when we construct a specific isomorphic mapping, called a ψ-*map* (where ψ stands for *p*reservation of *s*ystem *i*ntegrity), from the sources to the global schema, that we will obtain this result of no information loss.

On the other side of the spectrum, modelling can be used to identify outsourcing opportunities and for specifications for the suppliers, hence providing a formal description of outsourcing that can be used as a basis for a contract between the outsourcing party and the outside supplier. Specifying a typical SLA places high demands on the expressiveness and precision of the modelling language employed. We will employ *exact views* on top of existing information systems in order to eventually capture the formal requirements of the outsourcing relation. Furthermore, we will show how to construct a mapping from the source model to the target model (i.e., the model of the supplier) preserving the SLA. Such a mapping, called an ω-*mapping* (where ω stands for *o*utsourcing) will be shown to abide to a so-called *abstract outsourcing implementation schema* (called an ω-*schema*) in UML/OCL, ensuring correct outsourcing of a source operation. Our correctness criterion will be given in terms of an ω-schema.

Even though outsourcing is already common practice and currently attracts much attention in business circles, it should be noted that *research* on outsourcing (and in broader sense on unbundling) of business and information systems is very much in the stage of infancy. Theory and methodology for business unbundling has yet largely to be developed. Our paper focuses on modelling issues; for architectural aspects pertaining to outsourcing of information systems, we refer the reader to Grefen, Ludwig, and Angelov (2003).

We wish to emphasize that by investigating federating and outsourcing, we address both the *process* aspect and the *end-result* aspect of outsourcing; that is, we intend to address the process of federating and outsourcing existing monolithic systems. The process aspect mainly concerns *methodology* of modelling and design, while the end-result aspect deals with *correctness criteria* applied to models and designs of both federated and outsourced information systems.

This chapter is organized as follows. The first section offers a description of the correctness problem pertaining to federating, whereas the following section is devoted to outsourcing. Next, we offer an introduction to views in UML/OCL, and so-called *exact views* to model federated systems. After that, we examine a general framework for federating constraints. Then we use exact views to model outsourcing based on so-called ω-schemas and ω-maps; this section also contains an illustrative example of an outsourcing relation. We also discuss the duality relation between federating and outsourcing and in particular, advocates exact views as a uniform approach in both federating and outsourcing. Finally, we discuss future trends, and offer conclusions and directions for further research.

The Integration Problem: Inconsistency and Incompleteness

As pointed out in Sheth and Larson (1990), schema integration has to satisfy certain completeness and consistency requirements in order to reflect correct semantics of the different local schemata on the global integrated level. These requirements can be summarized as follows: each object on the local level should correspond to exactly one object on the global federated level, and each object on the global level should correspond to exactly one combination of objects on the various local component levels. Both requirements can only be satisfied if there exists an adequate mapping from the global federated database states to the component database states. In this paper, we will coin such a mapping from the collection of local database states to the collection of global federated states as a ψ-map.

Constructing a ψ-map can be a very challenging task. First of all, there are certain matters concerning inconsistency stemming from the problem area of *data extraction*. The process of data extraction (Balsters & de Brock, 2004a) can give rise to various inconsistencies due to matters pertaining to the *ontologies* (Rahm & Bernstein, 2001) of the different component databases. Ontology deals with the connection between syntax and semantics, and how to classify and resolve difficulties and classification between syntactical representations on the one hand, and semantics providing interpretations on the other hand. Matters such as naming conflicts (e.g., homonyms and synonyms), conflicts due to different underlying data types of attributes and/or scaling, and missing attributes, all deal with differences in structure and semantics of the different local databases. Careful analysis of these problems usually reveal that these conflicts are not real inconsistencies, but rather that by employing techniques such as renaming, conversion functions, default values, and addition of suitable extra attributes can result in the construction of a common data model in which these (quasi-) inconsistencies are resolved. Data extraction deals with the alignment of both syntax and semantics of data schemas between the existing local components on the one hand, and the global system to be constructed on the other hand.

A ψ-map also has to capture the requirement that local integrity constraints restrict the set of correct database states, and also has to capture the requirement that global integrity constraints on the federated level restrict the set of correct federated database states. Hence, a ψ-map has to deal with the *data reconciliation* problem pertaining to the real inconsistencies due to conflicting integrity constraints. We will explain these inconsistencies following Türker and Saake (2000), using the terms local and global understandability.

In databases, *transparency* means that users do not see the internals of a database, for example, the location of data on a disk. In the context of federated schemata, *global transparency* requires that global users do not see the local schemata, and also that the local users do not see the global schema. At the global level, *global understandability* demands that global transactions (updates, queries) are not rejected whenever they satisfy the global integrity constraints. *Local understandability*, on the other hand, demands that local transactions are not rejected whenever the local integrity constraints are satisfied in the corresponding local component database.

The problem of global understandability arises when a global update operation that satisfies the global integrity constraints is rejected without an obvious reason to the global user. This can occur when the local integrity constraints are not reflected in the federated schema; due to global transparency, the global user does not see the local constraints that are possibly not satisfied. On the other hand, the problem of local understandability arises when a local update operation satisfies the local integrity constraints, but is rejected without an obvious reason to the local user. The latter situation can occur when the local update gives rise to a conflict with an integrity constraint defined in the federated schema. Again, due to global transparency, the local user does not see this conflicting constraint on the global level.

Both problems of global and local understandability deal with the fact that any update on the global level is propagated to a corresponding update (or combination of updates) on the local level, and vice versa. This is due to the fact that a federated database is not materialized, and only exists in a virtual sense in terms of a certain view defined on the local databases. Ideally, both global and local understandability should be satisfied, meaning (Türker & Saake, 2000) that:

1.   Local integrity constraints of the component schemata must be reflected in the feder-ated schema in order to avoid the problem of global understandability;
2.   Global integrity constraints on the federation level, such as pure federation constraints defined by the database integrator, must be reflected in the component schemata in order to avoid the problem of local understandability.

In this paper, we will demonstrate that global understandability is indeed always fea-sible. Local understandability, however, is generally not feasible due to the general character that federation constraints can have. Should there be no extra purely federated constraints on the global level, then we can ensure local understandability. These two conditions, one in full strength and the other weakened, together constitute a criterion that we will coin as the *criterion of preservation of system integrity*, or psi-criterion (ψ-criterion). When this ψ-criterion is met, will there be a completeness result in the sense that:

1.   Each correct global update will correspond to exactly one combination of correct local updates, and;
2.   Each correct local update, without the presence of purely federated constraints on the global level, will correspond to exactly one correct global update.

We will next examine how to construct a corresponding federated schema and a ψ-map linking the collection of local schemas and the federated schema given an arbitrary collec-tion of component database schema.

The Outsourcing Problem: Schema Alignment

In outsourcing, one typically has the situation that a source company wishes to hand over parts of its functionality to an outside party. This outside party is called the supplier to which the functionality (or service) is outsourced. In terms of models, this situation translates to a (source) model having one or more operations that will be outsourced to an outside (target) model. To be able to perform this outsourcing activity, one not only has to locate within the source model which operation O is to be outsourced, but also all relevant attributes, relations, constraints, and auxiliary operations that are used in the definition of that particular operation O. For example, consider the situation of a company that wishes to outsource payment and calculation services pertaining to employee salaries. In order to perform outsourcing of this operation, here called *calcNetSal*, one might need information regarding present status, date, employee function, employee age, employee address, number of hours that the employee works, initial date of employment, employee department, and possibly more. Once it has been decided that an operation like *calcNetSal* is to be outsourced, one tries to locate an outside party supplying the functionality of this operation. Once such an outside (target) party is found, the source party and the target party enter negotiations regarding the quality of the outsourcing service that the target has to provide. Once an agreement has been reached, a so-called service level agreement (SLA) is drawn up to which both parties are bound. An SLA is crucial in outsourcing, since it is the sole basis on which source and target parties provide input (responsibility of the source company) and output material (responsibility of the target company). In terms of models, the source model offers the outsourced operation, say O, as well as all relevant attributes, relations, constraints, and auxiliary operations that are used in the definition of that particular operation O. Furthermore, the source model offers its initial conditions that have to be met by a target model. These conditions are the basis for an SLA pertaining to source and target model, and could typically be given in terms of pre- and postconditions. In the case of our example, we could stipulate the following conditions (written in UML/OCL):

```
context Employee::calcNetSal(presentDate:Date): Integer
pre: status=payrolled
post: age>40 implies result>3000 and
result < (self.manager).presentDate.calcNetSal and
self.department.depNm=`toy' implies result<4000
```

This specification states that within the class Employee, an operation called calcNetSal satisfies the postcondition that all employees over the age of 40 earn at least 3,000, that no employee earns more than his manager, and that all employees belonging to the department named "toy" earn at most 4,000.

Should one wish to outsource this operation, then the supplier is bound to this specification. This entails that the supplier is to offer an implementation calcNetSal' of calcNetSal, such that calcNetSal' has a pre- and postcondition that are consistent with respect to the pre- and postconditions of calcNetSal. For preconditions, this means that calcNetSal' should not accept arguments that are not accepted by calcNetSal, and for postconditions it holds that calcNetSal' should never produce results contradicting a postcondition of calcNetSal.

In our approach, the SLA between an outsourcing party and a supplier provides the input for a contract binding both parties. The SLA is then used to produce a formal specification, in terms of pre- and postconditions, in which it is precisely (unambiguously) and completely stated what the supplier is expected to deliver. Such a formal counterpart of the SLA is coined a σ-*constraint*.

The problem that we are now faced with, in terms of models, is to offer a *mapping* from the model of the outsourcing party (the source model) to the model of the supplying party (the target model) that preserves the σ-constraint. This mapping serves as a (correctness) specification of the outsourcing relation between source and target. Generally speaking, constructing such a mapping is no trivial matter, and it is the topic of this chapter to offer a methodology and a definition of a correct end result for an outsourcing mapping (or ω-*map* for short).

The ω-maps that we are looking for show many resemblances to certain mappings encountered in the field of data integration. In data integration, we have to map a collection of (local) source models to a (global) target model integrating various aspects of the source models. Typically, these local models are models of legacy systems that have to be mapped to a newly defined global system, and is known as the problem of global as view (or GAV, cf. Balsters & de Brock, 2004b; Bouzeghoub & Lenzerini, 2001; Lenzerini, 2002). In outsourcing we are faced with a more-or-less dual situation: here we are moving from a global system (the system of which a part will be outsourced) to a (possibly collection of) local system(s). Typically, the global system is a legacy system that has to be mapped to an existing local system that will supply the desired outsourcing service. Mapping an existing (global) model to an existing (local) model is known as the problem of *data exchange* (Miller et al., 2000, Rahm & Bernstein, 2001). In general, there are no algorithms for constructing mappings solving the data exchange problem. What we can do, however, as will be done in this paper, is provide criteria by which it can be judged, *in retrospect*, whether the construction of an outsourcing mapping from an existing model to another existing model has been performed correctly. In our case, we will offer a criterion, formulated in terms of a so-called *ω-schema*, by which we can judge that an ω-map ensures correctness of the outsourcing relation between source and target models.

We emphasize that in this chapter we do not offer a recipe for constructing an ω-map. What we do offer, however, is a criterion by which we can judge whether our outsourcing has indeed been performed correctly; that is, by offering a construction of an ω-map, we offer a guarantee that the outsourcing of the operation will yield results on the supplier side that are completely consistent with the original desired results from the side of the outsourcer. This process of constructing a schema on the supplier side that corresponds with a schema on the side of the outsourcing party is called *schema alignment*. We could also phrase this by saying that the intention of our approach is to guarantee *outsourcing transparency*. Moreover, we show that a *strategy* for constructing an ω-map could consist of devising a specific ψ-map that eventually will yield the desired ω-map.

The next section is devoted to views in UML/OCL; views will be used in subsequent sections of this chapter for constructing exact views, ψ-maps, and ω-maps in the context of federating and outsourcing.

Views in UML/OCL

Consider the case that in the context of some company, we have a class called Emp1 with attributes nm1 and sal1, indicating the name and salary (in Euros) of an employee object belonging to class Emp1:

Now consider the case where we want to add a class, say Emp2, that is defined as a class whose objects are completely derivable from objects coming from class Emp1, but with the salaries expressed in cents. The calculation is performed in the following manner. Assume that the attributes of Emp2 are nm2 and sal2 respectively (indicating name and salary attributes for Emp2 objects), and assume that for each object e1:Emp1, we can obtain an object e2:Emp2 by stipulating that e2.nm2=e1.nm1 and e2.sal2=(100 * e1.sal1). By definition the total set of instances of Emp2 is the set obtained from the total set of instances from Emp1 by applying the calculation rules as described above. Hence, class Emp2 is a *view* of class Emp1, in accordance with the concept of a view as known from the relational database literature. In UML terminology, we can say that Emp2 is a *derived class*, since it is completely derivable from other already existing class elements in the model description containing model type Emp1.

We will now show how to faithfully describe Emp2 as a derived class in UML/OCL (Balsters, 2003, Warmer & Kleppe, 2003) in such a way that it satisfies the requirements of a (relational) view. First of all, we must satisfy the requirement that the set of instances of class Emp2 is the result of a calculation applied to the set of instances of class Emp1. The basic idea is that we introduce a class called DB that has an association to class Emp1, and that we define within the context of the database DB an attribute called Emp2. A database object will reflect the actual state of the database, and the system class DB will only consist of one object in any of its states. Hence, the variable *self* in the context of the class DB will always denote the actual state of the database that we are considering. In the context of this database class, we can then define the calculation obtaining the set of instances of Emp2 by taking the set of instances of Emp1 as input.

```
context DB
def: Emp2: Set(Tupletype{nm2:String, sal2: Integer}) =
    (self.emp1-> collect(e:Emp1 |
    Tuple{nm2=e.nm1, sal2=(100*e.sal1)}))-> asSet
```

In this way, we specify Emp2 as the result of a calculation performed on base class Emp1. Graphically, Emp2 could be represented as follows:

$$\tag{1}$$

where the slash-prefix of Emp2 indicates that Emp2 is a derived attribute. Since, in practice, such a graphical representation could give rise to rather large box diagrams (due to lengthy type definitions), we will use the following (slightly abused) graphical notation to indicate this derived class:

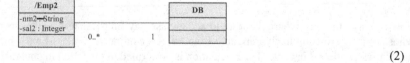

$$\tag{2}$$

The intention is that these two graphical representations are equivalent; that is, graphical representation (2) is offered as a diagrammatical convention with the sole purpose that it be formally equivalent (*translatable*) to graphical representation (1). Note that we have introduced a root class DB as an aid to represent the derived class Emp2. Since in OCL we only have the possibility to define attributes and operations within the context of a certain class, and class Emp1 is clearly not sufficient to offer the right context for the definition of such a derived construct as derived class Emp2, we had to move up one level in abstraction towards a class such as DB. A derived class then becomes a derived attribute on the level of the root class DB. In subsequent sections, we will use the concept of (exact) view to model integrating and outsourcing of information systems.

Exact Views

In the case that a derived class in UML is the result of a so-called ψ-map (Balsters & de Brock, 2004ab), then we speak of an *exact view*. Exact views belong to the domain of data extraction, and are constructed from a certain collection of injective conversion functions. Exact views have the property that they are correctly updatable, in the sense that any update on an exact view corresponds to exactly one (combination of) correct update(s) on the base class(es) it stems from. To get a flavour of what a ψ-map looks like, consider the following class Pers and a view /Emp.

Pers	/Emp
prsno: Integer	
name: String	pno: Integer
sal: Integer— in S	pname: String
street: String	sal: Integer— in €
hnr: String	
city: String	addr: String
telint: String	city: String
	tel: String

The view /Emp could function as an interface between various classes pertaining to descriptions of personnel, and often such interfaces have to meet the requirement that one can move freely from such class objects to the common interface, and vice versa. In such cases, we have to find a one-to-one mapping from a class like Pers to a view like /Emp. We will now discuss properties of such a mapping. Notice that:

- Attributes prsno and pno are *homonyms*, as are name and pname (*name conflicts*)
- Attribute sal in Pers is in $, and sal in Emp is in € (*conversion problem*)
- Attribute addr in Emp is already a combination of street and house number (again, conversion problem)
- Pers only has an internal telephone number (conversion problem)

These are typical aspects that one encounters in the realm of data extraction. We now try to get Pers-objects in line with corresponding Emp-tuples. To do so, we first define the underlying tupletype of the view Emp (using OCL syntax)

```
EmpType = TupleType(pno: Integer, pname: String, sal:
Integer, addr: String, city: String, tel: String)
context Pers
def: convertToEmp( ): EmpType =
```

```
Tuple{pno=self.prsn, pname = self.name,
sal = (self.sal).convertToEuro,
addr = self.street ->concat((` ') ->concat(self.hnr)),
city = self.city, tel= `+31-50-363'->concat(self.
telint)}
```

In the definition of convertToEmp, we have assumed the existence of a function convert-ToEuro used to convert dollars to euros. Furthermore, we assume that the internal telephone numbers can be extended to full telephone numbers by adding some standard prefix. Notice that the function convertToEmp is injective, and hence can be used to uniquely map Pers-objects to Emp-tuples (and vice versa). Such one-to-one functions are called ψ-maps, and a view like Emp is generated from the class Pers by applying the function convertToEmp to each object in the set of instances of Pers; hence, Emp is the result of a particular view on Pers. A view based on a ψ-map is called an *exact view*. For a more elaborate discussion on properties of exact views and ψ-maps, we refer the reader to Balsters and de Brock (2004ab).

Integration and Exact Views

Papers (Cali et al., 2002; Miller et al., 2000; Reddy, Prasad, & Gupta, 1995; Spac-capietra et al., 1992; Türker & Saake, 2000; Vermeer & Apers, 1996) have all investigated the problem of integrity constraint integration, and each (with exception of Türker & Saake, 2000), fall short in coming up with a satisfactory solution, in the sense that all constraint information offered on the local level is precisely (consistently and completely) represented on the global level of the integration. The approach adopted in these papers (with exception of Türker & Saakem 2000) basically boils down to so-called *loose constraining*, meaning that at least one of the contradicting integrity constraints is logically weakened on the global level. As we have seen in the previous section, this solution strategy does not solve the problem of global understandability. In contrast, we propose an approach based on so-called *tight constraining*, meaning that we faithfully (consistently and completely) represent all local constraint information on the global level of the federation. We will do so by employing so-called *exact views*; this in contrast with sound views (Lenzerini, 2002) that more or less comply with the approach based on loose constraining. We will develop an algorithm (cf. Balsters & de Brock, 2004b) that will calculate the appropriate exact view representing the (virtual) federated database state, given a collection of local database states. We will consider a so-called *component frame* of a collection of local databases, and define a derived attribute within this component frame in order to calculate the accompanying federated database state. This derived attribute will correspond to a view defined on top of the collection of local databases.

A component frame is a structure consisting of a collection of local databases, is depicted here:

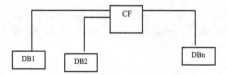

We will offer a definition in terms of UML and OCL (Balsters, 2003; Warmer & Kleppe, 2003) of both the component frame and the exact view corresponding to the federated database that we are targeting for.

A component frame can be modelled as a root class with relations to the respective local databases. Each database, in turn, is modelled as a root class with relations to the associated database tables (modelled as classes). Hence, if there are n local databases to be considered in the component frame, then a component-frame state consists of one object with a collection of n relations, each to a database object; each database object has a number of relations, each to a class representing a table of objects. For example, consider a component frame CF consisting of two databases (DB1 and DB2), and consider the situation that DB1 has a class C1 (a.o.) representing one of its tables, and that DB2 has a class C2 (a.o.) representing one of its tables. This can be depicted as follows:

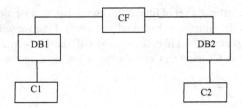

Hence, a state of CF consists of two database states, one for DB1 and one DB2, and each database state consists of a collection of tables, where a table is represented as the set of current object instances of a certain class. Let us consider the situation that we wish to integrate databases DB1 and DB2, and that classes C1 and C2 are related in the sense that they might have some characteristics in common. We will proceed by offering a general methodology to integrate these two classes C1 and C2, resulting in a collection of classes on the global level of a database federation. But before we do so, we first have to make explicit a number of assumptions to describe the context of our approach.

Basically, we wish to concentrate in this particular section on *constraint integration* and therefore, wish to abstract from other features that, in themselves, are possibly very relevant in the context of integration. In an earlier part of this paper, we made mention of the problem category coined as data extraction. This category deals with matters such as naming conflicts (e.g., homonyms and synonyms), conflicts due to different underlying data types of attributes and/or scaling, and missing attributes. These conflicts all deal with differences in structure and semantics of the different local databases. By employing techniques such as renaming, conversion functions, default values, and addition of suitable extra attributes, one can construct a common data model in which these (quasi-) inconsistencies are resolved. Since these techniques are well known and rather standard, in this section we will abstract from such *data extraction* problems, and assume that there exists a common uniform data model in which to represent the various component database schemata. The problem category we will focus on is coined as *data reconciliation*, and in particular we will concentrate on problems concerning constraint integration in order to tackle the problems of global and local understandability.

Consider the situation that C1 and C2 have a collection of attributes in common, and that this (maximal) collection is denoted by α. Assume that β (resp. γ) is that set of attributes in C1 (resp. C2) not common to the set of attributes in C2 (res. C1). Furthermore, assume that C1 has a subclass S with a specific set of attributes (denoted by σ), and assume that C2 has a relation with a class D with a specific set of attributes denoted by δ. This situation gives a general account of the problems that can occur when trying to integrate two classes such as C1 and C2. This situation can be depicted as follows:

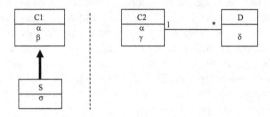

What we will now show is how to construct a set of (derived) classes that, as a whole, are the result of integration of the two model situations described previously. First we will show what the integrated class-attribute structure looks like, and then we will show how to integrate the possibly occurring constraints in C1 and C2. Consider the following diagram:

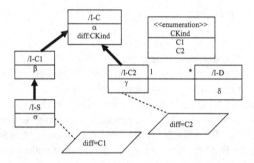

The slashes prefixing the class names in this model diagram indicate that we are dealing with derived classes (as discussed in earlier). This diagram will serve as a visual aid to show the result on the global level of the integration of classes C1 and C2. Basically, we have introduced a common super class I-C consisting of an attribute section that is common to both C1 and C2. We then introduce two subclasses, I-C1 and I-C2, with attribute sections that are specific as possibly differentiating them from the common class I-C. In order to differentiate between C1 and C2, we have introduced an enumeration class CKind. Class I-C1 is added with a constraint stating "diff=C1," and class I-C2 is added with the constraint "diff=C2."

INTEGRATING THE CONSTRAINTS

This section concerns the second step in the integration process. Once we have constructed a common underlying data structure for FDB as described in the previous section, we have to add the local and global integrity constraints. First we will offer a categorization of the various constraints, and then show one by one how each category of constraints obtains its place on the level of FDB.

We will discern between five categories of constraints (Balsters & de Brock, 2004b), and subsequently show how each category is integrated on the level of FDB. We will first do so by some specific examples, and then treat constraint integration in more general terms.

Attribute Constraints

Such a constraint deals solely with a restriction on possible values of one attribute inside a class. As an example, consider the following constraint specification:

> **context** Emp
> **inv** attrcons: age>30

where we have assumed that an employee class Emp has an attribute called age, and that each age value is required to be larger than 30.

Object Constraints

Such a constraint deals solely with a restriction on possible values of a combination of attributes on the level of an arbitrary object within a class. As an example consider:

> **context** Emp
> **inv** objcons: age>30 implies sal> 5000

stating that each employee older than 30 earns a salary higher than 5,000.

Class Constraints

Such a constraint pertains to the set of all instances of a class in an arbitrary database state. As an example consider:

> **context** Emp
> **inv** classcons: (Emp.allInstances -> size)<1000

stating that the number of instances of the Emp-class is always less than 1,000.

Database Constraints

Such a constraint states an invariant property between different classes inside one database. As an example consider:

> **context** DB
> **inv** dbcons: (Emp.allInstances -> size) > 10*(Man.allInstances -> size)

stating that in some database DB, the number of managers (Man is a subclass of Emp) is always less than 10% of the total number of employees.

Federation Constraints

Such a constraint is imposed on the collection of local databases participating in the federation; hence, it is an integrity constraint pertaining to the component frame, and it obtains its final representation within the derived class /FDB. As an example consider:

```
context CF
inv fedcons:
(DB1.Emp.allInstances -> size) < (DB2.Man.allInstances -> size)
```

stating that the number of employees of the Emp class in database DB1 is always smaller than the number of managers in the Man class of database DB2.

We will now show how to tackle the problem of global understandability within the context of our representation of FDB. We will offer a general algorithm for treating the constraints as described previously per category. We then proceed by offering a general approach to including federation constraints on the global level, and treat the problem of local understandability.

The Context

Consider the situation as depicted in our component frame. What we want is to describe the integration of local constraints occurring in classes C1 and C2. That is, we want to represent the integration as a set of constraints that will be placed somewhere in classes /I-C, /I-C1, /I-C2, /I-S, /I-D, and possibly also /FDB.

The Algorithm

We will define our algorithm per constraint category, and show how to represent local integrity constraints within FDB.

Attribute Constraints

Suppose that the attribute in question is a and that $\varphi(a)$ denotes the constraint in the local class Ci (i=1,2). On the global level, this constraint is now represented by the following prescription:

If attribute $a \in \alpha$ then the constraint moves up to class I-C and is changed to "if diff=Ci then $\varphi(a)$" else the constraint remains unchanged and is placed in I-Ci

Remark: Note that attribute constraints are inherited by subclasses.

Object Constraints

Denote the set of attributes involved in the object constraint by attr. If the object constraint in question pertains to class Ci (I=1,2) and is denoted by $\varphi(attr)$ then the following prescription applies:

If attribute set $attr \subseteq \alpha$ then the constraint moves up to class I-C and is changed to "if diff=Ci then $\varphi(attr)$" else the constraint remains unchanged and is placed in I-Ci

Remark: Note that object constraints are inherited by subclasses.

Class Constraints

Suppose that the class constraint in question pertains to class Ci (I=1,2); denote this constraint by $\varphi(Ci)$ and let attr denote the set of attributes involved in $\varphi(Ci)$, then the following prescription applies:

If attribute set attr$\subseteq\alpha$ then the constraint moves up to class I-C and I-C is constrained by $\varphi((o \in /I-C \mid o.diff=Ci))$ else the constraint remains unchanged and is placed in I-Ci

Remark: Note that class constraints are, in general, ***not*** always inherited by subclasses.

Database Constraints

These constraints remain unchanged, except for being applied to the I-prefixed versions of the classes involved in the database constraint in question.

Federation Constraints

Such a constraint is actually not really available before integration of a set of local databases. Once one has agreed to integrate, then possible federation constraints can arrive on the scene. The proper place to include them is on the global level of FDB. An example of a federation constraint is that class C1 always has less instances than class C2. Such a constraint could be represented in FDB as follows:

```
context CF
inv fedcons:
(FDB.I-C1.allInstances -> size) < (FDB.I-C2.allInstances -> size)
```

being an attribute (!) constraint (namely on the attribute FDB) within the component frame class CF.

In summary, what we have done is show how to lift local constraints to the integrated level of FDB by giving them suitable new classes to which they apply. The context of FDB can now be depicted by:

CF
/FDB = ...
λ φ

where λ denotes the set of local integrity constraints pertaining to FDB, and φ denotes the set of pure federation constraints pertaining to FDB.

The next section concerns a discussion on properties of our algorithm.

Properties of the Algorithm Computing the Database Federation

Our algorithm has the following properties:

1. The algorithm applies to all possible categories of constraints.
2. The integrated database FDB as the result of our algorithm satisfies the ψ-criterion.
3. Algorithm complexity is of order O(n), where n denotes the number of local constraints.
4. The resulting FDB does not contain indeterminate or-branches in order to integrate local constraints.

These four properties are an improvement over the algorithm offered in Türker and Saake (2000): the latter algorithm applies only to very specific (so-called *decidable*) local constraint sets; its complexity is of exponential order; and it introduces a possibly large number of indeterminate or-branches on the global level in order to integrate local constraints. Also, our ψ-criterion offers a sharper correctness criterion, offering a clear maintenance strategy when dealing with updates subjected to constraints on the federated level.

As mentioned earlier, our algorithm is symmetric (of course), but not necessarily associative; that is, first applying our algorithm to two classes C1 and C2, and then using this intermediate result to apply the algorithm again to a class C3, will not necessarily (and often will usually not) yield the same result when applying the algorithm first to say C2 and C3, and then using that intermediate result again to apply to C1. Associativity, however, is not an issue here; since the computation of our federated database (no matter how it arises) always satisfies the desired ψ-criterion. We refer the interested reader to Balsters and de Brock (2004b) for details on the properties of our algorithm.

We now (re)turn our attention to the dual process of integration, namely the process of outsourcing of the global functionality of an existing information system to a suitable local component. The next section deals with an outsourcing schema for moving from source models to target models. This outsourcing schema will rely heavily on employing exact views; these exact views will provide the mechanism to eventually construct ω-maps. We will also describe a running example of an information system used to register data concerning employees; the company owning this information system wishes to outsource payment and calculation services pertaining to employee salaries.

Outsourcing and Exact Views

It is important to note that this section has as its context the material pertaining to an outsourcing example described in the second section (called *The outsourcing problem*) of this chapter.

We recall that problem that we are faced with, in terms of models, is to offer a *mapping* from the model of the outsourcing party (the source model) to the model of the supplying party (the target model) that preserves a so-called σ-constraint (reflecting the formal counterpart of a service level agreement between outsourcer and supplier). This mapping serves as a specification of the outsourcing relation between source and target. Generally speaking, constructing such a mapping is no trivial matter, and it is the topic of this section to offer a methodology and a definition of a correct end result for an outsourcing mapping (or ω-*map* for short).

The ω-maps that we are looking for show many resemblances with certain mappings encountered in the field of data integration. In data integration, we have to map a collection of (local) source models to a (global) target model integrating various aspects of the source models. Typically, these local models are models of legacy systems that have to be mapped to a newly defined global system, and is known as the problem of global as view. When constructing such mappings from local models to a global model in data integration, we encounter problems pertaining to so-called *data extraction* and *data reconciliation*. As we have seen in previous sections, both data extraction and data reconciliation can be hard to realize, because of the severe restrictions placed on the mapping from local models to the global model. It is only when such a mapping satisfies certain isomorphism properties that the mapping will ensure correct resolution of the data reconciliation problem. As mentioned previously, such constraint preserving mappings have been coined *ψ-maps*.

In outsourcing, we are faced with a more-or-less dual situation: here we are moving from a global system (the system of which a part will be outsourced) to a (possibly collection of) local system(s). Typically, the global system is a legacy system that has to be mapped to an existing local system that will supply the desired outsourcing service.

We will provide criteria by which it can be judged, in retrospect, whether the construction of an outsourcing mapping from an existing model to another existing model has been performed correctly. In our case, we will offer a criterion, formulated in terms of a so-called *ω-schema*, by which we can judge that a ω-map ensures correctness of the outsourcing relation between source and target models.

Consider the case of an outsourcing example, provided earlier. We can discern within our source model (called SM, for short), the following model elements:

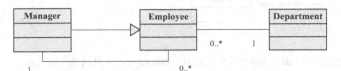

The class Manager is a subclass of Employee, a manager supervises n ($n \geq 0$) employees, employees belong to exactly one department, and departments have m ($m \geq 0$) employees. In our example, we (i.e., the company) wish to outsource payment and calculation services pertaining to employee salaries. To be more precise, the company wishes to outsource calculation of the net salary of a given set of employees on the basis of:

- Status (pay rolled, or not)
- Present date
- Employee function
- Employee age
- Number of hours that the employee works
- Initial date of employment
- Employee department

Moreover, the company wishes to obtain for each employee an overview listing all amounts deducted from the employee's gross salary. In terms of SM, not all elements of the class Employee are relevant for outsourcing of these operations. To this end, we will construct a view on the class Employee containing, in general, only those attributes, relations, operations, and constraints that are relevant for our particular outsourcing application. This particular view is called /SalView and is depicted in the following example:

/SalView
status: Set(payrolled, notPayrolled) function: String age: Integer hours: Integer
employedSince: Date depNm: String man-id: Integer
calcNetSal(presentDate:Date): Integer deductionOverview:Report

The operation *deductionOverview* will result in an overview listing all amounts deducted from the employee's gross salary. A view such as /SalView is called a *source view*.

In order to ensure a one-to-one correspondence between the view /SalView and the original class Employee (necessary to obtain a unique association between an employee object and his salary), we will proceed and provide a ψ-map ensuring that each object in the set of instances of class Employee corresponds to exactly one object in the view /SalView, and vice versa. In our example, we shall *assume* that there exists a ψ-map, say ψ_0, between Employee and /SalView, that we, using informal (i.e., non-UML) notation, will depict.

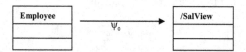

Recall that we have the following σ-constraint pertaining to the SLA that the outsourcing party demands from a prospective supplier:

context Employee::calcNetSal(presentDate:Date): Integer
pre: status=payrolled
post: age>40 implies result>3000 and
result < (self.manager).presentDate.calcNetSal and
self.department.depNm=`toy' implies result<4000

We shall now consider the side of the supplying party, determining the target model (or TM, for short). Should the company wish to outsource the operation calcNetSal, then the supplier is bound to the σ-constraint specified. This σ-constraint entails that the supplier is to offer an implementation calcNetSal' of calcNetSal, such that calcNetSal' has a pre- and postcondition that are consistent with respect to the pre- and postconditions of calcNetSal.

In general, in a context of outsourcing, a supplier has to abide to the following (abstract) implementation schema (employing informal (i.e., non-UML) notation), shown in Figure 1.

This schema (called an ω-*schema*) is to be read as follows: **op2** is (by definition) a *correct implementation* (or *refinement*) of **op1**, if and only if precondition *pre1* logically

Figure 1. ω-schema

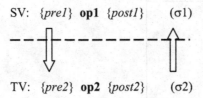

$$SV: \quad \{prel\} \ \textbf{op1} \ \{post1\} \qquad (\sigma1)$$

$$TV: \quad \{pre2\} \ \textbf{op2} \ \{post2\} \qquad (\sigma2)$$

implies precondition *pre2*, and postcondition *post2* logically implies postcondition *post1*. We also say that σ-constraint σ2 *implements* (or *respects*) σ-constraint σ1. An ω-schema prescribes a consistency and completeness condition with respect to pre- and postconditions of the outsourcer and the supplier operation involved.

The challenge of finding a correctly implemented outsourcing now boils down to constructing a mapping from a view SV (on the source model SM) to a view TV (on the target model TM), such that this mapping respects an ω-schema for outsourcing as described previously. We will offer a description of the requirements to be placed on these views SV and TV. Such a mapping is called an *ω-map*. In Balsters and de Brock (2004b) it has been shown that exact views (i.e., views constructed from ψ-maps) preserve constraint specifications in the transition from base classes (on which the view is defined) to the view in question. Hence, a mapping between source model (with its respective corresponding SLA specified as a σ-constraint) and target model consisting of a ψ-map, will automatically abide to an ω-schema, and therefore such a ψ-map constitutes an ω-map. In the remainder of this paper, we will employ this strategy to construct ω-maps as particular ψ-maps.

We will assume that a target model TM is already given (defined in terms of an existing external information system, for example a specific information system that can calculate net salaries and can generate deduction reports), and we are then faced with the problem to define a view on TM-a so-called target view (say TV)-having two important properties:

1.   TV contains all relevant information also available in the source view SV; we could also say that TV offers the *mirror content* of the data available in SV
2.   TV additionally contains from the target side extra attributes, operations, and relations (e.g., auxiliary tables with input data for operations) necessary to actually provide the calculations for the outsourced operations

Moreover, TV will typically be defined as a view on the complete target model TM. Hence, we will *assume* the existence of some ψ-map, say ψ_0', between TM and TV to ensure a one-to-one correspondence between an object from the view TV and some object from the original class TM. This situation is depicted as follows:

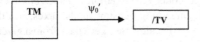

In our example, the supplying party has to offer an operation calcNetSal' (or deductionOverview', respectively) as an implementation of calcNetSal (or deductionOverview, respectively). Hence, a typical appearance of the target view could be depicted as follows:

/TV –including Employee mirror data
empid'—internal employee identifier status' function' age' hours' employedSince' depNm' man-id' presentDate'

The view TV contains mirrored data from the Employee class relevant for the view SalView. We will use the prime-notation to reflect this mirroring aspect. As an example, attribute age' in TV will typically represent the associated syntax for the original age attribute in SalView, and will typically also have a possibly different domaintype associated to it; for example, in Salview age could have domaintype integer, while in TV the domaintype is string, but we assume that we can somehow transform the integer representation to the string representation, and vice versa, as is common practice in the data extraction process. We will, therefore, also *assume* that there exists some ψ-map, say ψ_1, between SalView and TV, as depicted in:

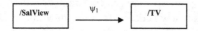

Existence of a ψ-map like ψ_1 is necessary for two reasons:

1. ψ_1 maps object data from SalView to TV, solving data extraction problems in the transition from the source model SM to the target model TM. Typically, attributes in TM (primed) corresponding to attributes to SM (nonprimed), will suffer from name anomalies and differences in type domains. These are all well-known problems in the field of data integration, where ψ-maps are used to resolve matters pertaining to data extraction ([5]).
2. We have to ensure that each object in the set of instances of view SalView corresponds to exactly one object in the view TV, and vice versa. Only in this way can we freely and unambiguously move between the source and the target models.

Remark: Note that we have not offered a concrete specification of ψ-maps like ψ_0, ψ_0', and ψ_1: we only assume that such ψ-maps can *somehow* be constructed. Without the existence of such ψ-maps, no guarantee can be offered for correctness of the outsourcing process.

In order to actually provide sufficient material to implement calNetSal and deductionOverview by calcNetSal' and deductionOverview' in the view TV, we will typically employ auxiliary data found in classes in the target model TM. Examples of such auxiliary classes contain data, operations, and constraints concerning pension funds, taxes, health insurance, vacation savings, and so forth: all necessary to calculate a net salary from a given gross salary, and to describe how amounts are deducted from gross salaries to obtain a net salary. Data from the view TV, together with such auxiliary data and operations from the target model TM offer input material for a function actually enabling the concrete calculation of net salary and its accompanying deduction report. This function will offer the material to define a new view (as the result of some suitable ψ-map), in which we find, neatly organized, those attributes pertaining to an employee's net salary and deduction report. Hence, view TV is used to obtain yet another view, say TV', containing the following data:

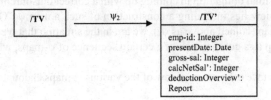

where we have assumed the existence of some ψ-map, say ψ_2, to map TV-objects to TV'-objects. TV' will also be used to registrate-in OCL-style-the constraint information defining the actual calculations of net salary and deduction overview.

If we split our original view SalView into two parts, one called SV containing purely the attributes, and the other called SV' containing purely the desired operations and the original σ-constraint, then we would arrive at the following situation:

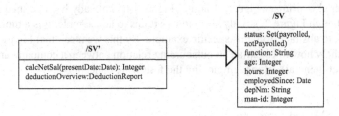

Figure 2. ω-schema ensuring correctness of outsourcing

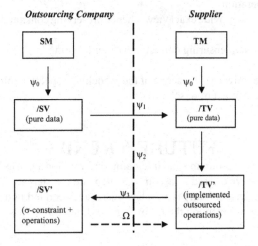

where SV' is a subclass of SV containing the desired operations defining net salary and deduction report. If we now could provide a suitable ψ-map, say ψ_3, to map TV' to SV, then we could actually, in turn, provide SV' with the desired calculations of calcNetSal and deductionOverview. Hence, our final obligation in coming up with a correct outsourcing of calcNetSal and deductionOverview lies in finding a construction of such a map ψ_3. Once we have constructed such a ψ-map (coined above as ψ_3), we are in the situation that we can construct our sought after ω-map as a composition of a certain sequence of ψ-maps, which we now explain.

Consider Figure 2, in which we offer an overview of the various ψ-maps encountered in our example thus far

The desired ω-map, say Ω (mapping the source view to the target view), can now be defined as the *inverse* of the map ψ_3. Note that ψ-maps ψ_1 and ψ_2 are essential in defining Ω, since these two ψ-maps determine the target view TV'.

In the next section, we will offer a general schema for outsourcing, and discuss scope and limitations of our approach.

A General Schema for Outsourcing

Generally speaking, our method for modelling outsourcing of operations in terms of ω-schemas is offered in primary Figures 1 and 2. Figure 1 had already been defined in general terms, and though Figure 2, strictly speaking, pertains to an example, it is a more-or-less simple matter to abstract from this specific example. By this we mean that Figure 2 can also be used to show how to construct an outsourcing relation between a company and supplier in an abstract (general) setting, employing the following concepts:

1. *Outsourcing company* and *Supplier*
2. *Source Model* (SM) and *Target model* (TM)
3. *Source View* (SV) and *Target View* (TV), purely pertaining to data (source data in the source view, and mirrored data in the target view)
4. *Source View'* (SV'), as that subclass of SV containing both the outsourced operation and the σ-constraint (offering the formal counterpart of the SLA)
5. *Target View'* (TV'), as that result of TV containing the actual implementations of the outsourced operation
6. *ψ-maps* in order to provide exact views (hence preserving constraints from base classes to views)
7. An eventual *ω-map* ensuring correctness of outsourcing

Figure 2, hence, offers a clear scope of the modelling aspects employed in the process of outsourcing in the context of ω-schemas.

FUTURE TRENDS

Not all aspects in outsourcing and integrating information systems have been covered in our approach. We have offered a basis from which one can start semantical analysis and move on to a correct design. Many issues, however, have been left untreated.

For outsourcing, we mention the following (possible) limitations in our approach:

1.   Can all aspects of outsourcing of information systems be modelled in terms of UML/ OCL?
2.   Are outsourced operations always query operations, or are update operations (those that result in a state change of an object) also candidates for outsourcing?
3.   Are outsourced operations only object operations, or can they also be operations that apply to complete sets of class instances, or even complete databases?

We offer the following comments on these possible limitations of our approach:

1.   There are aspects of outsourcing that we have not addressed in this chapter. Our outsourcing has dealt mainly with more-or-less *technical* aspects, and not with other more business-oriented aspects of outsourcing. For example, we have not discussed the matter of *costs* when trying to get two parties to agree to an SLA, or matters pertaining to *penalties* should a party not respect the SLA in practice. We think that UML/OCL is an extremely powerful modelling tool, and perhaps it is possible to also, eventually, model such aspects as those described in the UML/OCL framework, but this is still largely an open question.
2.   Query operations are not the only operations suitable for outsourcing in our approach. Update operations are equally suitable for outsourcing, due to the fact that our outsourcing schema employs exact views, hence ensuring preservation of integrity constraints (including those pertaining to state changes) from the source to the target. Update operations, however, fall into the category of transactions, and are therefore also subject to transaction protocols (of particular interest in a multiuser environment). In our case, we have to devise a transaction protocol between an outsourcer and a supplier, somehow keeping them in sync. Constructing transaction specifications and/or protocols in outsourced information systems is the next step in outsourcing of information systems.
3.   The question whether something is called an *object operation* or not, is of no significance when dealing with matters of complexity or operation expressiveness. For example, if an operation is to handle a whole set of instances (say of some class C) at the same time, then we construct a root class, say RC, from which we have a relation to C. We can then define an object operation inside class RC that can manipulate the class C. We can use a similar approach for an operation that has to handle a complete database. In this case, we just construct a database object containing relations to the base classes the database consists of. An operation on this database object can then refer to any collection of classes inside the database. Hence, an operation being an *object* operation, places no real limitations on its expressiveness.

Federating (information) systems has been the subject of a large research community in the field of databases and information systems in general. There are, however, still some topics in need of more research, of which we mention a number.

1.   We have a good idea what data integration (*data extraction*) and (static) constraint integration (*data reconciliation*) looks like. A next step could be to offer a theory of *operation integration*; that is, given some local operation (that we wish to share at the global level of the federation), how could we represent it at the global level, taking into account all possible data extraction and data reconciliation problems, and also

taking into account the pre- and postconditions (i.e., *dynamic constraints*) associated to that operation? This is an interesting and intriguing problem that is of particular interest in the context of EAI (enterprise application integration). Once this problem is solved, the way is open towards the beginning of a theory of transactions on federated information systems (transaction specifications and protocols in a multiuser environment).

2.   One might protest against the current state of affairs that we are only able at the moment to tackle data extraction and data reconciliation problems in federated systems, while actual transactions on a federated system are the core of the matter that we are aiming at. There are, however, applications in the context of data warehouses that could benefit immensely from relatively recent results in the field of federated information systems. Data warehouses, from the point of view of conceptual design, have mainly benefitted from current insights in data extraction, while the theory of constraint integration (i.e. data reconciliation) has hardly been addressed as being relative to data warehouse applications. We advocate, however, that data warehouse applications (largely being query applications) could use constraint information at the global integrated level to write more effective (and efficient) queries. Anybody involved in standard database applications already knows that knowledge of constraints is essential in the way one specifies queries: knowledge of key constraints, foreign keys and so forth, are used to the maximum to obtain correct and efficient queries. By having general knowledge of representing (ad hoc) local constraints at the global integrated level, data warehouse users could greatly improve the quality of their query specifications.

CONCLUSION

Federating and outsourcing are more-or-less dual processes. Federating (or: integrating) deals with moving from a given collection of local component systems to an encompassing global system, while outsourcing deals with moving from (a part of) an existing global system to a local system. Integration, as described in this chapter, employs the *global as view* (GAV) approach in constructing an appropriate global system, while in outsourcing one employs a *local as view* (LAV) approach in constructing an appropriate local system. In both approaches, *exact views* provide the basis for constructing the required systems. Data extraction deals with the alignment of syntax and semantics of data schemas of the local and global systems involved. The integration process and data reconciliation subsequently addresses the issue of correctly integrating local integrity constraints, where the existence of a corresponding ψ-*map* offers the criterion for successful integration of data and constraints. In the outsourcing process, schema alignment tries to match an outsourcer schema with a supplier schema, where the existence of a corresponding ω-*map* offers the criterion for successful outsourcing of an operation, together with accompanying data and pre/postconditions.

In summary, we can say that there is a *partial duality relation* between integrating and outsourcing. Both integration and outsourcing employ exact views to obtain their goals; the integration process, however, is subsequently aimed at the systematic construction of a suitable ψ-map, while the outsourcing process systematically tries to construct a suitable ω-map.

REFERENCES

Balsters, H. (2003). Modelling database views with derived classes in the UML/OCL framework. *«UML» 2003 6ᵗʰ International Conference* (LNCS 2863). New York: Springer.

Balsters, H., & de Brock, E. O. (2003a). An object-oriented framework for managing cooperating legacy databases. In *Proceedings of the 9ᵗʰ International Conference Object-Oriented Information Systems* (LNCS 2817). New York: Springer.

Balsters, H., & de Brock, E. O. (2003b). Integration of integrity constraints in database federations. In *Proceedings of the 6ᵗʰ IFIP TC-11 WG 11.5 Conference on Integrity and Internal Control in Information Systems*. Norwell, MA: Kluwer Academic Press.

Balsters, H., & de Brock, E. O. (2004a). An object-oriented framework for reconciliation and extraction in heterogeneous data federations. In *Proceedings of the 3ʳᵈ International Conference, ADVIS2004, Advances in Information Systems* (LNCS 3261). New York: Springer.

Balsters, H., & de Brock, E. O. (2004b). Integration of integrity constraints in federated schemata based on tight constraining. In *Proceedings OTM Confederated International Conference CoopIS, DOA, and ODBASE* (LNCS 3290). New York: Springer.

Blaha, M., & Premerlani, W. (1998). *Object-oriented modelling and design for database applications*. NJ: Prentice Hall.

Bouzeghoub, M., & Lenzerini, M (2001). Introduction to data extraction, cleaning, and reconciliation. *Information Systems, 26*(8), 535-536. Elsevier Science.

Cali, A., Calvanese, D., De Giacomo, G., & Lenzerini, M. (2002). Data integration under integrity constraints. In *Proceedings of the CAISE 2002* (LNCS 2348). New York: Springer.

de Looff, L. A. (1995). Information systems outsourcing decision making: A framework, organizational theories, and case studies. *Journal of Information Technology, 10*(4).

Demuth, B., & Hussmann, H. (1999). Using UML/OCL constraints for relational database design. *«UML» '99: 2ⁿᵈ International Conference* (LNCS 1723). New York: Springer.

Demuth, B., Hussmann, H., & Loecher, S. (2001). OCL as a specification language for business rules in database applications. *«UML» 2001, 4ᵗʰ International Conference* (LNCS 2185). Springer.

Eriksson, H. E., &Penker, M. (2000). *Business modelling with UML. Business patterns at work*. Hoboken, NJ: Wiley.

Forrester (2004). *Tracking Europe's outsourcing stampede*. Cambridge, MA: Forrester Research.

Gera, J. (2003). *Outsourcing management: Align management techniques to the outsourcing model*. Cambridge, MA: Giga Research (Forrester Research Inc.).

Grefen, P., Ludwig, H. & Angelov, S. (2003). A three-level framework for process and data management of complex e-services. *International Journal of Cooperative Information Systems, 12*(4), 487-531.

Lenzerini, M. (2002). Data integration: A theoretical perspective. *ACM PODS'02*. New York: ACM Press.

Miller, R. J., Haas, L. M., & Hernandez, M. A. (2000). Schema mapping as query discovery. In *Proceedings of the 26ᵗʰ VLDB Conference*. San Francisco: Morgan Kaufmann.

Rahm, E., & Bernstein, P. A. (2001). A survey of approaches to automatic schema matching. *VLDB Journal, 10*(4), 334-350.

Reddy, M. P., Prasad, B. P., & Gupta, A. (1995). Formulating global integrity constraints during derivation of global schemas. *Data & Knowledge Engineering, 16*(3), 241-268.

Sheth, A. P., & Larson, J. A. (1990). Federated database systems for managing distributed,h eterogeneous and autonomous databases. *ACM Computing Surveys, 22*(3), 183-236.

Smith, M. A., Mitra, S., & Narasimhan, S. (1998). Information systems outsourcing: A study of pre-event firm characteristics. *Journal of Management Information Systems, 15*(2).

Spaccapietra, S., Parent, C., & Dupont, Y. (1992). Model independent assertions for integration of heterogeneous schemas. *VLDB Journal, 1*(1), 81-126.

Sparrow, E. (2003). *Successful IT ousourcing, from choosing a provider to managing the project.* New York: Springer.

Türker, C., & Saake, G. (2000). Global extensional assertions and local integrity constraints in federated schemata. *Information Systems, 25*(8), 503-526.

Vermeer, M., & Apers, P. G. M. (1996). The role of integrity constraints in database interoperation. In *Proceedings of the 22ⁿᵈ VLDB Conference.* San Francisco: Morgan Kaufmann.

Warmer, J. B., & Kleppe, A. G. (2003). *The object constraint language* (2ⁿᵈ ed.). Boston: Addison Wesley.

Chapter XII

Verification and Validation of Nonfunctional Aspects in Enterprise Modeling

András Pataricza, Budapest University of Technology and Economics, Hungary

András Balogh, Budapest University of Technology and Economics, Hungary

Lázló Gönczy, Budapest University of Technology and Economics, Hungary

ABSTRACT

Dependability consolidation is a novel solution for complex problems. It includes in-depth analysis of business systems and their technology infrastructure for identification of risk areas. Results include the generation of precise metrics to quantify the risk. Once areas of low dependability have been identified solutions that minimize risk are defined. With Dependability consolidation techniques it is possible to make precise value assessments of entities like outsourced business operations or complex IT systems. In the case of IT systems, the use of dependability consolidation techniques enables the smooth integration of existing and new applications. Through the use of dependability consolidation techniques it is possible to seamlessly integrate modern systems design approaches like model driven architecture (MDA), system integration principles like service oriented architecture (SOA) and operating environments that contain supervised dependability.

INTRODUCTION

This chapter intends to provide a sound technical basis for the analysis and solution of issues of high interest in the e-business world. For example existing software applications represent a huge asset for industry but in most cases their design has addressed only the functional requirements with little or no attention given to dependability. Using dependability consolidation techniques such existing software can now be upgraded to create dependability assuring environments. Dependability consolidation makes use of formal analysis, proof of correctness and optimization methods to guarantee a proper quality of service.

The main notions related to the dependability of applications are presented in a self-contained way to make them accessible to non-experts. Topics include the formulation of modeling requirements in UML, the evolving UML profiles, the use of design patterns for best practices and basic means for testing. Validation based on formal methods and verification of designs are also covered. Another topic addressed is the use of model transformation techniques that allow quality of service driven optimization of enterprise systems architectures. The methods and techniques are illustrated with practical models and problems.

PROBLEM FOUNDATION

Impact of MDA

Recently, e-business came to be one of the main drivers in the development of economy. In the broadest sense, e-business is a standardized way for different service providers to share information and to cooperate.

The widespread use of computer-based business solutions has led to new challenges in the field of information technologies. The steady evolution of business and technology necessitates a high degree of flexibility and adaptability on the information technology side. Simultaneously, the reuse of existing intellectual property in the form of business logic designs has become a crucial factor in keeping the costs related to the development of e-business applications at a reasonable level.

The most promising answer is the model driven architecture (MDA) initiative by the Object Management Group. The basic idea in MDA is that the intended functionality of the target system under development will be described by means of a platform independent model (PIM). Automated transformations perform the resource allocation to these functions, map the PIM onto a platform specific model (PSM), and perform the generation of the runtime code (Figure 1).

Figure 1. Model driven architecture

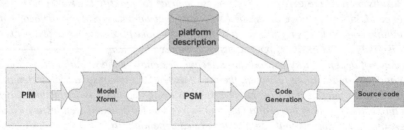

While the technology for MDA is still rapidly developing, its advantages are obvious. The formulation of the business know-how in the form of a PIM protects this essential intellectual property against rapid changes in the technology; moreover, best practices can be made available for the wide public in the form of business design patterns. The underlying easy-to-understand graphic annotation in the form of UML diagrams provides a proper means to develop interdisciplinary applications.

The productivity of the implementation is expected to grow by one order of magnitude. This increase in productivity results partially from the elimination or drastic reduction of tedious manual programming tasks needed to implement an e-business application. The other source of productivity increase is due to the lack of ambiguity in semiformal specifications like those prepared in UML. The avoidance of large redesign cycles, prompted by design defects originated in insufficient or incorrect specifications of the target system under design, is an important factor.

A third important benefit is the potential of a formal analysis of UML models to detect design faults in the early phases of the design. The main advantage of applying sophisticated mathematical formal analysis methods and tools to UML models is that an exhaustive analysis, checking all possible cases, can be carried out, thus guaranteeing a proper quality of the design and its implementation. Quality predictions indicate that the decrease of the remaining faults in an IT implementation may reach a factor as high as one and one half orders of magnitude.

Dependability Foundations

Dependability is the property of a system that makes it possible for the user to rely on its services. The importance of dependability is continuously increasing as society relies more and more on the services delivered by the underlying IT infrastructure. The meaning of dependability from a constructive point of view is that the system has to incorporate the ability to avoid unacceptable service failures.

In subsequent material, we refer to failures as deviations of the system-delivered services from their specifications in a way observable by the user of the services. We refer to the origin of misbehavior of the system as a fault that may propagate along a chain of faulty states through the system in the form of errors.

Faults can be developmental or operational, depending on the phase of creation or occurrence; internal or external according to the location of their occurrence in relation to the system boundaries; they may be natural or human-made, depending on the cause; and they can be malicious or nonmalicious according to the objective.

Dependability covers several attributes of a system. For e-business applications, availability, reliability, and maintainability are the most relevant ones, as they characterize the readiness and continuity of correct services and the ability to undergo modifications and repairs.

Security refers to the protection against unauthorized accesses and/or modifications of data. Assurance of a proper level of dependability can only be addressed in full detail at the level of the platform specific model, as the majority of faults and error propagation mechanisms depend highly on the implementation.

During the last decade, the dependability of the application and that of the underlying platform became two interacting but separately defined and implemented parts of the design for dependability solutions. The assurance of a fault-free, dependable platform became a primary objective of the IT hardware and software industries, and numerous commercial products are already available to fulfill this objective. Recently available products include high-assurance, enterprise-class servers that provide high availability by some form of cluster computing with failover capabilities upon detection of a critical error, firewalls, and intrusion detection engines to detect security threads.

The main driving forces related to design for dependability methodologies and technologies are the following ones:

- **Awareness:** Consumers of e-business are increasingly aware of dependability, and especially of security aspects. However, the process of the elaboration of an exact definition in the form of quantitative measures for dependability of complex services is still in its initial phase. No widely accepted standards and methodologies exist covering all the related aspects in a seamless way (with the exception of the field of security where some established methodologies are widely used to evaluate existing or designated systems). The increasing extent of outsourcing, to IT service providers, the computing infrastructures running e-business applications stresses the importance of measurable dependability. SLA (service level agreement) definitions still rely on ad hoc approaches.

- **Design:** The main trend in IT system design is the model driven architecture initiative, which aims at a high-level, model-based, platform-independent specification of the target system, and a subsequent highly automated implementation. Valuable initial work was done to combine this paradigm with formal analysis methods covering nonfunctional attributes as well, but there is still a lack of an industrial strength technology complementing the state of the art technologies from the point of view of nonfunctional requirements analysis.

- **Services-based integration:** One important evolving trend in IT is service-oriented system integration in which a user application is created by invoking and integrating third-party services via standardized interfaces over the Internet. A major business benefit in a Web services-based system composition originates in the possibility of selecting each service from the offerings of a highly specialized provider, assuring a high quality of the particular subservice. This way, the interoperability offered by the standardization of the interfaces results in a direct and easy way of creating highly professional cooperative businesses and services. The main advantage from the point of view of technology is that service-oriented architectures hide the implementation details behind standard interfaces describing the services offered. Such technologies, combined with dynamic deployment, may lead to a fast convergence of grid-based solutions and service-oriented architectures. However, the dependability of such invoked services is out of the control of the service integrator. There is a requirement for the SLA to offer standardized ways to declare, measure, and analyze QoS parameters of such services.

- **Operations:** Several industrial solutions exist that perform the monitoring and, if necessary, control or reconfiguration of a system from the point of view of performance, security, and dependability. Such systems form the basis for operating large-scale infrastructures. The most advanced supervisory systems support the creation of highly adaptive systems like those used in autonomic computing or self-healing systems. However, these systems protect the entire platform, and they normally use a purely heuristic way of designing the protection rules of the individual, critical applications. The integration of the MDA-based application design methodology and its run-time environment is expected to have a major impact, but configuration management remains a major dependability bottleneck.

Dependability Consolidation

The process of upgrading the dependability of already existing applications and harmonizing them with the functional design of applications under development will be referred to as dependability consolidation. A distinguished criterion for a successful dependability consolidation is the proper harmonization and integration of software reengineering and MDA-driven design for dependability methods and tools.

Existing software applications represent a huge asset for industry but in most cases, their design only considers the functional requirements, with little or no attention given to dependability. There are several possibilities for upgrading their dependability:

- One can go ahead with application reengineering. Often it is necessary to upgrade the applications, starting from code level, by reverse engineering, but this is a tedious and costly task.
- An emerging solution comes from MDA; its main promise is the reusability of the design. After reconstructing the model of an application by manual remodeling or by automated remodeling, all the technologies for dependability analysis and consolidation can be applied.
- Another possibility is to integrate the existing applications into dependability assuring environments. This includes the use of dependability enforcing add-ons for application-specific measures to increase the system robustness and the use of platforms that provide services for dependability (like those developed in the SA Forum platforms).

The seamless integration of modern design methodologies like MDA, system integration principles like service-oriented architecture, and supervised dependability-increasing operating environments is crucial and needs the support of formal analysis, proof of correctness, and optimization methods to guarantee a proper quality of service. The use of dependability consolidation techniques enables the smooth integration of existing and new applications.

WORKFLOW DESIGN AND ANALYSIS

The first step in the development after the definition of high-level services and functionalities is the estimation of the operation sequences in the form of a workflow. This workflow is specific to the organization implementing the functionality and at the same time, it serves as a basic model:

- For analyzing the business service to be provided,
- To estimate its resource requirements, and
- To provide the implementation with a high-level specification.

Accordingly, the model-based system development starts with the description of the workflows. Based on the analysis of workflows, the changes driven by real business needs can be collected, and the design or redesign of IT systems can follow the demands of the enterprise organization.

The definition of the activity diagram notation serves, simultaneously, two purposes:

- The language resembles strongly the most widely used business process modeling (BPM) languages not only by sharing the same mathematical background, but also using similar notions and notations to ease the communication between the system developer and the end user.
- The recent version of activity diagrams, which was enriched by a large set of newly introduced notations compared to the UML standard 1.0, should provide a notational richness and expressive power enough to support a direct implementation of a business workflow over an intelligent platform like business process execution language for Web services (BPEL).

This kind of simultaneous support of the business objectives and their IT implementation is beneficial not only from the reduced development time and cost point of view, but it also allows a rapid adaptation to the frequently chancy economic environment by offering the full flexibility of the model driven architecture approach.

Accordingly, activity diagrams provide a proper means to define and implement a wide spectrum of business applications where no very dedicated solutions are required. Frequently, especially in the case of small and medium enterprises, only a typical business goal and service-oriented solution is required, which is built over some high-level primitives of the runtime platforms. For instance, small e-catalog, e-commerce applications, or applications relying on service integration by Web services share the same set of primitive operations that are now directly supported by activity diagrams.

However, as the definition of a workflow becomes, in this category, the core concept of the implementation, the design quality of the BPM becomes not only a crucial but a decisive factor from the point of view of the quality of business services and the underlying IT solutions as well.

This way, an analysis of the workflow may essentially contribute to a correct operation:

- By revealing potential design faults in the formal description of the workflow,
- By providing uniform specifications for a thoroughgoing analysis of nonfunctional requirements like security, authorization, and availability at the high, algorithmic level.

In the subsequent chapter, we provide the reader with an overview on this topmost level of model-based system design and analysis techniques.

Naturally, activity diagrams do not provide a perfect solution for all kinds of problems. In the case of highly custom-tailored systems, the activity diagrams serve only to specify the control and data flow in the system, and the functionalities have to be specified in a more refined form by means of other UML diagrams like class diagrams, state machines, and so forth. Even in this later category of diagrams, the topmost level of dependability assurance mechanisms, like algorithm based fault tolerance (ABFT), rely on the algorithm implemented in the system: thus, they can be analyzed by using activity diagrams. Typi-

Figure 2. The activity diagram of the travel agency

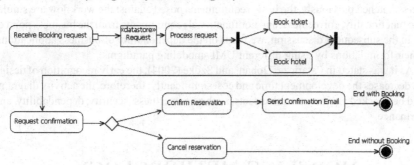

cally, the separation of concerns strategy means that a platform of proper characteristics conforming to the particular needs of the application is selected. For instance, in the case of a business critical application, a high-availability server can be used instead of a simple one as a deployment platform, to guarantee a sufficient availability for the entire application. However, this kind of measure appears from the top-level view of the system functionality only as parameters, both in the terms of required and guaranteed ones. This way, from the algorithmic point of view, implementation related aspects can be clearly separated from the objective and requirements view of the system. In the subsequent discussion, we assume only that the requirements formulated in the business flow can be fulfilled and be monitored with the proper technical means, without discussing the technical details.

The development based on activity diagrams is illustrated by the following simple example.

A travel agency offers online hotel and airplane ticket booking services. This process requires some input from the customer. For instance, the planned date and destination of the journey and some price limits have to be submitted via a Web form. Subsequently, the agency tries to reserve travel tickets and accommodation according to the input parameters and returns a confirmation request to the user. After confirmation and provision of credit card data, the reservation is committed.

This workflow can be implemented in multiple ways, depending on the economically and technology related constrains and facilities:

- If the travel agency can access some online databases directly, then the reservation takes only a few seconds and the application is reduced to a customized, standalone, enterprise software.
- If the agency is a division of a large company using a workflow management framework as a basis of its IT infrastructure, then the workflow logic is described in the vendor-specific representation language of the particular workflow engine.
- If the agency relies on some external services (for instance, a service provider offers unified access for multiple alternative accommodation databases), then only a loose integration is possible. This needs the usage of a standardized data exchange language and some remote procedure calling mechanisms, such as XML Web services and the business process execution language (Specification: BPEL, 2003) as workflow logic description language. In this case, the transaction is considered long running, and persistent storage of the request is necessary.

Please note that while technical alternatives essentially differ from the IT system architectures sketched previously, the basic requirements posed against the workflow are similar for the functionality, correctness, and nonfunctional requirements from the business point of view. In the subsequent discussion, we focus on the dependability of business applications, and their formulations by using different UML-modeling paradigms.

As it was stated in Pataricza, Dobán, and Szőke (2004), the early recognition of design faults decreases the development time and cost significantly; therefore, the activity diagrams should be checked against several aspects, such as correctness, security, dependability, and performance.

MODELING METHODOLOGY

The first step in the enterprise modeling lifecycle is typically the definition of a high-level workflow describing the business logic serving as a basis of the enterprise functions. The requirements to be fulfilled by the implementation specified in the detailed UML models are derived from this workflow. Therefore, it is crucial to detect the design faults in the early phases of development.

The workflow should be checked against several qualitative criteria that help to eliminate the faults resulting in a failure during the operational life of the system. Activity diagrams are introduced to model the control flow and the data flow of the system. The notation and semantics of UML 2.0 will be followed, hereby, referring to UML 2.0 (2004).

A proper service by a workflow has to fulfill several classes of criteria:

- Some general criteria apply for all kinds of applications. For instance, an arbitrary workflow has to terminate sooner or later, delivering a service to the user, or by triggering a failure notification to the system operator. This way, an infinite operation is always a design fault. This kind of criteria will be referred to in the subsequent discussion as general requirements. They can be evaluated simply by criteria to be fulfilled by any mathematical model of workflow.
- General requirements appearing in an application-dependent form constitute a second large class. For instance, in business models, it is usually required that an operation may require some kind of authorization. The actual form of authorization depends on the workflow and business rules implemented by the particular organization: however, their checking may share the same mathematical principles.
- A third category is formed by the requirements that are application specific. For instance, in the case of a travel agency, some check of the passports may be required before issuing a ticket to some foreign country, depending on the legal and geographical environment. This category will be referred to as application-dependent requirements.

Naturally, the set of application-dependent requirements may include a set of non-functional requirements as well. In the subsequent chapters, we summarize the most typical representatives of these categories, and sketch the principles to check them formally. Please note that a formal check does not mean, necessarily, the use of sophisticated mathematics. Frequently, especially in the case of simple workflows, they can be performed by an expert review as well. However, complex workflows necessitate the automation of the checking procedure by means of model transformations to a mathematical analysis tool. This later requirement originates in the fact that a proper quality can be assured if and only if an exhaustive check is performed, systematically evaluating all the possibilities in the control flow and time. The boundary between the expert review and the automated checking methodologies lies in the order of magnitude of a few tens of operations, depending on the complexity of the operations involved.

First, the workflow model has to pass a formal validation that checks the fulfillment of the soundness requirements, defined in van der Aalst and van Hee (2002). These exclude the existence of several structural faults, described in detail in Section 3.1.1. If the process is considered sound, the requirements of confidentiality are checked against the Bell-LaPadula criteria (Bell & LaPadula, 1973).

General Requirements

This section discusses the most typical general faults in workflow models and their control mechanisms. These faults can be categorized as structural faults originating in improper process structure, security deficiencies violating the security and integrity criteria posed against the system, performance issues originating in a wrong or insufficient resource allocation to the tasks, and poor utilization of system resources resulting in overpowered system implementation and potential high total cost of ownership (TCO). The majority of these faults remain undiscovered by recent, simulation-based modeling tools and therefore, they constitute a risk of runtime failures due to hidden design faults. Please note that the large number of potential faults requires an extremely large number of simulation setups and runs. Even if only a few failure modes per component are taken into account, to check the reaction of the system to faults may require an extremely large set of experiments. These faults can be eliminated by using formal methods to exhaustively check the model. Such a check may contribute to an increase in the overall dependability and performance of the system that finally results in a reduced risk of failures, a lower TCO, and a higher customer satisfaction.

First, the structural faults that affect the correctness of the workflow are discussed and presented by a sample model. The following faults belong to this category:

- Hanging tasks
- Dead tasks
- Deadlocks
- Livelocks
- Activities running after termination (references remain in the system)

Figure 3. Hanging tasks

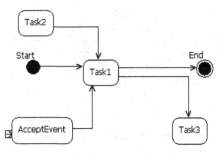

•   Infinite number of tokens

Before describing these faults in detail, the concept of token should be defined. A token represents a case: in other words, the executional state of a particular client request. If a request is submitted to a workflow (for instance, the travel agency gets an online booking request), a token is inserted into the initial node or event handling action of the activity diagram. The token is then passed through the model, representing the operation of the system.

A hanging task is an activity that does not have proper input or output conditions. Figure 3 shows a flow in which **Task2** does not have input condition, that is, no explicit route exists between the initial node and the task. **Task3** does not have a clear output condition and it is not needed for the successful completion of the flow. Note that the task "**Accept Event**" is an exception because it represents that the process may start upon an incoming message, and therefore can be considered as a possible entry point of the process.

Although the hanging tasks can be identified easily, most of the present modeling tools accept such models during the validation (even if they have such a feature).

A dead task is an activity that cannot be executed because it has improper input conditions, making its activation infeasible. Task4 in Figure 4 is dead because both of its inputs can never be active at the same time. This fault can be obviously recognized in this primitive example; however, a systematic check, covering the entire dynamics in the form of reachability analysis in the state space, is needed to identify such structural faults in the models of complex systems.

The problem of deadlocks is widely known in the different areas of computer theory (operating systems, database management systems, protocols, etc.); hereby a deadlock is a

Figure 4. Dead task

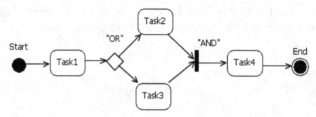

Figure 5. Deadlock

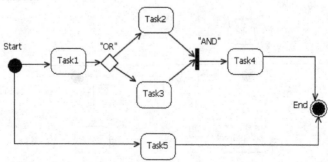

Figure 6. Livelock

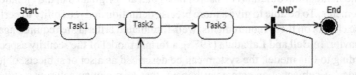

Figure 7. Tokens remaining in the process

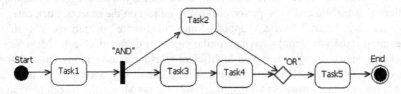

situation in which the end node can never be reached. In other words, a dead task is somewhere on the route to the end node. In the example shown in Figure 5, the execution of the process can never be terminated because **Task4** will never execute, and the final node will never get tokens on all incoming edges. Eliminating possible deadlocks from the model prevents the implemented software from getting "stuck."

A livelock (or trap) is the possibility that the process will never be terminated because of an infinite operation. Considering the UML activity diagrams, this infinite operation can be a loop that can be executed in an infinite number of times. Please note that both livelock and deadlock situations may appear not only due to the consequence of a simple structural design faults by including wrong loops or unsatisfiable mutual exclusions, but they may appear in a runtime context-sensitive form as well, if some branch operation has a wrong condition. In Figure 6, **Task2** and **Task3** will repeat continuously, and thus the process will never terminate.

If the process structure is not carefully designed, some unnecessary activities may remain live after the completion of the flow. These activities may produce tokens that will not disappear from the process. Figure 7 presents this situation: one of the two tokens (one on the path **Task2** and another on the path **Task3**-**Task4**) will remain in the flow after it has been completed (as the end node received tokens on all of its inputs). This means that a reference to the case (concrete flow instance) will remain in the system.

If the number of executions of a loop becomes infinite, then infinite number of tokens may arise if due to a flaw in the process design. This can happen in the example shown in Figure 6 where the system, remaining in a livelock, produces an infinite number of tokens on its output. Please note that this situation may happen despite a control condition: a feedback loop gets stuck at always enabled state due to an error in the data evaluation condition. If the activity itself is embedded into a higher-level model, this may raise severe runtime problems as tokens flood the system, which can cause a similar saturation and overflow effect like an infinite loop in traditional programming languages.

Security and Access Control

The second main group of faults consists of those that are originated in the violation of security requirements. To be able to give a more precise definition and the ability to perform general purpose checks on these requirements, well-formulated criteria are required against the system behavior. In Bell and LaPadula (1973), a formal model of the security aspects is defined. According to this model, the system can be described as a set of subjects, objects, and access modes. A subject is an active participant, that is, a human actor or a software component that initiates operations on the passive objects in the system (e.g. databases). Typically, these subjects appear in use case diagrams as actors.

The actions can be classified according to the access mode categories defining the operations that are allowed to be performed by the subject on the objects. Such categories are, for instance, "read," "write," "append," and "read-write" operations. The subjects can be categorized into groups having similar rights to different objects. Most security policies rely on access rights assigned to different roles in the operations. The role-based access control (RBAC) policies guarantee that in a central way, access rights are defined (and in some system management tools, like Tivoli Access Manager, this categorization is maintained and checked even during the operation). A mapping defines access rights of the individual role groups with respect to the individual objects or hierarchy levels in which the objects are organized.

The security requirements can be composed by using these concepts. For example, a rule can specify that "The group of students can only read the data in the table marks." More precisely, the objects and the subjects have security classifications (for instance, a number on a 0 to 9 scale). One of the most prominent representatives of security criteria in RBAC policies is the Bell-LaPadula system of criteria, supporting a general assessment of the overall system security. Of course, other application specific requirements may specify more strict security rules upon the system.

The Bell-LaPadula criteria are essentially two requirements that have to be fulfilled during the entire operational life of the system:

- The "no-read-up" rule prescribes that only the subjects with the proper level of privilege may access a document or other object. In other words, the security classification of the user has to dominate that of the object, that is, it must be more or equal on the same scale. This simple rule formulates the expectation that nobody should be able to access something above his level of confidence. These criteria assure that a data item may be revealed only to someone whom it concerns.
- The "no-write-down" criteria set up a more sophisticated (and more strict) requirement against the system: If a user reads an object with a security classification of i, then he can write only documents with a security classification that dominates i. This means that nobody can copy secret data to a nonsecret document; thus the intentional or unintentional revealing of confidential information is prevented.

General Resource Model

The general resource model (GRM) is part of the standard UML profile for schedulability, performance, and time specification (UML Profile for SPT, 2005). GRM offers a modeling language for describing resources (IT or non-IT, hardware, software, or human resources), resource dependencies, and basic quality of service values of these resources in a uniform way.

Figure 8. Core resource model (from OMG 2005)

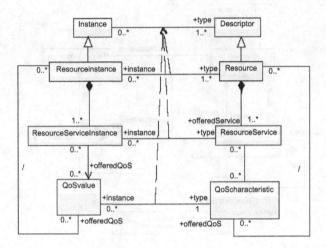

The core resource model, which can be seen in Figure 8, defines the relation between resources, resource instances, and QoS (Quality of Service) properties. A specific resource type has offered services, and each service may have defined QoS characteristics (for example mean response time), and all of its instances have a corresponding concrete QoS value. The resource-service model fits into today's service-oriented world, and expresses, from the service client's point of view, that the resource is defined by its offered services.

We can classify resources based on their purpose, activeness, and protection kind. Based on purpose, resources can be processor resources that represent either virtual or physical processing resources that can store and execute program code, communication resources

Figure 9. Static resource usage (From OMG 2005)

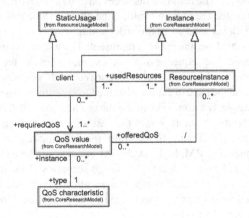

Figure 10. Dynamic resource usage model (From OMG 2005)

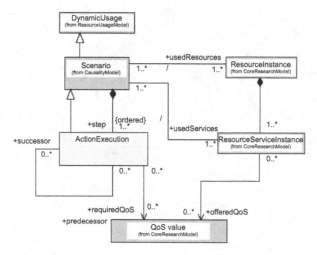

that transport information, or devices that represent all other resource types that are neither processors nor communication resources.

Based on activeness, resources can be either active, which are capable of generation stimuli (events) without the need to be explicitly stimulated before, or passive, which only react to incoming stimuli and do not generate any events without external triggering. Protected resources offer one or more protected execution instances, while unprotected resources do not have any execution protection.

Besides resources, GRM also defines usage scenarios that support the modeling of resource usage in the system. There are two types of resource usage: static and dynamic. Static usage modeling is used in cases where the client-service relationship can be considered as static from the modeling point of view. Figure 9 illustrates the structure of static resource usage. The client is connected to several used resources, and requires several QoS values (for example, a customer in a Web store requires that the response time of the Web server shall be less than 5 seconds). The resource instances have their own offered QoS values. If the offered QoS values match the required values, the client will be satisfied.

Dynamic usage model is used when the order and time of resource usages is relevant to the model analysis. In this case, the usage is represented by a scenario instance that has an associated action sequence. The sequence of action execution defines the order of resource usages. Action executions may have used resources and required QoS values associated. This complex modeling type can be used to express that the QoS requirements may vary during a usage scenario. For example, if a user is browsing the products of a Web store, the expected response time may be relatively short, but in the case of credit card check, the user will tolerate a longer response time. Figure 10 illustrates the dynamic resource usage model.

Using the techniques of GRM, high-level UML models can be easily extended with resource usage models, and even with complex usage scenarios. This enables the system designer to define the required resources and QoS values already on the platform independent model (PIM) level, and these modeling aspects can be mapped to the implementation level in the platform specific model (PSM).

Figure 11. Sample flow for the reachability problem

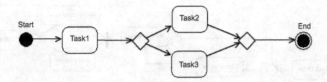

VALIDATION OF THE REQUIREMENTS
Qualitative Analysis of Process Models
General Criteria

This section presents some selected solutions and methods to eliminate the faults described in the previous section from the workflow model. Despite the fact that the notion of soundness and security differ essentially from a business point of view, as the checks share the same principles, they will be analyzed in the same chapter.

Obviously, these general criteria need a thoroughgoing check for all the possible rounds potentially occurring during the execution of the workflow.

The dynamics of a flow can be analyzed by introducing the concept of reachability graph. The reachability graph of a process flow (a UML activity diagram) is a directed graph, the root of which is the initial state (when all initial nodes are active). According to the UML 2.0 specification, when an activity becomes active, all of its initial nodes are active. The next nodes of the reachability graph are the possible active states of the flow, and so on. This is illustrated by a simple activity flow, shown in Figure 11.

The reachability graph of this flow is presented in Figure 12. The nodes in the graph show the active actions of the flow, and the arrows are the possible transition between the active actions.

In most cases, the minimal requirement that every process must fulfill is that there are no unnecessary tasks, and every case (i.e., request) submitted to the process is fully served, without any references remaining in the process. A process that fulfils these requirements

Figure 12. Reachability graph of the sample flow

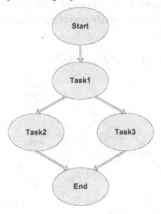

Figure 13. Delivery example flow before structural analysis

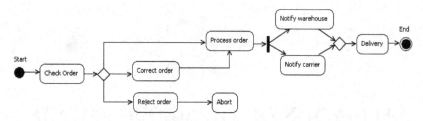

is called sound. Soundness means that every task in the flow is on a directed route between a start and an end node (as the UML 2.0 standard allows multiple start and end nodes in the process).

It can be proved that a sound process is free from the faults presented in section 3.1.1, namely it has no hanging or dead tasks, deadlocks, livelocks, stuck activities, neither may arise infinite tokens in the system.

To illustrate the usage of reachability graphs, a sample model is presented (that, in its initial form, has several structural faults). This example is only for demonstration purposes, as the size of the reachability graph of a real model is usually more complex. However, this simple structure helps to understand the validation methods. The following process models the delivery of an online shop. However, this process will not work correctly, as the careful reader may notice.

This flow is intended to work in the following way. Incoming orders are checked. If an order is fault free (that is, every data field is filled correctly), the order is processed. Otherwise, if the order contains small errors that can be corrected automatically (for instance, a ZIP code is missing, but the city and the street fields are filled), the order is corrected and then processed. If the order cannot be corrected or some other complication occurs, for instance, the ordered amount of an article is not presently available in the repository, then the order is rejected. If an order is approved, the warehouse and the carrier are notified about it.

Even this simple flow has several faults due to improper structure definition. First, there is a dead task in the flow. As the **"Process order"** task needs all of its inputs, which are two different choices of the same decision, it never can be executed. Therefore, this execution path can be considered a deadlock. Second, the **"Abort"** task is hanging because it does not yield any output (never terminates in a final node). Finally, there will remain some tokens in the process after termination, as the **"Notify warehouse"** and the **"Notify carrier"** tasks are

Figure 14. Reachability graph of the delivery flow

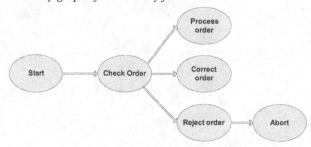

connected in an OR-join (merge element) instead of an AND-join (join element). Therefore, the task **"Delivery"** can run after getting the first input. This means that a reference to the case will remain in the flow in the moment of termination. Moreover, as the **"Delivery"** task is executed twice, the number of produced tokens is more than one.

All these faults can be strained off by three independent checks, all based on the reachability graph of the example shown in Figure 14.

The first check looks for dead tasks. These can be identified by the simple fact that they are not in the reachability graph. The task **"Delivery"** and all the subsequent actions are therefore dead. Note that the generation and analysis of the reachability graph can be done systematically by hand (this method is, however, rather time consuming) or by automated methods. We propose model transformation to help the automated analysis by the following steps:

1. The UML model is parsed to the (graph) representation language of the transformation tool, for example, VIATRA2 (Balogh, Németh, Schmidt, Ráth, Vágó, Varró, & Pataricza, 2005). This language stores the model elements as a set of graph nodes, where these nodes have attributes (e.g., the name of the task is an attribute of the corresponding graph node) and the relationships between the nodes describe the composition of the model (for instance, the arrows of the activity flow are relationships between the nodes).
2. The directed reachability graph is generated by model transformation.
3. The tasks of the original model are systematically checked in the reachability graph of the model.

In this example, the requirement is that every task should be available from the initial node. The node **"Delivery"** violates this requirement; therefore, it is a dead task (according to our expectations). Dead execution paths that is, those that do not end in an explicit Activity final or Flow final node, are also discovered. In our example, the path **"Check order"–"Reject order"–"Abort"** is such a path.

The nonterminating tasks that still run when the process should have been terminated can also be eliminated. This needs the generation of an inverse reachability graph in which the arrows of the model are reversed, and the generation of the reachability graph starts from the final node. Let us suppose that the model was corrected and extended with an explicit "End2" node to eliminate the hanging task from the system, and the AND join before the task "Process request" has also been replaced by an OR-join (merge control node) as shown in Figure 15.

Figure 15. The delivery flow after the first corrections

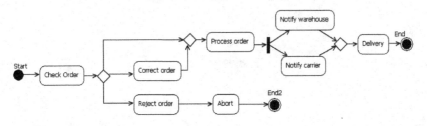

Figure 16. The inverse reachability graph of the corrected example

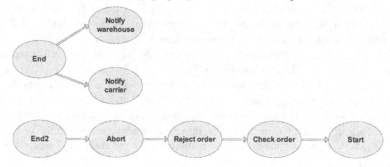

Figure 17. The corrected delivery flow

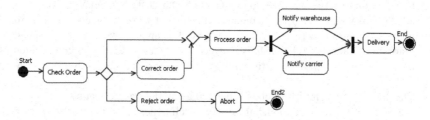

The inverse reachability graph of the corrected example is shown in Figure 16.

As the tasks **"Notify warehouse"** and **"Notify carrier"** are not on a directed path from the end nodes to the start node, these are tasks that do not necessarily terminate at the end of the process (i.e., when an explicit end node is reached).

Finally, the corrected delivery flow looks like Figure 16 (of course, this is not the only possible correction).

Figure 18. Error propagation and damage confinement region

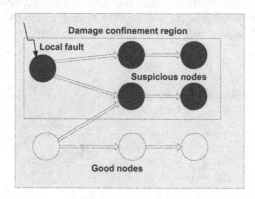

Robustness and Fault Tolerance

The validation of the process structure that is, the functional design itself does not prevent the system from unintended operations. To be able to answer questions like "How will the system function in the presence of faults?" a more detailed analysis has to be performed considering the interaction between hardware and software faults. This needs the modeling of resources and task-resource assignments. Once the local faults are modeled, their impact on the system has to be tracked in order to identify the critical points in the system. This is called error propagation. The result of this is the system-level failure caused by a low-level fault. For instance, if a network link to a server is broken, the end user may observe that he does not get answer for a query. Considering the delivery example, if a data field of an order request form is filled in badly, it may result in a bad delivery. The set of system components that can be affected by a particular fault is called damage confinement region while these components are suspicious. That part of the system that cannot be affected by the fault is considered to work properly, that is, the components in it are good. The propagation method needs the system components and their dependencies to build a directed graph upon which the damage confinement region can be determined, as illustrated by Figure 18.

To execute error propagation, the faults of system resources and software components have to be modeled. The GRM profile, presented in the previous section, can be extended, according to Pataricza (2002), to describe the actual state of **resources** as some enumerated value (e.g., good-faulty). The **software** components (i.e., objects implementing the required functionalities) are also modeled according to qualitative aspects. This includes the qualitative classification of attributes, such as good, faulty, illegal, and so forth. Note that the

Figure 19. Fault modeling architecture (from Pataricza, 2002)

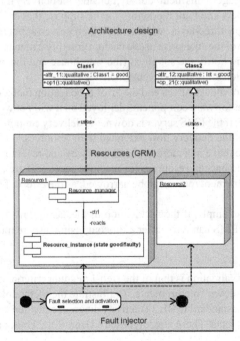

Figure 20. Delivery flow extended with resources

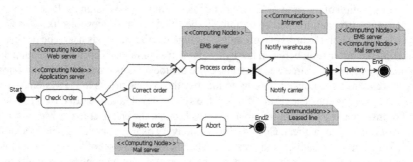

concrete values of the attributes are out of scope, only their classification is relevant. For instance, the date of an order can be valid (10/20/1996), faulty (00/00/9951), or suspicious (10/20/1960). The concrete definition of these categories is not needed for the error propagation. On the other hand, working with a few values instead of all possible data speeds up the analysis. For instance, all dates between 1990 and the present date are considered valid, therefore it is not needed to distinguish between them. This kind of system description is called uninterpreted modeling.

The hardware-software **configuration**, that is, the set of dependencies between the hardware and the software, also has to be known. Finally, a **fault injector** is needed to simulate faults. This accesses the resources and indicates a good-faulty transition in the resource state (to simulate permanent faults like a disk failure), or a good-faulty-good transition (to simulate transient faults like noise in the communication channel).

To illustrate the usage of this methodology, consider the delivery flow example, extended with resource parameters and fault modeling. Let us suppose that orders are submitted via a Web browser using a three-layer architecture (Web server-application server-database server). The employee of the enterprise uses a custom enterprise management system (EMS) to review the order and notify the suppliers (the warehouse and the carrier). The decision and delivery information are sent to the customer via e-mail.

The fault model of the resources and the error propagation method are quite simple: if a resource is faulty, the software components deployed on it will not work and the workflow will stop. For instance, if the EMS server is down, the delivery cannot be completed. Figure 20 shows the model of the delivery flow extended with resources.

The system can behave in a more sophisticated way and react to the occurred faults if exception handling and backup resources (or resource recovery) are also considered. This way, the damage confinement region can be narrowed, as the effect of a fault cannot spread in the system.

In this case, for example, if the notification of the carrier fails because of the failure of the leased line, the EMS can retry, after a timeout, using a spare modem.

Security Validation

The next kind of validation is that of the Bell-LaPadula criteria, namely the "no-read-up" and the "no-write-down" requirements. To illustrate the methodology, a sample model is presented, which is a standard UML 2.0 activity diagram extended with some stereotypes to describe security aspects. These stereotypes are User, Role, Unit, and Document, refer-

Figure 21. Order review example

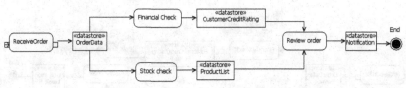

ring to enterprise users, roles, units, and documents, respectively. These stereotypes have properties like SecurityLevel, which describes the security level of a particular user of the enterprise system or a (sensitive) enterprise document.

These concepts are similar to those used by the main workflow modeling tools and workflow management systems.

The sample model in Figure 21 implements the following functionality:

If an order is received, it is tested against two respects; whether the user has enough credit and the articles are available in stock. These activities yield two different outputs: a customer credit rating and a product list. Then the order is reviewed considering whether it can be fulfilled or not. This flow could also be injected into the previous example, for example, instead of the process order task. The basic example – not containing the security aspects– is shown in Figure 21.

The documents in this example (**OrderData**, **CustomerCreditRating** and **ProductList**) may have different security classifications. For instance, the order data has a security level of 6 and the product list has a level of 5, while the customer credit rating is of a level 8 (on a scale from 0 to 9). The employees can be categorized according to their organizational units (e.g., Fabrication, Logistics, Sales, Marketing, Finance, etc.) and their actual role or scope of activities (Controller, Storekeeper, Financial Supervisor, etc.). These categories also have security classification assigned and therefore, a simple relation can be defined on them. According to the usual pessimistic (or restrictive) strategy, the actual privileges of a user (subject in the Bell-LaPadula terminology) are determined by the lowest classification regarding the user. In this case, the minimum of the actual Employee, Unit, and Role security levels is applied. Now consider the model in Figure 21, extended with security classifications for the different actors and units of the organization (Table 1).

The actual configuration of the system is the following (considering that the **ReceiveOrder** task represents the receiving of an online order request):

Table 1. Security classifications

Employees	Units	Roles
Alice: 9	Fabrication: 4	Clerk: 8
Bob: 6	Logistics: 6	Storekeeper: 6
Charlie: 7	Finance: 9	Financial Supervisor: 9
	Sales: 5	Salesman: 5
	Marketing: 6	

Figure 22. Order review flow with organizational extension

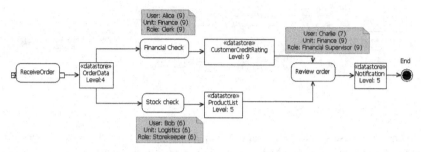

The first check that can be executed upon this configuration is the validation against the "no-read-up" criterion. This needs a simple check of the activities: the input and output documents and the assigned employees have to be compared. In this case, there are errors in the actual configuration as the following operations violate the "no-read-up" criteria:

- The security classification of Alice is 8, the minimum of (9, 9, 8), while the document she writes needs a level of 9.
- The security classification of Charlie is 7, the minimum of (7, 9, 9), while for one of the incoming documents he reads, a classification of 9 is needed.

These problems can be eliminated by assigning other employees to the tasks, introducing new roles with higher security classification, or reviewing the classification of the documents. In general, it is a good principle to separate sensitive and nonsensitive data; in this case, it is enough for the supervisor to see the result of the financial check and not all customer data, and so forth

The "no-write-down" criterion is also violated because the task "**ReviewOrder**" has input with a higher security classification than its output. This enables one to copy sensitive data to a nonsensitive document. This can be solved in several ways: by slicing the documents to separate the sensitive and nonsensitive data, or by inserting a new automated task that converts the detailed customer data into a simple Y/N answer, and so forth. The criterion itself can be too rigorous for some systems: if the tasks are validated (i.e., no direct copy is possible between documents of different security levels), the criterion can be ignored. A sample solution is presented in Figure 23: the "**Financial Check**" task does not need to ac-

Figure 23. The corrected order review process

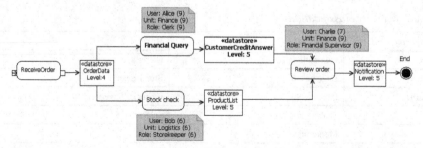

cess customer data directly; rather, it uses some external service (e.g., a custom component of the enterprise framework) that returns with a simple Yes/No answer. To visualize this change, the name of the task is changed to **"Financial Query."** The modified elements of the model are represented with **bold** letters. In complex systems with many organizational actors, documents, and tasks, the correction of security deficiencies is more difficult, but the Bell-LaPadula criteria help to check the model in a formalized, systematic way.

Generally, these security checks could be done by a custom software component that takes the UML model as input, and examines the activities and other assigned entities (e.g., users). However, as described in the next section, using model transformation can, on the one hand, enhance the integration of new or custom security tests, and increases the maintainability of the validation process, on the other hand. To illustrate the steps of security validation by model transformation, a possible scenario of the validation is presented

1.   The UML model is parsed into a graph representation (as described at the first step of the structural validation).
2.   A model is generated in a formal representation language that makes it appropriate for precise analysis.
3.   A set of linear temporal logic (LTL) and graph transformation rules is used to check the model. For instance, the "no-read-up" criteria can be described as a composition of one graph transformation rule that places a token in the error signal channel of the node under analysis, and one simple LTL formula (independent from the concrete model) that defines the global criteria that every error channel must be empty, that is, every node has to pass the test of the "no-read-up" criteria. Note that the test itself is made by a graph transformation rule driven by the model parameters: in this case, the security classification of the elements.

The check of the "no-write-down" criteria is similar, with the difference that the security classifications of input and output documents are compared.

Model Transformations

The proof of correctness at the model level necessitates the use of a variety of mathematical analysis techniques. Automated transformations are able to map design models, like the UML of the target applications to mathematical analysis models, in order to perform an exhaustive check from a specific aspect.

Figure 24 illustrates the most common usage scenario for a model transformation framework. It connects two different modeling domains to each other. In this example, the first (application) domain is the business process modeling domain, and the user works with

Figure 24. Transformations between the application and analysis domains

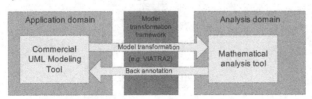

a commercial UML tool. The mathematical analysis tools, which offer model checking and optimization capabilities, work in a different domain, for example in the domain of linear equation systems or Petri nets (Gönczy, 2005).

A model transformation maps the source UML model from the application domain to the analysis domain to allow the mathematical analysis of the model, and after the analysis, another transformation to project back the results to the source domain.

Designing model transformation, in general, is a very complex problem. We have to treat with the concrete and abstract syntax of the source and target languages, and the semantic correctness of the mapping. There are several model transformation frameworks like VIATRA2 (Balogh et al., 2005) that ease the transformation development with powerful metamodeling capabilities, syntactical and semantic checking of models, and formal transformation languages. This increases the productivity of transformation development, and the quality of transformation programs.

Typical Enterprise-Level IT Design Patterns

There are several enterprise-level design patterns that can be used in infrastructure planning. These patterns are built to achieve high availability or capacity of server computers, and to introduce fault tolerance to the architecture.

Probably the simplest design pattern is the workload balancing cluster. It consists of several identical servers that run the same application. The incoming client requests are distributed among the servers by a dedicated load balancer node. This is a simple computer that monitors the load of the cluster member servers, and routes the new requests to the node that has the lowest utilization. Figure 25 illustrates this pattern using the notation defined by GRM.

Figure 25. Load balancing cluster pattern

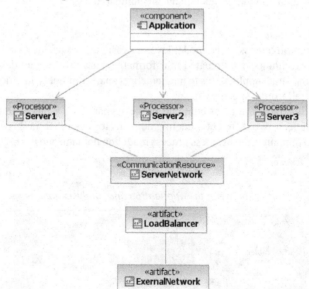

Figure 26. Tiered servers pattern

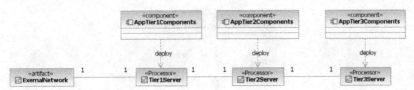

The next pattern supports the tiered load balancing. This means that the application is divided into several tiers (or layers), and the tiers are distributed across machines. This distributes the load of the server as a request is served in multiple parts by multiple servers. Figure 26 illustrates the pattern. The request is arriving at the tier 1 server that processes it and generates a new request for further processing to tier 2, and so on. After the last tier has completed the processing, the response is passed back through the tiers in reverse order, and the client will receive the completed response.

The two patterns that have been introduced can be combined; any tier can be extended to be a workload-balancing cluster. These solutions offer, however, minimal fault tolerance. The following patterns define methods for increasing the fault tolerance of the server infrastructure.

The cold-spare pattern consists of n+1 servers, where n means the number of active servers in the cluster. The n+1th server is a standby node that is only activated if one of the active servers fails. This results in a reduced performance while the standby is booting (several minutes, typically): then the performance of the server will be equal to the original. The structure of this pattern is nearly identical to the workload-balancing cluster and is illustrated by Figure 27.

Figure 27. Cold-spare pattern

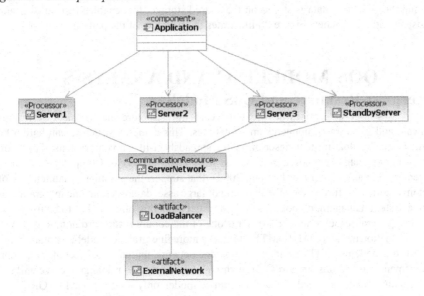

Figure 28. Failover cluster pattern

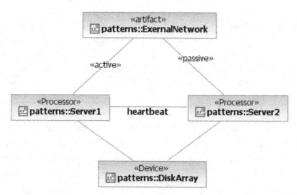

The hot-spare pattern is identical to the workload-balancing cluster, but the capacity of the servers is higher than the required level. This means that if a server fails, the remaining capacity of the cluster will also be sufficient to serve all requests and maintaining the proper QoS level. This can be imagined as if one of the servers would be a standby, but it is running to avoid the transient performance loss in case of failure.

The failover cluster pattern can be used where the servers have to store large amounts of persistent data. Examples of such applications are message queuing servers and database servers. The data that is part of the internal state of the applications must be available even if a server node fails, because the proper functioning of the application needs a consistent view of the current internal state (the current data). To achieve this, the data is stored on a shared storage device (storage area network, multi-port disk array) that is reachable from all of the server nodes. All nodes are running but only one is active (is serving user requests) at a time. The nodes continuously monitor each other and if a failure of the active node is detected, a new node will be elected to take over the service. The current state of application and the persistent data is stored on the shared storage; this enables fast failover and consistent data persistency. Figure 28 illustrates the structure of the pattern.

QOS MODELING AND ANALYSIS
Enterprise Resource and QoS Modeling

Today's large enterprises have extensive IT infrastructure that consists of various hardware and software components and databases. This complex structure can hardly be handled only by floating-text descriptions or spreadsheet-like inventory lists. There are more system management solutions (such as IBM Tivoli (2005), or Computer Associates Unicenter (Gupta, Weinberg, & LeClair, 2004)) that support the automatic maintenance of asset inventories. To further ease the handling of large asset databases and the integration of diverse system management tools, a standard visual modeling notation has to be used.

The general resource model (GRM) is one of the common standard notations. Common information model (CIM) (DMTF, 2005) is a more fine-grained modeling notation that supports the modeling of IT resources (computers, network appliances). Most of the system management applications support CIM. Although CIM is a standard language, we will not use it because we do not need such a fine-grained model, only a course one like GRM.

UML Profile for Modeling Quality of Service and Fault Tolerance

This section presents one OMG specification that is really driven by the actual business needs: the UML profile for modeling quality of service and fault tolerance (UML Profile for QoS, 2004). First, the business background is briefly described, then, the most important parts of the standard will be introduced.

Business Background: Outsourcing and Service Level Agreements

One of the greatest challenges in today's service oriented computing world is to provide correct services under specified circumstances. Correct means that the result of the service is appropriate in a functional sense, while "under specified circumstances" means that the nonfunctional parameters (availability, response time, security) of the service must meet the needs of the customer (or a predefined service level agreement).

There is a growing tendency of outsourcing, which means that companies make contracts with external partners and let the supporting functions be performed by the supplier. This helps focus on the core competencies of the enterprise. For instance, a shoe manufacturing company may decide that maintaining an IT infrastructure is not in its business profile. Therefore, this task is delegated to a professional IT company that can do it in a more efficient way and of a higher quality. The delegation of this task raises several important questions about the quantitative aspects of the infrastructure maintenance: such questions like "What is the guaranteed minimal number of users who can connect to the Internet with a guaranteed bandwidth?" or "How long is the downtime due to scheduled maintenance activities?" On the other hand, divisions and organizational units of the same company may make internal contracts to describe their relationships and obligations. This tendency reasons the need for a precise, automated way of contracting and defining conditions of services.

In most cases, the services are functionally correct, as many methods are worked out to support the functional modeling, analysis, and testing of applications. Problems are mostly with nonfunctional parameters, as they are neglected by the conventional software development process methodologies. These parameters are only determined by measurements in the software integration-testing phase, at the end of the development cycle. This leads to expensive reengineering of software, or the complete failure of the development project.

With the growing importance of IT outsourcing, service level agreements (SLAs) do have an important role as the acceptance criteria of services. Services can be infrastructural ones like leased lines and backup servers, or high-level ones like credit-card payment handling or electronic ordering service. As the service consumer builds on these services, the failure of them can cause significant downtime on the consumer side and significant financial disadvantages. Therefore, the violation of SLA parameters leads to penalties for the service provider. As penalties may be quite high, service providers have to prepare to failures, and have to design services with embedded QoS modeling and fault tolerance.

UML itself does not offer any QoS modeling capabilities; therefore, OMG introduced the UML profile for modeling QoS and fault tolerance (currently in finalization phase) to integrate nonfunctional modeling to the language. However, this profile also lacks the capability of defining actions for the case of violating the contract and defining exact measurement parameters (who, what, how, and when to measure).

QoS Modeling Basics

QoS specification languages are based on a set of constructors that provide support to describe the main QoS elements of the problem. The QoS and FT profile defines two levels of abstraction for QoS specification. The first level is the application architecture level that supports the QoS analysis of existing systems; the second level is the application analysis level that supports the development-time elaboration of solutions. The general model for the QoS application architecture of the profile is based on ISO general QoS architecture (ISO, 1998).

The basic functional elements that are considered are the resource-consuming component (RCC) for the application architectures, and the QoS-aware specification function (QASF) for the application analysis level. QASFs are significant services (for example, high-level Web services) of the new systems that have associated QoS requirements. These services (or functions) have both functional and nonfunctional requirements. RCC is a processing entity that has interfaces, event queues, and event sources (synchronous and asynchronous access points). RCC interfaces can be service-providing interfaces (that contain the provided functions of the component) or service-consuming interfaces (used to connect to other services to consume their services).

RCCs and QASFs have nonfunctional characteristics associated that can be either general purpose (maximum response time, availability), or domain-specific (surge protection level for a leased line). The quantification of these characteristics is fundamental for the expression of QoS values, the monitoring of the characteristics, and the evaluation of fulfillment of service-level agreements. The QoS characteristics that do not have objective quantification are very hard to measure; therefore, suppliers and consumers concentrate on the measurable ones.

A quality characteristic includes a set of quality attributes that define the dimensions to express quality satisfaction. For example, a "response time" characteristic of a service may include the following attributes:

- Mean service time
- Maximal jitter (variance) of time
- Soft deadline (request served after this time results in a limited usability)
- Hard deadline (requests served later than this may cause potential dangerous situations)
- Maximal load (workloads above this limit can affect the response time)

Figure 29. QoS attribute propagation

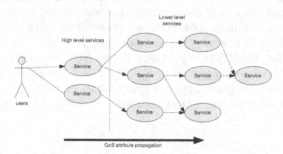

Figure 30. QoS characteristic metamodel

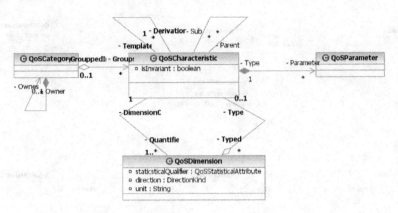

These attributes together build up a single QoS characteristic that defines the response time of a service. Service level agreements have to specify the various attributes precisely to allow the easy evaluation of QoS characteristics.

Quality levels express the quantifiable level of satisfaction of a nonfunctional property. An RCC can associate multiple quality levels to its service providing interfaces. These are the provided contracts of the component. To support the provided quality contract, RCCs can define some required quality levels on its service-consuming interfaces. These quality levels express the required quality contracts. This leads to the propagation of quality attributes from the high-level (public) services to the lower level ones (as illustrated in Figure 29).

QoS Framework

The profile defines a modeling language that supports modeling general QoS concepts. The metamodel of the language defines the abstract syntax, while the mapping to UML defines the concrete syntax. This language defines a framework that supports the characterization and integration of different kinds of QoS values including design-time and runtime values.

The profile contains a model of QoS characteristics, dimensions, and values. Figure 30 illustrates these concepts.

- **QoS characteristic** represents quantifiable characteristics of services. It is defined independently of the element is qualifies. It serves as the constructor for the description of nonfunctional aspects of system components.

  The relation Subparent in the metamodel provides support for the extension-specialization and the reuse of characteristics. The generic description of characteristics may require the parameterization of the units and types for the description of value definitions. QoS parameter supports these parameters. The isInvariant property defines whether the value of QoS characteristic can be updated dynamically or not.

- **QoS dimension**s are dimensions for the quantification of QoS characteristics. We can quantify QoS characteristics in different ways (e.g., absolute values, minimum or maximum values, statistical values). Examples of dimensions for response time are mean response time, minimum response time, hard deadline, and variance of

Figure 31. QoS context and constraints metamodel

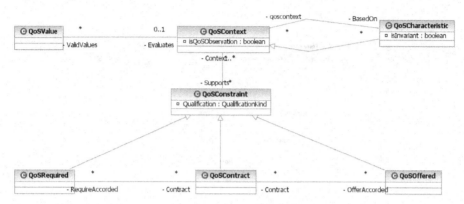

response time. We can also define QoS dimension for a QoS characteristics based on another QoS characteristic (for example, mean response time in the case of a defined maximum workload).

To make relational comparison between two QoS values, we have to define the ordering of the QoS dimension domain. For example, in the case of availability (%), the greatest absolute value is the "higher" or better QoS value, but in the case of response time, the lower absolute value is the "higher" QoS value.

- **QoS categories** provide grouping of various QoS characteristics. The typical groups are performance, dependability, and security, but users can freely create custom groups and groupings.
- **QoS contexts** support the definition of multiple functional and nonfunctional elements in a context of a single quality expression. A single QoS characteristic defines a context for an expression if the expression references only to that particular QoS characteristic. QoS context can be defined based on other QoS contexts or QoS characteristics. Attribute isQoSObservation specifies whether this context is a QoS observation point. Observation points record the QoS characteristics that they are based on.
- **QoS constraint** is an abstract metaclass, and limits the allowed values for one or more QoS characteristics. The QoS constraints define the constraints of the QoS values for model elements. These constraints originate either in architectural decisions or in system requirements. The QoS context associated with the constraint defines its vocabulary, and the QoS constraint defines the allowed values for characteristics.
- **QoS required** is defined by clients or consumers who want to use a service, and the provider (supplier) has to fulfill these requirements as well as the functional requirements. Often, an end-to-end quality requirement is decomposed to several required QoS constraints to achieve the quality needed.
- **QoS offered** is defined by the service providers (or suppliers) and serves the quality-based categorization of the services. If a specific QoS attribute is not appearing in the offered QoS constraint, the supplier does not take it into account. That means that clients must not expect any level of fulfillment regarding that attribute.

Figure 32. Sample component QoS definition in UML

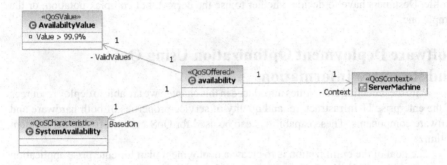

- **QoS contract** represents the agreement between service providers and clients. The client defines the required QoS constraints, the provider defines the offered QoS constraints, and finally, if the constraints can be matched, an agreement (or contract) between the two parties is created.
- **QoS level** defines an operating mode for a subsystem. A component (or subsystem) can support multiple operating modes and hereby, multiple QoS levels. QoS constraints can be defined for each level separately. We can also define the probability of level changes.

The profile for QoS and fault tolerance defines special subprofiles for special aspects of QoS modeling, including risk assessment and FT architectures that can be found in the specification of the profile. We will use only the basic elements introduced here to model nonfunctional aspects of enterprise IT systems.

Assigning QoS Values to System Components

The profile also defines the mapping of metamodel elements to UML constructs to support the UML-based representation of QoS models. The metamodel elements are mostly mapped to stereotypes that can be applied to classes that represent the QoS elements in our models.

In this section, we introduce several examples to help understand the QoS model representation.

Figure 32 illustrates the usage of QoS elements in UML. There is a server machine that acts as a QoS context. The server offers a QoS constraint that states that the system availability is greater than 99.9%. This representation form is a bit complicated; therefore, we suggest the usage of a more compact form that expresses the same concept but results in a much smaller model. The compact variant of the example can be seen in Figure 33.

Figure 33. Simplified QoS definition

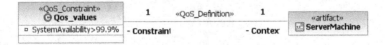

However, this representation is simple; it does not fully correspond to the standard profile. Designers have to decide whether to use the correct, but complex notation, or the simple one.

Software Deployment Optimization Using QoS and Resource Information

With the modeling techniques introduced in this chapter, we are able to deploy resources of the enterprise IT infrastructure, and quality of service properties of both hardware and software components. These capabilities can be used for QoS-based software deployment optimization.

The goal of the optimization is to create a deployment plan for enterprise application components that fulfils the QoS requirements of service consumers (users) and is optimal from the financial point of view.

The first step of this process is to determine the fault model of the system. We will refer to the J2EE (Shannon et al., 2003) architecture, as it is a typical distributed, enterprise application environment.

J2EE Architecture

To help the understanding of the optimization process, we have to introduce, shortly, the J2EE architecture and its typical redundancy patterns. The basic architecture of J2EE (see Figure 34) is built up from at least three tiers.

The first tier is responsible for data persistence, and contains so-called entity beans. The second tier of the architecture is responsible for the implementation of business logic, and contains session beans and message-driven beans that collect the (synchronous or asynchronous) business methods that build up the application logic. Beans represent the smallest independent software components in Java. Session beans can also be exposed as Web services and can be called from other applications.

The third (presentation) layer of the architecture is responsible for the implementation of application user interfaces. Web clients use the HTTP interface of the server that connects them to the servlet container of the J2EE server. The servlet container executes special Java

Figure 34. J2EE architecture

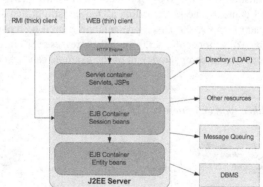

components (called servlets) that produce HTML pages that build up the user interface in the client browser. The advantage of this type of client is that standard Web browsers are used as client programs, so no application components need to be deployed on client machines. The drawback is that this HTML interface has several limitations, for example, in event handling or multimedia content handling.

A remote method invocation (RMI) client can directly connect to the session beans (the business logic) of the application. This interface is used by rich client applications. The advantage of this client technology (in contrast with the Web clients) is that many functions can be integrated to the GUI like input preprocessing, event handling, and so forth.

The J2EE architecture defines the infrastructural services that are needed to execute enterprise applications; therefore, the developers do not need to create custom interfaces to naming, authentication, message queuing, and database servers. This eases the development and the integration of applications.

The various tiers of the architecture can be distributed to separate machines to allow the independent scaling of the application components.

Several large software vendors support the J2EE platform, such as IBM, BEA, SUN, and so on, and several open-source implementations of the platform (for example, JBoss and Jonas) are available even for commercial use.

Redundancy Patterns in J2EE

There are several patterns for creating redundant J2EE server architecture for high availability and load-balancing solutions. The basic concept behind these techniques is clustering. A cluster is a set of computers that all run the same J2EE application, and communicate with each other to determine the set of currently active nodes, and to synchronize their internal state.

The incoming requests are distributed between the running nodes to provide load balancing. If a node goes down, the other nodes take over its workload. This results in higher availability, because the failure of a single node does not directly affect the availability of the services and applications.

Running Example

Our example is a simple order processing and stock management system. It receives orders from customers, prints invoices, and generates backorders to parts suppliers, if necessary. It consists of several services (implemented as session beans):

- The **partner service** is responsible for storing and retrieving the partner data, such as name, address, payment, and discount options.
- The **product service** offers access to the various data of the companies' products such as name, price, and description.
- The **stock service** manages the administration of the product's stocking and movements. It relies on the product service.
- The **accounting service** is used to create invoices for customers who order goods from the company. This service relies on the partner service.
- The **ordering service** that relies on the product, the stock, and the accounting services manages the incoming product orders.

Figure 35. Services of the sample system

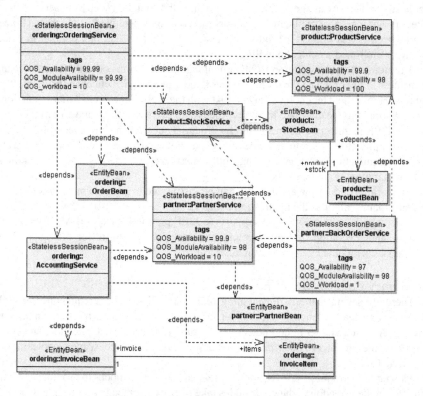

- The **backorder service** is responsible for the creation of backorders to parts suppliers if a specific product runs out of stock. This service uses the product, stock, and partner services.

Each session bean uses an entity bean to get access to business entity data. For example, the ordering service uses the OrderBean to access the data of living orders in the system. All entity beans use the same database to store their data. Figure 35 illustrates the components (the database module is not shown).

The services are grouped into three EJB modules and a database module (Figure 36). These modules are represented using UML packages. Entity beans are deployed together with the session bean that is accessing them. The database module represents the database server software.

To make the presentation form more compact, we represent the QoS values of services as tagged values in the diagram. QoS_Availability and QoS_Capacity specify the availability and capacity requirements for the service, respectively.

The QoS values are specified for single services, while the basic deployment units in the J2EE architecture are the EJB modules. This requires the propagation of QoS attributes

Figure 36. Deployment units in the system

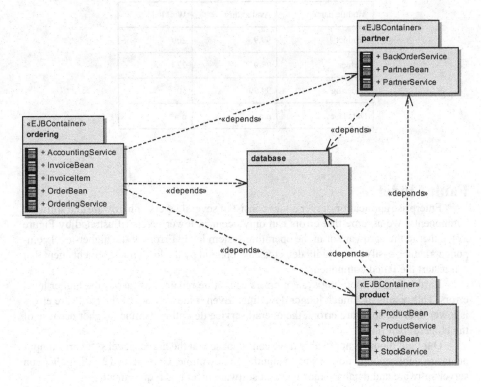

Figure 37. Application server components

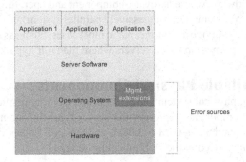

from service level to module level. The availability requirement of the module is the strongest requirement of its beans (the maximal availability in the module), while the capacity requirement is the aggregate capacity requirements of all its beans. The results of the QoS attribute propagation are illustrated in Table 2. (n/a means that no explicit constraints are defined).

Table 2. Calculated QoS parameters for the EJB modules

Module name	Availability	Workload
Product	99.9	200
Partner	99.9	22
Ordering	99.99	50
Database	n/a	n/a

Fault Model

Enterprise application server nodes consist of several layers of hardware and software components. We assume that errors can only occur in lower levels (illustrated by Figure 37), either in the hardware or in the operating system level. Errors of the higher-level components can be easily and rapidly detected and repaired by the local management agent that can restart the failed component.

Hardware and operating system errors cannot be repaired as fast as the higher level errors. This results in a much longer downtime. Even if the severity of the hardware errors is lower than the software errors, the overall service downtime is much higher because of the longer repair time.

Our fault model is applicable if we can suppose that the higher-level software components are stable enough not to cause a significant downtime. Commercial J2EE application server software and database management software meet this requirement.

The fault model introduced here has several limitations. If running on a dependable, highly redundant hardware, where hardware component and operating system errors do not cause system restart (for example, in a massively parallel system), higher level software errors will be dominant in service downtime, but in most cases, business software components are running on entry- or medium-level servers where the fault hypothesis is satisfied.

Modeling Available Physical Components

In our scenario, physical system components are server computers that can run J2EE applications. UML components represent the server types in our model. The hardware resources can be modeled using CIM or GRM, and the QoS values discussed next can be attached to them as described in the QoS modeling section.

Performance Metrics

There are several industrial standard benchmarks that measure the overall performance of a server system with all of its hardware and software components. One of these is the TPC-W benchmark developed by the Transaction Processing Performance Council. This test measures the performance of a Web-based transactional system. As enterprise services are Web services, this benchmark can be used as a reference for the overall system performance.

COMPONENT COSTS

The server components also have an associated cost value that indicates the TCO (total cost of ownership) value of the server, including the cost of all hardware (processor, memory, disks, UPS, and so on) and software (OS, application server, management tools) components, and all associated services (extended warranty, on-site service) for a given period of time.

The time factor depends on the desired lifetime of the service or application that is served. In case of applications with long life cycles, the basis of the calculation could be the expended life cycle of the server farm. The typical length of the life cycle of servers is around 2-3 years. To make the cost of the possible server choices comparable, the time factor should be universal for the whole model.

Component Availability

The third QoS value that is attached to servers is the availability. This attribute depends on the hardware, software, and also on the value added services offered to the specific server. Hardware suppliers specify the MTBF (mean time between failures) value for computer hardware. This can act as a starting point of availability calculation.

If we want to achieve high availability, software errors also play an important role, as the 30-60 second typical restarting time of a J2EE application server can also affect the availability of a critical service. In this case, the system adds extra redundancy to avoid the unavailability of service.

Availability (A) can be calculated from the MTBF value and the MRT (mean repair time) by the following formula (1).

$$A = (MTBF-MRT)/MTBF \tag{1}$$

Mean repair time depends on the QoS values of the service support of the hardware manufacturer (the maximum time of arrival of the service personnel in case of failure), and the average repair time. For example, a large server manufacturer guarantees a 4-hour response time, and the typical repair time is 1 hour. This results in MRT = 5 hours.

Figure 38. QoS values of sample server computers

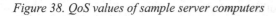
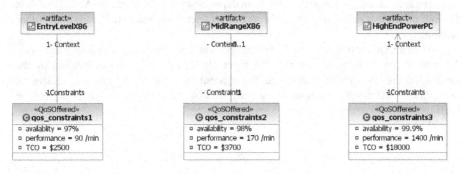

Figure 39. Model processing workflow

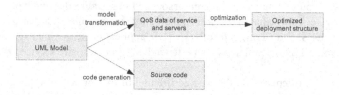

Hardware Units in the Sample System

We use three types of server computers (an entry-level x86, a multi-processor x86, and a high-end PowerPC server) in our example. The QoS values of the servers can be seen in Figure 38. We use the simplified QoS definition introduced earlier.

The Optimization Workflow

A sample code generation and architecture synthesis method is introduced in this section. A general-purpose model transformation system can be used for the implementation of the required transformations and code generation scripts. For example, VIATRA2 (Balogh et al., 2005) is such a tool.

Architecture Synthesis

The process synthesis consists of two main steps (see Figure 39). The first step is the transformation of the UML model of the system to a special format that can be imported to the optimization program. The program that is used for the synthesis is the second step of our workflow. The result of the process is the recommended architecture of the system. Parallel to the optimization, the source code of the system components can also be generated with one of the available UML to J2EE code generators. Most UML tools contain code generators that produce source code and deployment descriptors for various J2EE application servers.

Model Transformation

The first basic step of the transformation is the propagation of the bean QoS values to the EJB modules, as described earlier. Each EJB module inherits the maximum availability and aggregates the performance value of its beans.

The second step is to propagate the bean dependencies to the modules. An EJB module depends on another one if at least one of its beans depends on one of the beans in the other container.

After all QoS attributes and dependencies have been propagated to EJB containers, the transformation program generates the input file for the optimization program by the traversal of the UML package structure. It prints out the defined capacity and availability requirements and dependencies for every UML package that is marked with the stereotype EJBModule.

Deployment Optimization

The optimization itself is a linear programming problem, where the variables are the number of various servers used in the deployment. There are two possible subproblems for optimization. The first one is the arrangement of services in an existing infrastructure, where the number of servers is determined; the second one is the planning of a new hardware infrastructure for service deployment, where the number of servers is unlimited. Both problems can be solved using the same equation system, but the limited number of servers introduces several new constraints for the optimization variables. The goal of the optimization process is to minimize the overall system cost while providing the necessary system availability and capacity.

The Mathematical Model for Optimization

Optimization, in general, means a method that searches a point in the problem space that satisfies the defined constraints, and the objective function has a maximum (or minimum) value. Several special optimization problem classes have been defined, for example, the travel agent problem.

Initial Steps

The first step of the optimization process is the calculation of the aggregate workload of software modules. The developer only has to specify the direct workload for a specific container (the actual requests from clients), but the capacity needs to depend also on the indirect workload (calls from depending services). In our simple model, we suppose that a dependency represents a single call to the target service.

The calculation of aggregate workload is a recursive expression that calculates the workload as a sum of the direct workload and the additional workload of depending services (expression (2)). The depends(i) is a set of services that depend on service i.

$$Workload(i) = Capacity\_need(i) + \sum_{j \in depends(i)} Workload(j).$$

$$(2)$$

There are two important constraints that specify the capacity and availability restrictions of services: the workload and the availability constraints.

The Workload Constraint

The workload constraint means that the aggregated capacity of all deployed software modules on a specific machine must not exceed the capacity of the machine. A further tuning possibility is to define a saturation factor (SF) that specifies the maximum rate of workload on machines. This enables the developer, for example, to define a maximum of 60% for workloads that is widely used in the capacity planning of enterprise Web systems. Equation (3) specifies the workload constraint.

$$\forall m \in HW : Capacity(m) * SF \geq \sum_{s \in deployed(m)} Workload(s)$$

$$(3)$$

The Availability Constraint

The availability constraint specifies that the actual availability of each service must be at least as high as the required availability. The actual availability of a service can be calculated from the availability of the hardware that runs the service, and the availability of depending services. Equation (4) specifies the availability constraint. (A denotes the availability of a component)

A service is available if the hardware it is running on is available, and all the required services of the specific service are available. We suppose that if a hardware unit is running then all services deployed on it are running as well. We also suppose that all hardware nodes are independent, which means that all of them have their own uninterruptible power supply, disk subsystem, and so on. For independent components, the probability of the product event equals the product of the basic events.

$$
\begin{aligned}
A_{act}(i) &= P(HW\ available \wedge All\ needed\ services\ available) = \\
&= P(HW\ available) * \prod_{all\ HW\ running\ required\ service} P(HW\ available) = \\
&= A_{HW(i)} * \prod_{\forall j, HW(j)\ running\ needed\ service} A_{HW(j)} \\
\forall i &\in services: A_{act}(i) \geq A_{required}(i)
\end{aligned}
$$

$$(4)$$

The Objective Function

The objective function of the optimization process is the overall cost of the system, as described by equation (3). The total cost of the system is the aggregation of the product of the cost and the actual number of the defined hardware components.

$$
TCO_{System} = \sum_{m \in HW} TCO(m) * number\_used(m) .
$$

$$(5)$$

The Solutions

A solution of the problem is a mapping between computers and software modules that satisfies all constraints. Solutions are computed by a backtrack algorithm that tries to build the mapping step-by-step while maintaining the constraints. The optimal solution is the solution that has the lowest overall cost.

FURTHER ANALYSIS AND OPTIMIZATION STEPS

Business Continuity Planning and Disaster Recovery

There are several risk factors that are not considered by the architecture synthesis method introduced in the previous sections. We have considered the internal risk factors (HW and SW faults), but there are also several external factors. Typical external risk factors include lightning, flood, fire, earthquake, and so forth. The probability of the occurrence of these events is very low, but the damage they can cause to IT infrastructure can be extremely high: the whole infrastructure can be destroyed.

If the IT system is business-critical, these catastrophic events must also be considered when planning the infrastructure. We can choose two types of proactive actions: the first group is the business continuity planning that ensures the operation of the system, even in the case of catastrophic events; and the second group contains disaster recovery mechanisms that support the recovery of the IT infrastructure after a catastrophic event.

Business continuity planning includes, for example, the geographical distribution of the infrastructure. This protects the IT system against fire or flood damages. The different sites of computers need to be connected to enable the state synchronization between them. The connection can be online (leased line), or off-line (transferring tape backups). If we want to have exact and fast state synchronization, we have to use online connections with a relatively high bandwidth.

If we consider this example with the four-node cluster of servers, the cluster is distributed between two sites, and the proper load balancing between the sites is assured, then the same availability and performance is achieved as in the original configuration. In the case of a disaster, one of the sites will, hopefully, work and take over all of the requests. This will cause performance degradation, but the services will be available.

Disaster recovery actions include data backup-restore strategies, spare hardware elements, and so forth. It is important, for example, that the backup media must be stored in a separate location (to protect it from fire, or other damage), but in case of restore, it has to be transported back to the computing centre as fast as possible.

In our example, we have to create backups from the databases that the servers are using, and transport the backup media sets to a separate location. In case of disaster, these backups can be used to restore the system state. If we want to rapidly recover the perished site, we also have to store several spare components (servers, network devices) in a safe location. The degree of this redundancy depends on the financial conditions (income from customers, cost of reduced QoS).

The two aspects of proactive actions that must be taken to avoid the total destruction of the infrastructure together can guarantee the continuity of services from the customer point of view, and the continuity of business and avoidance of penalties from the supplier point of view.

Additional Steps

If the required availability or performance levels cannot be reached using the basic hardware types defined in the model, the optimizer applies the J2EE redundancy patterns for the design. This means that we have to create clusters from the basic hardware nodes to raise the availability and performance of a server. If the availability requirements do not allow single point of failure in the system, the developer can specify that only redundant arrays of machines can be used during architecture synthesis. This means that the optimization process has to create clusters, even if the performance and availability of a single computer could satisfy the needs of the services.

The capacity of a cluster consisting of several nodes can be lower than the sum of the capacity of the nodes. That is because various synchronization messages and algorithms are running on nodes. The typical value of performance loss depends highly on the actual server software, but it can be measured or taken from server benchmarks. We can define a "performance loss percent" that is subtracted from the sum performance of the cluster nodes. If the services only use stateless session beans and entity beans, this loss is negligible in most cases.

More components (EJB modules) can be deployed on the same server if the hardware has enough capacity for running all the services. This ensures that the workload of the servers will be nearly equal, and the hardware costs will be minimized. The optimization process defines a method for calculating the optimal configuration of services and hardware nodes using the explained equations and constraints. The output of the process is a list of services and the associated hardware nodes. This defines the suggested configuration of the system.

Result of the Deployment Optimization of the Example

The optimal configuration of the example is a four-node cluster from the second type of machines (supposing that the number of available machines is at least four). This cluster has a calculated availability of 99.9999%, and a total cost of $14,800. All services are deployed to this single cluster.

This result shows that the high availability needs that are introduced by the end users may result in a complex infrastructure, but fortunately, clustering of J2EE application servers is supported by all software vendors. Clustering introduces automatic failover and workload balancing.

REFERENCES

Avizienis, A., Laprie, J. C., Randell, B., & Landwehr, C. (2004). Basic concepts and taxonomy of dependable and secure computing. *IEEE Transactions on Dependable and Secure Computing, 1*, 11-33, 2004.

Balogh, A., Németh, A., Schmidt, A., Ráth, I., Vágó, D., Varró, D., & Pataricza, A. (2005). *The VIATRA2 model transformation framework.* Accepted to ECMDA 2005 — Tools Track.

Bell, D., & LaPadula, L. (1973, November). *Secure computer systems: Mathematical foundations.* ESD-TR-73-278, Vol. I, Electronic Systems Division, Air Force Systems Command, Hanscom AFB, Bedford, MA 01731.

Clark, E. M. Jr., Grumberg, O., & Peled, D. A. (1999). *Model checking.* Cambridge, MA: MIT Press.

Distributed Management Task Force (DMTF). (1999). *Common information model specification* (Version 2.2). Retrieved July 20, 2005, from http://www.dmtf.org/standards/documents/CIM/DSP0004.pdf

Distributed Management Task Force (DMTF). (2005). *CIM schema specification* (Version 2.9.0). Retrieved July 20, 2005, from http://www.dmtf.org/standards/cim/cim_schema_v29

Ehrig, H., Engels, G., Kreowski, H. J., & Rozenberg, R. (Eds.). (1999). *Handbook on graph grammars and computing by graph transformation, Vol. 2: Applications, languages and tools.* World Scientific.

Gönczy, L. (2005). Dependability analysis of Web service-based business processes by model transformations. In *Proceedings of the First European Young Researchers Workshop* on Service Oriented Computing (YR-SOC), De Montfort University, University of Sheffield, University of Leicester, UK.

Gupta, Y., Weinberg, L., & LeClair, D. (2004). *Managing on-demand computing*. Retrieved July 20, 2005, from http://www3.ca.com/Files/WhitePapers/managing_on_demand_computing_whitepaper.pdf

IBM. (n.d.). *IBM tivoli management software information portal*. Retrieved July 20, 2005, from http://www-306.ibm.com/software/tivoli/

IBM. (2003). *Specification: Business process execution language for Web services* (Version 1.1). Retrieved July 20, 2005, from http://www-128.ibm.com/developerworks/library/ws-bpel/

International Organization for Standardization (ISO). (1998). *CD15935 information technology: Open distributed processing — Reference model — Quality of service*. (ISO document ISO/IEC JTC1/SC7 N1996).

Menascé, D. A., & Almeida, V. A. F. (2002). *Capacity planning for Web services*. Upper Saddle River, NJ: Prentice Hall.

Object Management Group (OMG). (2002). *Metaobject facility specification* (Version 1.4). Retrieved July 20, 2005, from http://www.omg.org/cgi-bin/doc?formal/2002-04-03

Object Management Group (OMG). (2004). *UML profile for quality of service and fault tolerance characteristics and metrics*. Retrieved July 20, 2005, from http://www.omg.org/cgi-bin/apps/doc?ptc/04-09-01.pdf

Object Management Group (OMG). (2004). *UML 2.0 superstructure specification*. Revised Final Adopted Specification. Retrieved July 18, 2005, from http://omg.org/cgi-bin/doc?ptc/2004-10-02

Object Management Group (OMG). (2005). *UML profile for schedulability, performance, and time specification* (Version 1.1). Retrieved July 20, 2005, from http://www.omg.org/cgi-bin/apps/doc?formal/05-01-02.pdf

Pataricza, A. (2002). From the general resource model to a general fault modeling paradigm? In *Proceedings of the Workshop on Critical Systems Development with UML at UML 2002*, Dresden, Germany. Retrieved July 20, 2005, from http://www.inf.mit.bme.hu/FTSRG/Publications/UML2002_Pataric.pdf

Pataricza, A., Dobán, O., & Szöke, A. (2004). Costs/benefits of using formal methods. In *Proceedings of DSN 2004 - Supplemental Volume of the 2004 International Conference on Dependable Systems and Networks,* Florence, Italy (pp. 104-105). Los Alamitos, CA: IEEE Computer Society.

Shannon, B., et al. (2003). *Java 2 platform enterprise edition specification 1.4*. Retrieved July 20, 2005, from http://java.sun.com/j2ee/j2ee-1_4-fr-spec.pdf

van der Aalst, W., & van Hee, K. (January, 2002). Workflow management. *Models, methods and systems*. The MIT Press.

Varró, D., & Pataricza, A. (2003). VPM: A visual, precise, and multilevel metamodeling framework for describing mathematical domains and UML. *Journal of Software and Systems Modeling, 2,* 187-210, 2003.

About the Authors

Peter Rittgen earned an MSc in computer science and computational linguistics from University Koblenz-Landau, Germany, and a PhD in economics and business administration from Frankfurt University, Germany. He is currently a senior lecturer at the School of Business and Informatics of the University College of Borås, Sweden. He has been doing research on business processes and the development of information systems since 1997 and published many articles in these areas. For further details, visit http://www.adm.hb.se/~PRI/.

* * *

Lars Bækgaard is an associate professor at Department of Business Studies, Århus School of Business. Also, he works as an independent consultant. He received a PhD in computer science in 1993 from Aalborg University. He has worked at Aalborg University, Denmark, at the IT-University, Denmark, and at University of Maryland, USA. His current research interests are analysis and design of information systems, conceptual modeling, interaction modeling, activity modeling, and event modeling. More information can be found at www.baekgaard.biz

András Balogh graduated from the Budapest University of Technology and Economics, and currently, he is a second year PhD student with the Department of Measurement and

Information Systems. His main research interest is the application of model-driven development techniques for business and safety critical systems, with special focus on guaranteed functional correctness and QoS levels. He works on several EU projects regarding model-driven development, domain-specific modeling and model transformations. He is the main architect of VIATRA2, an open-source model transformation framework.

Herman Balsters earned his PhD in computer science at the Technical University of Eindhoven, The Netherlands (1986). From 1986-2001 he held the positions of assistant and associate professor in the field of database design in the Faculty of Computer Science at the University of Twente, The Netherlands. Since 2001 he has been an associate professor in the field of information systems design in the Faculty of Management and Organization at the University of Groningen, The Netherlands. He has published more than 50 scientific papers, mainly in the field of databases and object orientation. Currently, his main research interests are in the field of federated databases (integration of data, constraints, and transactions), object-orientation (UML/OCL, MDA), data management in legacy systems, and business modelling.

Artur Caetano is an information systems lecturer at the Instituto Superior Técnico, Technical University of Lisbon, Portugal, and a PhD candidate at the same university on the topic of business process modeling with separation of concerns. He holds a master's degree in computer engineering and information systems from Technical University of Lisbon, and his education has a background in computer science and software engineering. He has worked in several international projects concerning enterprise architecture and enterprise-distributed object computing. His research interests include business process modeling, role modeling, enterprise architecture and object-oriented frameworks.

Omar Chiotti was born in Argentina in 1959. He earned his degree in chemical engineering from UTN (1984) and his PhD in engineering from UNL, Argentina (1989). Since 1984 he has been working for CONICET (Argentina's National Council of Scientific and Technical Research), currently as a senior researcher. He has been a professor of information systems engineering at UTN – FRSF since 1986. He currently teaches management systems. He has been the director of the CIDISI (Center of Research and Development in Information Systems Engineering) since 2004. His current research interests are focused on collaborative commerce and semantic integration of information systems.

Stefan Dietze studied business information systems at the University of Cooperative Education in Heidenheim, Germany (1998-2001). Afterwards, he finished his PhD in applied computer science at the Potsdam University with a dissertation about collaborative open source software development processes (2004). Since 2001 he has been working as a research associate at the Fraunhofer Institute for Software and Systems Engineering (ISST) in Berlin. There, he is engaged in several research activities as well as in consultation projects for science and industry. His main research focuses are in the fields of software engineering processes, software and process modeling and knowledge management.

Peter Fettke earned a master's degree in information systems (Diplom-Wirtschaftsinformatiker) from the University of Muenster, Germany. Since 2002 he has been a research assistant at the Chair of Information Systems and Business Administration, Johannes

Gutenberg-University Mainz, Germany. His research interests include information systems analysis and design, especially the use of conceptual modeling and component-based system paradigm. Peter has published numerous articles on reference modeling, conceptual modeling and component-based engineering in both national and international journals and conferences. Furthermore, he is a member of the editorial board of the *Journal of Cases on Information Technology (JCIT)* and *Journal of System and the Management Sciences (JSMS)* and serves as a referee for the *Information Resources Management Journal (IRMJ)*, *Data & Knowledge Engineering (DKE)*, the *DATA BASE for Advances in Information Systems* and numerous national and international conferences. Currently, he has finished his PhD thesis and is moving to the German Research Center for Artificial Intelligence (DFKI), Saarbruecken, Germany.

Olov Forsgren earned a doctor's degree in informatics from Umeå University, Sweden. Forsgren is Sjuhärad distinguished professor at the University College of Borås and has 20 years research experience from Umeå University, Mid Sweden University and Örebro University. He has also been visiting professor at the University of Southern California, the University of California, Berkeley, and the Southern Methodist University, Dallas. He has been the scientific principal investigator responsible for a number of successful pioneering national and international research projects on information systems development in collaboration with multiple academic and industrial research partners.

László Gönczy earned an MSc in software engineering in 2003 at the Budapest University of Technology and Economics. He is a third year PhD student with the Department of Measurement and Information Systems. His research topics are Web service systems, service oriented architectures, business process analysis, dependability evaluation and model driven development. He is a participant of an FP6 EU research project regarding to the modeling and deployment of service oriented architectures.

Sandra Haraldson is a doctoral student in informatics from the School of Business and Informatics at the University College of Borås, Sweden. Her research is characterised by design of information systems and business development in the area of third-party logistics cooperation. In her thesis, she elaborates on how third-party logistics cooperation should be coordinated and organised, as a knowledge foundation for IS design. She is a member of the research network VITS in Sweden. She has been conducting a several action-research projects in third-party logistics setting with focus on business processes and information systems.

Mikael Lind is an assistant professor with the School of Business and Informatics at the University College of Borås, Sweden. He is the leader of the Informatics Department. His current research interests are business process management, method engineering, co-design of business and IT, design and evaluation of business process oriented information systems, and research methods for information systems development. He is a member of the research network VITS in Sweden. His research is mainly characterised by empirically driven theory and method development. He is involved in several action-research projects in different settings focusing business processes and information systems.

Peter Loos (1960) is director of the Institute for Information Systems (IWi) at the German Research Center for Artificial Intelligence (DFKI) and head of the chair for Business Administration and Information Systems at Saarland University. His research activities include business process management, information modeling, enterprise systems, software development as well as implementation of information systems. Professor Loos studied business administration and information systems at the University of Saarland and completed his degree (Dipl.Kfm.) in 1984. He wrote his PhD thesis on the issue of data modeling in manufacturing systems — awarded with the Dr. Eduard-Martin-Preis — in 1991 as a research assistant at the Institute for Information Systems (directed by Prof. Dr. Dr. h.c. mult. August-Wilhelm Scheer). In 1997, Professor Loos received the venia legendi in business administration. During his earlier career Professor Loos had been chair of information systems & management at University of Mainz (2002-2005), chair of information systems & management at Chemnitz University of Technology (1998-2002), deputy chair at University of Muenster as well as lecturer (Privatdozent) at Saarland University. Furthermore, he had worked for 6 years as manager of the Software Development Department at the software and consulting company IDS Scheer. Professor Loos has written several books, contributed to 30 books and published more than 100 papers in journals and proceedings.

Anna Medve is an assistant professor of software engineering with formal methods in the Department of Information Systems at the Faculty of Information Technology at the University of Veszprem, Hungary. Was educated at University Transylvania, Brasov, Roumania (MSc equivalent, matemathics and informatics science, 1977) and University Eotvos Lorand, Budapest, Hungary (MSc equivalent, computer science, 1990). She spent 14 years in industry as a computer scientist, and has extensive experience with techniques modeling process and design, implementation, maintenance and workgroups management. She has actively worked in projects that have spanned industries such as logistics, manufacturing, insurance, banking, telecommunications, government and education. Her research interests primarily concentrate on the field of requirements engineering and design for testability and maintainability. She has absoled PhD courses at University Eotvos Lorand Budapest (2001), and is continuing her research at Pannon University, Hungary to prepare her dissertation on software engineering processes with standardized formal methods. She is a member of the J. Neumann Society, the SDL Forum Society, the IEEE and the IEEE Computer Society.

Jan Olausson is a doctoral student in informatics from the School of Business and Informatics at the University College of Borås, Sweden. His research is characterised by design of information systems and business development in the area of transaction intensive settings like mail-order and third-party logistics. In his thesis, he discusses how to secure business success through the design of process oriented information systems. He is a member of the research network VITS in Sweden. He has been conducting a several action-research projects in mail-order and third-party logistics settings with focus on business processes and information systems.

András Pataricza, PhD, is an associate professor with the Department of Measurement and Information System at Budapest University of Technology and Economics. He leads the Fault Tolerance Systems Research Group. He served at several international conferences in the related field. He was the leader of an IBM sponsored project aiming at the creation of the courses for an e-Business Academy. He edited two books on formal methods and published more than 100 papers. He is the founder of OptXware, a spin-off company active in the field of model-based design, analysis and dependability consolidation of large scale applications.

Carla Marques Pereira has an MSc in computer science at the Technical University of Lisbon (IST). She is reading for a PhD on the subject of business and IT alignment. Carla is a member of Link Consulting SA's Enterprise Architects team.

Enrique Salomone has been a senior researcher of the Argentina's National Council of Scientific and Technical Research (CONICET) since 1997. He holds both bachelor's and PhD degrees in chemical engineering from Universidad Nacional del Litoral, Argentina. He was professor of information systems at Universidad Tecnológica Nacional – Facultad Regional Santa Fe, Argentina and research assistant at the Laboratory for Intelligent Systems for Process Engineering (LISPE), Department of Chemical Engineering, Massachusetts Institute of Technology, Cambridge. His current research interests are focused on decision support systems for industrial processes.

Kamyar Sarshar earned a master's degree in computer science (Diplom-Informatik) from the University of Hamburg, Germany, and a Master of Business Administration (MBA) from Cardiff University, UK. From 2002-2005 he worked as a research assistant at the Chair of Information Systems and Business Administration, Johannes Gutenberg-University Mainz, Germany. Since 2005 he has been a research assistant and PhD student at the Institute for Information Systems (IWi) at the German Research Center for Artificial Intelligence (DFKI) in Saarbruecken. Kamyar's research interests include information modeling, especially modeling languages as well as healthcare information systems. Kamyar has published numerous articles on modeling with Petri nets in healthcare.

Pedro Sousa is an associate professor of Computer Engineering and Information Technology at Instituto Superior Técnico, Technical University of Lisbon, Portugal, where he also earned his PhD in electrical and computer engineering. He has worked in several international projects concerning software and system engineering. He currently plays an active role in the enterprise engineering area, being involved in research and consultancy projects concerning enterprise engineering and architecture. His research interests include information system architecture, information system re-engineering, business process modelling and enterprise architecture.

José Tribolet is a full professor of computer engineering and information technology at Instituto Superior Técnico, Technical University of Lisbon, Portugal. He earned his PhD in electrical and computer engineering from the Massachusetts Institute of Technology, USA. In 1998 he was a visiting fellow at the Center for Coordination Sciences in MIT's Sloan School of Management and participated in the project "Inventing the Organizations of the XXI Century". He leads the Organizational Engineering Center at the Institute for Systems and Computer Engineering (INESC), a private sector, contract-based research organization, which he has co-founded in 1980. He currently plays an active role in the organizational engineering area, being involved in both research and consultancy projects concerning enterprise engineering and architecture. His main research interests are organizational modeling, business process engineering and information systems architecture.

Sandy Tyndale-Biscoe has spent nearly 30 years in IT. His technical experience encompasses business and enterprise modelling, open systems standardisation, and command, control, communications and intelligence (C3I) systems. For the past 9 years, Sandy has been increasingly involved in two major international standardization activities: ISO's RM-ODP, and OMG's UML related standards. He was the Convener of ISO/JTC1/SC7/WG17, which developed the RM-ODP enterprise language (IS 15414), and is currently one of the two joint editors of the UML for ODP standard (IS 19793 | ITU-T X.906). He is a contributor to the OMG activity in developing the new model driven architecture (MDA), and was the editor for the final adopted specification for UML Profiles for EDOC.

Antonio Vallecillo holds BSc and MSc degrees in mathematics, and a PhD in computer science. Most of his professional experience comes from the computer industry, where he has worked for several IT international companies such as Fujitsu and ICL plc. Since 1996 he has worked at Málaga University, where he is currently an associate professor, and has been head of the Málaga University IT Services. His research interests include model-driven software development, componentware and open distributed processing. He is the representative of University of Málaga at ISO, the OMG, and AENOR (the Spanish National Body for Standardization), and a member of several organizations, including ACM, the IEEE and the IEEE Computer Society.

André Vasconcelos is an information systems lecturer at the Instituto Superior Técnico, Technical University of Lisbon, Portugal, and a PhD candidate on the subject of information system architectures. He holds a master's degree in computer engineering and information systems from the Technical University of Lisbon. His research interests include information system architecture, information system architecture evaluation, enterprise modelling, organizational engineering, and business process modelling.

Pablo David Villarreal has been a postdoctoral researcher at the Argentina's National Council of Scientific and Technical Research (CONICET) since 2005. He holds both his bachelor's and PhD degrees in information systems engineering from the National Technological University (UTN), Argentina. He is an assistant professor at the National Technological University - Santa Fe Regional Faculty (UTN-FRSF). He is also a member of the CIDISI (Center of Research and Development in Information Systems Engineering) at the UTN-FRSF. His current research interests are focused on collaborative commerce, collaborative business processes, business process management and integration, MDA, model transformations, Web services composition and multi-agent systems.

Bryan Wood is a systems architect at Open-IT Ltd. Before joining Open-IT, Bryan spent 25 years with Sema Group plc. where his experience covered language design, compiler design and implementation, operating systems, real-time and communications-based systems, performance analysis and system consultancy. With Open-IT, his activity has included a UK MOD programme to develop a methodology for specification of command, control, communications and intelligence (C3I) systems, and a European Commission project to develop a model-based approach to the implementation of interoperable enterprise component systems. He has been active in the development of Open System standards, including

ODP standards, since 1980. He is active in the OMG, contributing both to the EDOC UML profile specification and to the model driven architecture (MDA).

Jörg Zwicker earned a master's degree in information systems (Diplom-Wirtschaftsinformatiker) from the Chemnitz University of Technology, Germany (2004). From 2004-2005 he worked as a research assistant at the Chair of Information Systems and Business Administration, Johannes Gutenberg-University Mainz, Germany. Since 2005 he is a research assistant and PhD student at the Institute for Information Systems (IWi) at the German Research Center for Artificial Intelligence (DFKI) in Saarbruecken, Germany. Jörg's research interest include information modeling, especially reference modeling. In the context of a German research project, he currently researches at theoretical and technological foundations for creating and using reference model catalogs. Further research interests include business integration and business rule management. Jörg has published articles on reference modeling as well as an architecture in collaborative scenarios at international conferences.

Index

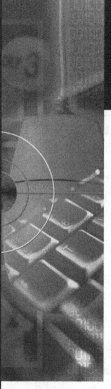